Promise Me

How a Sister's Love Launched the Global Movement to End Breast Cancer

NANCY G. BRINKER

Founder of SUSAN G. KOMEN FOR THE CURE

Broadway Books BROADWAY

Promise Me

Promise Me

How a Sister's Love
Launched the Global Movement
to End Breast Cancer

~

Nancy G. Brinker

FOUNDER AND CEO *of*

SUSAN G. KOMEN FOR THE CURE

~

with Joni Rodgers

CROWN ARCHETYPE · NEW YORK

Published in the United States by Crown Archetype, an imprint of the
Crown Publishing Group, a division of Random House, Inc., New York.
www.crownpublishing.com

Crown Archetype with colophon is a trademark of Random House, Inc.

Library of Congress Cataloging-in-Publication Data
Brinker, Nancy
Promise me / by Nancy G. Brinker; with Joni Rodgers
p.   cm.
1. Brinker, Nancy. 2. Komen, Susan G.—Health. 3. Breast—Cancer—Patients—
United States—Biography. 4. Breast—Cancer—Popular works. 5. Susan G. Komen
Breast Cancer Foundation. I. Rodgers, Joni, 1962–   II. Title.

RC280.B8B7287   2010
362.196'994490092—dc22
[B]   2010008731

ISBN 978-0-307-71812-9

PRINTED IN THE UNITED STATES OF AMERICA

Design by Elizabeth Rendfleisch

1   3   5   7   9   10   8   6   4   2

To Suzy . . . with love forever.
And to Mommy, Daddy, and Eric.
I dedicate my life's work to my fine colleagues and friends
who've made Susan G. Komen for the Cure come alive.
And to Norman.

CONTENTS

II EVOLUTION 153

III REVOLUTION 295

NOTE FROM THE AUTHOR

This book captures the spirit of my experiences to the best of my recollection with the help of letters, journals, press clippings, photos, and interviews. To create a readable story of manageable length, it was necessary to condense and combine some events and characters. Suzy's dialogue is based on her own words in letters to my family. Other dialogue was re-created for dramatic effect, based on interviews, letters, press clippings, and my recollections. Others may remember or interpret certain events and conversations differently. I don't pretend to remember every exchange verbatim, but I've done my best to remain true to the spirit of conversations and events.

Nothing in this book constitutes or is intended as a substitute for medical or legal advice. The opinions expressed are my personal opinions and may not necessarily reflect the opinions of Susan G. Komen for the Cure®, Susan G. Komen Race for the Cure®, Susan G. Komen 3-Day for the Cure®, private donors, corporate sponsors, local affiliates, or associated researchers and other medical professionals, or that of any corporate or nonprofit entity for which I serve, have served, or will serve as a board member now, in the past, or at any time in the future.

There's no such thing as a "tell all" memoir. Some things have to be omitted to protect the privacy of those involved. The people who've contributed time, energy, and rich experience to my life are far too many to mention by name in this book, but I would like to express my deepest thanks to the board of Susan G. Komen for the Cure for their dedication and insight; Alexine Clement Jackson, board chair; the staff at the SGK offices in Dallas and Washington, D.C., for their hard work and good hearts; the leadership at all our local affiliates worldwide for their passion and energy; my fabulous friends in Dallas, especially the founding members of SGK, who were there in the beginning and made this organization what it is; my family and friends in Peoria, the Land of Milk and Honey, and in Palm Beach, where Mommy and I have found a warm circle of laughter and love. I'd also like to thank everyone who helped make this book a reality: my brilliant literary agent, Dorian Karchmar at William Morris; our terrific editors, Lorraine Glennon, Sydny Minor, and Diane Salvatore; our publisher, Tina Constable, and everyone at Crown Archetype; my mother, who provided a wealth of photographs and memories; my son, Eric Brinker, who was a tremendous source of help and information; Barbara Rogoff, who participated in the live read and curates my Hungarian art collection; Jonathan Blum, Emily Callahan, Susan Carter Johns, Katrina McGhee, John Pearson, Pam Stevens, Elizabeth Thompson, Matt Wendel, Mike Williams; Dr. Eric Winer, and all the very special people who shared their stories.

To all those who aren't mentioned: Please know that I'm deeply grateful for your presence in the full story, which is written in my heart.

Nancy Goodman Brinker

September 2010

NOTE FROM THE COAUTHOR

Thanks to my agent, Wendy Sherman; my project assistant, Jerusha Rodgers; Gary and Malachi Rodgers, who provided help and support; and Colleen Thompson, Barbara Sissel, and Fred Ramey, who offered insightful critique on early versions of the manuscript. Much of this book was written at the Dakota Ramblers Writing Retreat in Montana. Thanks to the staff for their music and hospitality.

Joni Rodgers

September 2010

Promise Me

I

Suzy

Where Will Meets Way

My waking memories of my sister have grown hazy over the years, but Suzy still passes through my dreams as animate and vivid as a migrating butterfly. Her face is fresh and full of energy, her hair windblown but still beautiful. In a freshly ironed skirt and patent leather ballerina flats, she defies gravity, scrambling over a pile of slick rocks, Roman ruins stacked like unclaimed luggage on a hilly roadside in southern Spain.

Suzy, be careful, I call as she climbs higher.

Oh, Nanny, she waves me off, mugging for the boy with the camera. (Boys could never keep their eyes, or cameras, off her.) He tells Suzy to smile. *Say queso!* But she's already smiling. In studio and fashion photos, she was always slightly Mona Lisa, never *haute couture* haughty. Almost every candid photograph I have of Suzy seems to have been snapped just as she's bubbling up to giggle, that precise moment when you can see the laughter in her eyes and feel the active upturn of her mouth, but the not-quite sound of it is forever suspended in the air, teasing like the un-played eighth note of a full octave. Even in the dream, I ache for the unfinished music of her life.

Back home, Suzy would write something silly on the back of the photo of the Roman ruins—*I swear, it was like this when we got here!*—while I'd carefully record the date and precise location where the picture was taken. I'm simply not gifted with silliness like Suzy was. I appreciate it as an art form, and I try not to be frustrated by it, but gifted with it? No. I am not.

Suzy wasn't serious or "bookish" like me, but all her teachers loved her, and I always thought of her as the smart one. In addition to her sa-vant silliness, she was gifted with emotional intelligence, empathy, our mother's generous heart, an unfairly fabulous sense of style, and a humming, youthful happiness that made her naturally magnetic. She had a shy side, but people loved her to her dying day because she was just so much fun to be around.

I can be a bit of a task to be around, I'm afraid. I have no talent for sitting still. I'm not capable of pretending something is fine and dandy, when in fact it's not. If something needs to be said, I'm compelled to say it, and I do it as diplomatically as I can. But let's face it, candor's less endearing than coquettishness on any playground. My gifts were sturdy construction, a stalwart sense of justice, and the ability to whistle, ride horses bareback, and skip stones over water as well as any boy. I was a natural bridge builder. Even as a little girl, I was the ambassador between my high-spirited sister and our rightly starched father. She was three years older, but when Suzy was grounded, I was the hostage negotiator. When Suzy exceeded her curfew, I was the peace envoy.

When Suzy died, my life's work was born. Her meaning became my mission.

Born on Halloween, 1943, in Peoria, Illinois, a gentle and generous place that embodies the very soul of Americana, Suzy was three when I came along in December 1946. Mom says she peered at me over the edge of the bassinet and said, "Well! She's quite a character."

We were thick as thieves from that moment on. Suzy was always a queen bee in the neighborhood gang, and I was thrilled to be *Suzy Goodman's little sister.* I was her entourage, her liege, her cheerful sidekick, ambitiously pedaling my tricycle in the wake of her fleet-footed, inventive escapades. I can't remember a single instance of her telling me to buzz off or leave her alone or go play with the other kindergarten babies so she could hang out with the big girls who had more sophisticated things to do.

As our mother ages so gracefully, I can't help thinking what a couple of grand old ladies Suzy and I would have been together. That was our plan from the time we were little girls. My sister and I expected to age gracefully, set up housekeeping, cultivate a nice cutting garden, and sit in lawn chairs, watching our grandchildren play. We never discussed the fate of our beloved spouses; we just naturally assumed we'd outlive them in some "God's in his Heaven, all's right with the world" kind of way. It never crossed our minds that we'd be hip-broken or infirm. Not us. We'd be the spry old dames delivering Meals on Wheels, organizing holiday toy drives, knitting mittens for the underprivileged, quilting lap robes for all the tragic polio children.

The muggy summer of 1952 teemed with mosquitoes and clingy midwestern humidity. The school year ended (I was fresh out of first grade, Suzy liberated from fourth), but instead of that lazy, hazy wide-open summer feeling, we found ourselves in a world of closed doors and shuttered windows. It seemed to Suzy and me as if the city of Peoria had pulled into itself like a turtle, afraid to poke so much as a toe out to do anything. The ice cream parlor and candy store closed up shop. The streets and sidewalks felt muted and unfamiliar. Women hurried through the grocery store, holding the cart handle with a fresh hanky or dishcloth. We'd already been told there would be no movies, no carnivals, no concerts in the park. When Mother told us the municipal pool was closed, Suzy groaned.

"What about the lake?" she asked.

"They're letting a few people swim there," said Mother. "Invitation only."

I raised the possibility of the swimming pool at Uncle Bob and Aunt Helen's house or the wading pool at the park or even our little plastic pool in the backyard, but Mother shook her head.

"Dr. Moffet says children can get polio from going in the water."

"Clean water right out of the hose?" I said skeptically. "How would that give a kid polio?"

"I'm not sure," said Mom. "It's a virus, and it's very contagious. Now scientists are saying not to swim. I saw it in the newspaper. You girls should tell the other kids. Help spread the word about that. Even if it looks perfectly clean—and I don't care how hot it is—you girls don't go near the pool. Understand?" And knowing us as well as she did, she added, "Nancy, I'm counting on you to obey me."

Suzy tucked her knees under her chin, wrapping her arms around her legs, and I put my arm across her shoulders. She wasn't pouting; it made her sad to think about the poor polio children with their wizened limbs and squeaky little wheelchairs, their drawn curtains and dilated eyes longing for outside. It terrified her and broke her heart whenever we heard of another child in our neighborhood tumbling into the bottomless well of his own little bed.

These days we've all but forgotten what a scourge it was, but in 1952, there was a global epidemic. "Infantile paralysis" was a malevolent phantom that shadowed every summer day and haunted every cricket-filled night, poised to cripple and kill with one touch to the spine, the most deeply dreaded childhood disease of the twentieth century worldwide.

Mom stroked Suzy's strong shinbone.

"Right this minute, scientists are working to develop a vaccine," she said. "We have to do everything we can to help. Like this bake sale." She set a Tupperware container on the table. Through the milky-opaque plastic, we could just make out mounds of pink-tinted frosting topped with maraschino cherries. "Every little cupcake will do its part to end the epidemic. The money helps the scientists, the scientists help physicians, and if lots more mothers and daughters collect lots more money, and the scientists keep working, someday, they'll be able to give people a shot and—" She snapped her fingers. "No more polio."

Of course, in the oppressive heat of that long, sequestered summer, this grand vision sounded as ridiculous to me and Suzy as a cure for breast cancer sounds to all the naysayers presently telling me how impossible that is.

But in that first prosperous decade following World War II, the idea was still fresh in the American mind that we could accomplish anything when we all pulled together for the good of our nation. An entirely new form of media—*television*—swept the country faster and more infectiously than any virus, creating (or perhaps simply awakening) a scaly but softhearted dragon, the *mass audience*, provoking awareness that a viable vaccine was agonizingly close. Mothers saw their children standing on knobby pony legs just this side of that tipping point, mothers who'd recently awakened to the idea that the hands of women—women's voices, women's work—could build bombs as well as grow roses. In that moment, a singular need met its cultural match. Grassroots philanthropy sprang up, money rushed forth, and before the clock ticked into the sixties, a solution was discovered, a bridge was built between science and society, and the phantom was vanquished.

In the United States alone, 58,000 people were stricken with poliomyelitis in 1952. More than 3,000 died; another 21,000 were left disabled. Jonas Salk's vaccine was licensed in 1955 and was being widely distributed by 1959. In 1962, there were fewer than 1,000 cases of polio reported. In 1963, there were fewer than 100. These days, polio is a quarter-page sidebar in a history book.

Along the way, of course, skeptics in all their towering intellect persistently pointed out the many reasons the virtual eradication of polio could never be accomplished.

My mother respectfully disagreed, efficient and undeterred in her daily purpose. Suzy and I were bundled into the family station wagon every weekend to accompany Mom on her various missions. It wasn't up for debate; it's what we did. I'm in the habit of saying Mom was a "tireless volunteer," but putting that on paper, I realize it's ridiculous. Of course, she was tired. She must have been exhausted by all she did, but she did it anyway, and without complaint, which makes her all the more remarkable. In addition to her organized charity work, there were always little personal mercies: a casserole for someone just out of the hospital, a freshly folded laundry basket of diapers, the weeding of a flowerbed, whatever she could do to lighten a neighbor's load.

That summer she had to be careful. Rather than risk bringing the virus into our home, she'd put together a basket of food and other necessities and leave them on the recipient's porch with a light tap on the front door. The lady of the house would move the curtain aside and wave, waiting to open the door until Mommy was safely out on the sidewalk.

"Instead of dwelling on all the things you can't do," said Mother, "figure out what you *can* do. What you *will* do. My mother used to say, 'If you have to ask what to do, get out of the kitchen.' I'll bet you girls could come up with something if you put your heads together."

We piled into the station wagon and set out on our appointed rounds. Sweltering in the backseat, Suzy and I complained and deviled each other like a couple of spiny pill bugs.

"Girls, that's enough."

Mom sent a few ominous warnings over the transom as she negotiated the stop-and-go downtown traffic, but Suzy and I kept at it until the old station wagon swung to the side of the street and lurched to a halt. Suzy and I rarely saw our mother's patience fail. Every once in a great while, there might be a flare of angry words or a swift slam of the silverware drawer, but even that was as startling and incongruous as a griffin landing on the Sunday dinner table.

Mother didn't raise her voice, but her tone crackled with aggravation. *"Out."*

Suzy and I looked at each other, looked out at the unfamiliar neighborhood. Surely, she didn't mean—

"I said, *out.*"

Our parents didn't believe in corporal punishment; Mother disciplined by eye contact. We met her withering gaze in the rearview mirror for a tense *Don't test me* moment, then Suzy opened her door. We shuffled out onto the curb, and I instinctively reached for Suzy's hand, knowing she'd take care of me now that we were on our own in the world and would have to get jobs in factories or join the army or find a band of nomads to camp out with.

Mother stood in front of us in the blazing sun, shielding her eyes with her hand.

"People have died for this country," she said. "People have sacrificed their lives so you could live in peace and freedom, and all that's asked of you is that you take care of it. *Stewardship.* That's all. You care enough about your community to look after those who aren't as fortunate as you. When you see someone in need, you *give.* When you see something wrong, you *fix* it. Because this is *your* country, it's *your* community. You can't sit around on your duff waiting for someone else to make it better. It's up to *you.*"

She shook her finger at us, genuinely angry. Suzy and I stared down at our Mary Janes, waiting for something we hadn't heard a thousand times.

"If you girls devoted half the energy you use complaining and bickering to actually doing something for somebody else, I think you'd be amazed at what you can accomplish. So can I count on you? Are you willing to be good stewards for your country?" asked Mother. "Because

I'll tell you right now, you're not getting back in that car until I hear you say it. Both of you."

"I'll be a good steward," Suzy responded immediately.

Mother cut her pointed gaze over to me, but I locked my arms in front of my round little middle, sun prickling at the back of my neck. *I'm five,* I wanted to tell her. Big enough to know I wasn't big enough to do anything huge or meaningful or missionary. But there was no use arguing that angle with Ellie Goodman, Standard Bearer, Doer of Good, Righter of Wrongs, Mitzvah Maven.

Suzy jimmied me with her elbow and hissed, "Just say it so we can go."

"I'll be a good steward," I said without budging the square set of my jaw.

Mother opened the car door. Suzy and I climbed in, thoroughly abashed. Returning to the road before her, Mom steered back into the traffic and procceded with her errands, and we trooped dutifully, if not cheerfully, behind her. That night, as I lay thinking wistfully about cold hose water in a plastic pool, Suzy bounded onto my bed.

"Nanny! I know what we should do to be good stewards."

"What?" I yawned.

"*Variety show.*" Suzy hatched her brilliant idea like a magician turning a pigeon out of a top hat. "A song-and-dance variety show and you can sing and dance and I'll sell tickets. We'll get everybody to help."

It was an ambitious undertaking, but I had no doubt Suzy could rally all the neighborhood children into cast and crew and sell tickets to all the adults, because everyone loved Suzy and would pretty much give her whatever she asked for. I could belt out all the words to "The Secretary Song." (Remember that great old Rosemary Clooney number with the "bibidi boo bot" chorus?) Just in case, I fortified my stage presence with a Donald Duck hat that actually quacked. A bit of the razzle-dazzle, I figured, to compensate for any vocal prowess that might be slightly lacking.

By noon the next day, all twenty-three children who lived in our neighborhood were on board. Suzy and I were like a couple of Broadway impresarios, auditioning talent, casting acts, herding crew. Suzy had most of the roughneck little boys corralled with her irresistible smile, and I strong-armed the stragglers. A grand theater was jury-rigged, employing the side of our garage as a backdrop. Something right out of a Mickey Rooney movie. Suzy went out and sold sixty-four tickets. That evening, friends and neighbors gathered on the lawn with folding chairs and picnic blankets.

I can't begin to remember what was on the program. Some of the kids were genuinely talented, but there were a few painfully unpracticed performances on school band instruments, I suppose, maybe a mangled magic trick or two, a few fruits of tap and ballet class, some cheerleading and gymnastics, but of course, the whole program was inherently adorable because our appreciative audience was composed of people who adored us. I trotted out for my Rosemary Clooney number and delivered that thing like a wrecking ball.

Understand that I was a chubby little girl—and not endearingly chubby like Darla in *The Little Rascals*. More of an ungainly chubby. Like Chubby in *The Little Rascals*. But I'd never been made to feel self-conscious about it, so when the time came, I put myself out there, completely confident, uninhibited, the way consistently loved children naturally are. (How I wish I could go back and bottle a little of that chutzpah for my grown-up self.) Thinking back to that moment, it's plain to see that the first thing Mom did to prepare me and my sister for a life of service was to nurture in us a sense of self-worth. The very first step toward giving to others is grateful recognition of our own assets.

They say you're happiest doing what you did as a child, and those were the moments I remember most: when Suzy and I were fully engaged, *performing*—not in the sense of putting on a show to generate applause—performing in the sense of doing. Performing an act of kindness—or an act of will. Generating a response. I probably could have been a good theater producer.

"If there's a dog that needs biting," Daddy used to say, "Nancy's the one to bite it."

I've always excelled at backstage cat-herding and organization, but I'm a pretty good entertainer, too, and you have to entertain people at least a little if you want them truly on your side. Suzy was the visual artist. She understood the dynamics of drama and spectacle, what it takes to sweep people in and make them fall in love with an idea, a place, or a cause. In retrospect, I understand how moving it must have been for these terrified parents to see their healthy children dance. Our neighborhood variety show was a resounding success. There was no lack of applause for the Clooney number, but my "bibidi boo bot" may have been a little off, because the next day, Suzy tactfully suggested, "Next time, Nanny, it might be better if I sing and you sell tickets."

Mother drove us to St. Francis Hospital on Glen Oak Avenue. Elated, Suzy and I marched to the administrative desk in the front lobby and presented the receptionist with a crisp white envelope containing $50.14 in pure polio-killing, spine-saving, all-American do-gooding cash. A few days later we got a thank-you note from Sister Walburga, the hospital superintendent, assuring us the money would be "put to very good advantage."

Nuts and bolts. Dollars and cents. Cause and effect. The lesson wasn't lost on Suzy or me. This is where the rubber meets the road, I realized. This is where will meets way.

A fundraiser is born.

So began Suzy's and my charitable life together. It was my earliest inkling of what goes into the chemistry of change: moment meets messenger, information becomes action. Hearts and minds shift to a new paradigm, money happens, and it all comes together.

A Brief History of the Beast

THE EARLIEST documented cases of breast cancer appear in the Edwin Smith Papyrus, one of several existing papyri that detail ancient Egyptian medical practices. The unknown physician who crafted this document described a number of ailments and injuries and how they should be treated with surgery, magic, or medicinal herbs. Warm tumors in the breast were likely the result of an infection. The remedy: cauterization. A shuddering thought, but the patient probably lived to tell about it. In the case of hard, cold tumors deep within the breast, the scroll states simply, "There is no treatment."

This wasn't a disease the Egyptian physician saw often. Malignant tumors of all kinds were noted with about the same frequency in most of the same gender and age demographics that apply today. Since he recognized that breast tumors varied in nature, it's possible this physician may have also observed that those presenting in younger women tended to kill with a swift, unstoppable virulence. But breast cancer is far more prevalent in women over fifty, and most women in ancient Egypt didn't live past thirty-five, so this patient was rare.

One woman in thousands.

Given what we know about this disease and about ancient Egyptian culture, I imagine One Woman watched with interest as the physician carefully recorded her case. She almost certainly didn't know how to read or write. *There is no treatment,* he told her, straightforward but not without compassion, I think. He seems like a "good doctor" sort in his other writings. Perhaps he offered her a tincture made from alcohol and flowers, a prayer, a little stone god, some comfort she could cling to.

One Woman went home to her family and went on with her life. The tumor in her breast grew steadily over the coming months. The breast itself seemed larger, the skin thick and red, spidered with veins and stretch marks, but she felt strong and went about her daily business. Some days were better than others, and she felt a flash of hope. She laid fruit in front of the little stone god, whispered in its ear. Then came another day, and her hope faded.

The cancer metastasized, spreading from breast to breast, then riddling lymph nodes, lungs, spine, and liver. First, she felt a firm bulge under her right arm. Her fingers tingled and burned with neuralgia. She dropped things sometimes. Then there was a stabbing pain in her spine when she bent to lift her small child. Eventually, she had to sit on the floor and let him climb into her lap, holding him over on the side where she could still stand the pain if he leaned against her breast. When she laughed or yawned, there was a stitching pull deep inside her chest. It seemed to form a tight fist in her lung at times. She'd wake up coughing, struggling for breath. It made the baby cry, but when she tried to go to him, she was dizzy and nauseous. She was bent with the effort of getting up in the morning. Her complexion yellowed. The coughing spells settled into a nagging pattern of hoarse, painful barking.

Under her linen dress, her breasts were visibly misshapen and distended now. When she was naked, she could see a shadow rising to the surface. The skin became translucent purple and gradually gave way like a slit in a temple curtain. The lesions wept a thin blackish-bloody fluid. The skin crusted and opened, an unblinking eye with the slick, eel-colored tumor at its center. Her sisters tried to clean and care for her, but on a cellular level, the tumors were dying as rapidly as they multiplied, so the bulging tissue became necrotic, and the smell of death hung in the air, permeating the bedclothes, lingering in her hair. The woman's strength leaked out of her. Loved ones tried to feed her broth and soft meal cakes, but she was quickly wasting away, barely a thread of herself.

At the end, her sisters sat next to the bed, whispering to each other. *Is she breathing? Did you see her eyelids flicker?* They were terrified to touch her now. What if this dark disease was contagious? They had to think of their children. Lying in bed at night, they moved their hands over their own breasts, afraid to exhale. *Here? Didn't she say it started here, with a bump like a small pebble?*

It would be nice to think someone who loved her held her when she died.

A thousand years went by.

Four centuries before the birth of Jesus—about the time Siddhartha became the Buddha and Malachi the last of the Hebrew prophets—the Greek scientist Hippocrates observed coal-black tumors erupting through the skin of his patients and concluded that the malady was a manifestation of too much black bile or *melanchole* in a woman overly influenced by the element of earth, an internalization of autumn's dry cold. Tentacled tumors examined during autopsies spidered into the body, evoking the image of a crab.

Karkinos.

Cancer.

There was no hope of treatment or cure, so it was better, Hippocrates hypothesized, to prolong the life of the afflicted by making her as comfortable as possible in all other respects. He discouraged his students from surgically excising tumors from their patients' breasts, based on his assumption that pervasive black bile was a systemic problem. Barring intervention by the gods, the disease would invariably return with swiftly killing insistence.

For two thousand years, his conclusions remained the conventional wisdom. There was a glimmer in 200 C.E. when Galen, a devoted follower and biographer of Hippocrates, recorded his observation that not all breast tumors were created equal; some were slow and insidious, others quick and virulent. Not all had the iconic crab legs; some blossomed deep in the bosom and remained isolated from surrounding tissue like a lily floating in a pond. Galen treated patients with opium, licorice, castor oil, and incantations, but ultimately, he confirmed the six-hundred-year-old findings of Hippocrates: Breast cancer was a systemic disease caused by the darkest humor, surgery was contraindicated, sufferers were doomed. This remained the final word on breast cancer for another fifteen centuries.

Roughly around the time of the American Revolution, in an effort to discredit the time-honored ideas of humoral medicine, French physician Jean Astruc placed a slice of a breast cancer tumor in the oven next to a slice of beef, cooked both to a jerkylike consistency, chewed each one thoroughly, and declared that they tasted exactly the same, proving (among other things I can't even bear to joke about) that the breast cancer tumor contained neither bile nor acid.

Out with the old superstitions; in with empirical state-of-the-art methods. Now the true cause of breast cancer was wide open for speculation.

One school of thought pointed to the high incidence of breast cancer among nuns as evidence that breast cancer was caused by a lack of sex. Because breasts are sexual organs, *n'est-ce pas*? Without the fulfillment of their bountifully natural purpose, what could they do but atrophy and became cancerous? (I imagine there was no shortage of selfless lads willing to hurl themselves between innocent young women and this dreaded disease.) In women who did voluntarily engage in "relations"—randy wives and scurrilous hookers—tumors were said to arise from a lymphatic blockage caused by an overly vigorous libido. Another popular theory cited constriction of lymphatic vessels due to depression. Others blamed the curdling of unexpressed milk and the coagulation of blood caused by a sedentary lifestyle.

And so, in the enlightened age of Mozart, after three thousand years of observation and experimentation, it was scientifically deduced that if a woman presented with breast cancer, it was due to frigidity, promiscuity, craziness, laziness, or all of the above in some combination with the unknowable will of God.

One Woman after Another passed into ancient history, each less than a grain of sand, and there are places in the world where nothing has changed. Today women in developing countries echo the story of the woman in the papyrus and face their fate as if the last three thousand years never happened. I've seen One Woman's face, and I can't forget her. Sitting on a wooden stool by an ancient stone wall, wearing clothes right out of a Cecil B. DeMille Bible epic, she looked up at me and asked, "This disease—is it contagious?"

She has to think of her children.

At this writing, according to statistics, breast cancer is the leading cause of cancer death for American women between forty and fifty-five years of age. In One Woman's corner of the world, there are no statistics, never mind screening or even the possibility of treatment. Breast cancer comes and goes unnoted, misunderstood, taking thousands of lives with it.

One Woman at a time.

2

Founder Effect

Our father, Marvin Goodman, was of robust Russian and Lithu-anian ancestry. We suspected a little Irish, though for some rea-son, no one in his family would talk about it. Daddy and his sister, Ruth, had white hair, greenish eyes, and fair skin. The old family portraits are sharply angled with square jaws and stiff upper lips. Daddy's father was a deputy sheriff in Colorado, which was an extraordinary thing for a Jew-ish man to be back then. Daddy's mother was smart and articulate, but quick and unforgiving as a mousetrap. She ended up with Alzheimer's, but even as her mind and memories abandoned her, she remained con-stant about what mattered to her, most notably (it seemed to Suzy and me) the cleanliness, proper behavior, and mandatory silence of children.

Our hardworking father was a driven but principled businessman, and I'm glad to be my father's daughter in so many ways. In those days, it was hard to find any Jewish family who hadn't lost someone in the Ho-locaust, and our family was no exception. Yet Daddy never forfeited one ounce of his soul to hatred. I learned from him the empowering nature of purpose, how our own courage will rise up and surprise us when beck-oned in service of family, country, or passion for a cause greater than ourselves. I also saw what his driven nature cost him. The years have outfitted me with that same hard-earned hockey gear.

Suzy, of course, remains forever carefree and barelegged in a sum-mer dress. She has the advantage of never growing older, never knowing bereavement, never making it to a place where unwelcome wisdom inter-feres with a decent night's sleep.

I understand now that charity is a form of gratitude, and certainly, Suzy and I had much to be grateful for, but the dynamics of stewardship and volunteerism were central to our upbringing, a family tradition that stayed with us powerfully because we were shown, not told. Our parents were sincere but comfortably reformed Jews, and we attended a scandalously easygoing temple, Anshai Emeth, where people were zealous about service to their country, community, and each other, but fairly wide open when it came to religious dogma and ritual. The fun-loving, affectionate community met in a building that used to be a Baptist church. They had their share of family squabbles, but I think it speaks volumes that in several old photographs of temple events, the son of one of the members is surrounded by friends and beaming broadly, wearing a cocktail dress and full makeup.

Mom was far too busy to ponder the orthodoxy of charity, but she embodied the idea of *tzedakah,* which isn't about performing *acts* of kindness; it's about the state of *being* kind. This isn't something my mother has to think about. It's simply who she is. Her mother's daughter.

Mother's tribe was a boisterous, demonstrative bunch. This branch of the prosperous Silberstein family started over from scratch when Great-Grandpa Moses emigrated from Berlin to the United States in the late 1800s, but he prospered in America as well. Mommy's mother, Freda Newman—affectionately called "Fritzi"—was a founding member of the local Red Cross chapter in Peoria and dedicated most of her life to serving in hospitals and hospice. During World War I, Fritzi and her family took in soldiers, tended the wounded, comforted the dying. It offended her faith and her sense of justice to think that each of these brave young men had made it through the trenches and mustard gas, only to come home and die in his bed.

One day, Fritzi's nineteen-year-old sister, Esther, came home from work, disoriented and complaining of a strangely piercing headache. Fritzi and her big sister, Rose, made Esther lie down, and Fritzi ran for a doctor. According to the story that was passed down from Fritzi to Mother and from Mother to Suzy and me, the doctor came, briefly assessed the patient, dashed cold water in her face, and told her frantic family, "She'll get up." Ninety minutes later, Esther was dead.

"Aneurysm, maybe. Or an embolism." Mommy shakes her head when she talks about it now. "Nobody knew back then. Nobody questioned doctor's orders."

It's not likely that they could have done anything to save Esther, but doing *something* would have saved Fritzi from having to live with the fact that nothing had been done. Fueled by rage over the way her sister had been treated, she started asking questions from that day forward. She demanded answers, staunchly advocated for those who weren't in a position to stand up for themselves, and brought Mommy up to do the same.

My mother, Eleanor Tressa Newman, was born in 1920, effectively the only child of eight parents. Grandma Fritzi and Grandpa Leo (later affectionately dubbed "Boppie" by Suzy and me) lived in a big apartment with a constantly revolving cast of relatives, neighbors, friends, soldiers, and strangers—basically anyone who needed a place to stay. Growing up during the Great Depression, Mom was accustomed to sleeping in the dining room whenever some displaced drifter needed a bed for the night. When she was a little girl, if one of the uncles or a friend of the family was in the hospital, Fritzi would station her outside the hospital room and say, "Ellie, stay here while I dash home and make dinner for everyone. If anything happens, you run to the nurse's station and tell them to call me." Mommy took this responsibility very seriously. I think it brought out the guardian angel in her. Nothing was more important than looking out for each other.

Mom's flamboyant Aunt Rose came and went between husbands, and the dashing uncles all spoiled and doted on their little Ellie. She loved to travel with them to Atlantic City, the Illinois State Fair, or anywhere else someone would take her. She went to visit Aunt Rose and her husband of the moment in California or New York. Once a year, the whole family traveled south to see relatives still living in Kentucky, where they'd been raising hogs since before the Civil War, and Mommy had her own little billy goats there.

Mom was beautiful and stylish, making the most of everything, even when there was little money to work with. Aunt Rose passed along an evening dress with a beautifully crafted pearl and rhinestone collar. The fancy gown was too big and not something Mother had occasion to wear, but she snipped off the collar and sewed it onto a plain black dress Fritzi had made for her. And when that dress became faded and worn, Mommy snipped the collar off and sewed it onto the next generation. Old photographs show her blossoming into that collar. At first, on a girl of twelve, it seems a bit much, but by the time she was in her late teens, it looks elegant and proud. Instead of the collar glitzing her up, she's the one making the old hand-me-down look like something special.

When I was sixteen, the brilliant Betty Friedan published the now-legendary feminist classic *The Feminine Mystique*. Imagine how impressed I was to learn that Mommy and Ms. Friedan were actually classmates back in temple school. In my mind at the time, this was Mommy's only brush with greatness. They didn't dislike each other, but they weren't pals. Mom was one of the *It* girls who probably left Betty chronically perplexed.

"She was whip-smart and very serious," Mom says. "She didn't have much use for girls who were breezy and frivolous and not deep thinkers."

Mom went to college for a year, but there wasn't money for her to continue, and she's only a little wistful about that now. She met my father at a B'nai B'rith party when she was not quite twenty. He and his family had made their way to the Midwest. She'd just gotten home from California, where she'd been visiting Aunt Rose, and while she was gone, Fritzi had begun playing cards with Daddy's sister, Ruth. Daddy waltzed over to Mom, orchestrated a quick exchange of partners, and was immediately smitten, but Mommy was on a date with someone else. By the end of their first dance, it was all settled. She abandoned her other suitor and stayed out with Dad until four in the morning.

He told her right up front that he intended to be the head of his household and provide for his family; he envisioned a wife who'd devote herself to making a pleasant home, raising well-groomed, well-behaved children, and actively participating in community and charity projects. Though Mommy and Betty Friedan had more in common than either of them would have believed back in temple school, this proposal fit perfectly with Mom's vision for her own life. She understood the difference between service and servitude and wore her traditional role the same way she always wore perfect shoes: she liked feeling comfortable, functional, and beautiful. Mom never questioned or denigrated the different choices made by other women, but this was her choice, and she never regretted it. An unquestionably liberated woman, my mother did exactly what she wanted to do. Her parents loved my father. The uncles, impressed with young Marvin Goodman's entrepreneurial spirit and cast-iron work ethic, gladly brought him into the family real estate business.

A few months before my parents were married, Grandma Fritzi took ill with a kidney infection. A simple thing, these days: usually little more than an inconvenience. Ten minutes in the physician's office. Ninety seconds at the pharmacy drive-through. Penicillin, the drug that would have saved her, was discovered quite by accident in 1928 and first tested on human subjects in 1939. In 1940, when Fritzi's fever drove her to the hospital, that simple but effective remedy was in the pipeline and would be commonly available just a few years later—barely a breath in the scope of history. Meanwhile, sulfa drugs were all the rage, the most potent weapon there was against battlefield infection; soldiers were issued a powdered form in their first aid kits. But because of its low solubility, sulfanilamide tended to crystallize in the kidneys when taken internally. Fritzi's doctor—*drunk,* Mother maintains to this day—accidentally gave Fritzi a toxic dose.

Poor Mommy crouched in the corner of the hospital room as her mother, this angel of mercy, died in twisting agony. It left her grief-stricken, infuriated, and radicalized. From that day forward, contrary to the "doctor's orders" standard of the times, Mom was unfashionably fearless about questioning the judgments of God and doctors who think they're God's golf buddies, and she was utterly committed to the temple definition of stewardship Fritzi had instilled in her.

"Don't let the world fall apart on you, Ellie," Fritzi said before she died. "Just do those things that need to be done."

Mother had been Fritzi's right hand from the time she was little. Now it was her responsibility to clean, cook, and care for Boppie and the bachelor uncles, attempt to keep Rose on the straight and narrow, and tend to whatever strays and strangers needed her help.

She and Daddy got married later that year. Suzy and I came along on the leading edge of the baby boom. The war was over. Patriotism was a fervor. Optimism was a fever. Two weeks after I was born, movie theaters across the country were showing *It's a Wonderful Life,* and in Peoria, Illinois, this was most certainly true.

It was Boppie who taught me the gentle art of strong-arming when I was just a little girl. Every year he took me by the hand and escorted me through the buildings he managed, selling Girl Scout cookies. He was a jolly, beneficent landlord, and his tenants were always pleased to see him, but even I could see that my cookies enjoyed a whole different reception when I walked into the room under Boppie's corporate umbrella.

"Why, Leo!" the tenant would say. "Hello! How are you?"

"Very well, and you? How's your wife and the new baby? Of course, you remember my granddaughter, Nancy."

"Oh . . . is it that time of year already?"

My cue to pitch the Thin Mints, sandwich cookies, and shortbread squares stamped with the Girl Scout emblem along with a brief recitation on the illustrious history of the Girl Scouts of America and a couple of talking points on how the community would be served by a thriving population of healthy young women, all outfitted with skills in life and archery from Camp Tapawingo.

I learned a lot from our cookie sales excursions, and I loved being squired around by Boppie. His laugh was thunderous. His presence was huge. Doors seemed to open magically in front of him. He was no tycoon; Fritzi's brothers were the driving force behind the family business. But Boppie brought a healthy soul to their endeavors. He fostered good will and intangible assets that are just as bankable as wheels and deals at the end of the day—which is essentially what he did during our shortbread sorties. Boppie didn't sell any cookies for me; he just got me in the room. But it's amazing what a motivated person can do when partnered with someone who has the clout to get her in the room. And I was very motivated. Back then, there were no incentives or rewards for selling Girl Scout cookies; our reward was having Girl Scouts, and that meant a lot to us.

After the war, Mom banded together with a small group of friends to start the Girl Scouts chapter in Peoria. Boy Scouts had been going strong for decades, and it rankled Mommy that there was nothing like that for girls, but she heard the same dismissive arguments Girl Scout leaders had been getting since the 1920s. Conventional wisdom said girls didn't need the self-reliance skills boys needed. No money was going to be invested in that. So the mothers of invention came up with the Girl Scout cookie.

Once the Peoria chapter was up and running, Mom ascended the ranks in the Kickapoo Council, participating as a leader at the regional and national levels.

Mommy was deeply offended by racial segregation, which persisted through the 1950s. She made sure we understood how wrong it was when we came upon restrooms and water fountains marked "White" and "Colored."

"Think how you'd feel if that sign said 'Jew,'" she said. "We don't spend our money in a place that does that, and it's our duty to let them know it."

She didn't want Suzy and me to participate in racially segregated play groups or summer camps, so she spearheaded the efforts that eventually resulted in the acquisition of 640 wooded acres that became Camp Tapawingo, a culturally inclusive oasis of unabashed Girl Scout power.

"When you see a wrong, right it."

That's Mommy.

I lived for Camp Tapawingo every summer. Suzy wasn't much of a camper, so it gave me an opportunity to take the lead, and it was a powerful incentive as I trudged through each school year.

My first day of kindergarten, the teacher called my mother to report that I'd left the building, climbed a tree in the schoolyard, and refused to come down. Mommy hustled right over, and stood beneath the branch where I'd perched myself.

"Nancy? What on earth is going on?"

"This is stupid," I told her. "They're not doing it right."

"Come down," said Mom. "Tomorrow will be better." But it wasn't. It didn't take me long to figure out that everyone else saw things differently from the way I did. I realized that I was the one not doing it right and assumed I was the only one for whom learning was such labor. Numbers turned to a tangle of hieroglyphics and barbed wire somewhere between my eyes and the back of my brain. Back then, there was no testing, no diagnostics to identify the way numbers knotted in front of my eyes. Lacking any other terminology, I diagnosed myself as *dumb*. I knew I'd have to work harder than everyone else in order to compensate for that—and to conceal it.

I loved how proud it made my father when I did well in school; that alone was worth the struggle. I was willing to work as hard as I had to, but ultimately the effect of all that was a restless feeling that my nose would be forever pressed to the glass, that I'd always be double-tasking and still never quite measuring up.

It also trained me to think outside the box.

Daddy used to tell (with great amusement) the story of that particular Halloween. Mom had gone to Chicago for a national Girl Scout leadership conference. Dad had some important matter rumbling in his office, and Suzy and I were too small to go trick-or-treating on our own, so it was decided that she and I would stay home, staffing the front door and handing out candy to all the lucky little children with *nice* parents—children whose world had not collapsed into a wretched coal hod of inequity, as ours clearly had.

When the house was built, our resourceful dad had installed an intercom system at the front door, and equally resourceful, I hatched a brilliant plan just as a merrily costumed pair of trick-or-treaters skipped up to the door and rang the bell. Before they could shout the customary threat of extortion, I cranked up the intercom and mustered my deepest, most ferocious voice.

"*This is God,*" I intoned. "*Drop your candy and run.*"

Suzy's eyes went as big as saucers. There was a shriek and hasty scuffling out on the front stoop. After a moment, I opened the door a crack and—victory!—the spoils were mine. I quickly gathered the scattered candy into the abandoned bags and clapped the door shut as my next victims rounded the corner at the end of the block. I repeated my brilliant trick, gathering bag after bag of ill-gotten treats until—

Ding-dong.

"This is God! Drop your candy and—"

"*Nancy.*"

There was a heavy hand on my shoulder. My almighty father. He'd come out of his office to check on us. When Mother came home in the morning, she was surprised to find a row of candy bags banked against the wainscoting in the dining room and me, waiting in shame on a side chair. Needless to say, she was appalled to hear what had happened, and after a resounding lecture on the moral consequences of envy, fearmongering, and too much sugar, she sent me off on an all-day walkathon, schlepping those bags of candy all over the neighborhood until I'd returned every single one to its rightful owner.

Beyond reinforcement of the single overarching theme of my upbringing—"Do the right thing"—I'm not sure I learned any great lessons from this experience, but I try not to mess with divinity. I've met such a wealth of good people in my time—sincere, faithful, salt-of-the-earth people from every corner of the world, every conceivable religious tradition—that it's not possible for me to see any one cut-and-dried dogma that encompasses the human spirit. I have faith and doubt in equal parts most of the time. Having walked beside two popes and the Dalai Lama, I would never presume to question someone else's vision of God, and I'm immediately skeptical when I hear a voice saying the big-world equivalent of "This is God. Drop your candy and run."

For one thing, the Jewish faith doesn't include any threat of eternal damnation. To my mind, Hell is a place where people don't care about one another. Hell is the squandering of one's life on Earth without any good purpose. I don't believe cancer in general or Suzy's death in particular are part of God's plan. That puppet-master brand of theology removes responsibility from human hands, even as science persistently whispers that many cancers are caused by environmental and behavioral factors largely within our ability to control. I think God's plan (or at least His or Her desperate hope) is that we, the great and industrious anthill that is humanity, will love each other enough to apply ourselves to the scientific effort and figure out how to solve this problem.

Likewise, I'm skeptical when any scientific voice—be it physician, researcher, or school of thought—makes any sweeping declarations of what is true or untrue, absolutely right or absolutely wrong, in the arena of cancer research or cancer care. I've witnessed the lifesaving value of both chemotherapy and prayer, mastectomy and lumpectomy, allopathic medicine and complementary therapies. The only singular truth about breast cancer is this: There is no singular truth about breast cancer. Our best strategy is to respect and listen to one another, share what we learn, reach across the aisle, and make women's lives a higher priority than political agenda. Because I guess there actually is one absolute truth about breast cancer: *There shouldn't be any.*

Fear is a powerful weapon, and the rationalization that it's being wielded in the service of some imagined greater good doesn't make it any less immoral. Waiting in shame for my mother to come home, I suppose I sat there rationalizing that too much candy was terribly unhealthy for those little children, so in reality, I'd done them a healthy good service taking it away from them. Similarly, there are those who assert that routine mammograms are "uncomfortable" and cancer awareness is "depressing." There are still a few old-fashioned physicians out there who discourage women from seeking second—or third or fourth—opinions. In many cases, women would seek a second opinion but don't have access to it because of restrictions in their insurance policy, dictated by someone who isn't even a physician.

When Suzy and I were growing up, there were very few women physicians, and that undoubtedly contributed to the unwritten but unquestionable authority of male physicians over women patients. When a woman tried to assert some right of proprietorship over her own body, she was usually cowed with some variation of "I am God. Drop your candy and run."

Mom was wonderful about teaching Suzy and me to respect and care for our bodies. When my weight topped a hundred pounds during second grade, she gently intervened. Enlisting the guidance of our dear Dr. Moffet, the kindly family physician who'd expertly cared for us since we were born into his hands, she educated herself on the matter, and without making me feel ugly or obtuse, firmly guided me in the healthiest possible direction. In addition to a balanced diet, she encouraged my interest in competitive swimming, horseback riding, and other activities that nurtured my sporty side.

As Suzy and I grew, Mom encouraged our independence. We were active in Girl Scouts and B'nai B'rith, various charities, and temple activities. I begged for riding lessons, and once I discovered what it felt like to fly along at a full gallop, there was no stopping me. Suzy rode too, but she rode like a duchess in a parade, while I turned into an unbridled cowboy.

One day when I was nine and Suzy was twelve, we arrived at the barn just as they were preparing to geld a beautiful yearling. As they eased the tranquilized pony to the ground, Suzy and I hung back by the fence, but when the veterinarian drew his tools from a leather bag and got down to the business at hand, Suzy got horribly upset and ran away screaming. My initial reaction was "How silly!" but I realized later this wasn't about Suzy being a wimp or wanting attention. My sister was excruciatingly tenderhearted, empathetic, and easily upset by any thought of violence or mutilation.

I, on the other hand, scrambled up a tree for a better view, fascinated by the entire procedure, and when it was over I peppered the vet with a thousand questions. *Why do they do that? What's that thing? Will he be able to run as fast? Can I look in the bucket?* I tried to share what I learned with Suzy so she'd know it wasn't just some random atrocity.

"It *helps* him, Suzy. He'll be healthier and easier to ride and won't hurt himself scrapping with other horses."

Suzy wanted none of that. She covered her ears as if she could still hear the yearling's frightened whinnies.

"Nan, don't you know what that is? It means he can't—you know." She blushed pink, trying to think of a way to say it. "He can never have children. Don't you think that's sad?"

I was stumped. I'd been so fascinated with the basic mechanics of it that this aspect hadn't even occurred to me. Daddy and the wranglers were eager to point out all the good reasons for doing it, but this had never been brought up in their explanation of the procedure. It was all efficacy, no emotion. (Balancing the two continues to be one of the greatest challenges in cancer care.)

While the event didn't deter her from riding, Suzy was never quite as eager as I was to get to the barn. For me, riding was synonymous with joy, freedom, feeling alive. I learned everything I could about the history and science of horses, and knowing all that made it feel even more wonderful. It frustrated me that Suzy didn't see it that way, and I worried a little that what it really meant was that Suzy was just plain *sweeter* than me.

"We have to go to horse camp," I told Suzy when school ended the following summer. "It'll be tons of fun. Please, Mom, can we?"

"We'll see," said Mom, "but Aunt Rose would like you girls to visit. I think it would be a wonderful adventure for you."

"Just the two of us?" Suzy's fork poised halfway between her plate and her astonished expression. "We'd go to New York City all by ourselves?"

"Dad and I would put you on the plane in Peoria, and Aunt Rose would be right there to meet you when you land at LaGuardia. She wants you to stay a whole week."

Our father hushed Suzy's and my joyful trilling at that, but not very sternly. Suzy was immediately buzzing with packing strategy and general enthusiasm, while I interrogated Mom about agenda and logistics. We couldn't stop chattering about our plans as we cleared the table and did the dishes, imagining New York City as nothing less than the Emerald City, the only possible habitat for Aunt Rose, the most outrageously fabulous woman we'd ever encountered.

Suzy worshiped Aunt Rose because she was the epitome of fashion and femininity, stirring clouds of chiffon and perfume as she made her dramatic entrances and exits, filling the rooms between with flirtatious laughter and witty Hepburn banter. Men flocked and fell all over themselves in an effort to please and impress her, and she generally had her way when it came to everything from dinner reservations to travel destinations. I worshiped Aunt Rose because she was always in motion. Grand gestures illustrated her hilarious tales of passenger ships and love interests and African safaris. She was audacious, outspoken, and fiercely self-determined. She could do anything and feared nothing. Aunt Rose was barely middle aged and had already been married four times. (Daddy used to say, "Her husbands didn't die, they escaped!") She adored Suzy and me and brought us wonderful presents from wherever she happened to be. One summer she returned from Hawaii with hula gear and ukuleles for us, showed us a few island moves, and took pictures of us giggling in our grass skirts and coconut bras. Bottom line: Aunt Rose was *fun*.

At bedtime, Mom came to our room and said, "Before you go to New York, I need to remind you that Aunt Rose was very sick last year. She had breast cancer, and they did a mastectomy, which means . . ."

"We know what it means," Suzy said brusquely. "We don't need the details."

In fact, I *didn't* know and was intensely interested in the details, but Suzy obviously didn't want the conversation to go that way. This meant one of three things: Either Suzy had heard something earlier and hadn't had a chance to clue me in, or Suzy had heard something and didn't think I should be told, or Suzy had heard nothing and didn't want to hear it now.

"Do you have any questions, Nancy?" asked Mom.

I shook my head. I had only a vague idea of what mastectomy entailed, but judging from Suzy's response, I suspected it was something irredeemably brutal.

As our plane cruised over the water into LaGuardia, I nervously wondered if Aunt Rose would have the strength to make it to the gate to meet us. If she did manage that, would we still recognize her? I breathed a deep sigh of relief when we saw her standing at the end of the Jetway, slender and stylish and still very much Aunt Rose. She was as glamorous and animated as ever, madly in love with the man who'd recently become her fourth husband, and her husband clearly was crazy about her. We rushed to throw our arms around her, and she felt whole and warm. I felt sheepish and silly for thinking she'd ever be otherwise. If anything, she felt sturdier than ever, built up and tightly buttressed by the staunch whalebone corset that provided a functional prosthetic structure to her torso. At the time, I had no inkling of how unforgiving and painful that corset must have been; all I knew or cared about was Aunt Rose, standing tall, laughing out loud, and extending a strong hand to each of her nieces.

The first few days of our adventure were filled with shopping and lunching, striding down busy streets, strolling through quiet art galleries, the quintessential New York experiences. We were starstruck when we learned that Aunt Rose lived next door to Greer Garson in a co-op at Hampshire House on Central Park South. *My Fair Lady* had just opened on Broadway, and Suzy and I were very much the flower girls transformed into a couple of grand ladies. Every hour was thrilling in some oh-so-metropolitan way, but by the third night of our Big Apple adventure, Suzy and I were plain tuckered, and even Aunt Rose was showing signs of fatigue. She retired to her room that evening, after tucking Suzy and me into the guest room, where we fell into one of those typical sister-on-sister *did not, did so* squabbles. I don't remember what it was about any more than I remember other bones of contention we used to clash over, but eventually, Suzy decided to bust out the big guns and tattle to Aunt Rose. She stalked down the hall, and I sat seething on the bed, waiting for the sound of Aunt Rose's high-heeled pumps in the hallway. Instead there was the scuttle of Suzy's bare feet on the wooden floor, like the beating of a hummingbird's wings, as she dashed back to the guest room.

"*Oh, Nanny . . . oh, Nanny,*" she breathed with her back to the door-frame.

"What is it? What's wrong?" The squabble forgotten, I was instantly up with my arms around her.

"She was . . . her . . . it's awful," Suzy whispered, blinking back tears. "I don't know how anyone could live through a thing like that."

Peering down the hall toward Aunt Rose's room, I could hear her singing. Her husband said something and they laughed languid, romantic laughter together. I tiptoed toward the light that slanted from her open doorway and held my breath as I peeked around the edge of the jamb.

Propped on pillows in a sea of ruffled bedclothes, Aunt Rose had one elegant hand in her lap, the other on an open book at her side. Her silk robe had fallen open a little, exposing the startling remnant of her chest. Concave and burned bluish-purple by high-voltage cobalt treatments, her bosom looked hollowed out and fragile. I would have sworn I could see the chambers of her heart pumping through skin as thin and discolored as onion paper.

She glanced up and smiled inquisitively. "Why, hello there."

I swallowed hard and said, "Goodnight, Aunt Rose."

The Storyteller's Mastectomy

Fanny Burney was ten when she addressed her first journal entry: "To Miss Nobody." But Fanny was somebody now. A contemporary of Jane Austen and Mary Wollstonecraft, Fanny wrote wildly popular novels that helped launch a wave of literary women that included Mary Shelley and the Brontë sisters. Fanny married General Alexandre d'Arblay, a hero of the French Revolution. In 1811, they were living happily in Paris with their sixteen-year-old son, Alexander. One of Napoleon's own physicians, Dr. Larrey, gave Fanny the news.

"You have a cancer in the breast," he told her. "There's nothing for it but the knife."

By the eighteenth century, researchers had agreed: Breast cancer was not a systemic or spiritual problem, but a localized disease, with surgery the only logical response. From its inception, however, the mastectomy set at odds two guiding principles of the practice of medicine:

Primum succurrere, "First, hasten to help."

And *Primum non nocere,* "First, do no harm."

Before the time of anesthesia, before any concept of antiseptics or any reliable method for determining the difference between benign and malignant tumors, most women who underwent mastectomies died, either from the surgery itself or from rapidly raging infection. But some survived, lending credibility to the idea that mastectomy offered a potential "perfect cure."

Surgical procedures became more and more aggressive. Even when only a small portion of the breast was diseased, surgeons zealously went after the axillary lymph nodes by opening up the armpit. Soon surgeons in Paris were performing "en bloc" mastectomies, removing the entire breast, chest wall, and lymph nodes. The director of the cancer institute at England's Middlesex Hospital urged removal of the surrounding skin as well, rather than risk a return of the cancer owing to any "mistaken kindness to the patient."

"Madame, it's a small thing," Dr. Larrey assured Fanny Burney. "You sit in a chair. I excise the tumor. All over in a few minutes. I must caution you, Madame: The consequences of procrastination are dire."

Fanny later wrote to her sister Esther that she rose at eight on the appointed day and dressed with the help of her maid; the advancing cancer had left her right arm almost useless. Young Dr. Aumont arrived with a letter from Larrey, advising her that he and his colleagues would come at ten. Larrey reassured her of his dexterity and expertise, and admonished that, for sensibility and prudence, she should "secure the absence" of her husband and son.

Fanny made a pretense of lingering over the note, struggling to hide her growing apprehension. She had to protect her son from "the unavailing wretchedness of witnessing" what was about to happen. She dashed off a note to the *chef du division du Bureau* where her husband was at work, informing him of her situation and entreating him to trump up some urgent business to detain d'Arblay until it was over. She sent her maid down to Dr. Aumont—"the terrible Herald"—to inform him in no uncertain terms, she would not receive Larrey until one.

"I have an apartment to prepare for my banished Mate," she fussed. "Two engaged nurses are on the way. I have a bed, curtains, and Heaven knows what to prepare."

Dr. Aumont remained in the salon, stolidly folding stacks of linen. Word came that the surgeons couldn't come until three. Dr. Aumont left, promising to return at that time, leaving Fanny for two lonely hours with nothing to do but contemplate her fate. She tried to write letters to her family, but the debilitating ache in her arm prevented her. She wandered the apartment, finally forcing herself to open the door to the salon, where she discovered Dr. Aumont's immense supply of bandages, compresses, sponges. Clearly, significant blood loss was anticipated.

Fanny recoiled. In a state of torpid shock, she paced until the clock struck three. Gritting her teeth at the agony in her arm, she forced a few words onto paper, short notes for d'Arblay and Alex "in case of a fatal result." She rang for her maid and hired nurses, but before she could speak to them, seven men in black—Dr. Larrey, Monsieur Dubois, Dr. Moreau, Dr. Aumont, Dr. Ribe, a pupil of Dr. Larrey, and another of Monsieur Dubois—entered without announcement. Fanny was indignant, but she found herself unable to assemble a single syllable to object.

Why so many? she wondered. *And how dare they enter without leave?*

"Dubois acted as Commander in Chief," she wrote to Esther. "He ordered a bedstead into the middle of the room. Astonished, I turned to Larrey, who had promised that an arm chair would suffice, but he hung his head, and would not look at me."

"Two old mattresses and an old sheet," Dubois told the apprentices. Those arranged to his liking, he turned to Fanny. "If Madame would mount the bed, *s'il vous plaît.*"

She stood trembling, suspended in terror, eyes darting toward the door, windows, any avenue of escape. Her maid sobbed quietly by the door; the nurses stood frozen nearby.

Dubois issued a sharp command *en militaire.* "Let those women all go."

"No!" Fanny recovered her voice. "No, *qu'elles restent*—let them remain!"

But the maid and one of the nurses were already running down the stairs. A brief squabble broke out when the second nurse ignored Dubois and stood beside Fanny, who "resisted all that were resistible" as she was compelled to take off her long *robe de chambre*, which she'd meant to retain for the sake of modesty.

"Ah, then, how did I think of my sisters!" she wrote. "I regretted that I had refused my friends—anyone upon whom I could rely. My sister Susanna—dear departed Angel!—how did I think of her! How did I long—long for my Esther—my Charlotte!"

Seeing her distress, Dubois softened and tried to soothe her.

"*Oui—c'est peu de chose* . . . it is a little thing. . . ."

He took up a scrap of paper, nervously tearing it into small bits. No one else spoke. Larrey was aloof, pale as ash. Seeing his twisting discomfort, Fanny fully comprehended the mortal gravity of this thing within her breast. Fear of it filled the room. *What must the weight of its dangerous nature be,* she thought, *if this horrific exorcism is my only hope to escape it?* Fanny climbed onto the bed and lay back, her naked bosom fully exposed. Dubois spread a cambric handkerchief over her face, but it was opaque enough for Fanny to see the seven figures in black and one in white as they surrounded her. Through the lace edging, she glimpsed polished steel, then she closed her eyes.

Larrey's voice. "Who will hold the center?" Fanny's eyes flew open. She saw Dubois describe with his index finger a line from top to bottom, then across, then a wide circle. *They intended to take the entire breast.* Fanny sat up and cupped her breast with her hand. She had no intention of letting it go.

"Who will hold the *center*? I will, Monsieur! *C'est moi!*"

She tried to explain that the pain in her breast radiated from one small area; Dubois gently but firmly pressed her back into position and replaced the cambric hanky. Despairing, Fanny closed her eyes, "relinquishing all watching, all resistance, sadly resolute, wholly resigned."

My dearest Esther—and all my dears to whom she communicates this doleful ditty—you will rejoice to hear that this resolution once taken, was firmly adhered to in defiance of a terror that surpasses all description—and the most torturing pain. Yet when the dreadful steel was plunged into the breast, cutting through veins—arteries—flesh—nerves—I needed no injunctions not to restrain my cries. I began a scream that lasted unintermittingly during the whole time of the incision, and I marvel that it rings not in my ears still, so excruciating was the agony.

When the wound was made and the instrument withdrawn, the pain seemed undiminished, for the air that suddenly rushed into those delicate parts felt like a mass of minute but sharp and forked poniards, tearing the edges of the wound. When again I felt the instrument—now describing a curve—cutting against the grain, if I may so say, while the flesh resisted in a manner so forcible as to oppose and tire the hand of the operator, who was forced to change from the right to the left—and then, indeed, I thought I must have expired.

I attempted no more to open my eyes. They felt hermetically shut, so firmly closed the eyelids seemed indented into the cheeks. The instrument this second time withdrawn, I concluded the operation over—oh, no! Presently the terrible cutting was renewed, and worse than ever, to separate the bottom, the foundation of this dreadful gland from the parts to which it adhered. Again all description would be baffled—yet again, all was not over. Larrey rested but his own hand. Oh, Heaven! I felt the knife tackling against the breastbone—scraping it.

This performed, while I yet remained in utterly speechless torture, I heard Larrey (all others guarded a dead silence) in a tone nearly tragic, desire everyone present to pronounce if anything more remained to be done. The general voice was "yes." The finger of Dubois—which I literally felt elevated over the wound, though I saw nothing, and though he touched nothing, so indescribably sensitive was the spot—pointed to some further requisition. Again began the scraping. And after this, Moreau thought he discerned a peccant atom—and still and still and still, Dubois demanded atom after atom.

My dearest Esther, not for days, not for weeks, but for months I could not speak of this terrible business without nearly again going through it. I could not think of it with impunity! I was sick, I was disordered by a single question—even now, nine months after it is over, I have a headache from going on with the account—and this miserable account, which I began three months ago, I dare not revise, nor read, the recollection is still so painful.

The procedure took about twenty minutes, followed by the torturous dressing of the wound, during which Fanny briefly lost consciousness once or twice. In the rare moments she was able to speak, she didn't beg them to stop. Instead, she pleaded, *"Avertissez moi, Messieurs! Avertissez moi!"* Tell me! More than anything, she needed to know.

When it was over, strength annihilated, hands hanging lifeless, Fanny opened her eyes.

I saw my good Dr. Larrey, pale nearly as myself, his face streaked with blood, his expression depicting grief, apprehension, and horror. When I was in bed, my poor M. d'Arblay—who ought to write you himself his own history of this Morning—was called to me, and afterwards our Alex.

That same year, on the other side of the ocean, Nabby Adams, the daughter of Abigail and John Adams, underwent a similar procedure.

Both women were pronounced "cured." The following year Nabby returned to her parents' home, weak, ashen, and riddled with cancer. Abigail was overwhelmed with grief and horror, so Nabby's father cared for her in her final days. When she died in 1813, John Adams wrote to his friend, Thomas Jefferson:

> Your Friend, my only Daughter, expired, Yesterday Morning . . . in the 49th Year of Age, 46 of which She was the healthiest and firmest of Us all: Since which, She has been a monument to Suffering and to Patience.

Jefferson replied:

> . . . time and silence are the only medicine, and these but assuage, they never can suppress, the deep drawn sigh which recollection for ever brings up, until recollection and life are extinguished together.

But Fanny Burney lived to tell her stories. Nearly thirty years after enduring her wrenching mastectomy, she passed away peacefully at the ripe old age of eighty-seven.

In the 1840s, physicians at Mass General in Boston began using ether to render surgical patients blessedly unconscious. Anesthesia wasn't a new discovery; its increasingly common use was the result of a great shift in the culture of medicine, a step away from the idea that pain was not only natural but also sanctifying in some way. It was a dramatic improvement for those who could afford the best, most current care. For those who couldn't, there was the notion that suffering was God's way of building character. (And of course, using anesthesia on slave women would have been deemed a waste of money.) As the American Civil War raged with storied field amputations and dramatic gut-shot rescues, a doctor in Glasgow heroically performed an en bloc mastectomy on his sister as she lay splayed on the dining room table. It was hailed as a great triumph; the strapping girl endured the procedure with a minimum of thrashing and lived to set three more Christmas dinners on that table before dying in 1867 of the metastasis to her liver.

3

The Goodman Girls

"Goodnight," called Aunt Rose. "Sleep tight. Don't let the bedbugs bite."

As I gently pulled the door closed and crept down the hall, I heard her brightly singing.

"*I could have danced all night. . . .*"

Suzy was perched on the edge of the bed in the guest room, her face wrecked with tears.

"It looks bad," I conceded, "but she seems all right."

"*All right?*" Suzy huffed, incredulous.

"If it doesn't bother her, Suzy, why should it matter to us?"

"Nanny, of course it bothers her." Suzy hugged her knees to her chest. "How can she stand it? And how could he marry her after she was—she was *mutilated* like that?"

"Maybe because she's funny and beautiful, and she sings, and who cares if—"

"*Stop.* Just stop talking about it, Nancy. I don't ever want to think about it again."

But she did think about it. The image never left her. I didn't have the thousand words to erase that picture in her head. It didn't matter to her that Aunt Rose went on to live—and live large—for many years. Divested of the gorgeous fourth husband, she married a fifth and continued her travels, relishing the adventure that was her life until she was an old woman who carried this terrible scar and all her other scars, seen and unseen, with dignity and grace.

Suzy blossomed in the era of Jayne Mansfield and cashmere twin sets. Big breasts were—well, they were *big*. If you're not old enough to remember, take a look at the tight girdles and torpedo bras on *Mad*

Men. I was still flat as a pantry shelf and perfectly happy, but Suzy had begun to develop Mom's soft curves and enjoyed the way her body was evolving. A breezy model-in-the-making, Suzy turned thirteen in 1956, teeny-bopping to the tune of "Blueberry Hill." I was a rambunctious ten-year-old, athletic and easygoing. I started sprouting taller, quickly surpassing my big sister by several inches, and Mom's fashion sense and sensibility helped me adjust to and comfortably inhabit my changing body. As Suzy and I blossomed from little girls to young ladies, conversations about menstruation and reproduction were informative and not at all tortured. We felt free to ask questions, and Mom gave straight answers. If she didn't have the answer, she'd bring in Dr. Moffet.

Our gorgeous mother was as much a role model for womanhood as she was for stewardship. She never "let herself go"; to this day, she's feminine and impeccable from the moment she gets out of bed. Dr. Benjamin Spock's groundbreaking book on baby and child care was published the year I was born, so the world was awakening to a kinder, gentler view of parenting, but Mom was way ahead of her time in recognizing the importance of self-esteem in young women—and not just for Suzy and me. She periodically went through our wardrobes and weeded out anything that hadn't been worn recently (whether we were ready or not to part with it), and Mom impressed on Suzy and me the need to be sensitive about where our hand-me-down skirts and sweaters were going.

"If you see another girl at school wearing these clothes," Mother warned, "you don't ever say a word. *Ever.* If I hear a peep about it, you'll come home to a big closet full of nothing."

Mom wasn't one of the rich girls when she was in school, but she was popular because she was so kind, the personification of "pretty is as pretty does."

In 1957, the Everly Brothers were all over the radio with "Wake Up, Little Susie," and it was as if Suzy did. Fourteen years old, girly-girl going on womanhood, she was the most popular girl in school. She loved being beautiful, but it never seemed to go to her head because she loved being kind even more. Her friends had names like Peachy and Dottie, and Suzy went through a brief phase where she decided to be *Suzi* with an *i,* instead of plain old *Suzy.* They wore angora sweaters and felt poodle skirts that they exchanged among themselves so each girl could maximize her wardrobe options, and they always looked perfect, from their sparsely tweezed eyebrows to their pristine bobby socks. They gathered on our big front porch like so many butterflies in a rose garden, and their conversations were largely about their boyfriends, what their wedding dresses would look like, how they'd teach their husbands to dance, and whether or not it was wise to force their children to take piano lessons.

Our high school years overlapped for one wonderful year; Suzy was a senior when I was a freshman. Suzy tried to bring me into the butterfly tribe, doing her best to style me, coif me, make me over. It was no use. I was an unrepentant tomboy, galloping around with a hasty ponytail and cuffed-up jeans. My sister had stopped growing at a nicely filled out five-five or so, but I kept going—five-seven, five-eight, five-ten—I was taller than most of the boys in my class, almost as tall as *Daddy*. It made me feel alternately freakish and almighty and made it impossible for me to participate fully in the wardrobe exchange.

"It's all how you carry it," said Suzy. "It's whatcha do with whatcha got."

With great patience, she'd sit me down and open her cosmetics case between us, explaining each step as she played up my eyes with a soft sweep of shadow, carefully teased on a coat of mascara, told me to apple my cheeks and pout my mouth so she could apply rouge and lipstick.

Our house was at the top of the hill with a circular driveway, and as dusk fell on Friday and Saturday nights, I'd look out and see a parade of headlights, boys coming to hover and gawk. Suzy had them entranced with her shyly charming humor. All girl, but no Gidget. She was calm and put together. She knew exactly what she wanted and how to get it. Suzy wasn't one to play helpless or dumb, but she was more than happy to let a man take the lead, and she tried to coach me on the finer points of feminine wile.

"Nanny, if you just dive in there—*I'll fix it, I'll do it myself*—that drives men crazy. You can't take charge and expect them to think you're wonderful. Men don't want you to be the strong one. Not until they're old and sick and need you. Then it's okay."

This was not okay with me, but it was hard to argue with Suzy's success. She had an immaculately groomed and gallantly well-behaved date for every school function and all the social events at Anshai Emeth. She was conscious of maintaining her good-girl reputation, but the front porch saw a lot of within-accepted-parameters cuddling and canoodling late in the evening. Daddy paced between his study and the foyer, craning his neck at the living room window, eyeing the clock as it got closer to curfew. My task was to distract him, convince him the clock was broken, or at least deliver fair warning when he was on his way to the front door.

One night, he threw the front door open to discover that Suzy and her beau had hightailed it to the backyard. Daddy went for a flashlight and found them out there, lip-locked in the shadows.

"*Susan!* Get in here right now. It's your curfew. And *you . . .*" He steadied the beam on Suzy's beau. "Hold it right there."

The boy made a break for it, but Daddy chased him down and threw him bodily into the shrubs.

"And don't even think about coming back!" he bellowed.

Daddy came in, slammed the door, and berated Suzy all the way down the hall to her room. She was weeping, of course, decrying the fact that Daddy had ruined her life and she'd never be asked out again, but the following Friday, the parade of headlights floated up the hill, and Suzy and her friends held court as usual.

Richwoods High had just opened in 1957, so the class of '61 was the first four-year class to graduate. Suzy was elected homecoming queen. Mom and Daddy and I were huddled together on the bleachers at the football game the night before the dance when the announcement came over the loudspeaker. *Miss Susan Goodman.*

Everyone cheered. Last I heard, her trophy was still in the school lobby. It's odd to realize now, but this was actually very close to the midpoint of her life. Her middle age. She was not quite eighteen; she wouldn't live to see thirty-seven. More than half my years with her were already gone, and since so many of those last memories are fraught with fear and sorrow, Mommy and I hold on to Suzy's beautiful moments now. The ribbon of headlights. The roar of the crowd. Her rhinestone tiara and flash photo smile. The rustle of crinolines as she swept out the door. She wore a dress with a swan-white bodice, voluminous sky-blue skirt, and wide pink ribbon sash, and we shopped for the perfect pink satin pumps to match.

Peoria, Illinois, was and is a wonderful place to come of age: the quintessential American town. Elms and oaks shaded the friendly neighborhoods. The business climate hummed with fresh ideas and a strong work ethic. Suzy and I knew life wasn't so rosy for everyone living in Peoria County, but for us it was that idyllic place and time that anchors nostalgic Norman Rockwell images and "oldie but goodie" radio formats—that was our hometown in the 1950s.

Pleasantville, USA.

So, of course, we couldn't wait to make our escape. We lay in bed at night, talking about all the dragons just waiting to be slain.

In the fall, Suzy went off to the University of Missouri, and I felt utterly adrift without her. At first, we talked almost every day, but that was murder on the phone bill, and Dad let us know it. I kept my nose to the grindstone, because that's what it took for me to get the perfect grades I expected from myself, living for the weekends when Suzy came home and slept in her own bed, messed with my hair, and rounded things out with her laughter and breezy stories. She wasn't miserable at college, but she must have known from the start it wasn't where she wanted to be. Of course, she had a plethora of friends and boyfriends who adored her.

She was nominated for "Miss Mizzou," one of the more free-spirited titles in pageant-dom. This all-American beauty traditionally is awarded a trench coat, which she'd wear (according to campus legend) with little or nothing underneath. Suzy's campaign featured a full-length photo of her in a little dance leotard with the caption "This woman needs a raincoat!" I'm sure they've abolished this politically incorrect practice by now, but Suzy loved it. She was all over campus, involved in social and charity events. Her studies were barely a footnote.

Stuck at home, I doggedly applied myself to my schoolwork, living for spring break and summer vacation. The summer between junior and senior year, I joined the "Cherubs" at Northwestern University's National High School Institute. Honor students from all over the country came together in six divisions: Debate, Speech, Journalism, Music, Film and Video Production, and Theater Arts. In other words: Heaven. The founder of the Institute, Dean Ralph Dennis, started the program in the 1930s with this goal: "To bring together gifted young people and superior teachers in an atmosphere of affection, knowledge, and trust." An elegantly succinct description of the ideal educational endeavor, whether you're talking about a public school, a private tennis lesson, or a Saturday afternoon symposium for oncology nurses. It was hands-on, experiential, out-of-the-box learning, and I loved every minute.

In the fall of my sophomore year, President Kennedy spoke at Rice University in Houston. Riveted to the radio, I hung on every word.

We choose to go to the moon.

Another elegantly succinct statement of mission.

We choose to go to the moon in this decade and do other things, not because they are easy, but because they are hard, because that goal will serve to organize and measure the best of our energies and skills, because that challenge is one that we are willing to accept, one we are unwilling to postpone, and one which we intend to win.

Later in my life, while I was serving as U.S. ambassador to Hungary, I was starved sometimes to hear English, and the funny thing is, I didn't know how deeply I craved the sound of my own language until I heard someone speak a few words. I couldn't have identified this feeling when I was seventeen, but that's exactly the thrill I felt when I heard Kennedy speak. I didn't know it out loud yet, but this was my native tongue.

We choose to go to the moon.

Not "we hope to go" or "we plan to try."

We choose. To go. To do. To make real this thing that so many say is science fiction.

In the fall of my junior year, President Kennedy was assassinated.

Suzy majored in art history, as I recall. She never finished her degree, but she dabbled for a couple of years at an interesting course of study with all the makings of an appropriate pre-housewife degree. All she really wanted was a home and family: to live well, do good, and look great doing it. She wanted to be the same kind of quietly world-changing woman our mother was. Not me. I could feel the world shifting beneath my feet, and I wanted to be part of the earthquake. I wanted to make some noise.

Daddy had decided I should be a lawyer, but being a lawyer didn't really interest me, and beyond that was the reality of my well-hidden but ever-present learning differences. Since my first day of school, I'd turned myself inside out trying to maintain perfect grades, but the thought of keeping that up all the way through law school left me feeling utterly dwarfed, overwhelmed by the sheer number of words on paper. A stifling tension developed between my father and me. Now I know his high expectations were based on his love and respect for me, but at the time, I pinned it down as an extension of his deep disappointment that I wasn't born a boy. It burdened me to know I was failing him, but I was certain that if I waded into that ocean of reading and writing, it would sweep me out to sea and drown me.

College entrance exams shored up my lowball assessment of my own potential, so with a deep sigh of resignation, Dad wrote a check to the "safety school"—an excellent state university where I was guaranteed acceptance with my high school class rank. I intended to pursue subjects that actually interested me: sociology, anthropology, political science, and world cultures. These were also the makings of an appropriate pre-housewife degree, but at some fundamental level, I knew I'd find a way to turn my education into a career that would take me far from Peoria, Illinois.

In 1964, the Beatles appeared on Ed Sullivan, *Mary Poppins* appeared in theaters, and Suzy got married.

It was a lovely ceremony, and Suzy was a beautiful bride, but this was the completely wrong groom, a very odd fellow she was smitten with for reasons I couldn't understand and she couldn't articulate. But we were sisters, so I got myself up in maid of honor gear and stood beside her. In the midst of all the traditional this and that, the utterly wrong man passed out cold at the altar, overcome by nerves or the stench of lilies or maybe just unable to breathe under the pressure of the huge mistake taking place. The rabbi helped the groomsmen prop him up long enough to stammer his vows, but within a few months, Suzy sat on my bed sobbing.

"I should have taken the hint, Nanny. God was giving me one last chance to pick up my skirts and run."

Mom and Dad swooped in, brought her home, and helped her arrange a quick divorce. The only lasting artifact of the whole affair was a little black French poodle named Louie. Suzy had adopted him at some point during her marriage, which lasted only a little longer than the honeymoon, and sitting on her bed in our room at home, she clung to him for comfort as she tried to make sense of the incomprehensible situation.

"I don't understand, Nan. He was so smart . . . funny . . . cultured," she sniffled. "Not like other guys at all."

"It's not your fault, Suz." I put my arm around her and knuckled Louie's chin. "It was just a completely wrong match. It's good that you didn't try to drag on and on with it."

"Please tell me I'm not being a spoiled Jewish American Princess."

"You're not," I assured her. "I always thought he was a little . . . well . . . 'not like other guys' is one way to put it."

"He kicked Louie down the stairs," said Suzy. "How was I going to spend my life with a man who'd do something like that?"

"You couldn't," I said. "Of course, you couldn't, Suz." (Even now I find it remarkable that she was more concerned for that little dog than she was for herself.)

"I don't know how I would have gotten through this without you and Mom and Dad," said Suzy. "You've all been aces."

In proper little Peoria—or any midwestern town during the reign of *Father Knows Best*—being rashly married and hastily divorced would have spelled social disaster for a lot of girls, but Suzy's unstoppable charm coupled with Mom's get-on-with-it disposition simply didn't allow that. There was no energy wasted on chagrin, no time budgeted for wallowing. With her head held high, Suzy greeted people on the street and continued her charity work and good-neighborliness, being her fabulous self, going out on dates, winning friends and influencing people. We couldn't walk into the grocery store without meeting a dozen people who loved her. An elderly neighbor she'd taken time to sit with. A grieving widow to whom she'd brought flowers. A Girl Scout from whom she'd bought cookies. A teenager she'd cared for at the Florence Crittenton Home for unwed mothers.

There was a small space available in a shopping center Dad was developing, and Suzy opened a little art gallery that showcased and sold the work of local artists. She hosted parties that were packed to the rafters with smart, witty people and earned extra money modeling for department stores and catalogs. She played with Louie and toyed with learning guitar. To me at nineteen, it seemed like my big sister had it all together, but in retrospect I see she was flailing a bit in her search for herself.

We'd always taken an interest in politics and got involved early, stuffing envelopes and knocking on doors for Illinois' own Adlai Stevenson in the 1956 presidential primaries. We were both entranced with JFK in 1960, and I was insanely jealous that Suzy got to vote in 1964, squeaking under the wire and turning twenty-one a matter of days before the presidential election. I was still too young, but I was determined to make up for that by rabble-rousing to the best of my ability. We got a great education in political discourse during election years. Daddy was an old-school, fiscally conservative Republican, which—back in the day—meant pro-business and anti-nonsense. Mommy was a pragmatically moderate Roosevelt Democrat, which meant social consciousness with a firm nod to personal responsibility.

Growing up at that diverse dinner table, Suzy and I never equated a difference of opinion with hatred or disrespect, and to this day, I'm disappointed whenever I see it come down to that. We saw between our parents—in action and in rhetoric—the perfect model for a democracy; both sides of a debate are needed, and even the extremist views are valuable because they remind us where the middle is. Because I've witnessed the fundamental principles of both parties at their truest and best, I have respect and affection for people on both sides of the aisle, and I cherish the aisle itself as a welcoming middle ground, free of obstacles and hostilities.

I went off to college that fall and was up to my neck in activity within minutes. I knew I'd learn far more out of the classroom than in it, so I dove into student government and media. I was an eager volunteer when it came to organizing anything from a sorority dance to Trick or Treat for UNICEF. Even at eighteen, I knew my most lamentable weakness and my most marketable asset were one and the same: I simply had a different way of seeing things. Most people saw letters and numbers as clear and finite and viewed the boundaries and railroad tracks that separated class and culture with the same unbreachable clarity. My inverted vision turned a field of obstacles into an expanse of opportunities the same way it transposed *W* to *M*. Constantly circumventing this learning disability trained me to question what I was seeing, to ferret out the devilish details and look for an open window when confronted with a closed door.

I'd seldom been stranded without a date for homecoming and other high school functions, and the same held true in college, but I was way too busy to be swept off my feet by anyone in particular. First the pool was narrowed to men who were tall enough to dance with me at my full five-ten-plus-heels. Winnow from those the few who were smart and well informed enough to carry on a conversation. And among those, look for the one who didn't mind playing second fiddle to a crusade against the arming of campus security guards or fundraising for Radio Free Europe.

In January 1965, LBJ spoke of the "Great Society" in his State of the Union address.

> For today the state of the Union depends, in large measure, upon the state of the world. Our concern and interest, compassion and vigilance, extend to every corner of a dwindling planet. . . . We know that history is ours to make. And if there is great danger, there is now also the excitement of great expectations.

Looking back through the telescope of three decades in politics, I see the well-crafted wording, the agenda, the angles. But as I watched that speech on a grainy black-and-white TV in the dorm lounge, the vision of a society without poverty or racial prejudice formed a hard lump in my throat. I felt in my chest a whirlpool of possibility and yearning, youthful energy, a huge sense of future. I felt the excitement of great expectations.

> The Great Society asks not how much, but how good; not only how to create wealth but how to use it; not only how fast we are going, but where we are headed. It proposes as the first test for a nation: the quality of its people.

Our good friends, David and Michael, had evolved from little boys who engaged Suzy and me in water balloon wars to solid young men ready to see the world. When they told us they were going to Europe, Suzy's eyes came alive.

"Nanny, we have to go too," she said. "It'll be spectacular."

I was immediately on board. Mom and Dad took a little convincing. Suzy and I prepared an elaborate sales pitch and were prepared to pay for everything with money we'd saved.

"The boys are true-blue trustworthy escorts," said Suzy. "There won't be any shenanigans."

"We'll call you every week," I chimed in, "and send postcards and look out for each other."

"Think of the history and art. Very educational."

And so the lobbying went until Mom and Dad relented. Sitting at the kitchen table, poring over guidebooks and travel brochures, we felt terribly grown up. Real women of the world. We planned to fly to Spain, then go to Paris, where we'd buy a Volkswagen for cheap and spend the next three months driving an amorphous loop through France, Italy, Germany, Denmark, and England.

"Then we'll ship the car home from England, sell it here for twice what we paid, and split the money," I told Daddy, our oracle for all business advice. "What do you think?"

"You'd better have something on reserve," he said. "In case you shop beyond your budget."

"I just want to take in every speck of art my eyes can see," Suzy assured him. "I don't even care about buying anything. Other than gloves for Mom and Aunt Sylvia. Maybe a chic little suit if I see one that's inexpensive. Plus knitwear, of course. But that's it. Well—shoes. And if we end up going out a lot, we might need another evening dress or two. But other than that, I don't see us shopping much at all."

We judiciously packed summery, wrinkle-resistant Arnel shifts and sensible walking shoes for daytime, killer heels and *Mad Men* chic dresses for nightlife, and plenty of extra hosiery, because Suzy wouldn't be caught dead in Paris with a run in her hose.

The first week of June 1965, Mom and Dad threw a lovely bon voyage party for Suzy and me and drove us to O'Hare airport in Chicago. As we climbed the stairs to board the TWA flight bound for Madrid, I breathed in the heat radiating from the tarmac and said, with all the hope and hubris of a nineteen-year-old, "Ah, the intoxicating scent of freedom!"

"What a great life," Suzy smiled up at me. "We're so lucky, Nan. The luckiest."

We spent the first few hours engrossed in our phrase books, but out over the Atlantic, the air got choppy. With each dip and swell, unsettled gasps and murmurs rippled through the cabin. Mike and Dave were full of bravado, cracking jokes from across the aisle, but Suzy quickly became miserable.

Resting her cheek on my shoulder, she moaned, "I need Dramamine. And vodka."

When the food cart rolled past, I shook my head even though I was starving.

"You'll be okay," I said, stroking Suzy's hand. "Just think about Spain . . . Paris . . . Italy."

"Italy." She smiled wanly. "It's too wonderful to imagine."

Little Pearl Harbor

THE THRIVING port at Bari, Italy, was fully lit and hustling with activity the night of December 2, 1943. The Luftwaffe had no trouble finding it. During an hour-long raid, fuel gushed from a severed pipeline and flames bled across the bay, enveloping thirty cargo and transport vessels from America, England, Poland, and Norway, including a U.S. Liberty ship, which harbored a deadly secret. Hidden in the bowels of the foundering *John Harvey* were 2,000 hundred-pound mustard gas bombs.

In response to the hideous effects of World War I mustard gas attacks, an international pact forbade the use of chemical warfare, but nations quietly stockpiled supplies, fearing others might not be as good as their word. The Allied High Command knew Hitler had his own cache and suspected he'd use it without hesitation if the true nature of the *John Harvey's* cargo were discovered. In the days following the attack known as "Little Pearl Harbor," Eisenhower and Churchill scrambled to deny the existence of the mustard gas, which left medical personnel on the ground in Bari scrambling to determine what was happening to their patients.

Less than twenty-four hours after the attack, sailors who'd been plucked from the water relatively unharmed were in searing agony, blind, coughing blood, covered with chemical burn blisters that oozed a garlicky yellow substance. Blood tests revealed a dramatic change in body chemistry: lymphocytes—white blood cells that power the immune system—had been virtually wiped out. Autopsies showed severe damage to lymph node tissue. Soon, people from the nearby village where the smoke plume had settled were stumbling into the already burdened medical facilities, presenting the same symptoms. Within weeks, eighty-three sailors and uncounted civilians were dead, and hundreds more lay grievously debilitated.

On Churchill's order, the incident was stricken from the records, the casualties attributed to burns from the fuel spill, but U.S. documents regarding the incident at Bari were declassified in the late 1950s, confirming what physicians had suspected all along. Had the truth been known from the beginning, it's possible they would have missed a pivotal discovery in the history of chemotherapy. Now the Third Reich had fallen; researchers were contemplating the use of chemical warfare on a different kind of enemy. If the deadly alkylating agents in mustard gas killed lymphocytes, they theorized, mustard gas could kill lymphoma. And if it killed lymphoma, it could kill breast cancer that had metastasized to the lymph nodes.

If only there was a way to deliver the mustard gas without killing the patient.

Dr. Paul Ehrlich, a German Nobel Laureate known as "the Father of Chemotherapy," pioneered techniques for standardizing toxic chemical cocktails and delivering them intravenously prior to World War I. He was an immunologist and did significant work in cancer research, but the practical application that won over the most enthusiastic funding was Ehrlich's success in using arsenic-based drugs for the treatment of syphilis. Some say Ehrlich was the first to hypothesize about the "magic bullet" of cell-specific drugs. He accomplished a great deal before his death in 1915, but because he was a Jew, his work was discredited and the street signs bearing his name were torn down until after World War II.

Breast cancer treatment in postwar America hadn't advanced much since the time of Frankenstein. By the turn of the twentieth century, physicians and medical students from far and wide were packing into the observatory above an operating room at Johns Hopkins Hospital to watch and learn as Dr. William Stewart Halsted (usually braced by a pinch of cocaine) whisked away the breasts, chest wall, and lymph nodes, along with surrounding fatty tissue and skin, in one symphonic stroke. He was the undisputed Elvis of the super-radical mastectomy, hailed as the most brilliant surgeon who'd ever practiced, and the Halsted mastectomy remained the gold standard for breast cancer treatment for almost a hundred years. In Dorothy Parker's New York in the enlightened age of A-bombs and torpedo bras, offering anything less than the Halsted radical would have been deemed "a mistaken kindness" to my Aunt Rose.

Standard practice was to put a woman under general anesthesia and keep her under while pathologists did the biopsy. If the tumor was benign, she woke up with a small incision. If it was malignant, she woke up to an entirely different life, having had a radical mastectomy—or the new and improved super-radical mastectomy that went inside the rib cage, as technology advanced the limits of survivable surgery. If that didn't do it, hope was offered in the form of an oophorectomy, removing the ovaries. If the cancer recurred, sometimes removing the adrenal glands from the kidneys had some effect. Beyond that, there was brain surgery to remove the pituitary gland.

In the late 1950s, as a research fellow at the Postgraduate Medical School of London and subsequently as a professor of surgery at the University of Pittsburgh, Dr. Bernard Fisher was no longer buying into a mindset that looked at the frequent recurrence of breast cancer and said, "We're not cutting enough." Fisher, a scientist first and surgeon second, looked at the data and said, "We're cutting too much."

If breast cancer cells broke off and drifted through the lymphatic system long before the tumor was large enough to detect, Fisher said, it was therefore a systemic disease and surgery was far from the "perfect cure." At the time, of course, this view was heresy—a return to the bad old days of humoral medicine. With quiet confidence, Fisher conducted laboratory and clinical research that proved the efficacy of lumpectomy and radiation and eventually upended a century of conventional wisdom based on the Halsted approach. A new day was dawning. By the time *Dr. Strangelove* hit the movie theaters in the mid-1960s, radiation was improving survival rates, and clinical trials spearheaded by Fisher showed promising results for cyclophosphamide, the drug derived from mustard gas.

Statistics indicated there was no lifesaving advantage to the biopsy-mastectomy combo platter. Fisher argued that women should be given the opportunity to open their eyes, consider the unique circumstances of their individual situation, and make an informed decision about how they wanted to proceed. Essentially, the only argument against this humane, respectful approach was that because it required more than just one surgery, it caused a woman "inconvenience"—a word that makes me cringe when I hear it tossed up as a reason to abolish routine mammograms and breast self-exams.

For the record: Courtesy boarding, free Wi-Fi, a little plastic spoon attached to an ice cream cup—that's a "convenience." A canceled flight, a lost BlackBerry, a stain on your blouse—that's an "inconvenience." If the powers that be really want to help a gal out, they should offer to do our laundry, not relieve us of our power to make decisions about our own bodies.

Through the 1980s and 1990s, Fisher conducted clinical trials (funded in part by Susan G. Komen for the Cure) pioneering adjuvant and neo-adjuvant therapies, orchestrated campaigns that included chemo, radiation, and surgery. Preoperative chemo permitted less invasive surgery and killed off free-floating cancer cells in the lymphatic system before they could set up shop; postoperative radiation then zapped the vulnerable tissue where the tumor first presented. Given the improved chance of long-term survival, women were quick to sign on, despite the devastating side effects of chemotherapy.

And devastating they are: Cyclophosphamide (Cytoxin) and other alkylating agents strip away the immune system's ability to fight infection. Doxorubicin (Adriamycin) is essentially a toxic-caliber antibiotic that binds to fast-growing cells and destroys them, whether they're cancer cells or cells you'd prefer to hang on to—like hair follicles and the lining of your stomach. Fluorouracil (appropriately nicknamed "FU") and other antimetabolites disrupt the DNA that cells need to repair themselves.

All this translates to a firestorm of temporary side effects and sometimes lasting damage to every aspect of the body: total hair loss, debilitating fatigue, piercing headaches, vomiting, nosebleeds, raw sores in the mouth and throat, heart and lung damage, organ failure—a thousand strange anomalies, aches, and aftertastes that seem to (and often do) emanate from your very bone marrow. The early onset of menopause is common; loss of olfactory senses, a disjointed loss of memory referred to as "chemo brain," and even changes in eye color have been documented.

Every woman who's experienced this Little Pearl Harbor inside her own body knows exactly what I'm talking about, but I think those of us who survived to see our children grow up would agree: it was worth the "inconvenience."

In 1999, the first Susan G. Komen Race for the Cure in Rome—our first such event in Europe—drew a few thousand committed volunteers and advocates. Ten years later, my son, Eric, addressed a crowd of over fifty thousand runners and walkers gathered at the starting point in Terme di Caracalla Stadium. Led by Dr. Riccardo Masetti, a renowned breast surgeon and founding member of Komen Italia, dedicated volunteers extended outreach with a traveling Early Detection Village, a mobile facility offering free breast cancer screening to women across the country. In 2007, Komen Italia brought the Race for the Cure to Bologna and Bari.

On a bright spring morning, sixty-odd years after the deadly chemical plume stained the sky over the Bari harbor, the salt air was filled with pink balloons. And hope.

4

Women of the World

We arrived in Madrid at 6:30 A.M., ravenous, exhausted, and a little tipsy, but determined to milk every moment. Over the next ten weeks, we dutifully kept a diary, recording every sight we saw and every dime we spent. The first entry was a 15-cent cab ride to the hotel, where we dumped our bags, then headed out to walk the city.

"We'll have to do a little shopping first," Suzy informed Dave and Mike. "Nan forgot her patent heels. She can't go to dinner without them."

This didn't go down well with the boys. It was well before noon, and Dave had already pronounced it "hotter than hell's armpit." Somehow Suzy kept them tagging along in relatively good spirits, carrying our bags of shoes, dresses, books, and souvenir shot glasses until the shops closed for siesta. Back at the hotel, we collapsed until dinnertime, which for the jet set (and the jet-lagged) was ten-thirty at night. We ate like longshoremen, killed three bottles of wine, and ambled down the street to a club called Arco de Cuchilleros (*arch of the cutlers*, as near as we could figure from our dog-eared Spanish-to-English dictionary), where we downed a bottle of cognac and watched flamenco dancers, which Suzy called "flamingo dancers," and we were still laughing at that when we fell into bed a little after four in the morning.

Suzy's alarm went off three hours later. She rousted me out of bed, and I joined her at the open window looking out over Madrid.

"Look at the architecture," I said. "Marvin would plotz."

"I'm a little woozy, Nan." Suzy fanned herself with a folded map of the city. "We better pace ourselves."

I agreed, but the pace we settled into was nonstop fifty-five-hour days, traipsing past every painting in every museum, up every bell tower in every cathedral, down every alley in every straw market. Suzy was instantly in love with everything in this friendly, romantic country.

"I'm in love with Hieronymus Bosch," she said, standing worshipfully before his *Garden of Earthly Delights* in the Prado, and as we bused over to Segovia, she said, "I'm in love with those crinkly olive trees. Oh, Nan, look! I am in *love* with the Roman aqueducts."

I chatted up elderly British ladies, getting the lowdown on the cheapest hotels and essential historical markers. Suzy engaged the handsome tour guides, practicing her *español* so she could flirt fluently with the young men who flocked around her like goats every night in the cafés and clubs. The boys couldn't match our stride for sightseeing, but they managed to catch up with us every evening.

Dave had decided he was in charge, acting like the continental expert, and as we taxied across town, he educated us on the sport of bullfighting. "Also known as *tauromachy*," he informed us.

By the time we got to the Corrida de Toros, my curiosity had escalated to buzzing excitement and Suzy's enthusiasm had dwindled to unsettled dread.

"Maybe we could do some shopping instead," she suggested.

"Shops are closed," I said. "Some holiday having to do with Saint Peter."

"As if they need another darn excuse to close the shops. C'mere, Nan, you're shiny." Suzy powdered my nose, checked her hair, and dropped her compact in her purse. "There are no bargains here anyway. We should save our money for Paris."

"I think we should cut Paris short and go to Rome," said Dave. "I hear France is filthy. The people are rude. Everything costs an arm and a leg."

"I don't believe that," Suzy whispered in my ear. "I think I'll be in love with Paris."

Piling out of the cab at the Coliseum, we were instantly mobbed by little children begging, "Moneys? Moneys, Señorita? Cigarillos?" A woman thrust an empty baby bottle toward Suzy. Following the advice of the handsome tour guides but fighting everything in her nature, Suzy pushed past them without making eye contact. It upset her to brush by the needy, grasping hands, and neither of us was prepared for the bloody spectacle inside the Coliseum.

"Those bastards." Suzy shielded her eyes with a gloved hand as the picador went to work. "I hate this. This is a vulgar, disgusting sport."

"It's a cultural difference, Suz. We have to respect that and understand—"

"No. Some things I'll never understand. Jesus, Nan, why would you even want to? Some things are just—*oh no.*"

A beautiful young matador was gored horribly through the chest and groin. A shudder of delighted horror went through the crowd. Suzy nudged me and tipped her chin toward some men seated below us.

"Nan, they're saying he's dead."

"He's no such thing, Suzy. How could they know from way up here? They're just trying to impress you," I said, but angling for a better look, I felt guilty about rooting for the bull.

When the bullfight was over, despite my lofty worldview, I was no more able to eat dinner than Suzy was. Dave and Mike left us, and we wandered until midnight, then found a quiet little place where kindly Spanish grandmothers served us a simple salad with trout. Suzy and I sat for a long time, talking about everything we'd observed thus far about the treatment of women and the treatment of Jews. I was fascinated by Franco's staunch nationalism and the fervent anticommunist stand that made him sympathetic to so many Americans during the Cold War, though he himself was a dictator who'd sided with our enemies during World War II. Short-term memories yielded to the idea that "The enemy of my enemy is my friend."

Suzy was more taken with the politics of fashion, which wielded an influence more powerful than any de facto regent *por la gracia de Dios.* She was in awe of Balenciaga and understood something I didn't grasp until much later in life: that *fashion*—as both noun and verb—creates a collective. It graphically illustrates the ideas that bind a diverse population of individuals. Personal and professional intentions are made plain. Those of like mind recognize each other. Those who fear change are left behind. Leaders emerge, followers unite. Good ideas stand the test of time; faux pas of the past are forgiven with good humor. Perpetual evolution is not only embraced from one season to the next, it's celebrated.

"We must come back and tour Spain extensively," said Suzy. "We could spend fifty summers exploring the Prado alone and not see it all."

"We'll be the old ladies on the tour bus," I said.

She raised her glass to that. "Onward to Paris."

We faithfully wrote to Mom and Dad, Boppie, Aunt Rose, and everyone else in our leather address book, and our next letter home was written on gauzy gray stationery from a hotel near the Arc de Triomphe. At the top, Suzy wrote: *WARNING! This comes to you from Seventh Heaven!*

"Oh, Mommy, I can't stand to have this great experience locked up inside me," I wrote below. "I wish you could share it. The French have so much pride and patriotism. What a fantastic city!"

Suzy enclosed her P.S. on a fourteen-inch strip of stiff beige toilet paper. "So Marvin won't think we're living in luxury. Disregard everything people say. Courtesy, friendliness, and a cozy room with silk draperies. Louie would have a ball in Paris. Lots of girls for him. We can buy wine for 12 cents a bottle! Met some great kids and stayed up gabbing till 2 A.M.—up at 7:15 tomorrow. Sleep is the one thing we haven't overdone."

We floated through the week on a cloud of euphoria, perfume, and impulse purchases. Suzy bought a Degas lithograph (which almost certainly wasn't), and as we explored the streets of Montmartre and the Marais, I listened for echoes of V-E Day, relishing the idea that the little old men in the park might have been heroic figures of la Résistance. We traipsed the city for days and didn't miss a cobblestone. As we stumped up a hill in the Père-Lachaise Cemetery, the sole came right off the bottom of my beige walking shoe.

"Oh, Nanny," Suzy sighed. "And yesterday you broke a heel on the blue ones."

"I'll get a cheap pair," I said. "At that place near the American Express."

"Nan, that place has the most hideous shoes in the Western world."

"Who cares? They're just for walking. I'll dash in while you pick up our mail."

"I love getting letters from home," said Suzy, "but that Tom character I went out with before we left—he writes every day. Even called the hotel. He's really snowed. I'm trying to be nice, but wise up, for goodness sake."

"What a chore for you, to be so irresistible."

"Oh, shut up. Let's go buy your ugly shoes. Then we should turn in. The Louvre is free on Sunday. We want to be fresh."

We danced till four with Australians in a bar near the Moulin Rouge, but were at the museum when the doors opened. Somewhere between the Winged Victory of Samothrace and the Code of Hammurabi, we made the important discovery that tourists could sit in the bar at the Lido for less than $3, first drink included. We closed the place down and stumbled home in the wee hours, but bright and early the next morning, we met Mike and Dave, crammed an impossible cubic ton of baggage into the VW, and set out for the Riviera.

Dave did a fine job negotiating the winding mountain roads, but the lanes were so narrow, we held our breath every time we met another vehicle coming from the opposite direction. When we hit Saint-Tropez, the guys informed us they'd canceled their hotel reservation and were planning to stay at hostels and pensions for the rest of the trip.

"Suz, we should do that, too," I said. "Think of the money we'd save."

"I'm not staying anywhere I'd have to share a bathroom," said Suzy.

Our true-blue escorts dropped us in front of the hotel with our mountain of suitcases and headed for a nude beach they'd seen in *Playboy* magazine. We lugged our things to our room, then shopped our way down the sunny Strand.

"I'm in love with these knit suits," said Suzy.

"Daddy's going to kill us."

"Maybe so." Suzy bit her lip. "We should buy him a few of these fabulous ties."

The salesgirls quickly agreed this was the best remedy for our overspending and asked to see a photo of Daddy so they could tell us which fabulous ties were meant for him.

"Oh, cha cha, what a papa!" they exclaimed. "*Muy bello*—like a movie star!"

We met up with Mike and Dave the next morning to head for Geneva.

"You look sunburned," Suzy said tartly. "Or are you blushing?"

"Little of both," Dave grinned, but Mike slumped into the passenger seat without talking. He'd decided he was desperately in love with his girl back home and spent the rest of the trip mooning over her. Suzy found this absolutely precious, but I coughed irritably every time he started gassing on about it during the ten-hour drive to Rome, where it was stifling hot. The rhythm of the city felt ponderous and slow after the nightlife of Paris. The first thing Suzy did was purchase two little Mother Mary statuettes from a street vendor.

"Not expensive, Nanny. *Priceless,*" she said. "Blessed by the pope!"

Everywhere we went, Suzy attracted a flock of admirers. Tourists wanted to take her picture by fountains and doorways. Guys wanted to dance with her or buy our table a round of drinks, just so they could hover. Suzy welcomed anyone and everyone to join our happy company. David, Michael, and I laughed ourselves silly at the halting attempts of her suitors to speak English and Suzy's enthusiastic but not very successful efforts to speak Italian.

As we sat by Trevi Fountain in the cool of the morning, Suzy said, "Rome's a bit dirty, but the art is fantastic, and the Italian men . . . well, they stare, but they don't pinch like I heard. I haven't been pinched once, have you?"

"Not the slightest goose," I said. "I feel very insulted."

"Most of the Spanish men were a bit earthy for me, and most of the French men weren't tall enough, but Swiss men seem very strong and good looking. We'll reassess the men situation after Venice. I told Mommy I'd bring her back a rich prince."

"I don't want to have to be on date behavior," I said. "That's what I love about Europe. No social worries. Just learning."

"I can't believe you left your hair clips in Paris, Nan," Suzy said, smoothing a stray corkscrew away from my face. "I've lost half of mine running hither and thither, so don't look at me for spares."

We both had thick, impossibly curly hair that inflated to twice its original size in the humid heat. Earlier that morning, when Suzy plugged her hairdryer into the electrical adapter, the motor had fried with an acrid sizzle. She'd managed to tame her hair into a French twist with bobby pins and hairspray, but the moment we stepped outside, mine was total anarchy.

"I'm on my last pair of hose, too," I told her.

"Break down and buy some," said Suzy. "Stop being so tight."

"Nope. When these are gone, I'm going native."

"Nancy Goodman. You will not. Mommy would slip into a coma."

"It's not a Valentine dance, Suzy. It's *Roma,* it's *Fellini,* it's *Three Coins* in this very fountain!" I gestured to the spectacular stone hippocampus,

Oceanus, and his mighty Tritons—none of whom were wearing hose. "I'm not being tight. I'm being sensible. I counted our money, and I think we should skip lunch from now on."

"Maybe we should move on to Florence. *Firenze,* as the natives say. I hear it's much nicer and more affordable."

"Agreed. If Dave and Mike don't want to leave early, we can take the bus."

Suzy nixed that idea. "One: Hell could not be hotter than that bus. Two: Our hair would be so huge, we'd be combing chickens and goats out of it. And three: If we don't stick with the boys, we won't have anyone to go out with in the evening."

We devoted our last day in the city to Eva of Roma, a salon near the hotel.

"Without the hairdryer, it's a necessity," said my pragmatic sister. "We wouldn't be spending wisely if we didn't take advantage of the full treatment."

Similar logic was applied to a unique knit dress on the Via Veneto. My flight bag was already demolished, and as we were packing to leave, the zipper on my suitcase gave way.

Suzy took stock of the situation and said, "Ropes are the answer."

Down to the straw market we went. We found a serviceable length of twine, Suzy bought a darling little umbrella, and I managed to bargain a peddler down on a cigarette case by pretending to be flattered when he nibbled my wrist and professed his love in broken English.

Back at the hotel, we bumped into my friend Gail and her travel mate, Cis, who were following roughly the same itinerary we were. Reunion hugs all around, and we headed to the café next door to compare notes. Gail and Cis looked terrific, and they'd had dates almost every night since they hit the continent. Suzy's and my adventures hiking ruins and exploring museums suddenly seemed very pale next to wining and dining and getting squired about town by charming locals who knew the best places and paid for everything.

"We've found love in every country," Gail bubbled like fresh champagne.

I wanted to punch her. *Love?* In *every country?* While I got nibbled for the price of a lousy cigarette case? They sashayed off to hail a taxi, and I sat there on simmer until Suzy elbowed me in the ribs.

"All right, Lady Godiva. What's your problem?"

"I can't stand it that Gail and Cis are racking up romantic adventures—not to mention *free dinner*—wherever they go," I said. "Mike and Dave are such deadheads. Mike fancies himself so in love he won't go out. David thinks he's so sexy and full of grandeur—oh, I could knock the hell out of him sometimes, Suzy, and as long as we stick with them, we won't get asked on dates."

"Nancy, I'm not going out on a date with a total stranger."

"From now on, I'm boy-hunting. I don't care if I get ravaged on the street."

"*Nancy Lee Goodman.* Don't be insane."

"Heavens, no! I'm supposed to be the prudish one while you're the social butterfly."

"I don't pick up men in bars at home, and I'm not doing it here."

"I don't care if I have to go it alone. I'm not boating home with nothing to talk about but dusty relics and Hieronymus Bosch and how bloody beautiful everyone thinks *you* are."

"And to think, just this morning I wrote home about how well we're getting on." Suzy glared at me in stark annoyance. "*No fighting, Mommy. Nancy's being so mature. I almost forgot what a child you are.*"

Two young men at a table by the door were ordering a bottle of wine. One was quintessential tall, dark, and handsome, the other a not-so-bad nebbish, which could mean smart.

"Hi!" I called. Handsome looked up, and I waved like a yokel. "Hello there!"

He brightened at the sound of his own language. "Hi there. Are you American?"

"As apple pie! University of Illinois."

"UCLA. Mind if we join you?"

"Not at all," I bubbled.

Suzy sighed and mumbled, "Tell them to bring the wine."

They scuffed their chairs to our tiny table, and small talk ensued. It turned out Handsome actually knew a "dear acquaintance" of Suzy's (which in Suzy-speak usually meant "lovesick fool") in Los Angeles, and long story short, we had dates for our last night in Rome. Over our free dinner, Suzy mentioned that we were headed for Florence the next day.

"Maybe we'll bump into you there," said Handsome.

I was certain they would.

We were heartened by the beautiful drive to Florence, but arriving days ahead of our hotel reservation, we ended up with a room the size of Mom's linen closet. We flipped a coin, and I lost, but Suzy couldn't bear to make me lie on the floor next to the grubby bidet, so we huddled like spoons in the narrow single bed. Dave and Mike were even more disenchanted with their dodgy fifth-floor hostel.

"No bathroom and no elevator," said Dave. "And at this price. It's robbery."

"It's cheaper than Rome," I said. "Stop acting like they're prying gold out of your teeth."

"We're going to Venice. And if it stinks like everyone says, we're going to Munich."

"But *Firenze*—it's a dream," Suzy protested. "We have to see Michelangelo's *David*."

"You boys go ahead," I suggested readily. "Suzy and I'll take the train to Germany next week. Right, Suzy?"

We'd already connected with our dates from Rome, and going out with them opened the door for other likely candidates. Suzy and I set forth an aggressive agenda of museums, galleries, and historic sites followed by dinner and dancing every night. Our skirts were hopelessly wrinkled, but every time we plugged in the travel iron, it blew out the lights on the entire floor of our shabby hotel, so we bought new evening dresses for dating and spent the days barelegged and frizzy haired in $3 jumpers from the straw market. It was mid-July now. By the time we left Florence, every zipper on every bag was broken. By the time we left Venice, neither of us had a decent pair of shoes.

"My feet are ruined with all this walking," Suzy remarked on the train to Munich. "Happily, my tush looks amazing."

"Oh, my God." A headline caught my eye, and I picked up a British newspaper from the floor. "Suzy, Adlai Stevenson died."

She scootched close to read over my shoulder. The great statesman, whom JFK had appointed U.S. ambassador to the United Nations, had suffered a heart attack as he strolled down a London sidewalk with his UN colleague Marietta Tree.

"I've heard he's a deplorable womanizer, but still . . . it's so sad," said Suzy. "For some reason it makes home seem even more far away."

"We should try to find a *New York Times* every week, Suz. So we know what's going on at home."

"Yes. With the space flight and everything. That's a good idea."

Marietta Tree smiled up, chic as can be, from the rumpled newsprint. She was an object of some fascination for Suzy and me, a socialite who'd used her brains, style, and impeccable party skills to influence presidential politics and eventually gain appointment to the United Nations Commission on Human Rights. Somehow she'd managed to do everything right, while simultaneously doing a thousand things that simply aren't done.

"I hope we haven't hurt Mike and David's feelings," said Suzy. "I can't believe I'm saying this, but I miss them a little."

"I don't. Some girls in Venice told me Munich is crawling with Canadian boys." But I felt a flush of guilt and added, "Still . . . they've been awfully good about carrying things."

A nice German lady sat down next to us and was kind enough to spend the rest of the train ride tutoring me on my *deutsche* phrases. Our first night in Munich, we were slated to go out with the boys from UCLA, but Nebbish bowed out at the last minute. Suzy didn't want to leave me alone at the hotel, but I insisted she go. The minute she was out the door, I got dressed and set out on my own. Knowing Suzy would plotz if she knew what I was up to made me feel even more ferociously elated. I found my way to a café where Americans were said to congregate, and sure enough, fell in with a group of Boston girls bound for a party at the Excelsior. I'd been successfully goosed a few times and was striking up a conversation with a chemistry teacher who looked like a surfer when I heard Suzy call my name.

"Fancy meeting you here," she said icily.

Back at our hotel that night, we discovered our room was next to a bell tower, where a great, beefy bell tolled every fifteen minutes like Quasimodo's life depended on it. We lay in the dark, dozing for a few minutes, getting gonged awake, dozing again. Toward dawn, Suzy groaned into her pillow.

"My nerves are shot to hell. We have to find another place to stay."

"It won't be hard to find something. The German people are so friendly and helpful."

"They should be," Suzy huffed. "*All things considered.*"

I knew what she meant, but I'd been trying not to think about it.

"I hear you get free beer on the brewery tour," I said. "The best beer in the world."

"Well," Suzy sniffed. "It's nice they can happily go about making beer after—"

The bell tolled, echoing off the walls. It disturbed me to hear Suzy sound so hard. She was a baby during the last two years of the war, and I was born just as it ended. In that brief period of time, the whole world changed. Everyone at the temple had lost family in the Holocaust: extended family, third cousins, great-grand-aunts and uncles-in-law—people unknown to us but dear to those we held dear. We grew up keenly aware that those were Our People, who looked like us and shared our blood and our beliefs. Mom and Daddy were less than thrilled to have Suzy and me spend time in this place that was such a fresh hell in their memories. I'd brushed it off before we left, but now I understood, and I couldn't bear to connect such dark history with the generous laughter of the old man in the bakery shop or the kindly tutoring of the woman on the train.

"How could good people get swept up in such a thing?" Suzy wondered.

"I don't know. They probably don't know themselves."

In Paris, I'd felt the lingering voices of la Résistance; Germany echoed with something else altogether. I couldn't begin to grasp what that feeling was, having come from a community where most people listened to their better angels, but now perhaps I'd equate it with having cancer. What begins as a small, unsettled dread, grows to a terrifying certainty and quickly becomes desperation. This malignancy threatens everything, but it's part of you. To kill it is to kill an aspect of your-self. The normal human response is thrashing anger, a need to blame, throat-gripping fear, and lashing efforts at self-preservation. What's left, if one survives, is a scarred heart of fear and sadness, the feeling of hav-ing been rocked on one's foundation, and a grim determination to make life normal again.

"Suzy."

"Yes, Nan?"

"You know what they call the sleeping car on the train?"

"No, what?"

"*Schlafwagen.*" For some reason, we broke into a fit of giggles over that.

"You're such a nut," said Suzy. "What does *Schlafwagen* have to do with anything?"

"*Nichts,*" I said. The bell tolled, and we broke into another inexpli-cable fit of giggles.

"I heard from that nice man we met in Italy. I told him I'd go out with him tomorrow night if he brings a friend for you."

I huffed, indignant. "I can get a date on my own."

"I know, Nanny, but I want us to stick together. Some of these guys are so phony-baloney. Not just Europeans. American tourists and ex-pats, too. In fact, as far as I've observed, men are pretty much the same all over the world. It's fine to go out and have a good time, but we can meet guys anywhere. I'm here to see as much of Europe as I can. I don't want you to be so distracted chasing boys that you miss everything."

Later that week, two men got into a fistfight over Suzy, breaking stuff all over the Hofbräuhaus, but other than that, we found everyone in Mu-nich to be wonderfully kind and pleasant. Suzy and I explored museums and funny little galleries tucked between butcher shops and bakeries, staring for hour after fascinated hour at images from the grotesque move-ment that had influenced German art in the decades leading up to World War II. Suzy moved quickly past a series of Otto Dix etchings of twisted soldiers in bulky gas masks. The unsettling undercurrents were palpa-ble, even in the portraiture. Tortured colors, nightmare expressions. The postwar art was even more conflicted. We stood in front of an installation of black-and-white photographs, searching the meticulous compositions and corners, trying to understand how such great shame and such great dignity could possibly coexist. I thought of Suzy's mandate over my broken suitcase.

Ropes are the answer.

There were times, I decided, when redemption could be found only in the simple act of keeping it together.

Suzy seemed to have a homing beacon for the small galleries and arty coffeehouses, and in these less stately places, the so-called "degenerate art"—*entartete Kunst*—that had been ridiculed and confiscated by the Third Reich enjoyed a triumphant return from exile. In 1937, the "decadent work of Bolsheviks and Jews," which included works by Picasso and Kandinsky, had been exhibited in Munich alongside paintings by psychotics and schizophrenics. Some of the sixteen thousand works were auctioned off in Switzerland and America to finance the efforts of the Nazi Party. The rest were burned.

"I can't stand to think what was lost," said Suzy. "Art is the soul of a people. I don't know if it's possible to get that back."

We met up with Dave and Mike and drove the heavily laden VW to Berlin.

In 1961, the government of East Germany had reinforced the expanse of electrified barbed wire with 26 miles of concrete that separated family members, friends, and neighbors who'd once lived in the same city. In the pubs at night we heard stories about how the West Berliners posted Christmas trees on pedestals and sang carols over the Wall. The East Berliners had been forbidden to wave at West Berlin friends and family, so groups of housewives conspired to all wash windows at the same time. (It's laughable, really: those fat old colonels in their war rooms imagining they were any match for the kaffeeklatsch ingenuity of womankind.)

Travel between East and West Germany had been severely restricted since the iron curtain had descended, but during this brief window of opportunity, we were able to get permission to go into East Germany for a few hours. (Permission from the German government, that is, not our parents. We decided they'd be happier not knowing until we had the photos developed.) We made our way through Checkpoint Charlie under the hard stares of heavily armed soldiers and snarling dogs. At the border, we were thoroughly searched, interrogated, and warned about the consequences of overstaying our welcome or making any attempt to abet the escape of East Germans. Foreigners were known to alter the undercarriages of their cars to accommodate illegal passengers, so guards routinely measured frames and fuel tanks. If they found any discrepancy, the car was dismantled and the travelers arrested.

Facing the Berlin Wall on its eastern side was a façade of tidy prefabricated buildings, but beyond that, the city was scarred with rust and studded with wreckage from the war that hadn't yet ended for the people who lived there. We drove past toppled bricks and jutting rebar, sagging shingles rotting in the sun, women in worn-out dresses scolding their children out of the street, men with downcast faces standing in line for whatever compels desperate men to stand docilely in lines. Dave occasionally pointed out monuments and architectural features, but for the most part, we rode in silence. Huddled in the backseat of the VW, Suzy and I held our breath and swallowed our tears. The atmosphere of despair was overwhelming.

But every once in a while, I felt a nudge of Suzy's elbow, and she'd nod toward an alley where children played or a doorway where a couple paused to kiss. Because even in a horrid, rusty snow globe of a city, laughter and kisses can be found. In the midst of injustice, poverty, oppression—in the midst of cancer—small, sweet things take on remarkable proportion. This was my first inkling of that.

We made our way out of the city and sped west along the winding road. The speed limit on most stretches of the Autobahn was 100 kilometers (62 miles) per hour, but we were warned that some stretches were in ill repair, and lower limits there were harshly enforced by the Volkspolizei. This was a beautiful country. I wanted to love the thick woods and green hills, but it was impossible to see a single wildflower without thinking about the fear and sorrow that permeated the soil. It was impossible to feel anything but humbly grateful for the outrageous privilege of living in darling old Peoria in the Land of the Free and the Home of the Brave.

Along the hilly roadsides in Spain, we'd seen the layers of civilization one on top of the other. In Medina-Sidonia, Suzy had waved to me from the bell tower of an ancient cathedral that was built on top of a ruined mosque, which was built on top of a ruined Roman temple. On the Autobahn, skimming over freshly repaired cement, then bumping over stretches of old road where the asphalt had buckled beneath the caterpillar treads of the retreating tanks, we saw those layers of history being laid down, a vivid illustration of old and new, destruction and construction, victory and defeat, on and on through circling years.

As darkness fell, we crossed back into the free world, and I was overwhelmed with a very grown-up love and appreciation for my own country. Never in my life had I ever been so piercingly aware of the pure sweetness of freedom, the magnitude of what it meant to me to be an American. Never for a moment since have I taken that privilege for granted.

One of the great gifts of our journey was the opportunity to view our own country through the lens of another culture. Surveying ages of creative process, knowing the history tangled up in it, Suzy and I could plainly see how the stirrings in music, art, and fashion both foreshadowed and echoed political movements. The world tilted with plunging necklines and shoes that showed a little ankle. Degenerate art kicked Hitler's you-know-what and remained standing long after all the fallen armies of righteous Aryan wrath.

Seeing all this from the tourist's perspective, I suddenly looked over my shoulder and saw the music, art, and fashion shifting in my own country. The skirts getting shorter and the hair getting longer. Jazz music and beat poetry. Andy Warhol and Jackson Pollock. There was a feeling of unrest, spirits on the move. It made some people uncomfortable, but I wasn't afraid. Suzy and I were just beginning to understand where we fit in the world, wondering how—or even if—it was possible for our lives to make a difference. To my mind, the most exciting thing in the world was civilized dissent and the dynamic of change. It meant people were alive and fully engaged, that people *cared*.

If Germany held one lesson for me, it's that apathy is more dangerous than any ideology.

Our survey of European men—I mean *art,* of course, art and culture—was a resounding success. Very educational. Back in West Berlin, we made our way from hotel to hotel, art gallery to museum, historic site to train station. It was unseasonably cold, but we didn't want to spend money on new coats, so we hustled down the drizzly streets huddled close together under one umbrella, my arm across Suzy's shoulder, her arm around my waist.

Logistics, directions, and connections were a constant juggling act. Everything is so touch-of-a-button nowadays that we often fail to appreciate what a gift it is to be connected to the bank in the blink of an eye or to hear a loved one's voice at the flip of a switch. Of course, what I failed to appreciate back then was that this would be my best, biggest experience of both Suzy and the world. This was truly the only time we spent together, just the two of us, as grown single women, and had I experienced the dramedy with anyone other than Suzy, it wouldn't have been the grand falling-in-love-with-everything adventure that it was.

We had dates every night in Germany.

"Darling boys. Nice Jewish men," Suzy reassured Mom, stretching that definition to include an Irish Catholic guy named Israel.

Our last night in Berlin, we had dinner in a restaurant where John F. Kennedy had eaten pig knuckles on the same famed trip during which he declared himself to be a jelly doughnut.

"He should have said *Ich bin 'Berliner* instead of *Ich bin ein Berliner*," Boppie had explained to me at the time, but later I read that, while certain members of the American press romped on the alleged faux pas, Berliners themselves didn't bat an eyelash, since they actually call the pastry *Pfannkuchen*. And if one wanted to parse the minute nuances of German grammar, Kennedy's usage was correct, anyway, because he wasn't literally "from Berlin."

Sitting in the pig knuckle place less than two years after JFK was assassinated, I wondered at how one small word (not even a verb or a noun, but a mere article!) could balloon into an embarrassment and in the context of another moment—*pop*—it was rendered small again, almost endearing. It made me think about the power of language and legacy, how one could be so swiftly transformed in public perception from king of Camelot to jelly doughnut to martyr and then to a memory that digested all of this efficiently but reflected none of it accurately.

When I tried to express all this to Suzy on the way to Copenhagen, she sighed and pressed her fingertips against her temple.

"Nan. Calm down. You're either raging about politics or chasing everything in pants."

"Why do you have to be such a prude?"

"Because I'm the big sister. You don't how difficult it is. But so be it." She made a magnanimous gesture. "As long as my strength holds, I'll watch out for you."

The boys dropped us off and went to Brussels. We'd missed our check-in time at the hotel in Copenhagen, so the clerk referred us to a pleasant family home for $4 a night, including a grand, starchy breakfast, after which we trooped off in search of Hans Christian Andersen's *Little Mermaid*.

"I wish we'd known sooner that we could stay in someone's home," said Suzy. "You learn more about the local sights and meet these interesting people. Europeans are so grown up. Culturally, I mean. Everyone here knows at least three languages. Nan, let's study French and German together. Let's speak at least three—"

Suzy froze in the middle of the sidewalk and pointed to a sign above the storefront.

Uhren & Schmuck.

We died laughing. Not very cultured of us, I know. Suzy consulted her phrase book. It means "watches and jewelry." We couldn't help ourselves; every time we saw another *Uhren & Schmuck* sign, we went to pieces.

The family in Copenhagen referred us to the Barton family in Amsterdam. They welcomed us warmly and fed us another lumberjack breakfast. During the thirty-five-minute tram ride into the city, we met two darling Danes, who escorted us to the Anne Frank House and Rijksmuseum. After dinner, we strolled down Canal Street, where the ladies of the night waved from their windows. Somehow, in the context of all that Vermeer and Brueghel, even the prostitutes seemed as rosy, plump, and healthy as apple crisp with powdered sugar.

The next day, we went to the Jewish Quarter around the Waterlooplein. Jews from Portugal, Poland, and Germany had taken refuge there in the sixteenth and seventeenth centuries. Rembrandt and his wife had lived there, and we visited the home where he spent his happiest, most productive years, painting scenes from the Bible and re-creating the simple loveliness he saw as he walked along the canals. Before the war, about 140,000 people populated the quaint neighborhood, flourishing in pleasant shops and busy businesses. After the Holocaust, about 28,000 remained, and now a wide swath was being razed to make room for a modern expressway.

Suzy and I were somber as we made our way back to the Bartons.' She'd worn out another pair of walking shoes and needed a new flight bag, so we stopped to buy a serviceable beige satchel and a pair of loafers with square toes and a thick, matronly heel.

"These are even more hideous than the ones you bought in France," she said.

"On the bright side, they match your hideous bag."

Out on the crowded sidewalk, I lagged a few paces behind her, laughing my head off. Here was Miss Susan Freda Goodman, connoisseur of all things pretty and delicate, tromping down the street in her cast-iron loafers with that tan monstrosity on her shoulder.

"Excuse me, Miss?" I called. "Miss, I couldn't help noticing those *smart* shoes you're wearing. And that darling bag! Wherever did you find that little gem?"

"Very funny." Suzy looped her arm through mine, and we fell into step side by side, plugging one ugly shoe in front of the other, laughing harder than we did over *Uhren & Schmuck.*

Mrs. Barton was such a dear hostess, we bought her a dozen sweetheart roses on the way home, and when we presented them to her, she invited us to have dinner with the family. Their daughter would be coming with her fiancé, she told us, a wonderful man who spoke fluent English and held degrees in government and law from Tel Aviv University. She didn't mention that he was black. When the happy couple showed up at the door, Suzy and I did our best not to act like we were seeing a unicorn. We'd been taught all our lives how wrong segregation was, but despite the Civil Rights Act that had passed the previous year, it was still very much the norm in the United States.

Just a few months earlier, Martin Luther King Jr. had called from the steps of the Alabama state capitol: *"How long? Not long, because no lie can live forever. . . . How long? Not long, because the arc of the moral universe is long, but it bends toward justice."*

I knew it was true, but sitting across the table from Miss Barton and her fiancé, I rankled with impatience. *How long?* It had already been too long.

Lying in bed next to Suzy, I marveled, "His race wasn't even a footnote in her description of him. No separate but equal. Just people. Without having to say anything about it. What a wonderful country."

"It'll be like that in the U.S.," Suzy said. "You'll see. Someday, it'll change."

"It'll change when people *make* it change. When we get off our duffs and—"

"Oh, Nanny, don't go on about it. We had such a lovely day. Just enjoy being here."

I turned away and punched my pillow into submission.

"Nan?"

"What?" I huffed.

"Don't be a bitch."

"I'm not!"

"Well, how would you describe that disposition?"

I didn't feel obligated to describe my disposition one way or another.

"Nan?"

"What?"

"Now that we know what we're doing, I'd love to tour South America . . . Asia . . . India. And we have to come back to Europe with Mom and Daddy. The only thing that could possibly be more fun than you and me would be the four of us together."

"I can't wait to get my hands on an American newspaper," I said. "I'm dying to know how the space flight is going. But I will miss the wonderful breakfast here."

"Four of the guys I've gone out with are going to be in London," said Suzy. "They're snowed, but I could care."

"Even the one with the guitar?"

"*Especially* the one with the guitar."

We met up with Mike and Dave in London, but they were catastrophically hung over, and the happy reunion devolved into an argument about the car, which they were having shipped back to New York. They were planning to drive from there to Peoria, and the Goodman sisters with all our bags and baggage were conspicuously not invited along for the ride. Things went downhill from there.

"David," Suzy said imperiously, "I hate to say this, but I'm sorry I met you, and right now, to be quite honest, I could wring your fat neck."

As we haughtily stalked off, I broke a heel on my last pair of shoes.

"Oh, terrific," Suzy groaned. "You're hobbled again, and there go Uhren & Schmuck with the car."

We splurged on a taxi back to our dingy hole of a hotel room, which was filthy and without hot water, so our first order of business the next day was to find new digs, which we liked so well, we wrote Mom and Daddy asking if we could stay an extra week.

"I love hearing English again," said Suzy. "I'm tired of being the one with the foreign tongue."

I liked the British, so staid and dignified, proud of their heritage. We went to Parliament and Westminster Abbey, checked our watches with Big Ben, walked Trafalgar Square, and visited the National Portrait Gallery. I was stirred by the pomp and ceremony at the Changing of the Guard, and Suzy was in seventh heaven standing in front of the Crown Jewels.

"Five hundred and thirty carats." She whistled softly. "How'd you like that on your little handilock?"

We bought a large postcard with a picture of Queen Elizabeth and wrote on the back:

Hi Ellie! Like my picture? Just wanted you to know I'm taking good care of the girls—they are such dolls! How lucky you are! Tomorrow night Phil and I are entertaining them at a state dinner and perhaps they'll meet some interesting people—you never know! Suzy is staying in the new guest rooms, but Nancy preferred to sleep in the guards' quarters. I wish they would stay here forever. Such poised young ladies! Phil and I send all our love to you and Marv!

Every night, we took the Tube to the West End to see the ballet or a play: *Oliver!, The Right Honourable Gentleman, Beyond the Fringe, Richard V, Little Me*. We both loved *Camelot*, and Suzy was surprised to see me cry through half of it.

"Goodness," she said, "I thought I was the sob sister."

"It was so . . . so . . . *alive*," I sniffled. "So idealistic and tragic."

On the nights the theaters were dark, we watched risqué film noirs in stuffy art houses, where cigarettes glowed like fireflies, appearing and disappearing here and there throughout the audience. Suzy and I made no attempt to flag down viable dates, and if any were eyeing us, they didn't let on.

"All the hair on these men here in Beatle Land," Suzy said on our way home from Madame Tussauds. "I can't tell if they're mods or rockers. Very confusing."

"I don't have anything to wear on a date anyway. Our clothes look like they've been dragged through three wars."

"I know, but we can't give them up for two days to be cleaned. We'll just keep dousing ourselves with French perfume to disguise any musky aroma. Mommy would do the same in our situation. It would be silly to miss any opportunity."

"Agreed."

Suzy rested her head on my shoulder, and we swayed with the subway.

"I'm glad we came, Nan. This trip will forever be the highlight of my life. Other than getting married and having children, I mean." She stuck her feet out in front of her. "Are my legs smaller?"

"No, your shoes are bigger."

"I'll bet I'm down to a size two. My hose have to be rolled three times at the top. And I've been eating like I'm getting shot in the morning."

"We must have walked another six miles today. That would do it," I said, wondering why that wasn't doing it for me.

Our excitement about laying hands on an American newspaper faded when we saw the front page. Escalating bloodshed and casualties in Vietnam. Thirty-four people dead after five days of race riots in Los Angeles. Close to home in Illinois, a plane had crashed into Lake Michigan, killing the crew and twenty-four passengers. That night, while I stared at the ceiling, despairing over the state of the world, Suzy thrashed and moaned until I shook her awake and crawled in bed with her.

"Are you okay?" I whispered. "You were having a nightmare."

"That plane crash . . . oh, Nan . . ." She hugged her arms around me, trembling. "I want to go home, but I feel sick when I think about getting on that airplane."

"We'll dose you with Dramamine. You'll see. No more shpilkes." I used Aunt Rose's word for nervous jitters. "If we're going to be world travelers for the next fifty years, you can't be afraid to get on an airplane."

"I hear they have fabulous parties on ships. Dancing every single night."

"Oh. Well, if you'd be more comfortable on the boat, I don't mind."

I miss the days of sprinting into the airport to catch a plane. No barriers, no fear, no standing in line with one's shoes in one's hand. We pride ourselves on our streamlined connectivity, but in some ways we're more segregated than ever, conferencing via video instead of face-to-face, thumb typing a quick text instead of making the call. Dashing down the concourse in those God-awful square-toed shoes, we felt like we were flying already. Every gate invited us on another adventure. Suzy charmed her way out of the extra luggage fees and fortified herself with root beer and Dramamine.

"I'm ready to get home," she said. "I'm going to take a long, hot bubble bath."

"I'm going to eat a slab of roast beef two inches thick."

"Nothing compares with good old America."

"My favorite place in the whole world."

"My favorite place is *everywhere*." She closed her eyes and gripped my hand as we took off over the Atlantic. "I don't want it to be over, Nanny. I can't believe how fast life flies by."

Forever Blonde

> Judy Holliday, whose portrayal of a junk dealer's doxy in *Born Yesterday* created a new kind of beautiful-but-dumb blonde, died of cancer yesterday. She was 43 years old.

THE OBITUARY had appeared in the *New York Times* the same week Suzy and I left for Spain in the late spring of 1965. Suzy probably saw the item or something similar that went out on the wire, but she wouldn't have known that Judy Holliday died of breast cancer. The *Times* obit mentioned something about "cancer surgery" but spared readers the specifics, sharing instead the more comforting detail that "She died in her sleep."

The obituary mentioned Miss Holliday's Oscar, Golden Globe, and Tony Awards, her genius IQ, and how she rallied friends to cook up a cabaret act while blacklisted from radio and television during the Red Scare. In 1960, she starred opposite Dean Martin in the film version of *Bells Are Ringing,* playing switchboard operator Ella Peterson, the Broadway role that won her the Tony. Ella has a second-act showstopper, "I'm Going Back," in which she sings about returning to happier days at the "Bonjour Tristesse Bra-zeer Company." In the movie, Holliday danced her hands across her décolletage and tossed in a sly little line about "modeling on the side."

Judy Holliday was hilarious and charming. Like my sister, she somehow managed to be sexy and wholesome at the same time, and that's how the mass audience liked to think about breasts back then. Torpedo bras were lifting and separating from coast to coast, but we kept it classy for the most part, a coquettish wink-and-a-smile that offered just a hint of sexuality, the way peep-toe shoes offer a hint of red nail polish.

The unwritten media rule on breasts was "Look but don't type"; most people probably wouldn't have recognized the word *mastectomy* anyway. When Judy Holliday had her left breast removed in October 1960, she and her PR people put out a cover story that she was in the hospital for a "bronchial infection."

Hoping she'd been cured by the surgery, Miss Holliday appeared on *Perry Como's Kraft Music Hall* TV show a few months later and subsequently returned to the stage. She went on *What's My Line?* in 1963 as part of a junket for a Broadway show called *Hot Spot*. It flopped despite her formidable star power, and the game show appearance would turn out to be Judy Holliday's last TV gig. According to later reports, well-meaning physicians and family members thought Miss Holliday, who was prone to depression, would be better off not knowing her cancer had metastasized, so she was told the increasing pain in her right breast was "inflammation of the sternum."

I strongly suspect that the dumb blonde with the genius IQ knew she was being lied to. The ravages of the spreading cancer quickly became undeniable. Whether or not it came up in conversation, she had to have known she was dying.

Would Judy Holliday be alive today had she known the truth about her diagnosis? Almost certainly not. Treatment options in the 1960s were few and ineffectual. At most—and it's a stretch—chemo might have bought her enough time to make it to her son's bar mitzvah. (Jonathan Oppenheim was twelve when he lost his mother.) Would she have died more peacefully or less peacefully had she been told up front about the terrible fate that awaited her? It's not appropriate for those of us who didn't know her to speculate.

The truly relevant question takes in a much bigger picture:

Is knowledge more dangerous to a woman's health than ignorance?

Women were being "protected" from the facts about their breast cancer long before Fanny Burney's surgeon assured her back in 1811 that a mastectomy was "but a little thing" to be carried out with the patient seated comfortably in a parlor chair. And it's still going on today. Every time I think we've come so far, gained so much ground, established open dialogue, claimed our right to make informed treatment decisions—every time I'm certain we can file this one under "No-Brainer"—we find ourselves rehashing it again.

As recently as November 2009, forty-four years after the death of Judy Holliday, the U.S. Preventive Services Task Force (which sounds like a government agency but is actually an "independent panel") revised its recommendations regarding breast cancer screening and early treatment. Instead of getting routine annual mammograms beginning at age forty, they said, women should forgo routine screening until age fifty and then get a mammogram every other year. They went on to say women shouldn't be taught proper breast self-exam (BSE) technique—that BSE was, in fact, *harmful*—because finding a lump in her breast causes a woman emotional distress and prompts her to take unnecessary action. The panel had based its recommendations on statistics that had been floating around for a long time, but as Mark Twain said: "People commonly use statistics the way a drunk uses a lamp post, for support rather than illumination."

Of course, the news hit the fan, and pundits rushed in where angels fear to tread. One anchorwoman sat down with the network's chief medical editor to ask the obvious questions. Scrimping on mammograms could at least be rationalized as a cost-cutting measure, but why discourage BSE—a no-cost, noninvasive procedure which simply encourages a woman to be aware of changes in her breasts?

"Amid the passionate response," said the anchorwoman, "are a lot of women who say the old guidelines saved their lives. For example, we have a woman from Pennsylvania. . . ." She produced a letter and read from it.

I am a woman who was diagnosed with breast cancer at the age of thirty-five. It was because of me and my self-exam that I found this cancer. It was grade three, invasive, with three lymph nodes positive. It infuriates me that this study is suggesting that self-exams are useless. If I'd not done my exam, I'd be dead right now.

The anchorwoman lowered the letter and looked the medical editor in the eye. "So what are we saying to women like this one?"

"What we're saying, with great sensitivity," said the medical editor, "is that there are big bodies of science, where we look at the numbers across all women and all age groups who've been getting mammograms, and then there are anecdotes. The personal stories. We all know women who've found their breast cancers and were diagnosed at twenty-eight or routine screening at forty, and those stories *matter*."

She really did say it with great sensitivity, too. *Great* sensitivity, I must say.

"But," she went on, "the recommendations say that for every story like that, there were nineteen hundred other women who got unnecessary radiation, for whom screening wasn't the issue. So cancer is always personal, but these recommendations are supposed to give us scientific guidelines."

"But if, in fact, self-exam shows you that you have a lump," said the anchorwoman, "even if the chance is overwhelming that you won't find anything—but there's a chance that you would—what does it hurt? Why not just let people self-exam?"

"If you do self-exam and you're comfortable with that, that's fine," said the medical editor, "but a lot of women have been taught to do this search-and-destroy mission on their bodies every month, that our breasts are our enemies . . . and for the average woman, the yield is very low."

A lot of women. (Certainly a scientific, nonanecdotal way to quantify it.)

Do a search-and-destroy mission.

Against their enemy breasts.

The clumsiness, inaccuracy, and disrespect in that statement literally took my breath away. That characterization is the antithesis of what BSE is.

We take our children to the pediatrician every year for a routine checkup before the start of school; it's never recommended that mothers should blow that off because "the yield is low" and the "average child" walks in and out as healthy as a polo pony. At regular dental exams, the hygienist never accuses us of "a search-and-destroy mission" on our gums. Driving the car into the mechanic's bay for a routine inspection, we aren't berated for treating the Chevy like an enemy. Yet for some reason, routine maintenance of breast health is constantly being scrutinized and blustered against. I'm just plain baffled by the assumption that women who drive eighteen-wheelers and perform brain surgery turn into hysterical nitwits when they walk into a doctor's office, so (as Judy Holliday's well-meaning physician believed back in 1965): *Women are better off not knowing.*

The problem with BSE is that it works too well. When a woman finds a lump, she usually insists on knowing what it is, and when it's a malignancy, she usually insists on getting rid of it. The vast majority of lumps are benign and even some of the malignant ones aren't life threatening. If you completely ignore your breasts—keep your hands in your pockets, slap anyone who tries for second base, go to the movies instead of going for mammograms—odds are in your favor; you very probably won't die as a result. That's a statistical fact. One out of eight women will be diagnosed with breast cancer, but look at the bright side: the other seven won't! A biopsy that rules out cancer is deemed "unnecessary"—a waste of a perfectly good panic attack. So, they conclude, why worry our pretty little heads? We'd be *healthier* not knowing, and the people who love and insure us would be happier if we weren't so high-maintenance.

I reject the notion that blissful ignorance is healthier than an informed choice or even an educated guess, which is often as good as it gets. Shame on any doctor who subscribes to that belief, and God help any woman so easily displaced from the driver's seat of her own life. We are the CEOs of our bodies. It's our responsibility to gather the information we need to make the decisions with which we alone will live or die. My definition of an "unnecessary biopsy" is one in which you already know there's a malignancy. If there's any question, a biopsy provides a definitive answer. Obviously, I'd love to see a reduction in the number of biopsies on benign tumors. That's one of the reasons Susan G. Komen for the Cure is convening a major national technology think tank in 2010 with the goal of developing better screening technology, including a more accurate, more predictive mammogram.

Early mammogram technology that emerged in the 1960s was a step forward from the blurry, nonspecific x-rays of yesteryear. The second-generation designs of the early 1980s reduced radiation exposure and increased accuracy with better film and the first motorized compression device. In the early 1990s, the introduction of rhodium filters again reduced radiation exposure and improved imaging. In 2000, we took a giant step forward when General Electric introduced the first FDA-approved digital mammography system. We've seen significant advances in mammogram technology like clockwork every ten years since it was introduced, and it's time for the next step.

Meanwhile, we have to use what we've got to our best advantage. I'm delighted that the "yield is low for the average woman." But does that mean I can safely assume *I'm* average? Or is that just the cover story I'm supposed to tell myself?

Judy Holliday used to sing a song called "The Party's Over"; with palpable sadness, she called it a day. "*They've burst your pretty balloon and taken the moon away....*"

Late in the spring of '65, while Suzy and I sat at the kitchen table with our maps and guidebooks, Judy Holliday was quietly admitted to Mount Sinai. By the time we reached Venice, she was dead. Suzy flew off to Spain, unaware of Judy's fate. Judy died in her sleep, unaware of Suzy's existence. Would it have changed Suzy's life if she'd known she was on that same terrible path? Would it have changed Judy's death to know that someday women would stand up and demand the truth?

I believe knowledge is power, but I don't deny that ignorance is bliss. The trouble with bliss, however, is that it's often short lived. There's only one way to stay blonde forever.

~ 5 ~

May Queen at Neiman Marcus

tan Komen made Suzy laugh.

S   "More importantly, he makes me happy," she said. "Nan . . . I love this man."

He wasn't the prince charming she'd requisitioned in Europe, just a foundationally good man who made her feel warm and domestic. They met and became good friends during her Miss Mizzou days at the University of Missouri. They dated for a while, but faded out. Then Suzy got swept up in that utterly wrong marriage, and we'd spent the following summer exploring Europe. Stan Komen patiently stayed in touch with her, biding his time, just like the Gershwin song.

"What can I say? He won me over," she said, when she called to tell me they were getting married.

"Are you sure, Suz?" I reminded her of our plan to return to Germany and get jobs and continue our adventures together.

"I'm positive."

Suzy sounded settled and content, like a woman whose traveling days were over.

After the wedding—a beautifully turned do-over in which the entire wedding party made it through the ceremony on their feet—she and Stan moved to a pleasant apartment in a nice neighborhood in St. Louis, and Suzy set up housekeeping with her distinctly artistic touch, nesting comfortably but with panache.

I was less than 100 miles away from home at the University of Illinois in Champaign, so I came home on a regular basis, and Suzy visited whenever she could for parties and special events. It was understood by our father and by Suzy's husband: There would be fearsome phone bills. Suzy and I talked for at least half an hour virtually every day, and sometimes chattered on until late at night. She wanted to be filled in on every detail of my classes, sorority doings, and campus rabble-rousing, and wanted me to know every detail about the perfect pitcher and juice glasses she'd found at the five-and-dime, the matching place mats and table runner she'd ordered from Sears, and the entire saga involved in the living room drapes she was having made.

Her life in St. Louis wasn't extravagant by any means, but it was *lovely.* That was important to her. She was on a mission to create a certain atmosphere in which she would flourish and have children, a home filled with beauty: music to fill the air, art to fill the soul, picture books in which to lose yourself. Stan was in sales and worked hard at it, but Suzy's taste ran a little beyond their means. Sometimes she'd look to Mom and Daddy for something she couldn't afford on her own budget, and they occasionally indulged her because she gave so much of what she had and devoted so much of her time and energy to those less fortunate than herself. She was trying to get pregnant, volunteering with Girl Scouts and at St. Jude Hospital, doing everything she could for children already in a world that seemed to be growing more complicated every day.

"I worry about you, Nanny," she said. "I keep hearing about all these campus demonstrations and lockouts. You won't get involved in anything like that, will you?"

"Suzy, when would I have time for that?"

I always carried a full load of credits, but more important, I'd gotten myself elected to the student judiciary committee and was involved in the student senate. Inside the classroom, I trained myself to do well on tests and somehow found the self-discipline to trudge along with the sole objective of maintaining good grades on paper. Outside the classroom, I actually learned. My mind came alive. Every once in a while, there was even a thrilling moment of feeling like I belonged. I had no interest in unrest or free love. I was one of the uncool kids who stayed in a single lane aimed at my degree. I did believe the war should end, and I was proud to be part of a generation that cared at the top of its lungs, but I mourned the effects of drugs on the bright minds around me. I had my own focus, but when traffic was stalled by a sit-in or class was interrupted by demonstrators outside, I was grateful for those who took to the streets. I learned from them and tried to apply that knowledge in an effort to build bridges, solve problems, and bring about change from the inside.

It had rankled me since my freshman year that the girls had a different curfew from the boys, and now I was determined to do something about it.

"It's for your own security," Suzy said. "They just want you to be safe."

"I can take care of my own safety," I said. "Why should I have to leave the library an hour before a boy studying for the same class?"

"It's different, Nan. You know it is."

"If we were being treated equally, maybe more girls around here would be serious about their studies. It wouldn't just be something to do while they wait for the MRS degree."

"I like my MRS degree," said Suzy. "I'm doing exactly what I want to do, and I'm good at it. I think a lot of nice girls would take no curfew as an opportunity to be loose."

"Nice girls aren't looking for an opportunity, and loose girls don't need one. Meanwhile, I just want to be at the library."

"Nan, there's a system of rules developed over the course of years by dedicated professionals—*experts*—who know what they're doing. That's not going to change just because this girl comes over from Peoria and doesn't like it."

"It's going to change," I assured her. "I'll *make* it change."

Suzy continued to urge moderation, but my mother egged me on.

"Before you were born, Boy Scouts were going great guns in Peoria," Mom said, "but there wasn't anything for girls, and girls really needed that. Mothers were working outside the home for the first time, everyone doing things for the war effort. Everybody said, 'Oh, there's no time or money for that,' but that's where the opportunity came in. You go where other people aren't, and you make the best of it."

I sank my teeth in, wrote letters, circulated petitions, and basically got nowhere.

"It's so frustrating," I told my mother. "Nobody's listening."

"There are five ways to Mecca," she said philosophically. "Five ways anywhere. The trouble is, people stop before they find the one that works. You're going along, highway's shut down—so what? Find another way."

One semester after another, while I kept my grades consistent, stayed involved in everything I could jam into my schedule, and even found time to date a few interesting men, I kept the issue simmering on the back burner, stirring it up if the opportunity arose.

"I wrote a scathing editorial for the paper," I told Suzy. "There was a big response."

"For or against you?" she asked.

"Against," I had to admit. "But at least people are talking about it."

Tides were shifting. I wasn't the only one making noise, but instead of marching or shouting, I gathered supporting documentation and politely, persistently complained my way up the ladder to the dean of students. I can't say what actually did the trick, but much to everyone's astonishment, the curfew was eventually lifted. I couldn't wait to call Suzy and tell her about this great triumph.

"It's a meaningful step in the cause of equal education for women," I said.

The next morning I awoke in my dorm room to find exactly two girls on the entire floor: me and the least attractive girl on campus.

"This is not at all what I had in mind," I told Mommy.

"Freedom is always the right thing to fight for," she said. "You can't stop believing in freedom just because some people use it to be stupid. Just make sure you're not one of them."

Suzy couldn't stop laughing about it for a month, but between giggles, she did say, "I'm proud of you, Nan. My sister, the crusader. You said you'd make it change, and you did."

My senior year, I threw caution to the wind for a while. Suzy was horrified when she came to visit and found me practically dancing on top of the piano and hooked up with a boyfriend who was the born-to-be-wild type. Mommy and Daddy almost disowned me over this guy, but I refused to break up with him. He was the first in a long parade of bad boys I've loved, so of course, he eventually broke my heart and moved on. I resumed my responsible persona, Mom and Dad were mollified, and Suzy continued scouting around St. Louis for nice men to fix me up with.

"Elegance," said Coco Chanel, "is not the prerogative of those who have just escaped from adolescence, but of those who have already taken possession of their future." I was hovering somewhere between the two by my senior year. With a little help from Suzy and our survey of

European fashionistas, I'd discovered a style that worked for me, and the result was an undercurrent of confidence I'd never experienced before. It wasn't about being pretty, it was about being put together. After years as a loose cannon in Saturday casual, I was learning to carry myself with a well-tailored self-control.

Honestly, I needed someone to encourage my feminine side. From the time I was in junior high, Suzy had dogged me about my posture, taught me how to do my makeup, and helped me coordinate the right clothes for my figure as I shed my baby fat and grew tall and lanky.

"There's no profession in which being fabulous isn't a boost," she used to tell me, and of course, she was absolutely right.

Just before graduation, I was elected May Queen, a title that honored academic achievement, charitable efforts, and civic service, with a nod to the added assets of well-groomed grace and style. For that exact minute, I was essentially everything my parents had brought me up to be, and they couldn't have been prouder. Suzy loved that I was turning out to be a get-going doer, enforcer, striver, but she was thrilled with the beauty queen aspect of it all and took no small amount of credit. She had a badly sprained ankle and was hobbling around on crutches, but she wasn't about to miss the coronation of the May Queen she'd helped create.

Balanced on one foot, Suzy took a picture of me with my tiara, white gloves, and roses, on the stage, flanked by Mom and Daddy. At the time, I looked at it and saw a girl on the brink of becoming herself, a fresh, elated face, eyes bright and looking forward. But finding that photo recently in a tucked-away bin of Mom's memorabilia—old family photos, yellowed clippings of my scathing (I thought) editorials, tear sheets from Suzy's department store modeling jobs—I was captivated by the faces of my parents. I never felt like their pride and joy at the time, but pride and joy are the only words with which I can describe the way they're looking at me. Mom is outright laughing, a study in gladness. Even in profile, the love is apparent in my father's expression. It makes me laugh to see his car keys in his hand, as if he's been waiting for me to make it to this point so he could hop in his Cadillac and make tracks toward his own goals without the second full-time job of subsidizing, spying on, and spotting for two lively daughters.

Daddy was a driver; I was driven. We belonged to each other in more ways than either of us could appreciate at the time.

Suzy was settled and happy. Now I was on my way with my degree in hand. The first challenge I faced was finding the right time to tell Daddy I was moving to Dallas.

Daddy's sister, Aunt Ruth, and her husband, Uncle Ted, had moved to Texas and started a small insurance business back before World War II, so twice a year while Suzy and I were growing up, we all took the Santa Fe Chief south from Chillicothe, Illinois, to visit them. From my earliest memories, I adored Texas with its grand, swaggering spirit, massive tracts of land and *can do* and cowboys, even the kitschy Roy Rogers décor in the roadside diners. I loved the warmth of the people and the mildness of the winter weather. I had no interest in New York or Chicago; to me, north Texas was the next best thing to nirvana. When I decided to move to Dallas after graduation, I had no idea what I was going to do there, but I was convinced it was going to be Wild West wonderful. My father was not about to subsidize such a nebulous goal. He made it clear that if I opted to move to Dallas instead of going to law school or finding a good entry-level position with a company close to home, I was going to be on my own nickel. Suzy couldn't understand why I would choose to leave the land of milk and honey that is Peoria, Illinois, for anything other than love, but if there were ever sides to be chosen in anything, Suzy was firmly on mine. That I could count on.

"You have to go where you want to go. He'll get over it," she said. "I'm going to miss you, Nan, but I think you're going to take Dallas by storm."

When I arrived, my uncle introduced me to his friend, Sam Bloom, who gave me a fundraising job out of his office at Bloom Advertising, working at Temple Emmanuel, raising a pot of funds for the care of an aging and beloved rabbi. Not quite the storm Suzy had envisioned, but the project sparked my interest in marketing, and I started hunting for innovative ways to learn more about it. I heard that Neiman Marcus was hiring women with an eye toward training them for leadership positions, so I haunted the store on my lunch hours, absorbing everything about the way it worked. I walked in one day wearing my sharpest suit and went to the office of the personnel manager, Dennis Worrell.

After a few minutes of small talk, he folded his hands on his desk and said, "So. Nancy. What do you want?"

"I want to work for a company where I know women are allowed to move up the ladder," I said. "I want to learn from smart people who love what they do. And I want to not go back to Peoria. My parents aren't happy about my moving to Texas. In order to stay, I need a good job, and I need it now."

"I see." He absorbed all that for a moment. "Well, it's true we're looking for upwardly mobile women. You'd have the opportunity to become a vice president, if you have the desire and you're willing to work for it."

"Oh, I do. I am."

"Executive trainees rotate through every department. You learn the business from the basement up, starting in the receiving room, where you learn how clothes are received, tagged, and inventoried. If you do well there, you move to the junior women's department, then circulate up to the couture division."

I liked the sound of circulating up.

"How long does that take?" I asked.

"As long as it takes," he said. "The buyers upstairs have their choice of the trainees they want to have as assistants, so if you haven't distinguished yourself as someone who's smart, hardworking, and rock solid, then . . ."

"I understand."

When I told Suzy about my new job at Neiman Marcus, you'd have thought we'd both won the lottery. My head was ringing with the possibility of being vice president of anything; hers was ringing with dreams of couture at a discount. I worked my way through receiving, made good friends with all the shipping guys, and stayed good friends with them when I moved up through the departments.

Every day Stanley Marcus walked the store. Everyone knew his sonorous voice before we glimpsed his shiny bald head or neatly trimmed beard above the shelving. He surveyed every detail of his empire, making his presence felt. If you were behind a counter, that counter had better be gleaming without a single thumbprint, and if you weren't actively helping a customer, you'd better have a bottle of Windex in one hand and a polishing cloth in the other. He wanted the inventory mixed up every day, wanted his employees to think beyond what we were told to do and to re-create our little corner of the store in a way that made it freshly engaging every time a customer walked in the door. Watching the way he connected with people was an education in itself. It wasn't hard sell; it was a strategic sort of showmanship, and the objective was helping people, not separating them from their money.

"Presentation, presentation, presentation," he'd intone.

Mr. Marcus was thought to be way out on the left. He was one of the very few employers who didn't believe in keeping a glass ceiling over the heads of the women in the company. He traveled the world collecting modern art and creative ideas. He was always reaching out, always learning, always curious.

I immediately understood his approach to merchandise because it reminded me so much of Suzy's; it wasn't about having more, bigger, better stuff, it was about creating an environment of good quality and graciousness. Maybe it was a capitalist brand of ahead-of-its-time feng shui. Mr. Marcus understood that people respond and grow toward beauty, and it gave him joy to help them make a physically and emotionally comfortable home where the world would be left outside. And that dynamic applies right down to the most intimate environment we live in: our clothes.

The first Neiman Marcus Fortnight event was described in *Time* magazine as "Dallas in Wonderland." For two weeks in the autumn of 1957, shoppers entered the store and were transported to France: Parisian décor, Gallic music—Coco Chanel herself came from Paris to visit. The first international flight ever to arrive in Dallas delivered her to Love Field, and there to meet her were Mr. Marcus and his vibrantly elegant wife, Billie. Dressed in full way-out-West regalia—ten-gallon hat, embroidered shirt, and pointy boots—he whisked Chanel off to a party at his and Billie's home and then on to the event at the flagship store. Coco swept all the guests off their feet, customers couldn't get enough French fashion and perfume, and Mr. Marcus knew he was onto something.

He'd come up with the idea as a way to lure in customers during an aggravating slump in sales that occurred every year before the holiday shopping season kicked in. Every year, Fortnight featured a different part of the world. Brilliant ideas and unique experiences unfurled from the Marcuses' love of travel, theater, and art. In the early 1960s, Mr. Marcus brought in Alvin Colt, a Tony Award-winning set and costume designer, and they worked together for the next twenty-three years. During a Spanish event, an elaborate china shop hosted a live bull. The British event made the main floor into a manor hall. Visitors included Sophia Loren, Joan Crawford, Princess Grace, and Prince Rainier. As the events grew more and more grandly enchanting, holiday sales figures were left in the dust by the cultural attraction and marketing miracle of Fortnight.

"Go where people aren't," Mom had said. This was a vivid illustration. My first Fortnight in 1968 couldn't have been more perfect.

"It's Italy!" I told Suzy. "You have to come. There's going to be music, food, huge paintings, incredible designer clothes. It's not even optional for you to miss this, Suz."

She stayed with me at my little apartment. We dressed to the nines and stepped through the front door at Neiman Marcus and back in time to our Italian adventures.

Fortnight 1969 was "East Meets West." Alvin Colt created a life-size elephant made of fuchsia orchids and parked it near the elevators. Weaving arm in arm through the elegantly done aisles, Suzy and I reminisced and compared notes on love and life. She kept busy with Junior League and her other activities. I was dating a wonderful man I'd met at a University of Illinois alumni event. He was handsome, smart, and Jewish, but he was almost twenty years older than me, so Mom and Daddy were less than thrilled about it.

"He is a bit old for you," said Suzy. "Nan, he's pushing forty. Think about it."

"I like older men," I said. "Every guy I meet who's my age either smokes dope or *is* a dope or just wants to climb all over me. This is a wonderful man. Funny, smart, industrious. We could have a good family together."

"That sounds nice," she said wistfully.

I studied her expression for a moment. "What . . ."

"Stan and I won't have babies. Dr. Moffet tested us. It's not going to happen."

"Oh, Suzy. What about . . . have you seen a specialist? You could go to Chicago. . . ."

"And discuss our private life with some *stranger*?" Suzy pushed my arm, appalled. "Certainly not. We just have to face it. It wasn't bashert. Not meant to be."

"I'm so sorry, Suz. Are you okay?"

"I'm fine." She nodded. "We've started working through the process to adopt a baby from the Jewish agency, and I actually love the idea. Instead of sitting here month after month, waiting for a baby to happen, now I know there's a baby waiting for me, needing a home, and all I want to do is find him and get my arms around him and give him a wonderful life like Mommy and Daddy gave us. The thing is, now that I'm not obsessing about the pregnancy part, I'm thinking about the part where you actually raise up this child—this *human being*. It's kind of intimidating, the idea of being responsible for leading another person from the cradle to adulthood. I want to get it right."

"You will, Suz." I linked my arm through hers, and she squeezed my hand.

At the time, artificial insemination was just emerging into common use; fertility drugs and in vitro were some researcher's distant dream. (And thank God. Hormone treatments might have done Suzy in even sooner.) We'd always commiserated on "womanly complaints"—stabbing cramps and aching breasts that arrived monthly with our periods.

"Nanny, I asked Dr. Moffet why my breasts get so lumpy and painful every month. I told him you had the same problem, and he said it's fibrocystic breasts—which sounds a lot worse than it is. It's a hormone thing. Very common. Nothing to worry about."

I told her I'd already gotten this explanation from my gynecologist in Dallas, with the added caveat that if a lump didn't go away, it should be biopsied.

"To see if it's infected or . . . something."

"Well, right," said Suzy. "But it always turns out to be nothing."

That year, Suzy did have a lump that wouldn't go away. She ignored it as long as she could, but Mother and I dogged her about it until she relented, swallowed her fear, and got the needle aspiration, which determined the lump was just another cyst.

"You see?" she chided. "I was a nervous wreck for nothing."

Not long after that, I had a needle biopsy on a lump that lingered.

Later, Suzy had another, and I had another, then she had another, and so it went over the years. They were successively less frightening, and Suzy was happily lulled into a complacent sense of confidence. It was an inconvenience we both learned to live with. There were always unnerving moments waiting for the results, but we certainly weren't paralyzed with anxiety over it; neither of us ever slowed down for a second. The paperwork always confirmed the result we fully expected, and we went on our way as if the procedure was less than the bite of a horsefly. We paid attention without allowing the issue to distract us from living our lives. Which was the right thing to do.

Stanley Marcus liked me. Some whispered that Mr. Marcus sometimes "took interest" in women for a lot of reasons, but I think a lot of that came from men—and some women—who simply couldn't believe any woman could ascend in the corporate setting purely by dint of industry and horse sense. In any case, there was never a hint of anything offsides in the way Mr. Marcus treated me. I can state with certainty that he liked me because I worked like a dog and almost never asked for days off.

"Never stop selling," he said. "I think you've got a future. I want you to learn."

And I did learn. My years at Neiman Marcus were thrilling and intensely educational. I didn't realize until much later how much I absorbed just being there every day. Mr. Marcus gathered all the assistants on the floor for a company meeting on a regular basis, assessing us with a congenial but unblinking eye.

"I'm going to challenge you," he said one day before we dispersed. "If any of you can accurately tell me what a customer is going to spend, I'll give you five hundred dollars."

We slapped our hands together, whipped out our notebooks and pens, and went off to bird-dog the front door. The game of selling, we'd been taught, began the moment a customer crossed the threshold. Sizing people up by the obvious yardsticks—the cars they drove, the caliber of their shoes, the way they talked—we invariably thought we had them pegged, and invariably, we were wrong.

"Don't make assumptions," Mr. Marcus told me. "You can't judge a book by its cover."

The logical conclusion: Every person should be treated with the deference and respect you would show your best customer. Princes and paupers, ladies who lunch and the waitress who served them—every person has the potential to make or break your day, because the way you treat people in general adds up to the kind of person you are.

Norman Brinker was a man who definitely defied his book cover. He was a quintessential Texas entrepreneur, a millionaire in white jeans and riding boots, who transcended his hardscrabble childhood but never forgot where he came from. After a stint in the navy, he earned a place on the U.S. Olympic Equestrian Team and competed at the summer games in Helsinki in 1952. He started Brink's Coffee Shop in Dallas in the early 1960s and ended up building an empire. While I was in college, Norman was opening Steak & Ale restaurants all over the Southwest. While I was working my way up from the basement at Neiman Marcus, he was taking his company public and effectively transforming the casual dining industry. (He's often credited as the inventor of the salad bar.)

I knew who he was, because I was active in various charities around town, and if there's one thing good fundraisers know, it's which pants have the most generous pockets. Norman Brinker was a familiar figure and a bighearted donor at the symphony and American Cancer Society events. His wife, the renowned tennis champion Maureen "Little Mo" Connolly, had died of cancer in 1969. Norman was famously dedicated to her and devastated by the loss. We'd see him in the store with his two beautiful daughters, Cindy and Brenda. Adorably inept at all things girlish, he was grateful for the attention of the salesgirls who swarmed like a school of minnows as soon as he walked in the door.

Wealthy widowers do not go undetected in Dallas. Especially not this rare specimen, who combined the disarming grin of a newspaper boy with the body of an Olympic athlete. Women loved him, and he loved women—even the ones who unabashedly viewed him as a prime piece of real estate. As the house-hunters circled, he came and went, making amiable conversation with Mr. Marcus and whoever happened to be on the floor. None of us was surprised to see him shopping for a diamond ring.

In 1970, Neiman Marcus Fortnight was a salute to Ruritania, Suzy became the mother of a darling little boy named Scott, and I made it to the second floor.

I was selected from the pool of assistant trainees to work with an ambitious, wise buyer, Loretta Blum, who was fabulously smart and stylish. She was fairly small in stature, and I think she took one look at me—this corn-fed midwestern girl almost six feet tall—and knew I'd be able to negotiate the freight elevator with ten coats on one arm and six suits on the other. Plus the rods. I suppose she figured, "So what if she doesn't look like a scrawny little fashion model? This girl's a pile driver!" And I turned out to be exactly that.

As soon as the buyers were given an opening to buy something, I was writing letters and making phone calls, hounding the manufacturer. It made them a little crazy, but we got our clothes faster. Loretta taught me a lot about fashion shows and how to work with the designers who visited the second floor. At any given moment, everyone in the room was selling, whether the customer knew it or not.

In walked, let's say, Mrs. Jones of Amarillo. I jumped and ran. My first task was to make sure she was set up with a salesperson in a room full of merchandise of appropriate size and function. If Mrs. Jones was there for a cut-and-trim suit, I dashed downstairs for a bolt of cashmere, and while the designer worked her magic, I was all over the store gathering costume jewelry, hats, gloves, shoes, shoes, and more shoes, filling up the room like a bazaar.

About halfway through the measuring, cutting, gathering, and selling, there was always a light tap on the door, and Mr. Marcus would step in.

"Oh, Mrs. Jones. So happy to see you today. I was wondering if you'd like to come and have dinner with me and Billie tonight at our house." One day, he added, "Nancy'll be there."

I was on. I couldn't wait to tell Suzy.

Stanley and Billie Marcus lived in a magnificent contemporary home with pre-Columbian sculptures and great art everywhere. The guest of honor was seated on his right. I was seated on his left. The first course arrived: a delicate crab dish. Genteel but animated conversation moved back and forth around the eclectic group of Dallas elite, store employees, and a few random artists, writers, and designers. You never knew who was going to be there.

"Mrs. Jones," said Mr. Marcus, "I'm so happy you could join us this evening. I was thinking of you during my recent visit to Japan." He drew an intricately carved box from his pocket and set it directly next to her plate. "I saw this interesting piece from the Tang Dynasty. It reminded me that you have horses."

"Oh, my," said Mrs. Jones. "That is lovely, isn't it?"

"Exquisite." Mr. Marcus opened it to reveal a pair of intricately carved ornaments. "These netsuke—they're made of Siberian mammoth ivory—come from the Edo period. I realized how perfectly they'd coordinate with a certain diamond and sapphire necklace in our fine jewelry department." Out came the necklace from his other pocket. "And knowing how beautifully you wear sapphires, I wanted to show you the two together."

By the end of the evening, Mrs. Jones—or Mrs. Smith or Mr. Smith or the Smiths' lovely daughter—would have spent literally thousands and thousands of dollars.

Being able to observe this salesman extraordinaire—this master showman—up close was the greatest thing to happen in my marketing education, right up there with everything I'd learned watching my father persevere in building his business year after year. Stanley Marcus had an infallible eye for the devilish details, and the way he forged connections with people was nothing short of brilliant. When he was out traveling the world, he always had a stack of postcards with him, and as he rode along on trains and airplanes, he spent hours neatly scribing personal notes by the hundreds, one after another.

Dear Mrs. Smith,

I've just returned from India. I'm going to be sending you a box of wonderful merchandise I know you will love!

Love, Stanley

He didn't waste time trying to talk people into things they didn't need or want; he intuited what they secretly craved and offered it to them along with a story that transformed the item into an artifact and a purchase into a coup de grâce, the same way Alvin Colt transformed the main floor of a department store into the *Fête des Fleurs*.

"Most people aren't creative," Mr. Marcus said. "But they're waiting for creation. They don't want to be changed, but they want to be entertained and educated. They want to learn in a way that excites their curiosity and convinces them to take action."

I was brought into the creative meetings for the fabulous Neiman Marcus catalog that year, and I had the opportunity to present one seasonal idea.

"What about boats?" I said.

"Go on," Mr. Marcus said after a moment.

"My parents started out with very little. A little sailboat and a willingness to work hard. Over the years, they got a little motorboat, and then a rickety sort of houseboat, and now—well, now my father is doing quite well. They have a very nice boat. It's not a yacht, but it's the kind of boat you could take around the world, if you chose to. And a few years ago, he bought my mother a lovely mink coat. These things aren't about status or self-indulgence. They envisioned a quality of life and worked toward it. Fashion—whether it's personal style or home décor—is an extension of those dreams we have for ourselves. The cut of our jib, if you will."

I felt the eyes of everyone around the table. I wasn't being judged, I was being *heard,* and it was exhilarating.

"Plus," I added, "everyone looks better in white."

Mr. Marcus put me in charge of his little boutique at the Fairmont Hotel, where it was my responsibility to serve the particular needs of the most spectacular customers. Suzy was beyond thrilled when I was given the task of escorting Princess Grace to Fortnight and when I was given the difficult task of finding a Dallas restaurant willing to serve our guests, Ike and Tina Turner. (It was a different time; Tina and Dallas both worked hard in subsequent years to rise above bullies and become free and flourishing.)

When a major Hollywood diva arrived with her entourage, I was summoned to her suite. This was the first time I heard the Hungarian language spoken, and I was fascinated by the sound, but the pressing matter at hand was the proper fitting of the diva.

"Those silly girls," she lamented. "They keep bringing things that don't fit, telling me I'm not a size six. I think I know what size I am!"

"Yes, ma'am. Of course," I said. "I'll be back with some items for you to choose from."

I sprinted back to the store and rallied help down in the basement, hastily snipping tags and labels from a number of size six garments and stitching them into their size twelve counterparts. The diva was delighted and spent buckets of money, which earned a few more stars in my crown as far as my boss was concerned.

"You're an evil genius," Suzy giggled when I told her. "Is that even legal?"

"I'm not sure," I said. "But she is who she is, and she's worked hard for it. If she wants to be a size six, let her be a size six. Why should the customer fit the clothes? The clothes should fit the customer."

Everything in my life seemed to be coming together. I adored my job, and was quite taken with Jake, that nice man I'd been dating. I was fairly certain I loved him, but we hadn't had time to build much history together. My father's disapproval was a major impediment, so we'd been taking the small steps people do in a blossoming relationship. Just as we began exploring the idea of a future together, Jake suffered a massive coronary and died. I couldn't have been more stunned, and as the numbness wore off, anger and guilt swamped me. I knew my being there wouldn't have prevented his death, and I had no idea how things would have worked out for us if he'd lived, but I knew for a fact that I hadn't followed my heart, and having failed in that, I felt oddly unentitled to the grief that weighed me down. I had no standing, no right to feel so widowed. For many days in a row, I called Suzy, weeping, and she stuck by me patiently as I cried it out.

"When a young person dies," she said, "it's not just the person you're grieving. It's the death of a dream. Everything that was possible."

She was right, I would later learn, but at the time, all I took from the experience was a core-deep determination to never make the same mistake again.

Cents and Sensibility

IT TAKES a lot to get noticed in Southern California.

The San Diego Susan G. Komen 3-Day for the Cure is a breathtaking, blistering, 60-mile spectacular, featuring ocean vistas, a sea of magenta pup tents, bikers in black leather and pink tutus, friends and strangers in tears and embraces, cheering crowds, flying banners. It's a celebration of diversity, and in 2009, when Jennifer Awrey walked it with her mom, Tina Herford, the event generated a whopping $9.5 million for breast cancer research and outreach.

Tina, who lives in Alaska and works for the United Way, was diagnosed with breast cancer in 1998 when Jennifer was a senior in high school. It was rough during treatment, but Tina's a do-what-needs-doing kind of woman, and Jennifer is her mother's daughter. Tina first suggested doing the SGK 3-Day for the Cure when Jen was fresh out of law school, but Jen was busy finding her stride in life. A few years later, she called her mom and said, "Let's do it."

They started training with the best of intentions. Jennifer walked her Los Angeles neighborhood; Tina did treadmill at home on the Kenai Peninsula. SGK coaches provided a walker's handbook, stretching workout, weekly guidance, and encouragement by e-mail—even a guide to selecting the right shoes—but life got busy, and Jennifer slacked off a bit. Plodding to the end of a Saturday practice hike, she felt like she'd whipped it good, until she realized she'd walked only 12 miles. Facing 20 miles a day three days in a row, she was a little nervous.

Bright and early on November 21, 2009, mother and daughter joined four thousand walkers and volunteers for the opening ceremony at Del Mar Fairgrounds.

"It was awesome to see my mom in the survivor's circle," Jen says.

"But the coolest part was all these people who'd come out to cheer us on. Thousands of people all along the way in crazy outfits and hats, waving signs, offering us candy and cookies and tequila shots."

Energizer had supplied tall pink Energizer Bunny ears for everyone. Upbeat music played. It was cold, but a wave of warm energy swept Jennifer and Tina along. They didn't talk about cancer; they talked about life, happily chatting, catching up. As the morning sun climbed higher, they took off their jackets and tied them around their waists, walking briskly. At the first of many pit stops, San Diego police officers working security danced with the ladies waiting in long lines at pink Porta-Pottys. Breast humor was everywhere.

Pins stitched like baseballs: SAVE SECOND BASE!

Scrawled on the back of a minivan: THESE BOOBS ARE MADE FOR WALKING!

On a sandwich board: STOP THE WAR IN MY RACK!

After lunch in La Jolla, the walkers pushed on through Torrey Pines to Pacific Beach, and finally arrived at the base camp in Mission Bay. Blues musicians warmed up on the lawn. Local youth groups had labored all day, setting up tents to create a temporary village. The extraordinary community came together, people of all ages, sizes, religions, races, and persuasions. This was one of those rare, precious moments when differences didn't matter. Everyone was there for a common purpose. Exhausted and limping with blisters, Jennifer and Tina toyed with the idea of checking into a hotel, but they decided to stick with the group.

"Mom and I were wiped out, but determined to see it through," Jen says. "We heard so many stories along the way. Mom met a lot of survivors who were two or three years out of chemo. When she said she'd made it more than ten years, they were so thrilled. I hadn't realized before what it means to someone going through it to see this woman *walking*, living her life, happy and healthy."

They iced their aching feet, crawled into sleeping bags, and crashed, not even vaguely aware of the breakfast crew up and working at three in the morning.

Day 2, rain threatened, but morning mist burned off to reveal another beautiful afternoon. Tromping a wide circle through Ocean Beach, Jen and Tina didn't talk much.

"We were just together, making it through, looking at the stunning scenery along the coast. A peaceful, bonding kind of thing."

Waiting in line for a shower that night, Jen met a woman who'd just finished chemo.

"My doctor advised against it," the woman said, "but I had to be here, even if I can only do two miles a day. I can't believe I finished two twenty-mile days with everyone else."

If she can do it, Jen figured, *so can I.* She spent some time in the party atmosphere of the supper tent, iced her feet, and hit the sack.

As the walkers made their way through Balboa Park on Day 3, bikers roared by, wearing helmets with nipples. Loudspeakers blared "I'm a Survivor." People danced. High school cheerleaders shook pink pom-poms. Families shouted *thank you,* holding up photos of loved ones they'd lost. Volunteers stood ready with cold water and warm hugs. With many walkers, including local CBS news anchor Barbara-Lee Edwards, blogging and tweeting along the way, the word was out, and crowds swelled. A San Diego Police Department chopper hovered over the finish line, cheering people in over the loudspeakers.

"The closing ceremony was incredibly powerful," says Jennifer. "We each had our triumph shirt. Mine was white; mom was in pink with the other survivors. I walked with these great people we'd met along the way, and as we came in, each of us was given a pink rose. There was this outpouring of gratitude. As exhausted as we all were, it meant so much."

The Susan G. Komen 3-Day for the Cure, from opening moment to closing ceremony, is a masterfully planned, professionally coordinated event that makes grown men cry. Even the coolest hipsters describe it as life changing. We live in a cynical world. Some roll their eyes at the idea of grown women in bunny ears, dogs in pink tuxedos, and bikers in nipple helmets. Some feel this sort of frivolity trivializes breast cancer. But it's an experience no one within shouting distance can ignore and no one in attendance will ever forget. The moment that always gets to me in the closing ceremony is the march of the survivors; as they enter the arena, all the walkers hold up one shoe. It's a simple thing, but it makes me weep. Here's someone who just *walked 60 miles,* saying to these survivors, "I did all I could, and I did it for you."

We can't overstate the importance of the millions of dollars generated for cancer research, but the impact of the SGK 3-Day for the Cure is in the lives it changes as well as the lives it saves. It speaks to the tandem goals of survival and survivorship: You fight for your life. Then you live your life, regardless of what others think of your particular mode of self-expression.

We'd like to think we've come a long way since Ike and Tina couldn't sit down at a Dallas lunch counter, but there are still private clubs in the United States that I, as a Jewish woman, would not be welcome to join. The diversity of participants at SGK events bears witness to what a brutally equalizing sledgehammer cancer is. Breast cancer has no religious or sexual preference, no race, no age, no political predilections. But in cancer *treatment,* those differences cost lives. At this writing, a woman diagnosed with breast cancer in predominantly African American Cook County, Illinois, is far more likely to die than her white counterpart in Peoria.

How long? asked Martin Luther King Jr., and we're determined to answer, *Not long.*

As we expand our global reach, cultural biases throw out as many roadblocks as scientific conundrums, but there are times—scientific collaborations, support functions, social gatherings—when we're able to sweep all that aside, if only for a moment, to illuminate our reason for being. It never happens as quickly or easily as we'd all love for it to happen, but every once in a while, crossing one bridge to build another, we hold hands and allow ourselves to speak the diplomatic language of light.

In October 2009, at the second Bosnia and Herzegovina Race for the Cure, more than 2,500 Bosnians, Muslims, Croats, Serbs, and Jews came together side by side with one goal. A regional conference was held by the Women's Health Empowerment Program, which cultivates leaders, creates support networks, and facilitates patient-physician communication throughout the former Soviet Union, eastern Europe, Israel, and the Palestinian territories. It's tremendously encouraging to see these meetings of disparate hearts and minds.

Thirty years ago, at Suzy's funeral service, the synagogue was jammed with people who had nothing in common but their love for Suzy. Rabbi Goff stood before the assembled crowd and said, "We gather here today as a community. Some of us are Jews and some of us are Christian, but at a time like this those kinds of distinctions are unimportant. Because Suzy loved people—all kinds of people—whether they were Jews or gentiles, rich or poor, black or white. Her commitment was to the goodness she tenaciously sought for in others, and inevitably found. There was nothing petty or parochial about her, and we who have gathered to celebrate her life, do so in keeping with the breath and the universality of her spirit."

That gathering of souls, that universality of spirit, has been a guiding vision for this organization.

Behind the scenes at the San Diego 3-Day for the Cure, an amazing team of diverse, committed volunteers works hard all year to create an experience that evokes deep feeling and a safe environment in which to express it. But the most profoundly moving moments are the ones we could never orchestrate. As Jennifer walked into the arena for the closing ceremony, she saw a woman at the side of the road, cheering on the walkers, calling out thanks.

"She was bald, really thin, clearly in chemo. It was obviously a struggle for her to be there. One of the walkers passing by had given her that pink rose, then somebody else gave her one, and another and another until she had sixty or seventy roses piled higher than her little arms could hold. They were spilling onto the ground around her feet as she stood there with tears streaming down her face."

In that moment, every mile, every step, every blister was worth it.

"We were all like . . . *yes*," Jennifer says. "This is why we're here."

We All Fall Down

Neiman Marcus Fortnight of 1973 had a British theme. The main floor was transformed into a grand manor hall with soaring banners, Celtic musicians, and mummers. When Suzy came to see it, she and I agreed that Robert Leitstein was perfect for me. In fact, we agreed that Robert Leitstein was perfect, *period,* with his electrifying good looks, timelessly upmarket style, and a seamless, witty brand of repartee that subtly but distinctly showcased how smart he was. Bob was on his way up the ladder at Neiman Marcus. And he was Jewish. I was starstruck the first time I met him and did everything but handsprings trying to get him to notice me. He finally invited me to a party he was giving, and I was further starstruck when I saw his lovely apartment: clean lines and cultured accents, the *haute* of everything, just like the man himself. I did my best audition material, he quickly zeroed in on me as prime mating material, and after a year or so, we were engaged. I knew my father wouldn't be thrilled about the difference in our ages, but if anything, that added to Bob's charm.

"He's a vice president," Suzy teased, "and you're his vice."

But in retrospect, I think I was more of a sociology experiment. There was a very Henry Higgins–Eliza Doolittle dynamic to our relationship. I'd come a long way and learned enough to recognize how much I could still learn. Now here was Bob, eager to be my Pygmalion. He was wise in the ways of style and had a brilliant vision of the exemplary wife he wanted me to be and the refined life he wanted us to live—right down to the *nth* ramekin and throw pillow. I had a lot of respect for Bob and welcomed his direction and constructive criticism. It was thrilling to envision myself through his eyes: a *moderne* Donna Reed who kept an immaculate, upscale home, raised beautiful, lockstep children, and maintained a thriving, upwardly mobile career.

Of course, that career couldn't be on the same track as my husband's. I'd have to leave Neiman Marcus.

Mr. Marcus was loath to lose me after all the time and energy the company had invested in me, but it wasn't even a question. These were the good old days; an assistant buyer didn't become the wife of a senior officer and stay with the company. I didn't necessarily accept this unwritten law of corporate nature, but I wasn't bullied into the decision. I was happy with it, and not just because I'd completely bought into Bob's Jewish *Wunderfrau* scenario. The truth is, I'd realized marketing was where I wanted to be. As much as I appreciated the art of couture, I never really had a burning passion for fashion like Suzy did.

"There's a lot more to life than retail," I told her. "It wasn't going to be a life of meaning for me."

Suzy readily agreed, probably thinking I was talking about the meaning I'd find as a wife and mother, because this was a moment when Suzy felt her own life had a lot of meaning. She and Stan had moved back to Peoria and were living in a cute little house not far from Mom and Daddy. After Scott came along, they'd adopted a baby girl, Stephanie (Steffie for short), which gave Suzy a sense of completeness about her family. She loved her husband, loved their comfortable existence in this homespun, salt-of-the-earth community. Suzy's dream was for the two of them to do well enough to have a little vacation condo in Florida someday, but other than that, she now had everything she'd ever really wanted.

She was a goddess when it came to throwing birthday parties—for her children, for children of her friends, for Boppie—it didn't matter how many candles were on the cake, the occasion was done up right with lavish decorations, innovative party themes, hats, favors, games, and music. Suzy was born on Halloween, so naturally, there were extravagant costumes and festivities every year.

She had a terrific circle of friends and was a bit of a local celebrity, in the paper on a regular basis, modeling for department stores and boutiques. People recognized her from the photo spreads and from Junior League and all her other charities and activities. She thoroughly enjoyed being a big fish in the little pond. Suzy also did a lot of things no one ever knew about. Sometimes in her volunteer work at St. Jude Children's Hospital, she'd become acquainted with a teenager who needed a shoulder or a mother who needed a day out. She never walked by someone in pain or need, but she never felt the need to broadcast that.

Having found this particularly sweet spot in her own life, Suzy was eager to see me settle down. Some of my romantic assignations during college and my first few years in Dallas had caused Suzy a lot of angst. Watching me edge into my late twenties, well past the point where a nice Jewish girl should be married, she was delighted to see me with this fabulous man who was going to turn me into a classically trained wife.

Mom was not quite as enthusiastic.

She didn't like the way Bob had taken charge of planning the wedding, which was to be a small but precisely tailored event at the Fairmont Hotel. He wouldn't let Mom or Suzy or me touch anything related to staging and particulars. He chose our china and silver patterns, designed the bouquets, orchestrated the wedding cakes and flower arrangements, presided over the linens, table settings, music, menu, seating chart—every swizzle stick and cocktail napkin.

When I took my parents out to dinner at a Chinese restaurant to "discuss" the arrangements from which they'd been pretty much excluded, my father folded his arms and made a blunt assessment: "There's something funny about the whole thing."

"I think he'd like it better if the bride and her family weren't there," Mom said. She was worried that I wasn't speaking up—which was very unlike me.

"Mommy," I said, "the truth is, Bob has better taste than I do. I could never come up with anything as chic and elegant as all this. Why should I argue about it?"

He'd selected a sophisticated Ungaro gown for me and had it sent to Neiman Marcus, where he stood frowning while a seamstress finessed the stiff, matronly collar. He arranged a practice run for my hair and makeup, and I hardly recognized myself. There was something unsettling about this total stranger in the mirror, but I must say, she looked *fabulous*. I'd never felt truly glamorous before, and it felt good. Daddy was just disgruntled about the age thing, I decided, and Mommy would be happy when she saw how gorgeous everything turned out.

The night before the wedding, Bob and I had a cocktail party at the beautifully done apartment that was to be our home. Waiting for guests to arrive, I was kidding around instead of focusing on where the hors d'oeuvres were supposed to be positioned. Bob took off his shoe and threw it. And not playfully.

"You think this is a joke?" he said sharply.

"No . . . I was . . . I'm sorry."

I stood there, stung and astonished as it dawned on me: I was going to be apologizing for the rest of my life. The only thing out of place in this immaculately appointed apartment was me. Perfection. Nice place to visit, as the saying goes, but you wouldn't want to live there. The moment Suzy arrived for the party, I dragged her into the bathroom and shut the door.

"Suz, you have to help me. I can't do this. This is a terrible mistake."

"What? What's wrong?"

"All I could see was—I was so *wowed* by him, but now—I don't know. I'm not sure we even know each other. He thinks he's getting this malleable, chubby Jewish girl—ten years younger, never got the memo. Oh, sure, I'm a quick study, so he can shape me however he wants, and what he wants is fat and happy and home while he's out traveling the world, and I'll be the mother of three children and never open my mouth."

"Nanny . . ." Suzy looked at me, nonplussed. "You are not chubby."

I sat on the edge of the tub and moaned into my hands.

"And *malleable*—are you kidding?" She sat next to me and put her arm around my shoulders. "Nan, what's this about?"

The only concrete thing I could come up with was the shoe, so I told her about that.

"Oh, dear." Suzy bit her lip, then shook her head. "He's nervous. You're nervous. Everyone's nervous. It'll be fine. You look beautiful, Nan, and Bob . . . he's *perfect*."

"He is. I know. And I want to do the right thing, but Suzy, I'll never make him happy."

I didn't know how to make sense of it. How could I not want to be with him? Made by him, I was more beautiful than I'd ever been. When he told me where to stand and how to act, I could be confident I'd never put a foot in the wrong place. There was no valid argument for backing out and countless valid arguments against it. I'd be humiliating our parents, embarrassing myself, wasting all that food, flowers, candelabras, and money—for what? To escape the certain hell of an affluent life with every girl's dream husband?

It was ridiculous even to consider such a thing at this stage in the game.

But a desperate feeling swept over me, and it was still with me the next day as I walked down the aisle toward this flawless man with whom I was not in love.

I'd made a lot of connections in and beyond Dallas through my involvement in a steady pace of arts, charity, and political endeavors. As president of the USA Film Festival, I'd brought some big names and illuminating cinema to Dallas and worked with other movers and shakers in the American Cancer Society to produce the annual Cattle Baron's Ball. I enrolled as a nontraditional student and started taking courses in film and broadcasting at Southern Methodist University, and this all came together in a job as a talk show host at a local radio station. By the time I was pregnant with Eric, I'd been given the title "Talk Editor" at WRR, a Dallas radio station that was owned by the city but which ran on ad revenue, not as nonprofit public radio.

Understandably, this caused some friction with other stations in the city, which for years called for WRR to be privatized in the interest of fair play. WRR (speaking of strange bedfellows) was a sometimes-troubled marriage of civic and commercial interests, but I loved the added challenge of that delicate balance. Our bottom line couldn't be about money, but we didn't have the luxury of preaching to the choir while someone else paid the light bill. We weren't in a position to adopt one political view or another or to bend facts in the service of a biased agenda, but we felt a responsibility to raise difficult questions and hold people accountable for the answers.

My on-air partner was the brilliant and hilarious Guy Gibson, WRR's managing editor. He was huge and jolly, but didn't spare the conversational lash, and people loved him. "Gibson and Goodman" brought together topical subjects, provocative discussions, lively audience participation, and an amazing lineup of guests ranging from artists and actors to politicians, doctors, and scientists. Every hour of the talk show required at least two hours of homework. I wasn't about to settle for the small amount of knowledge that makes a person dangerous. I made sure Guy and I were armed with the best available information, whether we were talking to the cast of a Broadway touring show or the grand master of the KKK. This was a real schooling in "consider the source" for me, a training ground where I first understood the toxic quality of misinformation and the motives of those who spread it. I had a high degree of confidence in science, but I started to understand what Mark Twain meant when he said, "There are three kinds of lies: lies, damn lies, and statistics."

Our conversation with renowned economist Eliot Janeway was particularly eye-opening. I came away from it understanding that, almost always, the truth could be found beyond the numbers in the practical application of science to life.

It was my responsibility to get people on the horn and convince them to be on our show, despite the fact that we had no budget to offer them any kind of fee or honorarium. It was a fascinating, creative learning experience. I talked to people I never would have talked to, read books I never would have read. I dashed through the airport with my portable tape recorder dangling from a strap around my shoulder, trying to catch up with my quarries as they changed planes or ran for a flight. I was utterly fearless, and that in itself was a joy. Bob arranged his lunch hour so he could critique my performance every day, and as much as that grated on me, I'd have to admit his comments were incisive and astute. I improved by leaps and bounds.

One of the most fascinating guests we brought in was Elisabeth Kübler-Ross, who came to talk about her groundbreaking views on death and dying. In her book *On Death and Dying,* published in 1969, Kübler-Ross introduced "the five stages of grief": denial, anger, bargaining, depression, and acceptance. In 1975, when I was at WRR, she was touring to promote her third book, *Death: The Final Stage of Growth,* a sort of compendium of voices: people facing death, families, survivors, physicians, and others. It furthered her study of the dynamics of death and dying, but it also reflected on how profoundly the way people die is affected by the way they live.

One thing that riveted me as I read her book was the description of the common near-death experience reported by so many people. I'd experienced it too, when I was a very little girl. After I had my appendix out, peritonitis had set in, fever and infection raged, and my intestines shut down. Mother and Daddy were terrified, but I remember feeling almost blissful, ascending through the rushing tunnel, emerging into golden fog and a feeling of immense peace.

"Before I read your book," I told Elisabeth, "I always thought it was a dream."

"Maybe it was," she shrugged. "Does it matter? Does it change what you gained from the experience?"

"Well, I don't know that I gained anything. It was just . . . interesting."

She nodded. "Or maybe you gained something and don't know it yet."

Every day that we were on the air, "Gibson and Goodman" was a sprinting, fourteen-hour-a-day job. My only complaint was that it didn't last nearly long enough. Audiences embraced the news-talk format on WRR, but advertisers were slow to latch on. Guy was fired in the spring of 1975. Station management tried to spin it as a budget cut, but Guy was quoted in *Texas Monthly* as saying his removal was "systematically engineered by the city manager's office" because our show was too controversial. A number of station employees walked out in solidarity, and for those of us who chose to stay—or stayed because we had no choice—the job wasn't much fun anymore.

For me, the situation was cut and dried. No one else was going to hire me. I was five months' pregnant.

Suzy was overjoyed. All her dreams of our side-by-side happy motherhood and doting grandmotherhood seemed to be coming together. She wanted my marriage to be as comfortable and enduring as hers and hoped the baby would smooth over or at least distract Bob and me from how ridiculously mismatched we were. I was thrilled about becoming a mother. I wanted to have a child . . . but not with Bob.

There's no point going into the particulars of a bad marriage thirty-odd years after it came apart. We were just catastrophically wrong for each other. I was deeply respectful of his talents, and I'd like to think he was of mine, but we were ill suited on every level, and because we were two hard-drivers unwilling to concede defeat, we trenched in and stuck it out a lot longer than we should have. I tried to tell myself it would all be different if we had a baby, and I tried. I did try. But the writing was on the wall.

"I don't know what to do, Suz." Our daily phone conversations began to center on this familiar refrain. "I don't think I can stay in this marriage."

"You know Stan and I are here for you. You can come home anytime you need to."

I did know that, but the thought of crawling back to Peoria, alone, unemployed, and pregnant—I couldn't face the idea of my father seeing me that way. One way or another, I was determined to tough it out in Dallas. My main concern now was making a life for this baby.

Eric was born in October 1975.

"Sunshine breaks through." Suzy pressed her lips to the top of his head, and he studied her with wide, interested eyes. "He's perfect, Nan."

She was gaga over him. Mom and Dad rushed over from their vacation home in Florida. Couldn't wait to lay their hands on him. My husband tried to dissuade Mom from her plan to stay a few weeks.

"It's really not necessary," Bob said. "I'm bringing in a private nurse."

That didn't go far with Mommy.

"A nurse," she said flatly. "Why? Are you ill?"

It was a tense couple of months. In fact, it was a tense couple of years. The radio station switched to a music format, so I couldn't go back after Eric was born. I wanted to work part-time so I could be with him, so I took a series of project-oriented jobs with various PR and advertising firms. Bob expected me to uphold my busy schedule of charity and social events. He expected the house to be sanitized, the baby food steamed and pureed by hand, and educational activities done by the book. He expected dinner every night on a formally set table with Baccarat crystal, fresh flowers, crisply ironed napkins, and polished silver. He expected the baby to be freshly powdered and dressed like the crown prince of Freedonia.

Divorce was less common back then than it is now; I knew I'd be stigmatizing my son and setting him up for struggle. But I'd grown up in such a happy home, I was equally devastated by the thought of burdening his childhood with the cold war his father and I lived with.

I took Eric to visit Mom and Dad in Florida as often as I could get away, and sometimes we went to Suzy's and spent long weekends in Peoria, sitting in the kiddy area at the municipal pool, raking autumn leaves, and throwing those over-the-top birthday parties. Between visits, Suzy and I talked on the phone for hours every day. She was genuinely anguished by the way things had turned out for me, and looking back, I cringe at the amount of time we spent beating that dead horse. If we'd known how loudly the clock was ticking, we surely would have spent that time talking about something else.

Suzy's and my "dense breast" issues continued throughout our twenties, and now in her early thirties, Suzy had undergone a number of needle aspirations for cysts. On a Tuesday afternoon in the fall of 1977, she called me as she did every day, but something in her voice was off-key, forcibly unafraid.

"This lump is different," she said. "It's hard. He did the needle biopsy. It wasn't a cyst. I guess they have to take it out so they can say for sure."

"Oh, my God. Suzy, let me go with you."

"No, no, no. That's not necessary, Nan. Don't be silly. I'll call you when I get the results. You know it's going to be nothing."

"Right," I said. "So I'll be there to celebrate with you when it comes back negative."

I made arrangements for Eric, called the airline for a ticket, told Bob I was going, called work and left a message, all the while feeling like my heart had shifted into an uncomfortable thrumming overdrive. Flying out of Dallas, I was acutely aware of the vast emptiness between me and the earth.

Daddy was waiting for me out on the tarmac in Peoria, his expression fixed and ashen. He didn't say a word when I came to him.

He didn't have to.

Suzy has cancer.

This was now the fulcrum on which everything balanced. When we sat down to dinner, we didn't know how to pray or pick up our spoons. How could we eat if *Suzy has cancer*? How could anyone lie down to sleep? Do you put sugar in your morning coffee when *Suzy has cancer*? Should I tie Steffie's little shoe and send Scott outside to play or tell them to sit quietly in a chair and wait for the sky to fall? We sat around her kitchen table like soldiers in a foxhole.

I could tell Suzy was terrified, because historically, in the everyday crises of life—a flat tire, a blown fuse, or a fender bender—she always required a lot of hand-holding. Now all she wanted to do was comfort me and Mom and stuff Stan and Daddy full of home cooking. She had the desperate bravado of someone rising to the occasion. Grace under pressure was something she'd always admired, and she was digging deep for it now.

"It'll be all right. You'll see," she said. "It's not like I'm sick or anything. I feel fine. The most important thing is to get through it quickly and quietly so it doesn't upset the kids."

"Yes. Of course. Right," I agreed too much. "We're not going to panic. Once we have all the information, we'll move to the problem-solving stage."

"I have all the information I need, Nan. All I want to know is what time to show up for the surgery so I can get it over with and never think about it again. The surgeon says there's no need for me to have a mastectomy like . . . like some people used to have."

"Suzy, a mastectomy wouldn't be like Aunt Rose's."

"I can't even think about that," she said. "Jesus. If anything like that happened to me, I'd just—I don't know. I'd want you to find a way to kill me. I'd rather be dead."

"*Don't say that.*" I bit my lip, tried to soften my tone. "Suz, it's not like that anymore."

"Not at all. It's just a small incision, then he puts in an implant, and you're cured."

"Cured?" I echoed. "He used the word *cured*? He didn't say *remission*?" My mind circled back through all the luncheon speakers I'd endured. Had any of them ever said *cured* in the same sentence with *cancer*? "Is he suggesting chemotherapy or radiation?"

"No, no, no." Suzy waved that off. "Dr. Moffet said something about radiation, but the surgeon says it can leave scars, and I don't want anything like that."

"Suzy, M. D. Anderson is one of the best cancer centers in the world. I've worked on fundraisers for them, had physicians and researchers on my show. I'm sure one of them could help us get in. Just to get a second opinion before the surgery."

Suzy shook her head, adamant. "Nobody knows me like Dr. Moffet does. He's been taking care of me since I was born. Why would I want some stranger?"

"Because the stranger is an *oncologist*. A cancer specialist. Suzy, you have to get a second opinion. Mommy? Tell her."

Mom started to say something, but Suzy held up her hand.

"Please. I'm not you, Nan. I need to get through this my own way. I love this surgeon. And I trust him. He and Dr. Moffet say I'll be fine, and I will be."

The day of Suzy's surgery, I met the surgeon and thought, *What's not to love?* He was striking and suave, extremely good-looking. Most attractive was the way he told us all exactly what we dearly needed to hear. Confident as a big brass bell, he strode into her hospital room and said, "I got it all. She's cured."

He didn't ask if we had questions, and when I tried to volunteer one, he made it clear that he was not there to discuss things with us—only to inform us. He'd bestowed the blessing of his great skills and was handing our girl back to us, sewn up with a bow. Our gratitude was the appropriate response; our questions would be an insult to his expertise, and the answers would be beyond the scope of our intelligence anyway. He'd done a subcutaneous mastectomy, removing tissue through a deep incision and leaving the outside of the breast intact for the most part. Ten days later, he did an implant. It wasn't beautiful work, but it made her feel whole again. Within a few weeks, Suzy seemed fine, a relatively small scar the only evidence of her narrow escape.

She was ecstatic and ready to blaze back into her life, but even after I went home to Dallas, I kept nudging her to get a second opinion. I tried to enlist Mom's help, but I think she was as grateful and as happy as Suzy was to embrace the prognosis the surgeon had declared so confidently as fact. And besides that, Mom was always better than me at an aspect of patient advocacy that eludes a lot of people: respect for the patient's autonomy. Ultimately, these were Suzy's decisions to make. This was her body, her life. As far as she was concerned, she'd been cured of her cancer and didn't want to spend any more of our daily phone conversations hashing it over.

"You have no idea how terrified I was," she said. "I just want to put it behind me."

"I know, Suz, but the thing is . . . I called a friend at M. D. Anderson and at the library this morning, I spent hours reading all about medullary carcinoma. What that means is . . ."

"Nancy. Please."

"Sometimes a surgeon or a physician who's not a cancer specialist—he sees the border of the tumor and thinks it's okay, but this book said a lot of oncologists say it should still be treated as if it's invasive."

She winced at the sound of the word.

"Just stop, all right? I don't want to hear about *carcinoma* and *tumors* right before I sit down to dinner. And I think the surgeon probably picked up a little more in medical school than you gathered in one morning at the library."

"Look . . ." I tried for a conciliatory tone. "Just come down for a visit. We'll run down to Houston for the afternoon, get the second opinion, then hit the Galleria. Shop till we drop."

"Nan, let it go," said Suzy. "You're just fixating on this so you don't have to deal with your own problems."

I suppose that may have been true. Suzy did appear to be fine. She was rosy and busy again, right as rain with the exception of a light, rasping cough that seemed to linger. It was a common postoperative complaint, she was told; a person's throat is always a little irritated by the intubation. Meanwhile, my life was on the edge of unbearable. I was back on the Baccarat-crystal-and-cut-flowers routine, trying to make up for lost time with Eric, working one of those "part-time" PR jobs that actually require ten hours a day, and hunting for work in which I could invest my heart and soul. Of course, no matter how hard I worked, it was never up to that standard of perfection, and I was getting tired of hearing what a lazy pig I was.

"You have a beautiful baby boy. That's all that matters," Suzy kept saying during a hundred marathon phone calls we spent agonizing over it.

Inevitably, one evening Bob came home to find nothing on the table but a white linen cloth. I was in the kitchen, hastily hacking a romaine salad into a Steuben bowl, the baby howling on my hip. My husband shook his head dolefully and said, "What have you been doing all day?"

This was not the right thing to say. All that whiteness, that smug church-bell rightness—it was too much. I picked up the salad and dumped it on his feet.

"*That's* what I've been doing. Now get the hell out."

He looked down at his expensive shoes, looked up at me, laughed uncertainly.

"I'm not kidding," I said. "Get some shirts and go. I'm changing the locks tonight—as soon as I can get someone over here."

He didn't believe I was serious until the locksmith arrived.

It was a powerful moment, but not a particularly liberating one. Now I was alone with this toddler to raise. But he didn't require Baccarat crystal and cut flowers—just a free exchange of unconditional love. Eric and I immediately settled into a hardworking but happy life together. All the time and energy I'd been investing in ironing napkins and tap-dancing on eggshells I now devoted to things that actually mattered: my family, interesting work, and worthy causes. I kept my ear to the ground for any new information about breast cancer, but no one said much about it. After a while, I relaxed into the assurances that Suzy was fine.

Elisabeth Kübler-Ross: "When you learn your lessons, the pain goes away."

It had been a hard year, but I wasn't hurting anymore.

Mystery and Method

SINCE SHE lost her best friend to cancer at age fifteen, Dr. Mary-Claire King has been asking the same questions asked by survivors, cosurvivors, caregivers, and scientists—any and all of us who've stared at the ceiling, needing to know one thing:

Why?

A brilliant mathematician, Mary-Claire graduated from Carleton College at nineteen and went on to earn her Ph.D. in genetics and epidemiology from the University of California at Berkeley. Her college years were a tumultuous mix of science and activism; she immersed herself in the origins of people and politics, wanting to know everything about who human beings are from the cultural level to the molecular. She shook things up when she demonstrated that the genetic profiles of humans and chimpanzees are 99 percent identical. She helped fight human rights abuses in South America, working with Las Abuelas—"the grandmothers"—using mitochondrial DNA to identify and return children who'd been abducted from mothers "disappeared" by the military during Argentina's Dirty War. But she spent most of her career curiously digging for genetic connections to the predisposition for breast cancer.

In the 1960s, scientific understanding of cancer was all about *what*. Researchers knew what cancer cells looked like, what they were capable of, what effect the disease would have on its host.

"But it was very frustrating," says Mary-Claire, "because we didn't have any understanding or sense of *why* these processes were occurring. Exactly what was happening, why it was it happening, when was it happening, how was it happening, all the questions you ask of mystery."

In President Nixon's State of the Union address in 1971, he famously declared war on cancer. Cynics viewed it as PR sleight of hand, particularly in light of subsequent events, but Nixon asked for an appropriation of $100 million to back it up and signed the National Cancer Act of 1971 into law, saying he hoped it would be viewed as "the most significant action taken during my administration." Fort Detrick, a biological warfare facility in Maryland, was converted to a cancer research center. The National Cancer Institute was given budgetary authority within the National Institutes of Health.

Another harmonic convergence of message, money, and moment.

Significant funding materialized just as the entirely new scientific field of molecular biology was finding its feet. Molecular genetics and genomics opened doors and windows, and light poured in, illuminating the most infinitesimal dark corners of the body human. The science translated to patient care in the form of clinical trials. Foundations were laid for future breakthroughs. Now scientists were able to remove tissue from the body and manipulate individual cells, evaluate individual genes, scrutinize every protein and base pair.

What became *what if.*

For hundreds of years, physicians and researchers had speculated that some cancers were inherited, but if Mary-Claire King had advanced the idea that all cancer is genetic back in the 1970s, she would have been laughed at. The influx of cancer research funding in the early 1970s swung the gate wide for molecular genetics to evolve into a working field; now molecular genetics of the 1980s would ignite an exciting new era in cancer research with the realization that, while not all cancer is inherited, all cancer *is* genetic.

If that seems counterintuitive, think about it this way: Your grandmother's opal ring is inherited, but it's not genetic. The mutation that turned Bruce Banner into the Incredible Hulk was genetic, but not inherited.

Only about 10 percent of cancers are passed from parent to child, but all cancers arise from some change in the DNA. The gene is mutated, and the cell malfunctions. Normally, cells grow, do their thing, and die off at a nice, steady pace. Imprinted on that tiny universe-unto-itself is a functional wisdom; each cell knows exactly what it is and what it's supposed to be doing. Cancer happens when that wisdom is short-circuited by genetic aberration. Cell growth takes off like a runaway train, forming tumors, invading tissues, hijacking resources the body needs to survive. That elegant wisdom every healthy cell is born with becomes a kamikaze intention to maximize the damage on its way to self-destruction.

Dr. Mary-Claire King was already a bit of a rock star in the exclusive, sterile universe of molecular biology, and she'd been pondering the inherited predisposition for breast cancer for a long time. Early in her career, she'd begun assiduously collecting tissue samples from hundreds of women in about two dozen families for whom breast cancer had been a scourge from one generation to the next, afflicting more than a third of the mothers, daughters, and granddaughters. Almost twenty years later, she had methodically narrowed her search to 50 million base pairs on chromosome 17.

And there it was: a clear path to one of the most important discoveries in the history of breast cancer research. Dr. King had proven the existence of a breast cancer gene, and she knew where to find it. She announced the breathtaking discovery in the fall of 1990. The entire scientific community was thrilled. This was beyond a needle in a haystack; this was a needle in a wheat field.

The dog race was on. Every research team in the field began tearing through chromosome 17 in an effort to isolate the gene. It would be a PR coup that would translate to additional funding and major bragging rights. Dr. King's team in Berkeley ramped up their pace, putting in endless hours, keeping their work a closely guarded secret. Their hearts sank when a team from the University of Utah called a press conference in 1994 to announce they'd successfully identified and cloned the mutated gene—called BRCA1, for "breast cancer susceptibility gene 1"—and a team from Surrey, England, followed suit within weeks.

People expected Mary-Claire to be bitter, but she told a reporter, "I keep asking myself, am I suddenly going to feel terrible about this? But I don't."

She was elated. It was the answer she'd always craved, not the accolades.

BRCA1 and a second mutated breast cancer susceptibility gene—BRCA2—are carried by one out of every two hundred women, and 80 to 90 percent of them will develop breast cancer. Between 40 and 50 percent of the women who carry the BRCA2 mutation will develop ovarian cancer as well. The goal now is to use this knowledge to develop methods of cell-specific detection. Mutations happen, to coin a phrase. It's not likely that gene mutations can be entirely avoided, but it is likely that we can make invasive cancer a thing of the past by circumventing its progress before it has a chance to even think about becoming a tumor. And it's entirely possible that this lifesaving treatment will be no more invasive than a needle biopsy. The genetic testing kit requires only a swish and spit from the subject.

I tested positive for the mutation, so I'm guessing Suzy would have too, if she'd lived to be tested. She died just as Dr. King was beginning to understand this spiraling ribbon that binds my sister and me at the wrist. It was part of our shared destiny, in us before we knew who we were, and we knew who we were from the day we were born. Suzy and I came from good people. The mutated BRCA1 and BRCA2 are handed down by both men and women, and they are particularly prominent among Ashkenazi Jews—Jews of German and northeastern European descent.

They call it a founder effect.

"It's been very interesting to understand at the molecular level what the nature of carcinogenesis is. For example in lung cancer, we now have a really clear understanding of why smoking causes lung cancer," says Mary-Claire. "Many cancers, though—breast, ovary, much of colon—develop despite their victims' having done everything right. Breast cancer, for example, is very much the consequence of the normal life cycle of healthy modern women. Risk factors for breast cancer are related to hormones. They are also minimally related to the use of hormone replacement therapy. But most of the risk of breast cancer has to do simply with our being the most successful mammals there have ever been.

"We are very good at reproducing at young ages and continuing to reproduce at what used to be old age, the forties. This means that the ductile cells of the breast—the cells that line the ducts that are responsible for lactation—have the richest possible environment in which to live. They also have that environment if they've gone mutant. So breast cancer in particular is a consequence of a very healthy way of life."

SGK began funding Mary-Claire King's research in the early 1990s. Including a recent grant that enables her team to continue the search for unidentified genes in high-risk families, we've provided almost $1 million for her important, ongoing work. In 1999, SGK presented her with the Komen Brinker Award for Scientific Distinction to recognize her stunning achievements and to honor a lifetime devoted to the science of saving lives.

I thanked her. She thanked me. We hugged. *Oh*, did we hug.

"I'm so proud of you," I told her. "It's been thrilling to watch. Some of the most important research we've ever funded—or ever will."

For me, the most difficult aspect of getting my head around cancer research (second only to the challenge of spelling things correctly) is the snail's pace it seems to take. Mary-Claire is able to take that in stride.

"It's easily twenty years between a first, very relevant discovery and an end product that reaches a patient at a bedside," she says. "It's remarkable to me—and enormously heartening—that this society understands that. That this society has been willing to put enormous amounts of resources into the work of a very large number of people with the expectation that collectively we will come up with answers."

~ 7 ~

Wake Up, Little Suzy

I didn't let much grass grow under my feet. Within a month of changing the locks, I went to work as an account executive at a terrific advertising agency in Dallas and started dating a great big swashbuckling rancher. Other than the cowboy boots and mud-spattered Mercedes and private jet, he was a throwback to that born-to-be-wild boyfriend I'd loved in college.

Suzy didn't like it one bit.

"Nan," she sighed. "It's hard enough to be a good mother without all these distractions."

"I hardly call life a distraction. Someday when you're old, you'll be sorry you never had any fun."

"I have fun. You were at Steffie's birthday party. What's more fun than sixteen four-year-olds?"

"You really want me to answer that?"

"No, I want you to meet a nice Jewish man who wears regular shoes and hasn't been divorced twelve times."

It was a joy to kibitz over sisterly things instead of the dark cloud. To ask each other, "What are you making for dinner?" or "Did you see *All in the Family* last night?" We laughed about the clothes people were wearing to Studio 54 and chattered over plans to visit Mom and Dad in Florida that summer. Those months were like an oasis. A luxury. I see that now. Once again, the heartbreak was that it didn't last.

Six months after her original diagnosis, Suzy called me, beyond distraught.

"Nan, there's a hard lump under my arm."

"Oh, God. Oh, Suzy. . . ."

I covered my mouth with my hand. Denial. Anger. Bargaining. Depression. I felt them all hit me at once. Everything except acceptance.

"You can fight this, Suz. We will fight this together."

"Nanny, I'm scared."

"I know. Me too."

I brought up the idea of M. D. Anderson again, but Suzy wanted to go somewhere familiar. When Mommy's uncle was dying, she'd taken him to the Mayo Clinic in Rochester, Minnesota, and Suzy had gone there to visit him and to support Mom. So Suzy went to Mayo.

She and Stan had chosen not to tell their children about any of this, and she was adamant about keeping it from them as long as possible. For me, not telling Eric was a simple choice; he was a preschooler, far too young to understand, and didn't see Suzy on a daily basis. It was a more difficult call for Suzy and Stan: Scott was a smart, sensitive boy already in elementary school, and Steffie was this tender, tiny girl still at that age where Mommy is everything—love, warmth, water, light, the house you live in, the center of the universe. Suzy loved them both with the ferocity and vigilance of a mama tiger, and what was best for them was the touchstone by which she made every decision over the next two years.

The first step would be to open her eyes, and she was ready to do that now. She was ready to know everything she didn't want to know. At the Mayo Clinic, she saw an oncologist and began a battery of tests. Scans showed the cancer metastasizing to lymph nodes under her arm. There was also a tumor in her right lung. Other "suspicious shadows" haunted the images elsewhere. The oncologist who assessed her recommended thirty days of radiation.

"Then what?" I asked when Suzy called to update me.

"Then we watch it for a while," she said.

I had to physically bite my tongue. We all felt like we'd just stepped out of a storm cellar into a tornado; *watching* wasn't a course of action that really resonated for me. Suzy considered it, talked it over with Stan, and decided to do the radiation, but at the end of the thirty days, scans showed the cancer advancing unabated, raging through her lymphatic system, lungs, and other organs. Watching wasn't even an option.

"The next step is an oophorectomy," she was told. "Sometimes there's remission or at least some shrinkage in the tumors after removal of the ovaries."

Of course, we now have a better understanding of the connection between estrogen receptors and certain types of breast cancer, particularly the type of breast cancer that strikes younger women—thanks in part to research funded in Suzy's name. Scientists had been speculating since the early 1900s, but in 1978, finding the estrogen–breast cancer connection was still a bit of a fishing expedition.

"What happens if that doesn't work?" Suzy asked.

The oncologist shook his head. Suzy went ahead with the surgery, hoping for the best, but we didn't see any immediate improvement.

Less than thrilled with the reconstruction she'd had after the subcutaneous mastectomy, Suzy had previously consulted a plastic surgeon in Peoria. She liked and trusted him, and when she asked his opinion, he recommended M. D. Anderson in Houston.

"I guess she needed to hear it from someone other than her little sister," Mom told me. "She's decided to go there."

However she got there, I didn't care. Weak-kneed with relief, I got on the phone to my Houston contacts.

Waiting to hear her name called in one of the many waiting rooms where we'd spend much of our remaining time together, Suzy elbowed me and said, "Fancy meeting you here."

In the moment, it felt good to laugh a little, and in retrospect, I cherish the way Suzy and I stayed ourselves, together, through all that was to come. We laughed, talked about our kids, made healthy observations about handsome young doctors, and never stinted on saying "I love you." All the good moments stand out with intense sweetness, because running through every waking hour was the deep undercurrent of fear and sadness. She felt betrayed, I think, by the handsome surgeon, by God, by her own body, and by her woman's intuition. The injustice of it was flatly infuriating to me.

"What kind of sense does it make?" I seethed. "Why should this happen to someone who does nothing but good for other people?"

"You're right," said Suzy. "I should be rich. Living on the French Riviera."

"Purely from a personnel management point of view, wouldn't it make more sense if this sort of thing would happen to an ax murderer?"

"God really should manage these things better."

"I'd be happy to provide Him with a list."

Suzy laughed and leaned her head on my shoulder. As an hour or more dragged by, we both nodded and drifted. For a moment we were on a train bound for Munich.

"Nan."

"Hmmm?"

"I was thinking about Betty Ford," she said. "She took the chemo. If she can do it, maybe I can too. And if the First Lady of the United States can stand up in front of the whole world and admit she has breast cancer and she intends to fight it, . . ."

A nurse opened the door and called, "Susan Komen?"

I squeezed her hand. "You can do it, Suz. Mrs. Ford did it. You can do it."

In a dangerous, high-speed polo match, the all-consuming objective is to hit the ball into the goal. In the process, the grass is torn up, palms are blistered, and noses bloodied. It would be an unusual match if no one was hurt to some degree, but there's an acceptance of that before the game begins. The players know there will be collateral damage, but they ride out anyway, in pursuit of that all-consuming objective. Not because it's easy, but because it's hard.

Perhaps that's too cavalier a way to describe the people who make their lives and livings in the cancer treatment industry, but I've observed that same brand of undeterred passion in one cancer ward after another. The oncologists, nurses, researchers—even many of the housekeeping and clerical staff—are focused on the goal. They know that sooner or later they'll be hurt, because they can't insulate themselves from caring, but they show up every day and care anyway.

Up to this point, Suzy was basically in the care of one physician at a time. He told her what to do, and she did it. That's the way it worked back then. People were trained to follow "doctor's orders," and a lot of physicians were autocratic—and undeniably sexist—in the way they doled out those orders. At M. D. Anderson, there was a completely different modus operandi. Doris Bechtold, the wonderful patient care coordinator, met us at the door the very first day. A team of people was assembled to respond to Suzy's individual situation. Each team member brought his or her particular strength and expertise, but Suzy was indisputably in charge as they rode out in tight formation.

Her oncologist, Dr. George Blumenschein, was a Cornell man who'd done his postgraduate work at Bellevue Hospital in New York; the National Cancer Institute in Bethesda, Maryland; and Duke University Hospital in North Carolina. His credentials were varied and impressive, his work was well known and respected, and his patients adored him for his gentle good humor. The entire staff at M. D. Anderson was (and is) so wonderful, it's impossible to list all their names and praise each of them adequately, but I remember being awed by Dr. Blumenschein's breadth of knowledge and so very grateful for the way he empowered Suzy with hard information and encouraged her with realistic hope. He had enough respect for her strength and intelligence to pull no punches.

"You're Stage IV," he said. "The most critical scenario possible. I'd put your chances of long-term survival at about 25 percent. But there are aggressive measures available to you here, if that's the way you want to go."

Suzy said, "I want to fight it."

"Okay," said Blumenschein. "As long as you won't give up, I won't give up."

"Okay." She nodded.

"Let's give it all we've got."

He recommended removing the lesion from her lung and offered her a place in a clinical trial—an experimental program researching a state-of-the-art treatment protocol. Suzy started receiving a chemotherapy cocktail of powerful drugs, including steroids intended to beef her up enough to withstand the onslaught of good old doxorubicin—"the red devil"—and other chemicals.

I suppose you could apply the polo dynamic to chemotherapy on a cellular level; you go into it knowing there will be collateral damage, but that all-consuming objective is worth risking everything. These days, far more options and better-targeted treatments are evolving, but in 1978, there were less than a dozen drugs commonly used against breast cancer, and it was very much a shotgun approach. Chemo was designed to attack fast-growing cells, and there was nothing "smart bomb" about it. The toxins didn't differentiate between the fast-growing cell in a malignant tumor or the fast-growing cell in a hair follicle, the endothelial tissue lining the stomach and mouth, or any other part of the body that specializes in constant growth and regeneration.

Within weeks, Suzy was bald and fatigued. Her mouth and throat were pocked with sores. There was a translucent, almost angelic cast to her complexion.

"My skin actually looks beautiful," she said. "Long way to go for a facial, though."

Over the many months she was treated at M. D. Anderson, we all tried hard to be with her as much as possible. Suzy's wonderful friends stepped in at home in Peoria so Stan could go with her sometimes, but Suzy was more concerned for her children than she was for herself, and she knew they needed their father when she was gone. Daddy had a terrible time dealing with the strong emotions that came with seeing Suzy in that setting, but Mommy was there for her every possible moment. I took as much time as I could, though I needed to keep my income alive and hated leaving Eric. Every time he saw me packing my bags, his expression clouded over.

"Mama, are you going *again*?"

He wasn't whining, just struggling to understand. I finally decided to tell him the truth.

"Honey, Aunt Suzy is very sick. I hate to leave you, but she needs me now."

I knew Eric needed me too, and it tore me in half, but astonishingly, that simple modicum of honesty made all the difference to him. He was a preschooler with no concept of cancer, chemo, flight schedules, comp time—all the heavily weighted factors I was constantly juggling. But he accepted without question that when someone you love needs you, you go to her. Of course you do. It really is that simple, and it grounded me to suddenly see it through his eyes.

Month after month, through grueling courses of chemotherapy and radiation, surgeries that left her feeling truncated and unsexed, Suzy

came and went through a revolving door of emotion: grace, anger, gratitude, sorrow, laughter, grace again. She was stronger than I ever expected
her to be—stronger than I wish she ever had to be.

Mommy, Daddy, Stan, and I worked together to make sure she was
never alone in Houston. At least one of us would travel with her and stay
at the little apartment across the street from the medical center. We were
grateful for the place, because it cost a lot less than hotels and offered
Suzy a little home away from home. My apartment in Dallas functioned
as the staging area, a sort of base camp where she could decompress on
her way to and from each treatment. She adjusted her expectations and
lifestyle to the treadmill that kept her alive—a little longer, another day,
one more step, one foot in front of the other. I tried to make those Dallas days a treat for her. If she was up to it, we went shopping at Neiman
Marcus, had lunch at her favorite places, took in a movie, or visited local
art galleries. Sometimes I arranged dinner dates for us with two of my
handsome friends, and we spent a good hour beforehand getting ourselves dressed to the nines, doing a full makeup job, playing with her
hairdo on the Styrofoam wig head. If she couldn't find the energy to go
out, I made sure she was tucked in with fresh lavender pillowcases, silky
pajamas, and a good book.

She looked beautiful, despite the effects of chemo and radiation.

"I'm not fat, I'm zaftig," she said, as steroids filled out her slight form
and softened her sculpted cheekbones. Her skin was luminous and lovely,
chemo being the epilating and exfoliating demon that it is. After axillary
lymph nodes were removed and the area irradiated, she fought off pain
and swelling from lymphedema in her arm, but she wore long sleeves
and worked around it. For her second course of chemo, they installed a
"Gershon"—a subclavian catheter—in a vein above her collarbone, creating a port through which she could receive IV drugs from a little pump
that she wore on a strap around her shoulder. A little Frankenstein-ish,
but the veins in her arm had collapsed from all the injections, and this
meant they didn't have to keep searching for new ways to stick a needle
in her.

Between treatments, Suzy went home and took care of her family, continued her charity work, even did some modeling jobs, wearing a sassy
little bobbed wig. I took Eric to Peoria to visit as often as I could, and Suzy

came up with any plausible excuse to make the occasion into a party for the cousins and neighbor kids. Watching them splash in a backyard pool or tear around playing cops and robbers, I was reminded how green and friendly Peoria is, what a gentle, generous oasis in the world. Suzy loved her life there, loved the people she met in the grocery store, Girl Scouts selling their cookies at the door, shade trees and picnic benches in the park. She was thrilled by the first snow flurries in winter and the first crocus in spring, the cricket-filled nights in summer, the blaze of color in autumn.

Suzy celebrated what would be her last birthday in October 1979.

The effects of treatment mounted with the effects of the steadily advancing cancer. Suzy continued to receive what I now recognize as palliative care—the kind of treatment that buys time with no real expectation of cure—and that time was precious. The whole family settled into a lifestyle that was contorted around all the big and small necessities of Suzy's survival. It was laborious and stressful, but not entirely unhappy because every day that we had Suzy, we had reason to be glad. Suzy had plenty of reason to despair and feel sorry for herself, but she refused to be sucked into that swamp. She never talked about the possibility—the probability, in truth—that she was going to die. She made plans and spoke eagerly of everything she was going to do "when I get better."

Suzy spent long hours in the pediatric cancer wards in Houston and Peoria. To this day, I hear from people who remember her reading to the children, talking to them about their treatment, listening to them when they needed to be heard, comforting them when they were afraid. She was deeply concerned for some of the other women receiving breast cancer treatment alongside her. Not all of them had the loving family and financial resources Suzy had. The more time she spent in waiting rooms, sitting on the floor when there weren't enough chairs available, the more the assembly-line atmosphere rankled her; she found the dowdiness of the waiting rooms and chemo wards so depressing.

"Somebody needs to make this place a little more upbeat. It's unbearably boring and sad, and that's the last thing we need right now." Suzy frowned at the framed dollar-store art. "There should be classical music and something beautiful and stimulating on the wall. Something to remind us how wonderful the world is outside all this."

"Agreed," I said, flipping through a seven-month-old magazine. "Some good books wouldn't hurt."

"Poetry, maybe. And a coat of paint on the walls. Maybe a cute little tea cart with ginger ale and shortbread and soda crackers to settle the stomach," said Suzy. "It's bad enough we have to come here. Maybe if it was a little more inviting, it would make people feel positive and hopeful. When I get better, I'm going to make some changes around here. We'll do it together."

I looked at her doubtfully. Frankly, I had no intention of setting foot in this place again.

"Oh, c'mon, Nanny. It'll be fun," said Suzy. "Promise me you'll help."

Semper Pink

PHUONG-THAO BARNES is pretty in pink. She's heard people say the color insults and sissifies the seriousness of breast cancer, but anyone wanting to say that to her face will have to catch up with her first.

"My dad met my mom in Vietnam on his second tour during the war," says Thao. "He went back for a third tour just to get her and marry her. They're both very strong people. I have the best parents in the world. I've always been proud that I'm half Vietnamese, and I love having a Vietnamese name."

After graduating from Oklahoma State University with a degree in veterinary science, Thao joined the Stillwater, Oklahoma, Police Department. In 2005, after Hurricane Katrina decimated New Orleans and left the NOPD with little more than a skeleton crew, Thao and five other officers used their leave time to go to Louisiana. They were deputized in a neighboring parish and sent into the city.

"The officers there needed a lot of help," Thao says. "They were scattered and taking fire, having problems getting supplies. We split in half and went with a Special Forces–commanded guard group doing rescue missions afloat. It was pretty rough seeing all the bodies, the hopeless look about the people, all the pets left behind. We slogged around in that contaminated water for fifteen hours each day, trying to make sure no one was left behind."

Thao received a Distinguished Service medal, and the experience changed her.

"It was an eye-opener. I watched the Coast Guard and thought they were pretty squared away. I love the mission of the Coast Guard. Their motto is *Semper Paratus,* which means 'Always Ready.' These people are out there saving lives, working that mission 24/7."

Leaving her amazingly understanding husband, David, to care for her horses on their ranch, Thao enlisted. At twenty-seven, she was the oldest graduate at boot camp, but she left the youngsters in the dust, taking the Honor Graduate Award and clocking one of the fastest qualifying times for boat crew. She started training for her first triathlon. It was spring. Life was good. Thao was stunned when she felt the lump in her breast.

Just six months earlier, she'd passed a thorough medical exam with flying colors. There was no history of breast cancer in her family. She'd never smoked or taken a drink. Genetic testing revealed no genetic markers. But suddenly, inexplicably, Thao was facing a grim prognosis; the aggressive metastatic disease had already invaded her lymph nodes. She was Stage III and in for the fight of her life.

"At first, it was like . . . *disbelief*," she says. "And then I got angry."

Her physician was told to process her for discharge from the Coast Guard, but Thao begged for a chance to resume active duty after treatment. She went home on medical leave. Throughout a punishing course of chemotherapy, Thao dug deep for the energy to work in the Oklahoma recruiting office and raise money for Susan G. Komen for the Cure. Chemo was followed by mastectomy and radiation. Thao participated in Saddle Up for the Cure, riding her horse, Scoutland, in the American Quarter Horses Association's World Championship Show while she was still recovering from surgery. Her brother, a certified chef, catered dinners for the Susan G. Komen Race for the Cure and the American Cancer Society Relay for Life. Soon the whole family was involved.

"My family was there for me every step of the way," says Thao. "My husband is like the strongest guy in the world. My parents, brothers, sisters—they're awesome."

When Thao was handed her randomly selected number at the Oklahoma City Race for the Cure, she showed her mom and said, "How cool is that?"

It was her old badge number from the Stillwater PD.

Thao took her last hit of radiation in January 2008 and joined her Coast Guard unit in Los Angeles on light duty, requesting full duty every day until they gave it to her. In October, practically floating in all the pink of Breast Cancer Awareness Month, she took the top spot in Coast Guard Gunner's Mate "A" school (weapons training that involves everything from pistols to 76-mm weapon systems), beating out her classmates, all of whom were male and at least five years younger.

On a recent Facebook posting, Thao quoted Edmund Burke: "The only thing necessary for the triumph of evil is for good men to do nothing." This remarkable young woman lives the calling "to protect and serve" and has been *semper paratus* for a host of challenges no one could have anticipated. When the massive 2010 earthquake shook Haiti to rubble and ash, Thao knew immediately where she needed to be, but she was awaiting results from MRIs and other tests she goes through every six months as part of her ongoing breast cancer follow-up.

Thao Barnes is, in short, a superhero. In pink.

Over the years, as breast cancer pink gained more and more exposure, the movement began to experience a backlash. It's a law of physics: To every action there's an equal and opposite reaction. I have no retort to the accusation that we're "pinkwashing the world," because that's exactly what we're trying to do. People used to complain about red, but now we have safe-sex awareness and antiretroviral drugs for the treatment of AIDS. Red activists plan to stay on task until they've rendered themselves obsolete. We plan to follow their fabulous example. The condescension and pink bashing do occasionally hurt my feelings, but far worse, it hurts my mother's feelings, and I'm ready to put up my dukes when anyone messes with Mommy. Mommy, however, is the first to remind me that, not unlike the Coast Guard, our mission is to save lives. If we're to remain *semper paratus,* we have to keep our eye on the ball.

What can I say? As long as women are dying of breast cancer, we're going to keep talking about it, and this is our style. It was Suzy's style, and this is my tribute to her. I applaud others who have their own style. Three cheers for chartreuse! Godspeed, indigo! With the survival of young women like Thao hanging in the balance, I'm not willing to divert attention to popularity contests, celebritized egos, or the so-called breast cancer wars between varying schools of thought. Tearing down the good done by others simply isn't a productive use of anyone's time and energy.

Sexism is a troubling component in the breast cancer equation. For a lot of reasons. Ironically, pink prejudice cuts most cruelly against men diagnosed with this "female" disease. About ten years ago, we set out to change this with the help of Richard Roundtree. When the ultra-macho star of the blaxploitation blockbuster *Shaft* walked out in front of a press junket with a pink ribbon on his lapel, it was like Iconoclasts-R-Us. People were astonished to learn he'd been diagnosed with breast cancer and had kept it a secret for eight years.

In 1993, Roundtree mentioned to his physician he'd felt a lump in his "pec muscle." The last thing he suspected was breast cancer. Like Thao Barnes, his initial reaction was disbelief. And anger.

"I thought, *No way*," he says. "Men don't get breast cancer."

But that year, approximately 1,500 men did, and almost a third of them didn't survive. When people compared that number with the 40,000 or so women who died of breast cancer that year, some questioned the wisdom of devoting significant money to men's breast cancer, but we chose to fund both research and awareness—and not just because it's impossible for us to look someone in the face and tell her the death of her husband, father, or son doesn't merit attention.

The low number of men affected slows research, since studies only move forward when new patients provide new data, but we've learned that men and women differ dramatically in their response to anti-estrogen therapies. Understanding that difference may help us map the molecular minefield and improve hormone therapy for women with breast cancer.

On the surface of some breast cells—both normal and abnormal—are hormone receptors that attract estrogen and/or progesterone. When the hormones talk, those cells listen. And the hormones are saying, *Grow*. If you're a fourteen-year-old girl trying to fill out a cashmere sweater, that's great. If you're a woman—or a man—with breast cancer, it can be lethal. We've learned that we can slow or even stop the growth of breast cancer with drugs that inhibit the reception of estrogen, progesterone, and a protein known as human epidermal growth factor receptor (HER2). In triple negative breast cancer, none of the three receptors is present, so the cancer doesn't respond to hormone therapies like tamoxifen. (HER2 responds to drugs like Herceptin.)

Additionally, we felt certain we could impact the higher mortality rate for men simply by raising awareness, because it's partly the macho factor that works against men with breast cancer. Dr. William Wood, chairman of the Ethics Committee and professor in the Surgical Oncology Division at Emory University, a regular at a major annual breast cancer symposium in San Antonio, spoke at one of our press junkets. "Women see a doctor if they feel something the size of an M&M in their chest," he said. "Most men won't even think about it until the lump is the size of a golf ball, which means the cancer has advanced and probably spread."

It was incredibly courageous of Richard Roundtree to come forward. As he underwent mastectomy, chemo, and radiation back in the 1990s, he was forced to keep his diagnosis carefully hidden. Along with his life—and his bigger-than-life image—his livelihood was at stake. To work in a major film or television production, actors have to be insured. Had the truth been known, his career would have been destroyed. It's ironic and a bit heartbreaking that for all the strides we'd made toward breaking the silence, all our efforts to eradicate the term *women's cancer* from the lexicon, for far too long, men with breast cancer were left behind.

Over the following decade, men's mortality rates dropped a whopping 25 percent. Dr. Wood says men's breast cancer is being detected earlier and treated more effectively.

Apparently, the guys just needed a little pinking. Fortunately, we had Shaft on our side.

Ten years after he joined our awareness effort, Richard Roundtree is still speaking out about breast cancer and appearing, appropriately enough, on the show *Heroes*.

As for Thao Barnes, Thursday, January 14, 2010, she updated her Facebook status:

"All breast cancer tests and MRIs for this six-month period were clear! May 16 will be two years in remission. Life is AWESOME. Going for a five-mile run to celebrate."

The Coast Guard was already on the ground in Haiti with additional troops being mobilized. Friday, Thao's unit was deployed.

"Hey, friends," she posted. "Won't be back for a while. Going out to save the world."

~ 8 ~

Make It Last

I lay in bed at night, passing my hands over my breasts, intensely aware of every anomaly. *Has this bump grown slightly since last week? Is this one a little firmer than the others?* I alternately chided myself for being a coward and castigated myself for falling into that false sense of security Suzy and I had embraced over the years.

"Don't worry. It's nothing."

We'd heard it a thousand times. But *nothing* isn't palpable. *Nothing* cannot be measured between the thumb and index finger. You can't needle biopsy *nothing*. A cyst is not nothing. A benign tumor is not nothing. You get credit for a *something* there, even if it's something other than a malignancy.

Long before Suzy was diagnosed, I was well aware—and well informed—on the "dense breast" thing. I'd done my homework on it and told her with library-book certainty, "Statistically, the vast majority of breast lumps are benign. It really would be silly to rush off and get a biopsy every five minutes."

And I was right. That absolutely correct information was no less correct just because Suzy had cancer, but statistics and certitude rang quite differently in the blizzard-white world of M. D. Anderson. We struggled to find a balance between the "normal" world and the cancer ward, where baldness and IV drips were the norm. Infusions of toxic chemicals were standard; breakfast, lunch, and dinner were remarkable events that warranted a detailed report on Suzy's thick medical chart.

What was I to make of my normally abnormal breasts now, as I lay alone in bed with my persistent *nothing*s?

Balance. That was the goal I was trying to achieve, and it was tough. Time away from my growing son versus time away from my dying sister.

The need to financially support myself versus the need to emotionally support my family. The fear of knowing something terrible versus the fear of not knowing something terrible.

Later, at Suzy's funeral, the rabbi read W. H. Auden's poem "If I Could Tell You."

The winds must come from somewhere when they blow, . . .
Time will say nothing but I told you so.

After Suzy's diagnosis, my own physician eyed me with a different level of suspicion. Certain words creep onto your medical chart and color it like a coffee stain. Cavalier "cop-a-feel-and-tell-me-it's-nothing" exams were a thing of the past. He lingered over the lumps, wanting to err on the side of caution, now that erring one way or the other seemed unavoidable. Three times during the course of Suzy's treatment, I choked down my fear and went in for biopsy surgery.

"Mommy . . ." I hated to burden her with it, given everything she was going through, but I needed her to know. "This one's not budging. They want to take a look at it."

"I'm on my way."

There was nothing in her voice but my grandmother Fritzi's last mandate: *Don't let the world fall apart on you.* For one of the procedures, Mom had to leave Suzy's bedside in Houston to meet me at the hospital in Dallas. Groggy from anesthesia, I opened my eyes to find her there, and guilty relief flooded over me.

"Eric—he's okay?" My first waking thought since the day he was born.

"He's fine," Mom assured me.

So was I. The tumor was benign.

"Thank God," I breathed. "Mommy, I'm so sorry to put you through this again."

"Shhh." She stroked my forehead. "Let's just take the good news today."

I floated on the feeling of being five years old again, grateful, drifting back to sleep to the sound of her voice.

We all did the best we could, but really, Mom was the one who kept everyone going through all of this. She was, without exception, gracious and polite in every encounter, charming her way around triage nurses, caseworkers, and radiology lab techs. But she also kept the trains running on time when it came to Suzy's care. She had the backstage lowdown on every hospital, clinic, and chemo infusion facility. She orchestrated logistics and travel and helped Suzy manage the endless childcare challenges and wrenching separation from her little ones. She oversaw the grand timetable to make sure Suzy had help, transportation, and companionship whenever she needed it. We continued taking turns traveling with her to treatments and surgeries, but there was one terrible stretch where Mommy stayed with Suzy for five and a half weeks in Houston and never saw the outside of the hospital.

Daddy had a hard time coping with the reality of what was happening to Suzy. Men of his generation were trained to batten down the emotional hatches, take hold of the ole bootstraps, and fix whatever needed mending. But this was beyond his control—both the situation and the depth of feeling roiling inside him—and he struggled as Suzy's decline became more and more obvious. Suzy continued to preface her intentions with "when I get better," but the rest of us gradually realized that this really meant "when I die." It was unspoken for the most part. Suzy didn't want to discuss any details, but one day after I brought her home from treatment, I stepped into the kitchen to make her a cup of tea, and I overheard her tell Dad with a small, choked sob, "Don't let them bury me in the ground, Daddy."

I heard him murmur in response, his voice low and comforting. She was always and forever his beautiful little girl. How, I wondered, would he ever recover from this?

Mommy suggested that the four of us—my parents and Stan and I—should visit with the rabbi at Stan and Suzy's temple for advice on how we could best help Suzy now. Rabbi Goff had known her for a long time, knew what sort of woman she was and why she didn't want to talk about what was happening to her.

"Stay hopeful. Keep encouraging her," he said, "but don't pretend she's not dying. Don't lie to her or put her in a position where she feels obligated to lie to you. There are limits to optimism and stiff upper lips. The suffering of a kind, loving, beautiful young woman—it offends our sense of justice. We feel angry at life's unfairness, angry at our own helplessness. But the way we respond to life and death as it flows, as it comes to us—that's the real test of our character and our humanity. I have the highest respect and admiration for the way your family has responded to the stress of this catastrophe. Suzy is a lucky woman in many ways. A lot of people live a long time and never know the quality of human relationships she has with her family and friends."

Lucky.

It wasn't the word I would have chosen at the time.

As her energy waned and her little body began to waste away, the good days became fewer, the long nights darker. Mom and I frantically researched whatever treatment or drug or twist of fate was on the table, trying to decipher acronyms, begging for clinical trial bulletins, desperately trying to connect some frame of reference to Suzy's blood count and vital signs.

"Don't get so excited," Suzy would say. "Calm down, Nan, and help me figure this out."

Initially, we'd await test results with an even mix of hope and apprehension. Now we rolled with the punches. Bad test results were just information, not a body slam; good test results were rare and regarded with cautious optimism. Suzy's buoyant outlook turned contemplative and somber.

For fifteen months, Blumenschein and the team at M. D. Anderson had managed to pump the brakes, never stopping the disease but definitely slowing its progress. Now Suzy's cancer was learning its way around the drugs. Her body acclimated to the onslaught and built up resistance. Dark shadows rose up under her skin. Lesions opened and oozed on her chest. One surgery after another was performed to close and cover them. Another procedure was done to remove the implant from her previous reconstruction, and muscle tissue from her back was used to replace the chest wall. Despite all the desperate measures of the previous two years—mastectomy, oophorectomy, more radiation, new drugs—the cancer caught hold and spread like a wildfire inside her.

We began a downward spiral toward the inevitable.

Trips to Houston were hard on Suzy, but she kept going. Mommy and I whispered back and forth on the phone, fretting over how to help Suzy as she became more and more weak and malnourished from vomiting. Having tried everything else, Mom went out—God knows where or how—and procured some marijuana. With her heart in her throat, Mommy taped the plastic bags to her legs before she boarded the airplane to meet us at M. D. Anderson. Unfortunately, by this time, Suzy was so ill, she couldn't eat the pot in cookies or brownies, and her lungs were so beleaguered, trying to smoke it made her cough, which made the horrendous nausea even worse.

Week after week, she sat shivering in the cold, drab waiting room until they called her name. Then she shuffled through the double doors and lay shivering in her hospital gown on a gurney in the hall, slipping in and out of fitful sleep.

I understand now why Suzy hated hospital gowns. At the time, I guess I thought, *Why wouldn't she hate them?* She was an impeccably stylish woman who cared a lot about how she looked. That's who she was. But in retrospect, I think there was more to it than that. The one-size-fits-all boxiness of the thing is dehumanizing. That pragmatic but potentially breezy opening in the back goes to the very etymology of the word *embarrassing,* and the very idea that one size does or can or should even attempt to *fit all* was offensive to Suzy, literally and metaphorically. This wasn't a matter of style or aesthetics—it was part of a larger dynamic that makes so many cancer patients feel dehumanized and stripped of their dignity.

Emerging from an uncomfortable doze on a gurney in the hospital hallway one day, Suzy discovered that her clavicle port had been bleeding and that her gown was stained with a dark blossom of dry brown blood.

"Excuse me? Nurse?" She kept trying to flag someone down. "Could I get a clean gown, please?"

I'd gone to take care of some paperwork while she was sleeping. By the time I got back, Suzy was beside herself, struggling to bite back her anger and swallow her weeping. I chased down a nurse who promised to bring the clean gown, but the facility was always overburdened with patients. The staff were stretched to the limits of what they could do, and the matter of Suzy's lifelong pride in her appearance—the fact that to feel in control of anything at all, she at least had to be in control of that—none of this could be taken into consideration when there were a hundred other patients on the ward, some of whom were even closer to death than Suzy was. And Suzy understood all that, but understanding that all the small things you care about have been lost in the grinding machinery that keeps you alive—well, that isn't very comforting, is it?

"All I want is a clean gown," she seethed. "I can't sit here in a dirty, stained . . ."

"Suzy, calm down. It's okay."

"It's not okay."

"No. I know," I said, thinking she was talking about herself.

"This isn't right, Nan. This shouldn't be."

It wasn't like Suzy to lose it, especially in a public place, but she did lose it a little, and maybe it was good for her. She cried, inconsolable, about the stained gown that was really her ruined beauty, about the thin white blankets, which were really the flimsy treatments that offered her such pitiful shelter from the creeping chill of this disease. She mourned the day away from her children, which was really her fear of missing the rest of their lives. She raged at the docile flock in the waiting room, who were really the women of the world, waiting to be heard, wanting to know more than they were being told. Suzy's hopes and dreams—all the things she'd planned to do and see and be in the world—had been flattened and boxed into framed dollar-store landscapes, and finally, for a moment, she allowed herself to be heartbroken by it.

I stood there, helpless, humbled by the enormity of what she was struggling to encompass, everything she could see so clearly behind her, and everything unknown that lay ahead. Denial, anger, bargaining, depression—there were even a few moments of reluctant acceptance. We'd been to all these places over and over, visiting and revisiting each stop like a shuttle circling beneath the airport terminals. Where do you get off? (I suppose that depends on your destination.)

Back at home, I drew a bath for Suzy. She never wanted me to come into the bathroom when she was uncovered or throwing up, but she was so weak and so violently ill that she needed me to undress her and help her into the tub.

"Oh, Nanny . . ."

The sight of herself in the mirror weakened her knees, and she sank into the water. She weighed not much more than a child in my arms. Holding her against my shoulder, I leaned in and washed her surgery-scarred back, then cupped water over her chest and dabbed at the broken skin. All the fighting spirit was gone out of me. Why the hell should anyone plaster on some vapid "positive attitude" in a situation like this? Rabbi Goff's advice resonated with comfort for both of us. Suzy was dying, and it was hideous and unfair and tragic. We both had good reason to give in and cry, and we did.

"Oh, God, Nan, I look so awful," Suzy wept. "This is horrible."

"It is horrible, Suzy. It's awful, and I hate it. I hate that this is happening to you."

"I feel so . . . so tired and so . . . ruined."

"I know, Suz." I touched my forehead to hers and wrapped a warm towel around her shoulders. "I also know that you are perfect. You are the perfect Suzy you always were, and nothing can change that, and nothing can change how much we love you."

Suzy's lungs filled up and had to be drained to keep her from essentially drowning inside her own body. They extracted almost a gallon of fluid from her chest as she lay gasping in agony.

When it was over, she clung to my arm as we made our way down the hall to the elevator. We stood quietly in the elevator, then made our way through the lobby. We pushed through the lobby doors, then made our way to the corner. I kept my eyes on the sidewalk, watching Suzy's ballerina flats, one in front of the other, wanting to make sure she didn't stumble. Every step was such an effort now. Her small frame felt as fragile as spun sugar.

Standing at the corner across the street from the little apartment, we waited for the light to change. Traffic roared by. A huge city bus loomed into view at the end of the block.

I'd want you to find a way to kill me. I'd rather be dead.

In the hitch of one breath, the thought passed through my head. How much easier it would be. A quick, merciful accident. Just to slip and fall through a crack between being and not being. Her suffering would be over, and I could scream loud and long and flail my fists against something solid. Suzy's back was to me, but I wonder now if I would have seen that thought flash at the corner of her eye. Summer wind stirred a baby-fine wisp of hair trying to grow at the nape of her delicate neck. The bus closed in, looming larger. The driver's face rose blank and focused as a gibbous moon beyond Suzy's bony shoulder.

I gripped my sister's hand and pulled her close to me.

The light changed, and she clung to my arm again as we crossed wordlessly to the little apartment, where she fought for another night of life, and I did everything I could to help her. Because this is the place you come to when someone you love is slowly dying: You're desperate for it to be over, and even more desperate to make it last.

Betty Rollin's groundbreaking bestseller *First, You Cry* was published in 1976, and I read it simply because everyone else was reading it. It was the big book that was being talked about, and that in itself was astonishing. In fact, much of the talk about the book, as I recall, centered on how remarkable it was that everyone was talking about it. The movie starring Mary Tyler Moore came out in 1978, the year after Suzy was diagnosed. Suzy saw it on TV and read the book while she was in treatment at M. D. Anderson. She was impressed with Rollin's candor about the physical and emotional wreckage breast cancer had brought into her life, but beyond that, it encouraged her to see this bright pinhole of light shining through the heavy curtain of silence and stigma. Breast cancer was still effectively barred from polite conversation, but it was no longer an obscenity. (Not in the rhetorical sense, anyway.)

"It needs to be talked about," said Suzy. "Betty Ford, Happy Rockefeller, Shirley Temple Black . . . They aren't the least bit afraid to talk about breast cancer—what it really is, what it does. We have to talk about it too. Promise me, Nan, when I get better, we'll do something with Junior League or B'nai B'rith. We could call the American Cancer Society and get some ideas."

"When I get better, Nan, you and I are going to do something about the hideous décor in this waiting room. It's usually all girls. It should be pretty and light."

"When I get better, Nan, we should have a luncheon to raise awareness for the new mammogram machines. So few women know about the newest technology."

"When I get better, Nanny, we have to do a tea—something educational, but fun and lovely with flowers and—oh! We could all wear hats. We could invite Dr. Blumenschein to speak. Promise you'll help me put it together."

These were plans she was making for me, not for herself, but I smiled and nodded, knowing that talking about doing these things made her feel included in some version of the future. She was still her mother's daughter, full of good intentions and good ideas to back them up. She didn't have to ask what to do, and she wasn't ready to get out of the kitchen.

As the summer wore on, her good days became few and far between.

Suzy rallied every ounce of strength she could to be with her children, but there were frustrating moments when there was no way to make it okay for them. Scott was ten years old now, old enough to know something was terribly wrong but not yet able to make sense out of it. He didn't want to talk about it, and he was sick of hearing that Mommy couldn't get out of bed today or Mommy was going away again or Mommy was too tired to talk on the phone. Stephanie was six and in school now, vaguely aware that her family didn't function the way her friends' families did, but unable to remember a time when things were different. Suzy had been in treatment for half of her little girl's life, so Steffie saw nothing odd about her mother disappearing for days at a time, sleeping in the daytime, or eating a soda cracker and ginger ale instead of whatever was on the dinner table for everyone else.

More and more often now, there were times when Steffie wanted and needed more than Suzy could give. It was agony for Suzy that she didn't have the strength to sweep her little girl up in her arms. She couldn't be there for every school program and PTA meeting. When Steffie tugged Suzy's hand, begging her to come into the swimming pool, Suzy had to pull away and adjust the neckline of her beach robe so Steffie wouldn't see the cath port and lesions on her mother's chest.

Suzy was torn between caring for herself and caring for her children. Mommy was torn between caring for her daughter and caring for her grandchildren. I did what I could do from Dallas. Stan and Daddy were there, strong and constant, in Peoria, along with Suzy's posse—a fabulous cadre of half a dozen true-blue friends who stuck close by her, took turns making dinner for her family, picked up the children for play dates and school events, and never for a moment left her without a shoulder. We all did our best to wrap our love around Scott and Steffie, wanting to shelter them from what was coming. It was like trying to pitch a tent in the path of a tornado.

One afternoon, Mom and Suzy stood at the kitchen window, watching Scott and Steffie dash back and forth in the cool spray of the lawn sprinkler.

Suzy said, "I worked so hard to get them, Mommy. Now I'll never know what happens."

Mom put her arm around Suzy. She would never have insulted Suzy by saying some platitude or making some empty promise that everything would be all right; they both knew it wouldn't be. We could surround these children with all the family we had, but without their mother, the landscape of their lives would be forever altered.

"I know you'll take care of everyone," Suzy said, and Mommy nodded. That she could promise, and they both knew what it meant. They didn't discuss any particulars.

As difficult as it was for her to leave her family, Suzy seemed relieved to be in Houston with me. She didn't have to be brave or perky when it was just the two of us. She could close her eyes when she needed to. She could cry or throw up without trying to hide. She could take care of herself without feeling torn in two. When the little apartment wasn't available, we stayed at a nice hotel near the medical center, and Suzy loved to stretch out by the swimming pool, reading paperback novels and soaking in the sun.

"I look healthier with a little color in my face," she said.

I agreed, though we both knew *healthier* was a relative term these days. Suzy was acutely aware of how visibly sick she was. People were ill at ease sitting near her in a restaurant or making eye contact in the mirror in the ladies' room. When we walked into a clothing boutique, the salesgirl's ready smile quickly faded. It made me furious, but I didn't want to make it worse for her by venting. It had always been next to impossible to walk into the grocery store in Peoria without meeting someone who loved Suzy. The folks behind the deli and bakery counters used to wave and call to her. Acquaintances from Junior League and PTA rushed to hug her in the produce section. Now people averted their eyes, scurried down the aisle, dodged behind a stack of canned goods. They crossed the street to avoid brushing by her on the sidewalk, recoiled from her as if she were contagious.

Certainly, Suzy noticed and was hurt by it, but it didn't change the way she conducted herself. She didn't leave the house without putting herself together: wig, makeup, the same stylish clothes she'd always worn. She was still as charitable and outgoing as ever, not about to be defined by this disease or by anyone's adverse reaction to it. Instead of decrying the acquaintances who migrated away from her, Suzy held fast to that fabulous little cadre of friends and told them often how much she loved and appreciated them.

Stretched out on the chaise by the hotel pool in Houston, Suzy wore Jackie O shades and a wide-brimmed hat with a tropical beachy cover-up that concealed the Gershon port below her collarbone but left her bare legs in the sunshine. Whatever she was reading had her fully engaged, so she didn't notice me watching her chest rise and fall with a soft, dry wheeze. Her limbs were so thin and knobby, she looked like a little girl playing dress-up. I had to smile, suddenly thinking of Suzy and me in the backyard, dancing for Aunt Rose in our coconut bras and hula skirts. Suzy and me at the stable, pretending our ponies were Royal Lipizzaner stallions. Suzy and me in Paris, tromping up a hill at Père Lachaise. Suzy and me on the porch at Mom and Dad's, playing patty-cake with our babies and planning another Halloween birthday.

Tears stung my eyes behind my sunglasses. Suzy's mainstay role in my life had begun with the sound of her voice before I was born, and she'd been with me for every major moment since. The memories flickered faster, a stream of images and emotion. The dizzying speed with which our time together had come and gone left me breathless. I tried to catch her as she flew by on her two-wheeler, so real I could hear the patter of the playing card stuck in the spokes. My heart called out to her as she skipped down the front steps in her pink ribbons and crinolines, but she was already sailing across the dance floor at the Excelsior with a handsome young Italian.

Don't go, Suzy. Don't leave me.

The unbearable weight of losing her crushed against my rib cage.

Where I live now there are cherry trees, and sometimes children run after the blossoms as they rain down in the spring wind, trying to catch and collect as many as they can. I think that must be what I was doing that day by the pool. I'd brought along the notebook in which we logged Suzy's office visits and recorded her meds, but I flipped past all that to a clean, white page and started scribbling one line after another, catching and collecting every moment I could grasp, frantic at the possibility that I would lose a single charm bracelet artifact or forget her expression when she heard the opening skiff of her favorite song on the radio.

> Bibity boo bot
> Party for Boppie's Eightieth
> Louie
> "I'm in love with Hieronymus Bosch!"
> Hadassah fashion show
> This woman needs a raincoat

Suzy's life was so much greater than the sum of all these small parts, but I could see in each moment of her—even the moments of anger and silliness—a gift for someone else. The list became a eulogy and then a prayer.

I took Suzy back to Peoria, and she was happy to be home. She wanted to avoid the hospital as long as possible, so Stan and Mommy did their best to care for her with the help of hired nurses, but she was in and out of the hospital a lot toward the end.

She was wasting away rapidly now, her lungs constantly clouding over with fluid, new lesions emerging all over the front of her body. I visited every other week and stayed as long as I could, but by Sunday afternoon, I was eager to get back to Dallas, where I could fetch Eric from my friend's house and immerse myself in another week of work. When Daddy took up his car keys to take me to the airport, Suzy always insisted on coming along. Anytime she wasn't in the hospital, she had to ride along to greet me and send me off. For the most part, she slept, curled up on the backseat of the car, but that gesture of being there for me was important to her, and looking back on it, it means the world to me.

The last time I saw Suzy was probably the last Sunday in July 1980.

"Can you stay another day or two, Nan?" she asked.

I shook my head. "Eric needs me."

This was a lie; the truth was, I needed him. He anchored my sanity these days with his sturdy little grin and self-reliant lunchbox. Daddy took up his keys, and I got in the backseat with Suzy. We rode in silence for a while. Her lungs were filling with fluid again, so when she did speak, it was barely above a whisper.

"We have to do something . . . to help . . . those women at the hospital. Make it better . . . for them . . . for their families."

"We will, Suz." I patted her hand, watching my hometown amble by the open window.

"*Nan.*" She gripped my wrist. "Promise me it'll be better."

"Suzy . . . I promise."

"It has to be talked about. Breast cancer —we have to talk about it. It has to change . . . so women know . . . so they don't die. *Promise me, Nanny.* Promise . . . you'll make it change."

It wasn't like the good intentions, couched in the optimistic time frame of "when I get better." This time there was no mention of pretty specifics, no inkling of a plan, only purpose burning in her sunken eyes, weighing on her emaciated shoulders. If she'd asked me to swim the length of the Nile, I would have found a way to do it. She said it like she was pleading for her life. I didn't understand until three years later that it was my life she was about to save.

I promised. I swore with all my broken heart.

"I promise, Suzy. I swear. Even if it takes the rest of my life. . . ."

I gave her a quick kiss on the cheek as Daddy pulled up to the curb, then gave Daddy a quick kiss on the cheek as I threw the car door open, needing to stretch my legs and get out in the air. Striding toward the terminal, I swung my bag onto my shoulder. Dallas. Eric. One foot in front of the other.

There was an odd little sound behind me. It felt more than sounded like my name.

Nan.

I turned and saw Suzy standing unsteadily next to the open car door, trying to smooth the front of her rumpled blouse. Her scrawny legs looked impossibly wobbly, and her wig had shifted a little to the side. But she smiled at me and opened her arms.

"Suzy . . ."

I dropped my bulky messenger bag and ran back to her. Knowing I should scold her and tuck her back in the car, I swept her into my arms instead. Abandoning the eggshell genteel hugs we'd been exchanging lately, we held each other as hard as we could.

"Goodbye, Nanny. I love you."

My throat closed before I could say a word. I'm not sure I could have said that particular word anyway. *Goodbye.* I just didn't have it in me. All I could do was hang on until Suzy couldn't hang on any longer. Then I helped her back in the car, scooped up my bag, and loped down the concourse to catch my flight.

A few days later, Mommy took Suzy to the hospital in Peoria. They drained her lungs again, did what they could to make her comfortable. She never wanted Scott and Stephanie to see her in that setting, but this time, she told Stan to bring them and asked Mom to help her into a pretty robe before they arrived. She watched them play together in the waiting room for a while, then managed a little walk with each of them alone.

Seeing them seemed to strengthen her. She wanted to go home again, wanted Mommy to stay with her and sit up with her at night to help her stay awake. She was afraid to fall asleep. Mom cared for her at home for a few days, but they both knew it couldn't last.

"Sweetheart, we have to go to the hospital," Mom told her one morning after Stan took the children to school. "We need to go over there and get you better."

Suzy tried to answer, but her tongue was swollen in her dry mouth.

"I know, I know," Mom soothed her, stroked her hand. "But I love you, your dad loves you, your sister loves you, your family loves you. . . . That's what you know for sure."

She was awake and trying to talk on the way to the hospital, but Mommy couldn't understand what she was saying. The moment they pulled in, the orderlies rushed out, and by the time Mom had parked the car and caught up with them, Suzy was in a bed and had slipped into unconsciousness. Mommy stayed beside her, unable to tear herself away as long as there was the slightest chance Suzy might drift to the surface for a moment.

Over the next few days, Stan came when he could get someone to be with the children. Daddy came when he could stand it. Suzy's closest friends—Linda, Patty, and Dee—took turns, keeping the quiet vigil with Mommy.

If we should stumble when musicians play,
Time will say nothing but I told you so. . . .

I made arrangements for Eric and lined up a flight from Dallas.

Because I love you more than I can say,
If I could tell you I would let you know. . . .

Looking down at the verdant green of the midwestern summer, I knew in my heart I was too late.

S uzy died August 4, 1980.
She was thirty-six years old. Her children were ten and six.

Mommy and Linda were there with her. I was on my way, but Daddy met me at the airport again, his eyes rimmed in red, his mouth drawn down to a tight line of self-control.

"She's gone," he said.

There was a shock wave of agony, relief, guilt, and sorrow. Then a strange state of white noise settled in my head. That night I slept with Steffie in her ruffled pink bed, drifting off for a few minutes, then jarring awake as if a bell tolled in a tower next to my head. I cried as quietly as I could for a while, then lay there feeling empty, listening to the soft, consistent breathing of Suzy's little girl beside me.

"Aunt Nan?"

The door creaked open, and Scott peeked in. I patted the bed beside me. He crept over and crawled in, and though he was a great big boy of ten, he let me pull him into a good snuggle.

"What's going to happen now?" he asked.

"It'll be like . . . when your mommy had to be away for a few days," I lied, but trying to make it true, I added, "Grammy will be here. And your daddy."

"Will you be here?"

"I . . . yes. Sure, Scott. I'll be here."

He looked up at me. Skeptical. Ten.

"I will, Scott. Maybe not as often as I have been lately, but I'll come to visit you, and you'll come see me and Eric in Dallas, and we'll all go to Florida to see Grammy and Grandpa. It'll be hard for a while. You have to be a good big brother, and we all have to . . . just . . . just cover each other up with love."

He burrowed into my side, and I stroked his hair away from his forehead, resting my other hand on Stephanie's back, and we stayed that way until morning.

We all walked through the next few days as if we were characters in an old TV show, negotiating the set pieces, speaking our lines through the static, our faces in grayscale, everything around us black and white. With a numb efficiency, Mommy and I ordered flowers and discussed appropriate readings with the rabbi. We agreed that Suzy personified Solomon's good woman in the Song of Songs.

I am a rose of Sharon, I am a lily of the valleys.
As a lily among thorns, so is my love among the daughters. . . .

Daddy made arrangements for the above-ground mausoleum. Stan nodded and agreed to things, ashen, exhausted. Suzy's wonderful friends stepped in with food and flowers and warmth for Scott and Steffie.

Set me as a seal upon thy heart . . . for love is strong as death. . . .

The casket was to be closed during Suzy's funeral, but there was a private viewing for the family before the service. I knew Suzy wasn't there, but I needed to see her.

A woman of valor, who can find? For her price is far above rubies. . . .
She stretcheth out her hand to the poor, yea, she reacheth forth her hands
to the needy. . . .

The absolute stillness of her body seemed to anchor the room. All the months of twisting frustration and abject terror disappeared now, drawn into a peaceful center of gravity. But when Mom and I stepped closer, the breath caught in my chest. Heavy-handed makeup covered Suzy's soft, expressive face. Everything about it was wrong. The eye shadow was blue as a bruise. Sweeps of rouge attempted to impart a blush of life in her cheeks, but the wrongness of the tone and the matte finish of foundation made her look plastic—almost puppetlike.

"No. No way."

I strode to the back of the room where the funeral director stood, trying not to hear the obvious punch line Suzy would have whispered with one hand cupped to my ear if it had been someone else lying there. "I wouldn't be caught dead looking like that."

"Excuse me." I was quiet but firm. "That makeup needs to be removed. That's not at all how my sister looked. Just take it off, please. I'll redo it myself."

Sensing there was no room for discussion, he quickly had it done. I took my own little makeup bag from my purse and leaned down over the edge of the coffin. Her skin was smooth and white as a pearl, her lips faded lavender, her eyelids porcelain gray.

Strength and dignity are her clothing, and she laugheth at the time to
come. . . .
She openeth her mouth with wisdom, and the law of kindness is on her
tongue. . . .

I clenched my teeth against the need to sob. Tried to breathe around it, but couldn't.

Mom watched from a chair off to the side. She didn't make a sound, but she didn't fight or push away her tears.

She looketh well to the ways of her household. . . .
Her children rise up and call her blessed, her husband also praiseth
    her. . . .
Grace is deceitful, and beauty is vain, but a woman that feareth the
Lord,
    she shall be praised. . . .

The light-handed way Suzy had always applied her makeup was as much about her personality as it was her sense of style. She had no desire to hide or alter anything about herself, only to make the most of what she had. There was a daytime look routine and a nighttime look routine. She'd taught me to do both and updated me periodically with new tricks and trendy products.

Give her the fruit of her hands and let her works praise her in the gates.

Suzy left us with the daytime look.

II

Evolution

9

A Seal Upon Thy Heart

In a garden square near the Szechényi Chain Bridge, which spans the Danube to connect the cities of Buda and Pest, the stylized Zero Kilometer Stone carved by Miklós Borsos symbolizes the starting point from which all major roads in Hungary count their distance. While serving as U.S. ambassador to Hungary, I spent some time staring at that stone, contemplating the starting points in my life. The moments from which I mark the distances I've traveled are not, in and of themselves, all that remarkable. They tend to be smooth and stylized, elegant and immovable, like the Zero Kilometer Stone.

Eight weeks after Suzy's death, I was so deeply entrenched in grief, I wouldn't have believed that a new beginning was possible, let alone so close that I could almost reach out and touch it.

In September, Eric started kindergarten, and I went back to work. I wasn't ready to face the reality of a daily life without Suzy, but I had rent to pay, a child to raise. People searched for the right thing to say and came up with, "I'm sorry for your loss." I'd grown immune to the words. My automatic response was a wooden "Thank you. You're very kind." But it didn't always feel like kindness. Sometimes it felt like politeness. This was the correct thing to say, and if I were a correct-thinking person, I would rise above this now. It was time to let go. But how do you let go of someone so thoroughly woven through your soul? How do you live without someone you would have died for? I read books on the psychology and methodology of grieving, feeling like a failure because I still couldn't sleep or eat or think straight.

"How long has it been?" someone would ask, and I didn't know how to answer. *How long has it been?* implied that this foundation-shifting event was over, and for me, it was still going on. My mother's unstoppable spirit was shattered on the floor. My father's bounding energy had aged to a weighted sigh. My own ability to help them or even make it through the day felt frozen. Literally. My heart and mind felt encased in ice. The only warmth I could feel was Eric. Sometimes I had to take hold of him and hug him until he squirmed away, complaining that my hands were cold.

"When can we visit Aunt Suzy?" he'd ask the same way he asked, "When can I go to Grammy's house?"

It tore my heart out that I'd let another person disappear from his life, but he was just asking out of curiosity. "Why are you crying?" was a candid, legitimate question coming from a four-year-old who was just as likely to ask in the next breath, "Why are fire trucks red?" or "Why do some dogs not have tails?" He didn't know there was any such thing as grief; he was just figuring things out, fitting life into his lunchbox. It was comforting, this tiny happy-talking refuge in the midst of all that emotional wreckage.

I lay in bed at night, staring at the ceiling, scenes from Suzy's life and death replaying in my head. We were there, on a street corner in Paris.

What a great life! We're so lucky, Nan. The luckiest.

The next moment, we were on the street corner in Houston, staring down the oncoming bus. Now it felt like I was the one who'd been slammed to the ground, stunned, run over.

Fancy meeting you here.

My father's dignity and the grace with which my mother faced all this were heartbreaking. Mommy had witnessed Suzy's first breath and her last and remained grateful for every day between. I should have felt lucky to be the tagalong little sister who got as much of Suzy's time as I did, but all I could feel were the missing hours, the wasted words, and all the thousands of days that Suzy should be here and wouldn't be. I couldn't fathom the character of a God who would turn his back on her.

"I'm not sure I can even believe in the existence of such a God," I told Mom. "I don't know where to put all this. Mommy, if you think I should move back home for a while, . . ."

"No," she said flatly. "That would be a disaster. Your life is in Dallas. You have your job. Eric has school. Live your life and take care of your responsibilities. That's the best way to get through it."

This was the hardest moment of my mother's life, but she was no stranger to loss. Her style of grieving was eminently pragmatic. Daddy was strong for her; she was strong for him. Scott and Steffie desperately needed a mother's love, and Mom was there with the closest possible approximation. It didn't surprise or hurt me that Suzy never asked me to step in and be a mother to her children. She knew I loved them, but we had very different mothering styles, and she knew our mother didn't have to be asked.

I know you'll take care of everyone, Mommy, she'd said.

She'd trusted Daddy to look after her. *Don't let them bury me in the ground.*

He was the one who'd always sheltered her. I was the one who'd challenged and perplexed her, so maybe she was getting a bit of her own back, leaving me with this impossible task.

Promise me, Nan.

I'd promised, and I meant it, but what was it she expected me to do? Paint the walls in the waiting room? Stand on the corner with a sandwich board? Was I supposed to find every woman who didn't know better and shake her till she listened? Did Suzy expect me to *cure breast cancer*?

"Knowing Suzy," Mom said wryly, "she expected all of the above with a pink ribbon on it. Plus a box of chocolates."

"So what am I supposed to do?"

"Go back to what you know. Volunteer. Raise money. Make noise."

I went back to what I knew, picked up where I'd left off. At the time Suzy died, my autumn and holiday season had already been booked full of various projects. The doing of those familiar things kept me busy and tenuously connected to the life I had when Suzy was alive. Charity functions. Fashion shows. Luncheons to support hospital wings. I did everything I could to sync my PR job with the charity work I wanted to do so that I'd learn from these events, connecting with people who knew people and spending time with the guest speakers, whether they were oncologists, researchers, or celebrities. At the annual Cattle Baron's Ball, a star-and-rhinestone-studded event benefiting the American Cancer Society, I ran into Dr. Blumenschein, and he greeted me with a warm embrace.

"How are you, Nancy? How's Miss Ellie and your dad?"

"We're fine, thank you." I went with the polite response; he already knew the real answer. "I'm glad to see you, Dr. B. I need your advice on something."

"Fire away."

"I have to cure breast cancer."

He smiled a pained, knowing smile. "Me too."

"No, I mean it. This has to be done. How do we do this?"

"Well, you start with . . . with this," he said, indicating the packed ballroom. "Keep doing what you're already doing. We need funding for research."

"Funding can be had," I said. "There's tons of oil money in Texas right now. We need to push breast cancer to the top of the list and get some of that money flowing our way."

"People tend to fund a general focus on cancer. Breast cancer specifically . . . that's a little difficult."

"Yes, so I've heard. People keep telling me it's not a major deal, which you and I both know is untrue. Or they tell me it's unseemly and makes people uncomfortable. But why should that be? How can people in the civilized world circa 1980 glorify Raquel Welch, eat up *Charlie's Angels* with a spoon, then turn around and tell me there's something unseemly about *breast cancer*? What is this antediluvian . . ."

"You're preaching to the choir, Nancy." Blumenschein held up his hand like a crossing guard. "I'm not disagreeing. Just saying . . . let's not get ahead of ourselves. That's how it is. We've learned to be realistic about it."

I studied the well-dressed assembly. There was a lot of décolletage in the room. If we couldn't champion the cause here, where on earth could we? When Dallas society came out to play, they did it in a great big, star-spangled, bouffant-and-bow-ties way. Bras and beehives were piled high, egos and checkbooks fully loaded. Generosity was a competitive obsession, second only to Friday night football. Texas was teeming with fabulously philanthropic movers and shakers like Joanne Herring, powerful politicos like the Bush and Connally families, brilliant business moguls like . . . like Norman Brinker.

He smiled at me from across the ballroom. I smiled back with an absent nod and returned to Blumenschein.

"It's a marketing issue, that's what it is," I said. "We need to work on education. That's imperative. To get the money ball rolling in a big way, we need awareness. We need *outrage*. We need people to care enough to get into the conversation. Rose Kushner, Betty Ford, Happy Rockefeller—they got things started, and the Betty Rollin book was a huge step forward. But it came out four years ago, and in terms of awareness, have we made any real progress since then? As far as the fund-raising piece—okay, we're here. This is a wonderful event, and I appreciate everyone's generosity, but it's too little, too late."

"Too late for Suzy, yes," said Blumenschein. "And for a lot of others. Believe me, I never forget a face. But what keeps me up at night are the ones walking in the door tomorrow. The ones we might be able to save."

"You're a great man, George Blumenschein." I gave him another quick hug, then clinked my champagne flute on his. "L'chaim."

He nodded firmly and raised his glass. "To life."

I saw Norman Brinker again the following Sunday.

My friends, Joyce and Selwin Belofsky—regulars at Dallas charity functions and in the *Dallas Morning News* society pages—had been very sweetly concerned about me over the previous year and had invited me to brunch at their country club. Norman did the standard table flyby.

"Joyce, so good to see you. Selly, how's it going?" He gave my tailored red suit an unabashed once-over. "And the lady in red. How are you, Nancy?"

We exchanged stock pleasantries, and Norman went on his way, working the room like a summer wind gust, stirring up a little flurry of conversation here and a little dust devil of laughter there. Joyce and Selly and I sat chatting in the sunshine until Norman made his way back to us again.

"Selly, what are these ladies buzzing about so intently?"

"Nancy's doing the most interesting work with M. D. Anderson," said Joyce. "She's studying all the medical journals and really making quite a project of it."

Norman raised one eyebrow. "Really."

"I met some Baylor research scientists at the Cattle Baron's Ball," I said. "They were very appreciative of everything you've done."

"I'm glad to help," said Norman. "Can't say I know much about the science, but I do know a good team when I see it, and they've got one."

A few more pleasantries and off he went. And back he came.

"Selly, I just want to know how you rate," he said. "Not one beautiful woman on your arm, but two? Don't you think that's a little greedy?"

Polite chuckles. Parting pleasantries. Off he went again, and we got up to leave.

"Well," Joyce said, "Norman Brinker is a good friend of ours. But not *that* good. He was hovering around our table like a honeybee."

"Had to be the red dress," said Selly.

The milestone moment. A crisp October morning at ten o'clock, my phone rang.

"Hello?"

"Is it true you walk on water?"

"Who is this?"

"Norman Brinker. "

I'm not going to sit here and pretend I didn't know why he was calling. Through the grapevine, I knew he and his second wife had divorced after five years. They'd had two children, but for whatever reason, they didn't appear to occupy the same sort of place in his life as Brenda and Cindy, his daughters with Little Mo. He was currently seeing a nice woman and wasn't one of those men who swaggers around playing the field or flying personal laundry out in the breeze. He was a father, the head of a huge corporation, an extremely wealthy and influential community leader; a man in his position has good reason to be guarded about the relationships he gets into. If I was interested in getting to know Norman—and I was—I could expect to be properly vetted. Which was fine with me. I had my son to consider; I wasn't about to get involved without knowing a man's true colors.

He asked me to meet him at Chateaubriand, a Dallas steak house that was upscale but not too self-important.

"Can you be there in ninety minutes?"

"Sure," I said. I was there in eighty.

Norman was still there ahead of me, glad-handing the waiter like the guy was his long-lost cousin. Something I quickly learned about Norman: No matter how many friends he had there when he walked in the door, you could multiply that times ten by the time he walked out. It was the secret of his success. He was the quintessential people person. He didn't lord it over a waiter or a line cook; he was in league with him, a comrade-in-arms. He made everyone on the totem pole feel like a partner in this great endeavor of dining, this noble enterprise of living a good life, eating good food, and making great, caring conversation with everyone in earshot.

I quickly learned a few other things as well. He didn't drink. (His mother was a staunch member of the Woman's Christian Temperance Union.) He didn't smoke. (His father had once made him eat a fistful of chewing tobacco.) He rarely ate lunch sitting down, but he accepted the table we were offered, held my chair, and sat down across from me. There was a bright light directly over my head. I felt a foursome of suits at a nearby table giving me the eye. A trio of ladies came in and exchanged pleasantries with Norman, then sat in the corner staring holes in the back of my neck.

"Tell me about yourself," he said.

"What do you want to know?"

"The usual. Where are you from?"

"Peoria, Illinois. Land of milk and honey."

"Are you a person of faith?"

"More like a person of doubt right now. It's been a trying year. But I was raised Jewish, and those teachings mean a lot to me. I hope God and I will eventually be on speaking terms again."

"What do you like to do when you're not at work?"

"My little boy keeps me busy. I'm involved in a lot of cancer-related charities. Working on fundraisers, trying to learn everything I can."

We riffed the way acquaintances do, starting with banter-weight small talk, then embarking on what felt like one of those long, casual job interviews, where you're not really sure you want the job, so you're not nervous, and the person conducting the interview isn't really sure he wants to hire you, but he's definitely reluctant to let you leave. Talking back and forth across the table, we both recognized a kindred spirit under the skin, but to the naked eye, we didn't have much in common.

Norman was sixteen years older than me, a Christian, with two grown daughters. Five years earlier, he'd founded the Willow Bend Polo and Hunt Club just outside Dallas, and while Norman himself was an egalitarian sort of guy, there were plenty of godly people in the country club set who chose not to mingle with God's Chosen People. I wasn't sure I'd be welcome there, even if I was associating with someone swanky enough to invite me.

We talked about our families—children and parents—and here again, our backgrounds were light-years apart. My childhood was far more privileged, idyllic compared with Norman's, but I could see that he cherished his upbringing the same way I cherished mine. His mother had died just a few months earlier, and he was still feeling raw about that loss, a feeling with which I could certainly identify. We traded our best stories about growing up and going out into the world. I shared a few amusing anecdotes from my travels with Suzy, and he regaled me with the tale of his great Hungarian horse-jumping mishap at the Modern Pentathlon in Budapest in 1954.

The first event was on horseback: a three-mile course with twenty-eight jumps. After that came fencing, pistol shooting, a four-hundred-meter swim, and a three-mile cross-country run. (Yes, I know. No shortage of testosterone there.) Toward the end of that first event, the horses had to jump over a fence onto a bridge, then go around a big tree.

"I figured I could save about three seconds if I took the fence at an angle and went under the tree," said Norman. "Unfortunately, the tree had other plans."

When Norman was snagged by a low branch, the horse's gait was thrown off. Going into the next jump immediately in their path, the horse fell and Norman flew from the saddle in one of those spectacularly terrifying, Superman-destroying moments that define this dangerous sport.

"I heard something when I hit the ground," he told me. "I knew something was broken, but I managed to grab hold of the reins and get back on. Finished eighth out of sixty, but I was out for the rest of the competition, which was unfortunate."

"What broke?" I asked.

"Collarbone. Right here." He indicated his left shoulder. "They hitched me up with a metal sling and knocked me out with painkillers for a few days."

"You were lucky," I said. "That could have ended badly."

"Don't I know it. But you can't think about that when you're in the saddle," he said.

"In 1954—the height of the Cold War—it's remarkable that they had Americans competing at all."

"Oh, the people were great. They're just grand, proud, strong people over there. But there were only about two dozen Americans in the whole Eastern Bloc. The next day, I came to in the hospital and found a crowd of Hungarians packed into the room, reading my American magazines, asking me about Jesse Owens and Bogey and Bacall, looking for news of the outside world. It was the darnedest thing—they were so isolated, so misinformed. These people didn't stand a chance under the Communist regime. No way to get out into the world or even know what was going on. No way to make anything of their lives other than what the government told them they could. Even at that age, I appreciated what it means to live in a free country."

I smiled, remembering Suzy. *Nothing compares with good old America.*

"I like your adventure stories," I said. "They're all about horses."

"I'm playing in a polo tournament down in Argentina later this month," said Norman. "We should go riding when I get back."

"I'd love to."

"Do you ride Western style? Or are you one of those DAR types who has to have an English saddle?"

"I can handle anything you put under me."

Norman raised one eyebrow.

"But I am a proud Daughter of the American Revolution," I added. "And a Daughter of the Confederacy."

"You don't say."

"My mother's grandfather came from Germany and settled in Kentucky."

"How'd he end up there?"

"No idea. We didn't spend much time with that side of the family, but I've seen pictures of my great-grandmother sitting on the front porch in

Hopkinsville, smoking a corncob pipe. They raised hogs. My Grandpa Leo was a butcher."

"Jewish hog farmers of the Confederacy. That's good stock." Norman laughed, crowing straight from the thorax, wide open, highly contagious.

"You have a terrific laugh," I told him. "I hate a pinched laugher. You're the polar opposite of that."

"Glad to hear it."

"So. Mr. Brinker. Is there anything else I should know about you?"

"I'm not easily smitten."

"Lucky you."

The suits were loitering over coffee and whiskeys now.

"Those gentlemen over there keep looking at us," I said.

"You're very easy to look at."

"Are you allowed to flirt with me?"

"That would be up to you," he said. "Do you play polo?"

"No, but I think I'd be good at it. Is it as dangerous as it looks?"

"People say it is." Norman shrugged. "If you took the danger out of it, I think I'd just as soon go do something else. It's like a business deal. If there's no risk, where's the fun in that?"

"I'd love to take some lessons. I really need to get . . . just get out of myself. Learn something new. Do something hard. I want to leave the last year behind and start the decade all over again."

"Why's that?"

"My sister . . . Suzy. She had breast cancer." I made a point of saying it now. Saying it the way it should have been said before. "She died."

"I'm sorry for your loss."

"Thank you. That's very kind," I said automatically.

"Cancer's a hard way to go. A hard thing on the family."

I nodded because saying anything risked my bawling like a calf. If he'd said another word, I would have had to leave the table, and what made me fall a little bit in love with this man right then was his respect for that. There was no searching for the right thing to say because he knew there were no words—or there was something beyond words—I don't know. I felt safe with him, that's all. Here was another small refuge from the wreckage: a quiet conversation with someone who had no expectation that we should rise above these losses we both knew would tower over us for the rest of our lives. There was, however, an expectation of redemption and the return of joy.

"Tell me about Little Mo," I said.

Norman's face lit up, and without hesitation, he brought her to the table with us, telling me how they met and fell in love, what she was like on the court, in the kitchen, in her business, how she shined, and how thrilled he was whenever he saw a spark of her in his daughters.

This, I realized, was how you let go of someone you love.

You don't.

When You Hear Hoofbeats

Maureen Connolly won her first Wimbledon championship in 1952. The city of San Diego was so proud of their hometown girl, they decided to present her with a car.

"Thank you," she said politely. "But could I have a horse instead?"

I imagine city council members were a bit taken aback. What seventeen-year-old girl wants a mare instead of a Mustang?

An unusual girl. To say the least.

Maureen's father, an athletic trainer for the navy, walked out when she was four. Her mother, Jessamine, was a pianist who aspired to play concert halls but wound up playing weddings. As a little girl, Maureen was wild about horses, but Jessamine couldn't afford riding lessons. What she could afford was $1.50 for a tennis racket.

A fireball is born.

Maureen was left-handed, but when she started playing on the public courts in San Diego, she was advised to switch. It felt unfamiliar, counterintuitive, but with singular focus and self-discipline, she did it. Her star began to rise. San Diego sportswriter Nelson Fisher dubbed her "Little Mo" when she was just eleven years old, comparing her backhand to the big guns on "Big Mo," the USS *Missouri*. Whether she was working out her abandonment issues or just doing what she was born to do, she tore up the courts, playing aggressively, intensely and unapologetically hypercompetitive. She wrote a sports column for the local paper, in which she waxed poetic about psyching herself up with utter loathing for her opponents.

"I have always believed greatness on a tennis court was my destiny," she wrote, "a dark destiny at times, where the court became my secret jungle and I, a lonely, fear-stricken hunter. I was a strange little girl armed with hate, fear, and a Golden Racket."

Oh, that hyperbole! Don't you love that? And who's better at it than sportswriters and seventeen-year-old girls? The two rolled into one nattily dressed sports legend who was just too fabulous for mortal kind. Back in the 1950s, Suzy and I and every other little girl in America worshipped Little Mo like she was a Marvel-made superhero. Cameras loved her, and the press decked her out in superlatives; she was the tiniest, the hugest, the fastest, the best. A new coach came into her life and taught her to play a kinder—but not gentler—tennis game. Powered by love for the sport instead of hatred for the girl on the other side of the net, Little Mo matured, as an extraordinary athlete and as an exceptional young woman. She abandoned her anger without losing that singular focus.

"All I see is my opponent," she told a reporter. "You could set off dynamite in the next court and I wouldn't notice."

During that terrible polio epidemic of 1952, at a moment when it meant so much to see this all-American phenom, so unstoppable and light on her feet, Little Mo won Wimbledon—along with the hearts of pretty much everyone in the world. The city of San Diego happily presented her with her mighty steed, Colonel Merryboy. She boarded the horse at a stable in the valley, where she met Norman Brinker, who was a born-and-bred fireball himself. He lived to ride and had earned a spot on the U.S. Equestrian Team, its youngest rider at the Olympic Games in Helsinki that summer. She asked him about horse training. He challenged her to a game of tennis. Sparks flew. About thirty minutes into the smashfest, a boy peering through the chain-link fence with about fifteen other onlookers said, "Boy, mister, do we feel sorry for you."

Norman had met his match, and he knew it.

The following year, Maureen won the Australian Open, the French Open, Wimbledon, and the U.S. Open. She was the first woman—one of only five players in the history of the game—to achieve the Grand Slam. In 1954, she won Wimbledon for a third time and for the third year in a row was voted Female Athlete of the Year by the Associated Press. That summer, she was ranked number one in the world, on a winning streak that showed no sign of slowing down, until one afternoon when she was riding Colonel Merryboy down a Mission Valley road. An oncoming cement truck startled the horse. He shied, spun sideways, and crushed Maureen's leg between his body and the moving vehicle. Her fibula was broken, muscles and tendons torn. She applied herself to rehab, and tried briefly for a comeback, but it wasn't going to happen.

At the ripe old age of nineteen, her extraordinary tennis career was over, but her extraordinary life had just begun. She'd lost none of her love for the game or for horses. All her drive, ambition, and hyperbole were perfectly intact. She just needed a new place to put all that, and because of the kind of woman she was, she didn't sit around whining about it. In the years that followed, she wrote, she rode, she taught, she brainstormed. She provided color commentary for tournament broadcasts on radio and television and shared her love of the sport, nurturing and mentoring young players around the world.

Maureen and Norman were married a year after the accident. He rose to oversee the expansion of Jack in the Box, led the team that took the company public, then left it behind to open his first coffee shop. She was by Norman's side as he laid the foundation for an empire. He was by her side as she was inducted into the International Tennis Hall of Fame and founded the Maureen Connolly Brinker Tennis Foundation. They were famously devoted to each other and had two beautiful daughters, Cindy and Brenda, who brought Maureen the full, loving family she'd longed for as a child.

"I've got everything I want," she said. "Everything I've had I got through tennis. It gave me a terribly exciting life. I met so many people in exalted positions. It opened so many doors, and it's still opening them. I've had a wonderful life. If I should leave tomorrow, I've had the experience of twenty people."

The Brinker family moved to Dallas in 1964, and Maureen enrolled at Southern Methodist University to finish the history degree she hadn't had time for when she was younger. Norman and his business partners had launched the Steak & Ale restaurant chain, and were rolling into a time of major expansion. Maureen was thirty years old and vibrantly healthy. When she began experiencing persistent back pain, it was reasonable to assume she'd pulled a muscle riding or maybe played a bit too hard with Cindy, who was starting to seriously hold her own on the tennis court.

Maureen and her physician reasonably proceeded on that reasonable assumption for several months. There's a tried-and-true philosophy applied to the practice of medicine: "When you hear hoofbeats, think horses, not zebras." It's essentially the same as Occam's razor, which states that the simplest solution is the best. It makes perfectly good sense.

Except when it doesn't.

Maureen was eventually diagnosed with ovarian cancer. Her hopes were high after surgeons initially told her they'd "gotten it all," but a year later, scans revealed the cancer metastasizing through her abdomen. Norman was beside himself. For the next year, the expansion of Steak & Ale, along with polo and everything else, took a backseat to tracking down the best care that could be found for Maureen.

The Brinkers were as tough and tenacious as they come—smart, resourceful, and financially well set. A golden couple. (In the 1978 movie *Little Mo*, Maureen was played by Glynnis O'Connor, and Mark Harmon played Norm.) The media, reporting that Maureen had "stomach" or in some cases "women's cancer," portrayed the spunky, determined champ everyone loved. If anyone could beat this, Little Mo could. But off-camera, Maureen knew she was dying, and she did an admirable job of preparing herself and her family for that eventuality. She kept up her business and charity activities and made time to visit friends, but her daughters were the center of her singular focus now. The lasting effect of her love for them is clearly evident in their lives today.

Despite his saddle-leather hide, Norman struggled under the weight of his emotions as Maureen lost ground. My heart ached when he told me about a telling incident during her last Christmas with the family. Norman left the company Christmas party to walk through the restaurant and greet customers as he always did. In the bar, a guy who'd had a few too many was throwing ice, giving the waitress a hard time, and generally being obnoxious.

Norman, who was invariably soft-spoken, kind, and unbelievably patient with this sort of thing, said, "Hey, fella. That just won't work. Why don't you go on outside and get some fresh air?"

The drunk, a head taller and a bushel of bricks heavier, sneered down at Norman.

"Sure," he slurred. "Let's go."

One thing led to another, burly words, back and forth, the guy called Norman something filthy, and Norman wheeled around with a right hook that sent the drunk flying back through the kitschy swinging saloon doors. He landed flat on his back in the vestibule. Norman's employees were stunned by this entirely aberrant event, but everyone knew what he was going through at home. If anything, it made them love and appreciate him even more. "That Time Mr. Brinker Decked the Guy" went down in restaurant history. (Frankly, it's probably the only public service the obnoxious drunk ever did; I can think of a few times when Suzy was ill where Daddy might have realized great therapeutic benefit from punching someone's lights out.)

After a last desperate trip to Memorial Sloan-Kettering Hospital in New York, Norman hired a nurse and had a hospital bed installed by a big bay window in the living room. Maureen spent a few peaceful weeks there, surrounded by a tight circle of love. She died in June 1969, the night before Wimbledon.

I owe a lot to Maureen Connolly Brinker. Wherever Norman and I went over the years, Little Mo's tennis racquet went with us, occupying a place of honor on a shelf or mantel in every home we lived in. I cherished it as a bit of women's history and a potent good luck charm. She taught my husband how to love a wife with a life of her own, how to appreciate a woman of singular focus. He was always a work-hard, play-hard kind of guy, and his marriage to Maureen taught him to respect and appreciate a woman as driven as he was.

Theirs was a rare partnership for that time and place. To understand the role of the executive's wife in the corporate culture of the 1960s, all you have to do is watch a few episodes of *Bewitched*. By and large, a wife who was decorative, quiet, and schooled in the social graces was considered an asset; a wife with talents, ideas, and ambitions of her own was quite often an *ex*. That mindset was still alive and well in the 1980s, but Norman never bought into it. Maureen had taught him the value of a life partner who has an entire life of her own. Because she was fully rounded and fully grounded in her own accomplishments, Maureen was able to stand beside him, a tower of strength, supporting him in his endeavors—and that made it a joy for him to support Maureen in hers. He found the equal partnership thrilling, and he wanted to have that—*expected* to have that—with me.

Norman's brilliance was in his ability to assess and mentor people. For him, there was no greater personal achievement than raising someone else to succeed. He had a keen sense of strategy, and he knew how to communicate direction without barking orders. Most CEOs (the good ones anyway) are visionary in the way they see the possibilities outside "business as usual"; Norman also saw the limitless possibilities inside people. And he knew how to bring them out. He loved women and thoroughly enjoyed them in all the ways you'd expect a roguish Texas millionaire to love and enjoy women. But he genuinely *liked* women, too, and it showed in his hiring practices. Like Stanley Marcus, he was eager to see women on high-trajectory career tracks, breaking through the old glass ceiling. In their early years together, Maureen was a famous professional athlete and Norman was on navy pay. As his star rose in the restaurant industry, it frustrated him to see promising careers stifled by the old folkway that claims a woman shouldn't out-earn her man, and he brought up his daughters to believe in their own potential.

Norman was enormously instrumental in the early success of Susan G. Komen for the Cure, not because of his money, but because of his dynamic participation on the board, his unique understanding of what's at stake for a family when a woman has cancer—and because of the way he mentored and believed in me.

In the management of a multimillion-dollar corporation or the emotion-fueled solar system of a giant nonprofit foundation, a firm grip on reality must be maintained. Certainly, a key component to managing one's own cancer treatment or the treatment of a loved one is managing expectations, which means chiseling some kind of reality-based tunnel between statistics and hope. There's no practical value in leaping to unlikely conclusions, whether you're talking about a fantastically unlikely good thing—such as a little girl with a dollar-and-a-half tennis racket achieving a Grand Slam—or an extremely unlikely bad thing—such as a back spasm turning out to be ovarian cancer.

To keep the chessboard moving and for the sake of our own sanity, when we hear hoofbeats, we think horses. It's reasonable to think horses. It's *comforting* to think horses. But it's sadly self-limiting—and occasionally dangerous—to pretend zebras don't exist.

Perhaps the legacy of Little Mo is the ability to keep both feet firmly on the asphalt while maintaining an unquestioning belief in the extraordinary. I see it in her daughters and in the children who compete in the "Little Mo" International Open.

I saw it in Norman, and he helped me see it in myself.

10

Flying into Love

The people staring at us from the neighboring tables at Chateaubriand eventually finished their lunches and made their way out. Norman and I lingered in the empty dining room. He listened and laughed as I told him about selling Girl Scout cookies with Boppie, riding horses with Suzy—the quiet adventure of my family's life together. I don't remember him glancing once at his watch.

He told me about his childhood in Roswell, New Mexico, about learning to jump horses with a Western saddle, and learning to play polo with the Ivy League boys. He talked about the navy, Little Mo, his children, his faith, and his booming business. Norman had invested $5,500 in the start-up of Steak & Ale in 1966. Ten years later, it was turning over millions of dollars in annual sales. Now he'd been brought into the Pillsbury Corporation and was on a fast track to the top of the second-largest food service company in the world. The business thrilled and energized him; he told restaurant war stories with the same relish as he told horse war stories, punctuating them with "Brinker Principles" like:

Begin with the end in mind.
Let natural curiosity lead the way.
And my favorite: 2 + 2 = 5.

Oh, how I would learn the truth of that one in years to come! Susan G. Komen for the Cure epitomizes the idea that the whole is far greater than the sum of its parts. Norman's business philosophy—which was really a way of life—fascinated me. So much of what he said resonated the way practical wisdom does when it connects with something you already know deep in your heart.

"Well, Norman," I said finally. "This has been delightful, but it's time for me to get my son from school."

We stood up, and I thought about giving him one of those casual hugs you give a man with potential—just enough to let him know what's what and sneak a deep breath near his collar—but while I was debating it, Norman offered his hand.

"It's been a pleasure, Nancy. I'm intrigued."

The grip was warm and firm, purposeful, but not like he was doing it on purpose. I could still feel it after he let go. We walked out into the sunshine and handed the valet our parking stubs. As we waited for our cars, Norman regarded me with his tilted smile.

"I like your hair," he said.

"Thank you." Of course, I felt the usual compulsion to say something about how out-of-control it was, but I felt a sharp glance from Suzy. She'd worked hard for years to teach me that *thank you* is the only proper response to a compliment.

"There's a surfeit of blondes in this town," said Norman. "It's refreshing to see a beautiful brunette."

The valet limped an ancient blue station wagon to the curb. When it lurched to a stop, the tailpipe bobbed like it was about to fall off, and something dark dribbled from the undercarriage. The valet hopped out and handed the keys to Norman. I laughed till I had tears in my eyes.

"Okay, now *I'm* intrigued," I said. "Would you like to have dinner with me?"

"I would, but . . ." He hesitated, then shook his head. "I'm not free to do that right now."

"I understand."

"I'll call you when I get back from Argentina."

"When is that?"

"Mid-November."

It sounded like a long time. I'd never made a practice of sitting by the phone, and I wasn't about to start now. But two days later, Norman called.

"Hey, Bruni. Let's go riding before I leave for Argentina."

Heading out to the barn, he noted that we had a "well-matched stride," and I laughed, because I was thinking the same thing. I was thinking a lot of things. Now I wondered if he was thinking, too, and it soon became apparent that he was.

I hadn't been on a horse in a while, but everything I'd always loved about riding lifted me up the moment I was in the saddle. It meant something to me that Norman didn't give me some docile old trudger, just as it meant something to me that Dr. Blumenschein never condescended when we talked science. My mount was as high-spirited as Norman's, and we lit out across the meadow shoulder to shoulder. Every once in a while, we slowed down to talk, easily picking up threads of conversation, revisiting some topics from our long lunch.

Norman was the single smartest man I'd ever met. He was a staunch conservative, but not the miserly kind; he was the same sort of old-school Republican my father was, a product of the Land of Opportunity, who genuinely believed in personal responsibility, civic duty, and the rising tide that floats all boats. He was a generous listener and an animated talker. I'd always thought he cut a pretty fine figure in his tux, but now I was seeing him in his natural habitat. Norman belonged outdoors. He wore his hat well and rode with the kind of confidence that makes a horse relaxed and brave. It was the sexiest thing I'd ever seen.

"Thank you for this, Norman." I must have said it a dozen times that afternoon. "It feels so good to be outside, stretching my legs and *doing* something."

I lay in bed that night, my whole body singing with life, my brain revving on everything we'd talked about, my heart opening up for the first time in years. Mae West used to say a man's kiss is his signature, and that was true of Norman. He was foursquare, straightforward, curious, unafraid. For the first time in my life, I felt like I could return a kiss without holding back. I was "snowed," as Suzy would have said: completely smitten, full of oxygen and light.

"Suzy? I think I love this man." I ached with everything I wanted to tell her. "If he doesn't call me when he gets back, . . ."

The phone rang.

"I was thinking about you," said Norman.

"I was thinking about you, too."

"Want to go riding with me tomorrow?"

"I want to do everything with you tomorrow."

"Careful. A reckless man would take you up on that."

"I dare you."

"Keep your boots on, Bruni. I can't get involved in anything until after the election."

"I understand," I said, and I did. It wouldn't work to have gossip distracting from his goals right now. I stretched, holding the phone close to my cheek. "My mother says if we lose Carter, we lose our soul. Daddy says Reagan is our only hope for solvency."

"Your daddy and I are going to get along just fine," said Norman. "Which side of the line are you on?"

"I don't believe there is a line. I vote my conscience. Right now, I have one political flour sifter: *What's best for women with breast cancer?* Republican or Democrat, he or she, I don't care where they stand on oil embargos, cattle prods, or how to fry an egg."

"Maybe that works on a local level, but in a presidential election, you have to set aside special interests and look at the big picture. It's rationale like that that got us into the state we're in with this economy."

"Norman, I'm not saying that if Idi Amin could cure breast cancer, I'd be out campaigning for him, but . . . wait a minute. When do you leave for Argentina? Norman, you won't miss voting, will you? Absentee ballots don't have the same zing. Not for a presidential election."

"I'm going the day after."

"Thank goodness. I'm not sure I could marry a man who votes absentee."

He huffed a startled chuff of laughter. "Let's not get ahead of ourselves."

"Why do people always say that? What are they worried about— falling off a cliff? Stepping on their own shadows? I *want* to get ahead of myself, Norman. I've been trying my whole life to leave myself in the rearview mirror and speed up to the person I'm supposed to be. Suzy's the only one who ever *dug* that about me. Other people tell me I'm being intense."

"You are intense," said Norman. "That's what I like about you. Drive, passion—that's how you get somewhere in this world."

He was quiet for a moment.

"Let's go riding tomorrow," he said. "I have to meet this guy to go over some building plans, but after that—well, we'd have to eat in, but if you don't mind my cooking, we could have dinner."

"That sounds nice."

It was nice.

We rode all afternoon, and Norman noted with pleasure that I took no longer than he did to shower, change, and get ready to meet the real estate developer. After dinner, Norman and I sat in front of the fire for a long time. Talking sometimes, sometimes not talking. I drifted off with my head on his shoulder, feeling like I'd never lived anywhere else. When I mumbled something to that effect, he pressed his mouth to the top of my head.

"I'm looking forward to seeing where you go," he said. "Once you figure out how to settle down and focus your efforts. You've got a lot of potential."

"So do you, Norman. So much inside you waiting to come out."

He laughed that wide-open laugh. "I can't believe you said that. You're incredible."

"I need to go. School night for the babysitter."

"Hey, Bruni." He caught my hand as I got up to go. "Come with me to Argentina."

"I appreciate the offer, Norman, but I won't travel with a man who's not my husband. I wasn't brought up that way. And my son's not being brought up that way either."

Norman nodded and walked me out to my car. "I'll call you when I get back."

"Who knows? I might be married to someone else by then."

"Not a chance," he said. "You're not everyone's cup of tea."

"All right. Fine. I'll marry you."

"On the other hand, there might be somebody out there crazier than me. Better let this dog hunt."

"What does that mean?" I asked Suzy as I drove to work the next day. "*Let this dog hunt.* I've been in Texas for twelve years. I thought I'd heard all the cryptic ranching aphorisms. Seriously, Suz. Am I the dog? Am I the hunter? Am I the subject of said hunt? I don't get it."

She'd been gone three months now. It was getting harder to hear the things she used to say, and that disturbed me. So much had happened since she died—her death itself being the most profoundly ground-shaking event of my life—and now here was this new thing. I was free-falling in love the way she'd always wished for me. When I was with Norman, I was completely happy. When I was alone, I kept tripping over little potholes of loss. Places where Suzy wasn't. Moments that didn't include her.

Jewish tradition doesn't embrace the idea of a literal afterlife where souls are assigned to either Heaven or Hell, but there's a lot of room in reformed thought for all kinds of possibilities, including Einstein's assertion that energy can't be destroyed, only transformed. Suzy's energy was formidable; the transformation of it had to cause a ripple somewhere in the universe. But where?

"I keep trying to feel her," I told Mom. "You know how people say they feel the presence of a loved one who's passed away."

"Oh, I know," she sighed. "Someone in the grocery store told me she was always finding pennies, and she just knew it was a sign from her dead husband. I scrutinized every penny I saw for days. Seemed more like a sign of how low the value of a penny is. Not even worth a knee bend for most people who drop one."

"I didn't think I could ever be happy again, and now whenever I am happy, I feel like a traitor."

"Oh, sweetheart, that's just . . . meshugah. Not right in the head. Live your life. You're happy? Be happy. I'm happy *for* you. And you know Suzy would be happy for you. Suzy loved for everybody to be in love."

"I talk to her sometimes, Mommy. Does that make me meshugah?"

"Of course not," she said. "You talked to her every day of your life for thirty-two years. You can't just quit cold turkey."

"What if Norman goes to Argentina and I never see him again?"

"Then you'll be happy with someone else," she said. "There's other fish in the sea."

"Not like this fish. This is an extremely good fish."

She didn't say anything about the difference in our ages. Or that he wasn't Jewish. Mom and Daddy had mellowed, I think. Issues that once seemed worth arguing over were no longer worth a disturbance of our fragile peace.

Norman called the next day. "Come over and watch the election results. Bring your boy with you."

"No," I said flatly. "I'll get a babysitter."

"I'd like to meet him."

"You will. If you call me when you get back from Argentina."

"I said I'll call you. That's my word."

"I'm glad to hear that, Norman, but this is my son. If you're not ready to eat dinner with us in a public place, you don't need to be in his life."

"I can respect that," he said tightly.

"Thank you."

We shared election night. Missed the returns. Woke up to find Reagan ready to restore hopes of solvency to my father and his fellow American Dreamers.

Norman asked me to go with him to the airport the next day. We had lunch with his daughter Cindy before he caught his flight to South America. The little girl I remembered from Neiman Marcus had evolved into an articulate, poised young woman just out of college, ready to take on the world. I suppose there was potential for awkwardness there—I was closer to Cindy's age than I was to Norman's, and things seemed to be moving pretty fast—but Cindy knew about Suzy, and because she had a sister she loved more than life, she met me with warmth and compassion.

I don't remember how the conversation meandered up to it, but we were talking about the general concept of stepparenting, and she asked me if I thought it was possible to truly love someone else's child. I'd been wondering about that myself; as hungry as I was for love in those days, Eric's well-being was my first concern. It felt so good to be head over heels that, selfishly, I didn't want to complicate things by piling a fleet of toy trucks and building blocks in Norman's lap. More important, I wasn't willing to risk Eric's heart being broken. I was already out there—ahead of myself—and there was no turning back, but I wasn't going to take Eric out there on the limb with me until I knew the answer to Cindy's question.

"Is it possible to truly love someone else's child?"

I looked at this girl who was the reflection of a woman I'd always admired and the man I'd decided I couldn't live without.

"It's possible," I said. "In fact, if you really love someone, . . . you can't help it."

A few days later, I got one of those crackly, echoing overseas phone calls we were grateful to get back then.

"Norman? Are you all right? How's the tournament?"

"It's good. Are you still single?"

"So far. Hurry back."

"I will."

He wrote me a letter telling me how beautiful it was and how beautiful I was and how much he wished we were together there. I wrote back in kind and heard not another word for eight interminable days. I was about to crawl out of my skin when he called me from Chicago.

"I'm back. I missed you."

"I missed you, too, Norman. I can't wait to see you."

"We're having dinner," he said. "Bring Eric."

In the early 1950s, a Dallas socialite named Nancy Ann Smith attended a spectacular charity ball at the Waldorf-Astoria. Swept up in the spectacle of New York City's upper crust in all its glory—and duly impressed by the amount of money raised for disadvantaged children—she returned to Texas, rallied a contingent of ladies who were up to her standards, and organized the first annual Crystal Charity Ball. The Crystal Ball quickly became *the* holiday event to see and be seen at, and in the fifty-odd years since then, the ball and related fashion shows, silent auctions, and luncheons have generated over $88 million to benefit children's charities in the Dallas area.

When Norman asked me to go with him, he felt the need to add, "The other lady I asked couldn't go."

I guess this was his way of applying the brakes, letting me know he wasn't about to be roped into anything.

"Norman," I said with an exaggerated sigh. "For the last time. I said I'd marry you. You don't have to keep trying to impress me."

I loved seeing the startled look on his face when I teased him like that.

~

My beautiful sister, Susan G. Komen. A homecoming queen in pink ribbons and matching pumps; looking very *Mad Men* at the World's Fair in 1965; modeling for a local furrier even after she'd started chemo.

A beautiful and industrious teenager during the Great Depression, Mommy took the dazzling collar she's wearing here from one of Aunt Rose's old evening gowns and sewed it on a succession of dresses.

My parents, Marvin and Ellie Goodman. They first saw each other when Mommy was on a date with someone else. She handily wrapped that up and met Daddy at ten; they were married just a few months later.

Suzy was born in 1943. Mommy wrote to Boppie, "Has there ever been a baby so loved and babbled over? No! We're inventing ways to spoil this child."

Me, mom, and Suzy, happily heading off on our rounds in wintery Peoria. Mommy instilled in us the joy of helping others.

The Goodman family in 1949: (l to r) Suzy, Daddy, Mommy, and me.

The Goodman girls out to dinner with the family. Mommy thinks this was the bon voyage party before our European adventure in 1965, but it could have been any of a thousand big and small occasions when we came together to celebrate as a family.

My proud parents came to see me being crowned May Queen just before I graduated from the University of Illinois in 1968.

Norman Brinker as I will always remember and love him. A fearless horseman, brilliant entrepreneur, generous mentor, and joyful spirit.

Valentine's Day, 1981. Mommy arrived for our engagement party and said, "You're grown-ups. Why not just go to city hall and get on with your lives?" We surprised everyone that night by celebrating our happy marriage instead of the world's shortest engagement.

Brenda and Cindy opened their hearts to Eric and me. Norman was so proud of his girls, and it's a great gift to still have them in my life.

Polo was a big part of our lives. I loved every minute. Still bald from chemo in 1984, I was back on that pony, sporting a new pink helmet, ready to take SGK to the next level.

Former First Lady Betty Ford was a terrific friend to our organization and to me personally. Eric and I were thrilled to meet her for the first time at the airport in Dallas.

Sharing a laugh with then New York governor Mario Cuomo (right after Eric and I stole his lamb chop). Even as a kid, Eric knew we were hanging out with some extraordinary people. Norm always told him, "Listen and learn." And Eric always did.

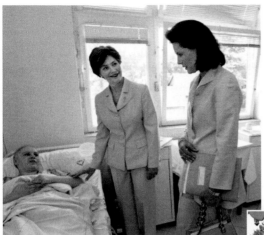

My friend Laura Bush visited me in Hungary in 2003, and we looked in on cancer patients in a Budapest hospital. Imagine what it meant to this woman to open her eyes and find the first lady of the United States smiling down at her, squeezing her hand, and saying, "You can do this. We're with you."

Leaving the White House with the Dalai Lama in 2007. Wherever he goes, he leaves an amazing wake of peace and joy.

We pinked the Chain Bridge in Hungary in 2003 and the Great Pyramids at Giza in 2009 (and illuminated the White House in between).

Scott and Marnie's home in St. Louis with Suzy's granddaughters, Maddie and Abbie Komen.

Today, Eric is a successful businessman and member of the SGK board. I'm so proud of the good man he's grown up to be.

Mom is filled with pride and wonder at what our amazing volunteer family has accomplished in Suzy's name. After the Medal of Freedom ceremony in 2009, we celebrated with friends and colleagues, full of hope and memories, envisioning a future without breast cancer.

Women on the prowl were supposed to be subtle about it. Don't scare the man off, heavens no. Norman liked it that I had no intention of prowling. And I wouldn't have been in love with a man who was that easily scared off.

I'd been to the Crystal Ball back in my Neiman Marcus days and to what felt like a thousand tony charity galas, brunches, and lunches since then. After a while they all started to blur together, but this one I do remember. Norman had been late with his RSVP, and the event had been oversold, so we were seated at one of the extra tables outside the ballroom. I'm sure the rest of the partygoers out in the hall were disgruntled about the arrangement, but we were thrilled. Not a soul got in or out of that ballroom without passing directly by us, and we made the most of the opportunity to meet and greet everyone.

As the evening went on, Norman and I worked the party in perfect harmony. The few people he didn't know from business or political functions, I knew from arts luncheons and cancer fundraisers.

"Norman. By the fountain." I tipped my chin toward someone I knew he needed to talk to. "Let's spend a few minutes there, swing left, sweep right, finish the room on a straight path toward the foyer."

"Sounds good, Bruni."

We reached the grandstand just as the mayor and his wife were being presented. The rest of the evening felt a lot like that big waltz number from *The King and I*.

A few days later, we went to a Christmas party for the Young Presidents' Organization, then the Steak & Ale corporate Christmas party, and a steady schedule of political and social events typical of the season. After a while, we didn't have to say a word. Walking in the door, he'd give me that unabashed once-over and a look that said, *Ready?* And I'd give him a look that said, *I'm with you.*

Norman was great in a ballroom. Affable, funny, full of great stories, but eager to listen to the great stories of others. He'd become friends with Stephen Covey long before we met (and long before Covey's book *The 7 Habits of Highly Effective People* switched on a guiding light for all kinds of leaders). Norm embodied the philosophy of "Seek first to understand, then to be understood." He wasn't one of those people who suck a lot of air out of the room. There was no holding forth or holding court. Norman wasn't there to make sure everyone knew who he was; he wanted to learn who they were and what they were doing and if there was anything he could do to help. I've never known anyone as guilelessly likable as Norman Brinker, and I suspect a lot of other people would tell you the same thing.

"It's a luxury to go to these things and not have to hold somebody's hand," he told me. "I don't have to look around to make sure you're okay or stop to coach you to talk to people. I always know we're together, even when you're on the other side of the room."

Neither of us was big on public displays of affection, but the chemistry between us must have been fairly apparent. I wasn't aware of the pointed looks at first. Many eyes on Norman Brinker and this new woman he was squiring around. This younger woman.

The truth is, I'd always dated older men largely because so many of the boys who came of age with me in the late 1960s smoked pot, and Suzy and I simply didn't want to be around that. Here I was, a nice girl from a nice family, seeing a nice man who drove a really awful car. I couldn't understand why someone would glare at me in the ladies' room or make a barbed remark at the coat check.

One evening, a woman dripping in diamonds cornered Norman as we stood in a receiving line. She kissed the air next to his cheek and said, "Norman, sugar! Call me. I have someone wonderful for you to meet. I mean . . . *really.*"

Of course, now that I'm a woman of a certain age, as they say, I understand. The talent pool gets pretty shallow when it comes to men in their fifties and sixties. It's hardly a pool at all. More like a birdbath. Men my age are dating women half theirs; if I dated a man half my age, the kindest thing I'd be called is a "cougar." Back then, many women of a certain age jumped to the harshest possible conclusion when they saw me walk in on Norman's arm, and I'm probably guilty, on occasion, of jumping to the same harsh conclusions about young women I see dating up today. But I do try to curb the impulse to be catty. I remember too well what the claws felt like.

The second week of December we attended an important dinner for the World Affairs Council. Some attendees were nodding off and checking their watches during a deeply troubling after-dinner speech about the depletion of natural resources, but I was riveted by this vivid illustration of the very concept I'd been trying to get my head around.

I passed Norman a note:

So like the cancer world—funding, politics, science, culture, human factor—key is interconnectedness of all.

Norman studied it for a moment, scribbled on the back, and passed it to me.

Are you for real?

I wrote back:

US foreign mineral dependence 80% v Soviet 20%? Scary!

Norman turned it over, scribbled, passed it again.

I love you.

We were married on Valentine's Day, 1981.
I wore a red dress.

Love and Other Cannonballs

THE PEOPLE who truly love us free us to be our true selves. This was Heather Gardner Starcher's last gift to her brother Shawn Gardner.

"I'm a co-survivor," Shawn says. "Five minutes before I knew Heather had breast cancer I wouldn't have guessed it would redefine who I am and what I do, rewrite everything about my life. It's not just inspiration—though she did inspire me, always—it's a passion and my duty to do whatever I can to fight this thing."

The day Heather was diagnosed, Shawn ran out of the hospital into the rain, and he's still running. He talks about breast cancer to everyone who'll listen, including media, women's groups, and the U.S. Senate. He rallies his students at South County Secondary School in Lorton, Virginia, to participate in talent shows and Wear Pink to School Day. He and his husband, Chris Barron, bring their families together with dozens of other members of Team Heather to participate in the Susan G. Komen Global Race for the Cure every year in Washington, D.C.

At this writing, about to run their tenth Global Race, Team Heather has raised almost a quarter of a million dollars—75 percent of which stays local, funding research, prevention, and screening, as well as services for underserved women.

Growing up on a quiet street in Manchester, Ohio, the Gardners were the quintessential all-American family on the block, with conservative Catholic parents and smart, well-behaved children: Shawn, Heather, and their sister, Renee. From the time she was a teenager, Heather volunteered with Big Brothers and Big Sisters and as a counselor at Camp Wonderlung, an Ohio summer camp for kids disabled by asthma. She was bright and beautiful, the type of young woman you hope your little girl will grow up to be.

One morning in the spring of 2001, twenty-five-year-old Heather rolled over in bed, and her arm brushed a lump in her breast. Her mother had already survived breast cancer, so Heather knew the drill. She immediately went in to the doctor, and when the doctor sent her home with assurances that "Women this age don't get breast cancer," she immediately pursued a second opinion.

"The surgeon came out and just crushed our world," says Shawn. "She told us it was Stage IV. It had spread to the surrounding lymph nodes, spidered everywhere. She said it would almost certainly take Heather's life."

Shawn ran out into the rain and called Renee. Then there was a blur of activity. Tests, phone calls, logistics. Heather was admitted to Ireland Cancer Center in Cleveland. A team of specialists was assembled. They were straightforward about the gravity of the situation and the long road ahead. Heather and her family knew it was going to be rough. They formed a treatment plan, but there was something Heather needed to do before she started down that rough road.

The first Saturday in June 2001, Heather stood at the starting line for the Susan G. Komen National (now the Global) Race for the Cure in Washington, D.C., and her family stood with her.

"I think she needed to connect with other people going through this and gather her forces for what was coming," Shawn says. "It was powerful. It gave us all a lot of strength. This was huge for my mom, who was a survivor, and now her daughter was diagnosed. A lot of tears and a lot of hope, sharing stories with so many people, so many families. We weren't even thinking about raising money that first year, but we did raise a few thousand dollars. It just kind of happened without trying."

The year that followed was a roller coaster of joy and sorrow. Heather underwent a TRAM flap procedure (a mastectomy with reconstruction using skin, adipose tissue, and minor muscles from the abdomen) along with chemo and radiation. She kept working at her father's insurance agency, traveled around northeast Ohio speaking about the importance of early detection, and in the spring of 2002 married her high school sweetheart, Jason Starcher.

"She'd go hatless and wigless to treatment," Shawn remembers, "because she wanted people to ask her about it. She was eager to talk about breast cancer to other young women, older women, girls, families, everybody."

The first week of June 2002, Team Heather was back at the starting line in D.C., having expanded to include even more family and friends.

Chris was there, and Heather asked Shawn, "Who is that guy?"

"He's a friend," Shawn hedged. "This lawyer I know."

It didn't seem like the appropriate time or place to "out" himself to his conservative family—if there was such a thing as an appropriate place to shift their world on its axis.

Over the summer, Heather's cancer continued to metastasize. It had reached her brain and raged like wildfire through her organs. There was more chemo, full brain radiation, music and massage therapy, frantic late-night hospital runs. As autumn leaves turned spectacular, Heather entered in-home hospice care. She'd lost much of her sight and hearing, but Shawn sat with her for long hours, talking, listening, being together.

"I couldn't bear to have anything separate us. Not at this point. I confided in her, told her this is who I am and who Chris is. She couldn't really talk anymore, so I wasn't even sure if she actually heard or understood me, but I wanted to tell her."

Later that evening, Heather struggled to speak.

"Lawyer . . . the lawyer . . . the lawyer," she finally managed. Then she told her parents, "Don't be mad at Shawn."

"She knew it was going to be hard for them," he says.

A priest came and pronounced the Anointing of the Sick. Loved ones made their last visits. Heather died on a peaceful evening in late September, surrounded by people who loved her, leaving a company of caregivers and co-survivors who were deeply battered and sleepless with grief.

"There was this overwhelming need to just huddle together after everything we'd been through," says Shawn. "My parents were so wounded. I was torn between wanting to be there for them and hating these little white lies that had to happen to protect them. In October, I told them I was gay, and it was hard, but my mom and dad were not about to lose another child. They just embraced me and embraced Chris as part of our family."

The first week of June 2003, Chris's family joined Team Heather at the National Race for the Cure in D.C., and in the seven years since, Shawn's efforts to raise research funds and awareness have taken on the dimension of a second full-time job. As an eighth-grade English teacher, he tells his students about the dynamic of purpose and the practical magic of grassroots activism. As a warrior in this cause, he's both relentless and hopeful.

"The first time I crossed the finish line without Heather, it was emotionally exhausting, but I promised I wouldn't stop until there's a cure. Losing my sister was a catalyst that sort of shot me out of a cannon. I thought I knew where my life was going. I had my work. I wasn't out, but I think I would have taken that step eventually. Probably. I don't know. The way this has consumed my life, it's hard to imagine what I'd be doing if things had gone differently." He clears his throat and adds, "I wish I'd had a chance to find out."

This is all agonizingly familiar to me. The first time I heard Shawn Gardner give voice to what co-survivorship means to him and his family—and to Chris and his family—I was instantly back in that year after Suzy died. *Cannonball* is an apt comparison. Or perhaps this is our coping mechanism of choice. All I know is that, for Shawn and me, there's nothing voluntary about this particular volunteer work, and the same is true for many people I meet at every SGK event. The loss of a sister or mother or daughter leaves a lit fuse. Something's going to happen. Perhaps one of the most important functions of the Race for the Cure is that it gives co-survivors an opportunity to come together. It's a powerfully positive way to release that explosive energy as they struggle to find and redefine themselves and each other. Almost without fail, the love conquers all, the petty falls away, the true selves shine through.

Shawn Gardner and Chris Barron were married in March 2010, when the Religious Freedom and Civil Marriage Equality Act took effect in Washington, D.C.

In the Catholic tradition, St. Augustine's Prayer for the Sick implores: "Tend your sick ones, O Lord Christ. Rest your weary ones. Bless your dying ones. Soothe your suffering ones. Pity your afflicted ones. Shield your joyous ones. And for all your love's sake. Amen."

How moving—and how appropriate—to include co-survivors in that blessing. For the suffering, there's comfort. For the weary, rest. For the afflicted, compassion. And for love's sake, joy.

11

Outside the Box

Oh, how I wish Suzy could have been with me for Sunday afternoons at the Willow Bend Polo and Hunt Club. The place was set on a beautiful tract of land north of Dallas—an old turkey farm originally. Tired of playing on ill-kempt, open-ended fields out in the hinterlands, Norman had approached the landowner with an offer to purchase half the tract back in 1976. His plan was to build a polo field and eventually an upscale clubhouse. The landowner was so taken with the idea that he proposed they go in on it together. Five years later, thousands of spectators were coming out every weekend to see the exciting matches.

Sprinkled in with the standard Western wear, there was a lot of fabulously tasteless early eighties fashion—men in *Miami Vice* blazers with the sleeves pushed up, women in hibiscus print skirts and jewel-tone blouses equipped with shoulder pads in which we could have played Friday night football. Debutantes in Dior and Chanel mixed with modern-day cowboys in Levis and nouveau riche oilmen in Ralph Lauren. Children wheeled around on their bicycles in the parking lot, learning early to keep their balance, work up their nerve, and hit the ball. The scrappy, up-and-coming spirit of Dallas was as pervasive as the scent of fresh-cut grass and Shalimar. Suzy would have loved it.

My first several months as Mrs. Norman Brinker, I embraced and bought into everything there was to love about the lifestyle to which I instantly became accustomed. I took Mommy to the spa, shopped for clothes, and gave money to the charities I'd always supported, but mostly with elbow grease and good wishes. I relished the freedom to spend time with Eric, and while he was at school, I threw myself into learning everything about the skill and strategy of polo, starting with the basic ability to close in and hit the ball without falling off the pony. Susie Welker, the wife of the club manager, played with me. It was more fun than anything I'd done since I was a kid, a return to the childlike ability to *play*, which I didn't even know I could do anymore.

Norman was a "three-goal poloist"—rated in the top 5 percent of amateur players nationwide—and he took on every match with serious passion. He was out there to win. There was always a team of paramedics standing by; not a match was played without a concussion or a broken wrist and a few dislocated fingers. I knew if I didn't understand polo, I'd never truly understand what made Norman tick, so in the beginning, it was a way for me to learn his language. But the game quickly pulled me in. Flying up and down the field on my favorite mount, I was ahead of myself at last. I was outside myself, elated, in love, and for a few glorious moments not thinking at all about cancer. Of all the gifts Norman gave me over the years, those honeymoon months of newlywed joy are among the most precious, and in many ways, the honeymoon lasted for twelve years.

That summer, Norman and I christened five private air-conditioned boxes above the polo field, which were pretty rustic compared with the private boxes in other sports stadiums but suited the sport and our personal tastes just fine. The boxes weren't closed in; you could chat with your neighbors across the hip-high wooden divider. They were outfitted with simple cane chairs and painted plank floors. It was a safe place for Eric to play and a pleasant spot to drink iced tea with Brenda and Cindy and Norman's administrative assistant, the remarkable, irreplaceable, indispensible Margaret Valentine.

Our box was built to seat fourteen, and it was always chock-full of Norman's old buddies and new business associates, who quickly became his friends, and their wives, who quickly became my friends. A lot of these women were doing important charity work, and I was eager to volunteer to help wherever, whenever, and however possible. I also invited people I'd met through my own work in PR, media, and various charities. It was a high-powered group of people doing big and interesting things. Animated conversation echoed off the paneled walls: politics, wheeling and dealing, society gossip, and almost universally good humor. Usually, a jolly group of a dozen or so migrated over to the big Victorian club-house for dinner at dusk, after a pleasant afternoon watching Norman tear up and down the field with his team.

Susie Welker and I put together a women's team with Susie as captain, and we made our debut on a gloriously sunny Saturday at the Women's Polo Classic. We rode out all spiffed up in white jeans and sky-blue uniform shirts designed by Milo and wowed the crowd by playing just as hard as the guys.

That night, I lay in bed with Norm, cherishing the day in every aching muscle, and thinking, *Suzy should have been here.*

The promise I made weighed heavily on my heart. Many nights I lay awake for hours, thinking, *How the hell can I do this?* I had access to a certain amount of money now, but that was only part of the equation, arguably the least important component. It took a while to dawn on me: What I really had now was a platform. Just like the days when Boppie got me in the door with my Girl Scout cookies. The question was how to make the most of this opportunity, and quite honestly, the loveliness of the life I was living made it very easy to tuck that question into the back of my mind for a while.

Despite his resources, Norman and I both wanted our home life to be relatively simple and centered on family. Norman, Eric, and I sat down to dinner together every night. Cindy and Brenda were busy with their own lives, but whenever they were with us, the kitchen was alive with laughter and conversation. They took Eric under big-sister wings, and he loved them with worshipful little-brother love. I relished doing the deliciously domestic things a wife and mother does, caring for my husband and son, doing little things for my blossoming stepdaughters. But even with home, ponies, and charity activities, I was getting restless. Other than that brief period when Eric was born, I'd always worked. It was never my intention not to have a career.

Mommy sent me a wooden box in which she'd collected all the letters Suzy and I wrote home from Europe, and I felt a little guilty when I read what I wrote on our arrival in London. We'd laid hands on an American newspaper as soon as we could, hoping for news of the space flight, but finding news of the Watts riots—six days of violence that left thirty-four dead and over a thousand injured—and the body count from a bloody summer in Vietnam. Suzy and I were both distraught.

> Please, Mom and Dad, don't think I'm being melodramatic, but I can't help feeling the need to be reassured of humanity. Are we in the U.S. civilized? No, adults throw the philosophical crap about: tolerate people, act mature, be good—but then they kill each other. Now I know why Kennedy's favorite play was *Camelot*—it was real. It ended in war. May God help us, and I mean it. I'm sorry to pour myself out like this, but I can't help it. I think I may never grow up or something. Or ever be able to believe adults are basically good or people are basically rational. I admire you more and more every day. I guess people manage to stay alive and not kill each other because of "guarders" of our world like you. I just pray every day that people will stop destroying each other.

"Where did all my outrage go?" I wondered when I read that. "Where did *everybody's* outrage go?"

Mulling the numbers in those headlines—thirty-four dead, a thousand injured—and remembering how it affected me, I did some digging on one of my regular excursions to the library and came up with a startling frame of reference.

"During the ten years of the Vietnam War, about 58,000 American men and women died," I told Norman the next morning at breakfast. "During that same ten years, 339,000 American women died of breast cancer."

"Wow. If that's correct, . . ." He glanced up from his newspaper, gauging his response the way most people do when they first hear those numbers, trying to decide if it could possibly be right. Norman knew me well enough to know that it was. "That's a powerful number."

"Isn't it? It's unthinkable. Why aren't we out on the streets with anger and protest signs and T-shirts? Where are the monuments and marches? How is it that so few people care about this cause when so many are directly affected by it?"

"You know how," said Norman. "You've done enough PR to know people don't care about a cause, they care about other people."

"Agreed. There has to be a face on it."

"And they have to know about it."

"So you think it starts with awareness?"

"It starts where everything else starts," he said. "Money."

"Funding," I nodded. "That's what Blumenschein said."

"That's going to be the easy part," said Norm. "I've seen you in action. Nobody's better at fundraising than you are."

"I do know how to raise money. What I don't know is how to spend it. It's not enough to fund research; we need awareness, advocacy, support services. There's a million components to each of those, and somehow it all has to be integrated."

Norman made a flat gesture with the palm of his hand and said, "Focus, focus, focus. Begin with the end in mind."

"Well, the end would be to cure breast cancer. And to keep as many women as possible alive while we do it."

"Okay. You've defined the vision. If you were building a business, your next step would be to set goals, then seek out people with the expertise to help you get there."

"That's the way to do it. Build it like a business." I toyed with my coffee cup, carefully considering my timing. "Norman, I've been thinking about starting a foundation in Suzy's memory. Specifically for breast cancer. To keep my promise to her and realize some of the things she talked about while she was sick. Little things in some cases, but I think if it was done right, . . . Mommy always said, 'Go where people aren't and do what's not being done.' God knows, there's a lot of *not* being done in the area of breast cancer."

"It's a big undertaking," said Norman.

"It is."

"But it sounds like something you really have to do."

I put my arms around his neck and kissed him. "Thank you for knowing that."

"Do me one favor," said Norman.

"Anything."

"Please, don't call my friends."

"Of course not," I said.

I'd already collected all their names and numbers and had them neatly organized in a shoebox.

B efore Suzy died, Dr. Blumenschein had asked me to participate in a study tracking the sisters and other female relatives of cancer patients. Every six months, I went to his office for an exam and took advantage of the opportunity to pepper him with questions about conferences and clinical trials.

"I've decided to start a foundation," I told him. "I was wondering if you'd help me figure out where we can most effectively make research grants."

"Sure," he said. "There's some very exciting stuff happening on the scientific front."

"Like what?"

"One big thing on the horizon right now is monoclonal antibody therapy."

"Monoclonal antibody therapy." I repeated it carefully, digging in my purse for a pen and notepad so I could write it down. "How does that work?"

"It doesn't. Yet. It's just a theory. But we know that a certain type of B-cell found in multiple myeloma produces a certain type of antibody, and the hypothesis is, if a compound could be made that would deliver a toxin to a particular type of tumor in a very targeted way, we could manufacture a sort of magic bullet for that specific type of cancer, and the side effects of treatment would be minimal."

"*Magic bullet*? That's perfect! Wonderful. So we'll raise the money to fund that. That'll take—what—a year? Maybe three?"

Knowing what I know now, I have to give George Blumenschein credit for not laughing out loud.

"It's going to take a while," he said. "Ten to fifteen years."

"Ten to fifteen . . . ," I echoed. It sounded like a prison sentence.

The meagerly built group of women in Blumenschein's waiting room didn't look like they could have scraped together fifteen years among the lot of them.

"FDA approval is even further off," he said. "That's just to get viable clinical trials in place. It's going to take time. And significant funding."

"How can I learn more about what's going on in the field?"

"I'll make you a list of seminars and symposiums. The presentations tend to be pretty academic, not really intended for the general public, but you'll be able to get the gist and make some interesting connections."

I gratefully accepted the list and dutifully went to the conferences, and yes, many of the presentations were mind numbing, but I did meet people, and a nebulous plan started forming in the back of my brain. Mommy always said about this sort of thing, "You might not get all the answers, but you usually come away knowing what the questions are." I followed up every dry presentation with phone calls, lunches if they'd meet me, and many trips to the library. I spent my afternoons on a wooden chair with a stack of books on my left and a yellow legal pad on my right and hardly looked up until it was time for Eric to get home from school. I called the National Institutes of Health and said, "Send me everything you have on breast cancer." I had enough knowledge to make myself dangerous now; possibilities were blossoming inside my head.

Armed with my binder and legal pads, I attended a breast cancer seminar at Baylor Hospital in the spring of 1982 and was pleased to see a senior officer from the American Cancer Society. I cornered him during the first coffee break and introduced myself, eager to tell him about my plans for Suzy's foundation.

"We're having an organizational tea at my home next month," I told him.

He nodded and said that was nice.

"I want to firm up plans ahead of time so these ladies know what we're raising this money for. People know and trust the American Cancer Society. Believe me, I know. They feel very comfortable giving money to you. It's the perfect umbrella for us to come in and do a major project specifically dedicated to breast cancer, encompassing the key elements—awareness, advocacy, and research funding—really setting things in motion."

"Well, I applaud your enthusiasm, Mrs. Brinker," he said diplomatically. "We certainly do appreciate your support, and I assure you, we're very conscientious about how we distribute funds raised in our name."

"Yes, absolutely. That's why this is such a perfect partnership. You've got the administrative machinery in place, and you're in the best position to help us figure out the clinical trials and research specifically dealing with breast cancer."

"That's not how we do things, Mrs. Brinker. If we did a breast cancer project, we'd have to do a lymphoma project and a pancreatic project—we don't single out one disease."

"But breast cancer is the number-two killer of women. I'm sure you know that better than I do. But thirty years ago, one in twenty women were diagnosed with breast cancer, now it's one in thirteen. Ten years from now . . ."

"Yes, I'm familiar with those numbers," he said.

"When people start hearing about this, there's going to be a ground-swell of great concern. There's going to be a real outcry."

"There should be," he nodded gravely. "But what experience has taught us—frankly, Mrs. Brinker, it won't work. People are receptive to general messages about cancer, but breast cancer is a very private matter for the patient and not something people want to see up on a billboard."

"But women *need* to see it on a billboard. They need to know it's out there and it's okay to talk about it. We have so little idea of what this thing is until it's in our lives in a very big way, and then—well, then you're in crisis mode. Then talking time is over. You need to access information immediately and be ready to take action."

"You're right about that. We've created some excellent brochures and booklets, and of course, we have our Reach to Recovery program."

"Yes, all that is terrific. I so appreciate everything you've done. But my vision for my sister's foundation . . ."

"Yes," he said, glancing at his watch. "As I said, you can be sure that whatever funds you raise will be put to very good use. We can certainly earmark donations for research related to breast cancer. A wonderful group of ladies in Houston supplied the Reach to Recovery gift bags today. We'd be happy to send some with you for your tea party."

"Actually, it's an organizational . . ." I bit my lip and offered my hand. "Thanks so much for your time. I truly do appreciate the work you've done."

Over the next thirty years, this gentleman and I laughed a lot about that conversation. Often in the context of Susan G. Komen for the Cure handing the American Cancer Society a check for $5 or $6 million. He was a great man, the ACS is a great organization, and I still believe in the importance of working collaboratively. We're happy to fund projects within the ACS and within other organizations—some of whom turn around and criticize us in the media, along with the critics who turn around and copy us. I don't care; as long as they're providing meaningful help for women with breast cancer, I support them.

And I have to wonder what would have happened if the response from the ACS had been different, if they'd taken us in. Or if any of the other hospitals, foundations, or institutions I approached had taken us in. Things would have turned out very differently, and I rather like the way things have turned out, aside from the fact that I really had planned to be done by now. I genuinely thought it would take ten years. The vaccine would be announced. The bells would ring. The factories would shut down for the day, and mothers would cover their faces and cry the way they did the day polio became an anachronism.

I had told Suzy, "I promise. Even if it takes the rest of my life . . ."

I had no inkling that it actually would.

When I told Norm my plan to find an umbrella organization had met with defeat, he could tell I was feeling stung.

"Did you really listen to what people were saying to you?" he asked.

"Yes," I said. "But they're saying a breast cancer–specific foundation isn't viable. And they seem to assume this is a whim—like I'm dabbling in this to keep myself busy between shopping sprees."

"That's understandable, based on the information they have."

"But they're wrong!"

"Prove it," he said with that tilted smile.

I invited about two dozen ladies to the first organizational tea for what would become the Susan G. Komen Breast Cancer Foundation on July 22, 1982. Ten or twelve attended, every one of them a smart, capable, fabulous woman who has my undying gratitude. I think all of us were there because we'd lost someone we loved to breast cancer. It was personal. The conversation was committed and energized, a deep breath of fresh air after all the nay-saying I'd been listening to.

We had a little over $200, which I'd squirreled away from my grocery budget. Someone brought a typewriter I could borrow. And I had my shoebox.

It made sense to have our first big event at Willow Bend because I knew the place like the back of my hand and figured I could get the biggest bang for our buck there.

"You always want to look bigger than you are," Norman sagely advised.

This happening was all about launching our tiny foundation in a very big way. Maximum visibility at minimum expense, diving for the deepest possible pockets. I had my shoebox of names, plus all the goodwill and the Rolodex fodder I'd built through years of helping others with their fundraising efforts. Annette Strauss, a city council member who went on to become mayor of Dallas, co-chaired the event with her charming daughter Nancy, and they had quite a shoebox of their own. Soon we had RSVPs for a very promising lawn party at the polo grounds.

I wanted so much for this to be a lovely, lovely day. I envisioned the women stepping out of their cars into the glorious sunshine of a classic Dallas autumn. We took great pains to decorate the place in a way that evoked elegance, femininity, and grace—my way of bringing Suzy's spirit to the place. Pink crepe paper streamers fluttered in the breeze below tufted pink paper roses. The porch rails and patios were festooned and pleated within an inch of their lives. The land once occupied by the polo club has been absorbed into the city suburbs now, but back then it was out in the country, a fairly substantial drive from the upscale neighborhoods in town. The parking lot was large but not paved. The dining room was spacious enough for the Sunday crowd, but we were going for the garden-party feel with attendees strolling about the beautifully green grounds.

Almost everything we said about our plans for the day included phrases like "as long as it doesn't rain" or "assuming the weather is on our side." Knock wood. Salt over the shoulder. Fingers crossed. It really wasn't a stretch to assume it would be lovely, because most Dallas autumn days feature the stunning cloudless blue sky the camera zooms in on during the opening theme of the television show *Dallas*.

Of course, speaking the very words *lawn party* is probably the most effective rain dance ever devised. We should dispatch to every drought-stricken area on Earth a contingent of well-heeled Junior Leaguers in white shoes and wide-brimmed hats with instructions to stage an elaborate afternoon social under the dependable sun. Storm clouds will roll in. Guaranteed. That morning, it looked like the entire Gulf of Mexico had evaporated into the atmosphere and was pouring down on us. Standing at my kitchen window, watching the sky fall, I felt Norman's hand on my shoulder.

"You okay?"

"No one's going to drive all the way out there in this downpour," I said. "We're going to have to hustle out our husbands, kids, dogs . . . anybody we can get. I feel sick thinking about the money we laid out for catering, flowers. . . ."

"I thought you got most of that donated."

"Well, it cost *them* money. And it cost us a favor we could have used on a better day."

"On the other hand," he said, "don't overlook the opportunity here. If people don't come out for the event, you can blame the weather. It's a freebie. You'd be able to try a different tack without looking like you got thrown off the horse."

He was good, I'm telling you. Norman Brinker was really good.

Heartened, I put myself together in a tailored pink suit, did my makeup, got ready to meet whatever the day had in store.

"Okay, Suzy. Let's go do this."

Walking out the door into the impenetrable humidity, I could physically feel my hair swelling like a sea urchin. The rain had slowed to a drizzle, but the drive to Willow Bend was treacherous and slow. The radio jabbered about the freak storm, telling people to stay home. Thanks a lot. The only vehicles in the parking lot belonged to the food service workers who'd braved the weather out of loyalty to Norman, I suppose. Our sodden crepe paper decorations dangled heavily from the front porch. Some of the pink streamers had been beaten down and lay in squiggles like earthworms on the flagstone patio. But my wonderful team of volunteers arrived on time, dashing through the rain with umbrellas flapping and hats pulled down over their ears, and we all gamely went about putting the finishing touches on our preparations.

A little while before the luncheon was scheduled to begin, I stepped out onto the porch. The rain had let up for the moment, but the gray sky hunkered low over the old turkey farm. It was quiet except for an occasional distant whinny from the stables. The outbuildings were all but invisible through the mist. Strangled bunting had blown down onto the polo field.

"Suzy, I'm sorry. I said I wouldn't fail you, and I have. This is a disaster."

With tears burning my eyes, I tramped across the driveway and minced out onto the lawn, my heels poking through the soggy Saint Augustine grass as I made my way out onto the field to pick up the trashed decorations. Mud sucked at my white pumps with every step. Every time I stooped to retrieve a piece of wet bunting, dots spattered my suit. It didn't matter now. Thunder growled, and I started weeping.

It wasn't supposed to be like this. Suzy and I were supposed to do it together.

Every once in a while, especially during the first few years she was gone, the loss of my sister hit me with a fresh vengeance, pulled a string deep in my chest, and unraveled me from the inside out. I stood there on the polo field and sobbed hard, wrenching sobs.

"I'm sorry, Suzy, I'm sorry. . . ."

When I could breathe again, I straightened my shoulders and cleared my throat. It was time to go in, thank people, and send them home with plastic bags and foil packets of petit fours and crudités. My ruined shoes made a slurping sound when I tried to move my feet. Suzy would have been hysterical at that, but because I couldn't hear her laughter, I started crying again, and then I was laughing, because Suzy would have known anything this tragic had to be hilarious.

I waded a few yards across the field, just to smell the wet grass and storm clouds.

A spark caught my eye on the horizon. What looked like a firefly. And then another and another, flickering, appearing and disappearing at the smudged hemline where the meadow met the glowering sky.

Headlights, I realized. Lots of them.

Pickup trucks and town cars, mom-style minivans, a small but steady trickle of vehicles wound its way up the country lane and through the gate, dropping passengers at the clubhouse, then wallowing out to the muddy parking area, sliding into crooked rows, wheels spinning in the mire. Dozens of cars turned into hundreds, a steady stream of headlights emerging from the mist. It reminded me of the stream of firefly headlights wending their way to our front porch in search of Suzy. Just like that bevy of boys, they came because they loved her. Maybe not my Suzy; none of these people had known her. They each had their own Suzy—or they were the Suzy for someone else.

I hurried back to the clubhouse, pausing to stuff the soggy bunting in a trash can as I dashed up to the porch. A pretty young girl from the local paper stood there.

"Looks like you struck a chord."

"I guess we did," I said, dabbing at my eye makeup, scuffing my ruined shoes on a welcome mat.

"My only personal experience with breast cancer was with my mother's best friend. She lived a block away, and no one knew she had breast cancer until she died. You just didn't speak of it. This is amazing." She nodded toward the wallowed parking lot. "You do know this is amazing, right?"

"*Yes.* I'm—I'm definitely amazed. I'm just so grateful they came."

And they kept coming.

I Hope You Dance

JUST SIXTEEN and already talking about majoring in business, Brooks Byers was about to learn one of Norman's prime Brinker Principles: "Be persistent. Keep knocking on doors."

I first learned this lesson from my father. Even as a child, when someone told me no, all I heard was the first two letters of "not yet." But Daddy, along with Boppie and my industrious uncles, also taught me that this is a good quality only when used for good instead of greed. In the ethical practice of business, the *why* of a deal is more important than the *how much*. The most powerful lesson every mentee learns is how to care for others. What you get is vanishingly unimportant compared with who you bring along.

In the fall of 2009, Brooks approached department stores in his hometown, Flower Mound, Texas, requesting permission to set up a table and wrap gifts during the Christmas season as a way to raise money for breast cancer research. He organized a list of stores, called around and collected the names of all the managers, typed up neatly addressed business letters, got into his church clothes, and went out to hand-deliver the polite requests.

"One just said no without a reason, one never responded, some said it was against store policy, somebody said a group in the past ruined it for everybody. The manager at the Christian bookstore was pretty nasty. That one was a surprise."

Brooks's dad, a marketing executive, told him, "When you're pitching, if you get five out of a hundred, that's successful."

"I only needed one," says Brooks. "I didn't expect it to be that hard."

He got his yes from Susan Held, manager of a local Belk Department Store.

"She was really excited," says Brooks. "Came down two or three times to check on us on Black Friday. The people who worked there were a lot more customer service–oriented in general. And a lot happier. To me, that says she's a great manager."

He roped in a few friends, and they wrapped gifts every weekend from Thanksgiving until Christmas, raising about $500 for Susan G. Komen for the Cure, about the same amount he'd raised for SGK that summer with a tennis clinic for neighborhood kids. Susan Held speculated that perhaps he got the negative responses initially because breast cancer seems like an unusual interest for a teenage boy. She suspected Brooks had a pretty solid *why*.

His great-grandmother died of breast cancer when he was two, but Brooks was seven when his grandmother died. He remembers. "Even when she was in chemo, she'd walk with me when I rode my bike or get down on the floor and play."

Brooks was fifteen when his mother was diagnosed.

His little sister, Annemarie, was eight, a blossoming ballerina.

"I didn't want to tell him right away," says Christy Baily-Byers, a communications teacher at Southern Methodist University. "Brooks was born going on forty. He's so responsible, such a caretaker by nature, I didn't want him to take too much of this on himself. I was determined the disease wouldn't define me. I kept teaching through it all—tamoxifen, Lupron, Taxotere, Cytoxin. Sometimes my back hurt so badly, Annemarie had to dress me, but I went to work. We ate a lot of takeout. I was too fatigued to do errands, so Brooks drove me around with his learner's permit."

Christy scheduled chemo around the family vacation to Europe that summer.

"We'd been planning it for a long time, and I wasn't sure how many more family trips there'd be," Christy says, but then she rushes to qualify, "because the kids grow up so fast."

She lost her hair in Paris. Annemarie went with her to the wig shop and charmed the French salesladies, dancing around in a bouffant do.

With a strong family history of breast cancer, Christy had done her homework. One of the regular guest speakers in her classroom was SGK communications specialist Melissa Anderson. Christy had herself tested for the BRCA genes, and the results were negative, but her oncologist cautioned that we've only just begun to understand other genetic factors. Some scientists think the age at diagnosis may drop with each generation in some families with hereditary cancer, and there does seem to be a pattern in Christy's family.

"My grandmother was in her seventies. My mom was fifty-six. I was forty-three. . . ." Christy looks over her shoulder at Annemarie. "I try not to go there in my head. I don't want her to grow up with a cloud over her, so I won't talk to her about it until some point in the future. Meanwhile, we do every little thing that might help. I've read and read. I'm careful to avoid hormones in meat or poultry. She's in ballet. They say exercise might help. Brooks is determined to do whatever he can to help find the answer before she gets there."

It's possible, if not probable, that Christy has passed on to Annemarie a genetic predisposition for breast cancer. But it's a solid certainty that she and her husband have also passed to their children life lessons in perseverance, grace under pressure, pragmatic optimism, and vigilance when it comes to caring for themselves and each other. Looking back, I see my father's guiding wisdom in every pivotal decision of my life. When he was living, he was always there, nudging me to ask the right questions instead of handing me the answers. His belief in me was unshakable, and the example he set guides me still.

LaSalle Leffall, another towering mentor in my life—and the lives of thousands of others—likes to quote Henry Brooks Adams: "A teacher affects an eternity."

As LaSalle was growing up in the segregated South, his godmother's husband was the only black physician in his hometown, but his parents and teachers instilled in him potent messages of purpose and possibility. As a black student in the 1940s, Howard University was one of only two medical schools open to him, but he graduated first in his class in 1952 and went on to become president of the American Cancer Society, the American College of Surgeons, and the American Society of Surgical Oncologists. He's taught 5,000 of the 7,500 physicians who've graduated from Howard.

When LaSalle was about the age Annemarie Byers is now, he found a bird with a broken wing.

"Why don't you try to put a splint on it?" his father suggested.

With shades of the exactitude that would one day make him a great surgeon, LaSalle carefully splinted the bird's wing and fed it bread crumbs and drops of water for several days. His eyes still shine when he tells how it eventually grew strong and flew away.

A beautiful metaphor for both medicine and mentoring.

Brooks Byers, with his innate sixteen-going-on-forty understanding of all this, will prosper in business school, I predict. But more than I enjoy imagining how far he'll fly, I relish the thought of those he'll take with him. He'll go out into the world and build on the lessons he's learned from his father and mother and other mentors who've shown him the way. And if all our vigilant prayers are heard, his little sister will grow up, grow old, and teach her granddaughters to dance.

12

Follow the Leader

Response to our soggy maiden voyage event was immediate and astounding, and it grew with every event we did that first year.

Susan Carter, the young reporter I met that rainy day at Willow Bend, worked for a group of community newspapers in the Dallas area, covering local events and human-interest stories. That day, she hurried back to the newspaper office with a raft of hastily scratched notes and a roll of great photos.

"My editor and I sat there trying to figure out how we were going to report this story," she told me later. "We could call it 'female cancer' or 'a woman's cancer' but you made it clear you wanted us to say 'breast cancer.' And the name of the organization made it impossible for us to avoid it."

Susan had graduated with a degree in journalism from Texas Christian University in the late 1970s, part of that forward-thinking *Our Bodies, Ourselves* generation, who grew up in jeans and tie-dye instead of girdles and crinoline. The lexicon was changing, and it was time for genteel Southern sensibilities to catch up. Susan pushed the story through and kept an eye on other SGK events over the next few years, making sure we got our share of column inches and volunteering whenever she could. She landed a job at a top PR firm in Dallas, eventually launched her own PR firm, and became Susan Carter Johns. Her major meat-and-potato accounts included Coors and Strohs, and on the side, she helped us define and refine branding for our events, including Race for the Cure and our annual awards luncheon. (It's been years since she came to work for us full-time, and we still tease her about the fact that her whole career has been beer and breasts.)

Thanks to the hard work of our volunteers and the generosity of our donors, in our very first year we were able to award two research grants, totaling $30,000, to M. D. Anderson and Baylor University. There was no question in my mind now; that groundswell I'd been certain of came from an aching need. So many women had been silent for so long, questions unanswered, stories untold. They wanted their voices to be heard and needed to know that someone would listen. Some came to honor a loved one they'd lost, others to fight for the life of a loved one who was still hanging on. Some were fighting for their own lives and were desperate for any kind of handhold. Some had lived with the specter of breast cancer in their family and were hungry for hard information about how to protect themselves and their daughters.

Armed with information and resources, we went to groups of professional women, PTA moms, proactive movers and shakers in churches and synagogues—those lionesses who get so much done—and we went to the media with a simple mandate: Shine a light on this disease. We wanted people to see the faces and know the numbers that summed up the real and alarming scope of emotional, physical, and financial damage being wreaked by breast cancer. During the early years of SGK, this work was tremendously time-consuming—almost like having another child who needed constant nurturing—but during that time, Norman and I were forging our small, ironclad family unit. He felt strongly that success in business was pointless, improbable even, if you weren't successful as a human being. To Norman, that meant being fully engaged in family life, active in the community, and willing to take a political stand. He did all that, along with ski trips and long afternoon rides, and still managed to fit in his passion for polo.

I have to back up for a moment and talk about Norman and Eric.

The two of them formed a bond all their own. They were the guys. Eric had been through a lot in his short years. Norman was strict but endlessly patient. He had high expectations for Eric, the way my father had for me, and that scared me a little because I'd begun to suspect that Eric saw the same tangled hieroglyphics I'd seen as a child. I couldn't bear the thought of this bright, motivated little boy growing up feeling like he'd always have his nose pressed to the glass. Early in his school years, we had him tested, and he was diagnosed with dyslexia. It had a name. It was real. And it could be dealt with. We expected no less from him; there were no excuses, no lowering of the bar. But we were determined to provide him with the tools he needed, not only to deal with this challenge but to turn it into the same backhanded blessing it ultimately was for me.

In the spring of 1983, while my friends and I were putting together our next event, Norman was getting restless with his job at Pillsbury. He'd headed up a restructuring of Burger King, which was a lot of fun for him, but now the chain was firmly on course in its new direction, and he was dealing with the ongoing operations (read "lumbering bureaucracy") and traveling 150,000 miles a year. He started looking around for something new, something challenging, and got into an interesting conversation with Larry Lavine, the founder of Chili's, which at that time was just a small burger chain. Norman tried hard to steer Pillsbury toward acquiring it. He wanted to grow the chain by sharpening the concept and incentivizing managers with stock and profit sharing. He called me, as he always did on his way out of a board meeting, and I could hear the disappointment in his voice.

"They decided not to go for it."

"Oh, Norm, I'm sorry."

"Oh, well," he sighed. "Onward and upward. No use dwelling. I just can't help feeling we're missing a real opportunity."

"Norman . . ." I hated to tell him, but I had to. "He sold it to Saga. It was in the paper today."

Norman was not a cussing man, but he gritted his teeth and groaned.

"Maybe you can salvage it," I said. "It couldn't possibly be a done deal yet. They're undoubtedly still working it out. You could call Larry Lavine and . . . Norman, you could do the deal yourself, if you wanted to."

"That's exactly what I was thinking."

"Norm, you should do it. Call him right now. I'll get everything ready for a meeting. Just bring him right here to the living room. No boardroom, just friends sitting around talking."

"It's a risk."

"If it wasn't a risk," I said, "what fun would it be?"

Fast-forward past all the horse trading; Norman ended up buying a large share of the company, with plans to take it public. He resigned from Pillsbury. I thought my father was going to have a stroke.

"He did *what*? Nancy, a marriage is a financial partnership. You're jointly responsible for any . . ."

"Daddy, calm down."

He pressed his palms together. "Help me understand. How did he finance this?"

Truthfully, I was cloudy on the finances of the whole thing. All I knew was that Norman would do whatever it took to make it work, and I'd do whatever I could to help him.

"Norman is brilliant," I said. "I trust him. It'll be a tremendous success."

"If something happens to him," said Daddy, "you and I are in the restaurant business, and I don't know anything about the restaurant business."

I waved that aside. "Daddy, relax. Nothing's going to happen."

Something promptly happened. My dad was no fool.

Over the Fourth of July weekend, Norm was playing in a polo tournament at Willow Bend. Tuesday was to be the first day of the new era at Chili's. All the managers were convening for a big meeting so Norm could set them on fire with his bold new strategy for the company. Saturday afternoon, tearing down the polo field, his horse's leg got nicked by another player's mount. The poor animal buckled and went down, hurling Norman out of the saddle and onto the hard ground. That night he lay in the hospital with broken ribs and a cracked pelvis.

"I don't have time for this," he told me.

"Tell me how I can help. Mom and Daddy are here, so Eric's covered. What can I do?"

"We need to gather the team together as planned. And I need to helm that. They need to see they can depend on me."

We decided to bring the mountain to Muhammad, as they say.

Norman called Ducky-Bob's party supply and ordered chairs while I wheeled the second bed out to the hallway. Mommy, Margaret Valentine, and I rushed around, getting everything we needed to cater the cramped but memorable event, and on Tuesday morning, about three dozen top members of the Chili's team jammed into Norman's room at Presbyterian Hospital. Norman didn't want his people to see him lying down, so I'd helped him get into a jogging suit and robe, and propped him up on one of those rolling carts they use to distribute meals. He was in unthinkable pain, but he spoke to them from his heart about how much he appreciated them, how committed he was to the success of the organization, and how far they could all go together.

That day was an education for me. I'll never forget it. Standing in the doorway, watching the reaction of the men and women gathered there, I witnessed the powerful effect of unwavering, uncomplaining, uncompromising leadership. It changed me. It was one of those moments when you say to yourself, *That's what I want to be when I grow up.* And you know you've grown up a little already, simply because you recognize it.

By 1984, our humble but proud $200 had become $150,000.

As word got out—what we were doing and what we were about—people came forward both asking for and offering help. News coverage on our research grants brought a flurry of requests from scientists, physicians, facilities, and support programs. The SGK office was in my guest room. We didn't have the science advisory board we have now; the board members and I spent long hours in marathon meetings, going through the grant requests. Relying on double-blind peer review to keep things impeccably honest, we depended on the expertise of Dr. Blumenschein and Dr. Bill McGuire, founder of the San Antonio Breast Cancer Symposium, as we weighed the possible impact of each proposal and made the difficult choices about where to put our funds. From early on, we were clear in our own minds about our mission: increase awareness, fund research, and improve access to care.

Norman was on the board of directors from the beginning, and we talked a lot about the responsibility we owed our generous patrons. These people had given large amounts of money with complete faith that we'd use it to save women's lives. We never for a moment took these gifts for granted—we still don't—so we were committed to keeping costs down and making the most of every dime. I had to be strategic about asking Norman's friends for money. He was growing a business, and there's an etiquette to that. Likewise, it wouldn't have been kosher for him to bankroll SGK at the expense of other good causes he'd always supported.

I was adamant about our organization staying in the black, setting aside enough for two grant cycles. We set up an endowment, resisting the urge to spend money on operating costs like a facility or staff. When it got to a point where our guest room was bursting at the seams, Norman offered us a small office space at Chili's corporate headquarters, and we gratefully moved in with borrowed chairs and desks and stacks of cardboard file boxes. We all worked on a volunteer basis, including the administrative assistant, who couldn't type, which didn't matter, because the typewriter didn't work.

Kay Bailey Hutchison was there from the start, a dynamic businesswoman just beginning her career in politics. Margaret Hunt Hill and Ruth Altshuler gave us our first $100,000 checks. (Ruth called me when I was on my way to Fort Worth, and I almost drove right off the road, I was so excited.) Sharon McCutchin, Alinda Wikirt, Margaret McDermott, Diana Strauss, Sydney Huffines—I probably shouldn't mention names because there were so many in this early band of angels, there's no way I can begin to acknowledge or introduce each of them. Mom was enthusiastically supportive, of course, and so were Brenda and Cindy and Margaret.

There were still a few people who disapproved and let me know it. Some people couldn't get past the idea that there was something inherently salacious in the word *breast,* and talking or hearing about breasts made them uncomfortable. I'm sure a lot of people scribbled that check as fast as they could in hopes that I'd just go away. (Nothing wrong with hoping.) I'm embarrassed now when I think about the way I bullied my way into every conversation with statistics, death counts, warning symptoms—tenderness, nipple leakage, nothing was off-limits—and always the earnest pitch for help in the form of time, energy, and money. More than a few times, I felt the gentle touch of Norman's index finger under the table at a dinner party or on my elbow in the lobby at the symphony. Never did he ever try to muzzle or quash me, but there were moments when I crossed the line, and he tried as gingerly as possible to let me know.

Naturally, a few cynics rolled their eyes at all the pink and the unabashed emotion at our events, but overwhelmingly, we heard from people who believed in what we were doing and wanted to be part of it. We felt our way forward, figuring out each step as we took it. We knew that in the big picture—the proverbial "30,000-foot view"—we wanted to have an impact on both the clinic and the culture, and we were certain we could do it with a savvy combination of corporate support and grass-roots activism.

Norman suggested that I consult Nancy Jeffet, a good friend who'd helped Maureen set up and administer her foundation. I was grateful to have her by my side from the beginning.

"Make an endowment right away," she told me. "Set that money aside and don't dip into it unless the world's coming to an end. Nonprofits should never go into debt by funding ahead. If you don't have it, don't commit to it."

To my mind, this meant we had to have it. And a lot of it. The work we'd set out to do towered in front of us, a mountain to climb. When we started talking about our First Annual Awards Luncheon, I planned to implement everything I'd learned working for Stanley Marcus. Go big or stay home. This was about creating a culture people would want to be part of, that would evoke huge emotion and provoke huge response. And we had something better than a giant orchid elephant.

We had Betty Ford.

The First Lady

Elizabeth Ann Bloomer grew up in the rambunctious company of two older brothers who insisted on calling her Betty.

"It was always my dream to be called Elizabeth," she said, but Betty she was and always will be, from head to toe. As a kid, she played football and ice hockey with the boys. Sitting on the sidelines like a girl simply wasn't her style. In many ways, she and I were a lot alike. She came from a good family and lived in a pleasant neighborhood in Grand Rapids, Michigan. Her father was a successful businessman who sold conveyor belts for the Royal Rubber Company. Betty's mother, Hortense, was active in local charities, president of the local hospital for crippled children. Hortense worked hard to make everything about their home perfect.

But there was a dark undercurrent. Betty could never quite grasp what it was until she was sixteen. Her father was found dead under his car in their garage, asphyxiated by carbon monoxide. The coroner ruled it accidental, not a suicide, but there was speculation. This was how Betty learned that her father was an alcoholic and that her mother had made a lifelong industry of concealing it. Betty turned into a bit of a wild child in high school, a founding member of the "Good Cheers," a sorority that lived up to their name by drinking, smoking, and chasing boys. She spent two summers studying dance with Martha Graham and during the school year modeled for a department store. Through a brief, unhappy first marriage and beyond, she kept working, kept dancing, kept being Betty.

She met her match in Gerald Ford, once a college football hero, now a lawyer with political aspirations. They had to postpone their wedding in 1948 to accommodate his run for Congress, but that was fine with Betty, who maintained a pragmatically balanced view of their personal and political life together. Their fifty-eight-year marriage was a partnership; she knew exactly what she was getting into, and she was up for it. The president stood by his wife when she felt the need to speak out and was equally outspoken about his love and respect for her. Of all the couples who've taken up residence in the West Wing, the Fords were among the most genuinely, demonstratively in love. She brought out the boyish charm in him, and he brought out the dancer in her.

It was naïve of the White House spin doctors to think they could keep a lid on her.

During the summer of 1974, tensions knotted around Watergate built to the August resignation of President Richard Nixon. Gerald Ford had become vice president less than a year earlier, when Spiro Agnew had resigned in disgrace in October 1973. Now Ford was the president, and Betty was First Lady. The country had been torn apart by scandal and distrust, and the Fords' first order of business was to reassure the nation that we were in good hands. Determined to set a straightforward tone of openness and honesty, they appeared at a joint press conference, during which the First Lady took questions from the White House Press Corps. Not everyone liked what she had to say, but no one could deny that Betty held her own.

Asked what she considered the best role for women in the effort to end future wars, Betty tartly replied, "Well, they can always enlist and make sure."

Asked if she'd be willing to advance the cause of cancer research in hopes of continuing Nixon's declared "War on Cancer," she said, "I'd be glad to. Only too happy."

Asked how she'd like to be remembered, her answer was appropriately circumspect: "In a very kind way. As a constructive wife to the president."

She spoke a little about continuing her efforts on behalf of her "profession"—meaning the arts—and on behalf of mentally disabled children. She was inches from a clean getaway. Then someone asked if her views were closer to those of New York senator James Buckley, a conservative calling for a ban on any and all abortions, or the soon-to-be vice president, Nelson Rockefeller, who advocated the liberalization of abortion laws.

"Definitely closer to Governor Rockefeller," Betty said without hesitation.

Not surprisingly, that was the headline grabber. A White House spokesperson tried to step in the next day with modifiers and mitigation, but Betty refused to back down from her opinion, even though it differed sharply from that of her husband, who'd adamantly spoken out against *Roe v. Wade*. A feeding frenzy of negative press troubled the waters for four days, then erupted into a firestorm when President Ford announced he'd granted Nixon a full pardon. Among the complaints being made about Gerald Ford was his failure—or more accurately, his refusal—to muzzle his wife.

As the brouhaha continued, Betty quietly went about her business. On September 26, she accompanied her friend, Nancy Howe, to an appointment for a scheduled breast exam at Bethesda Naval Hospital. Nancy encouraged Betty to undergo a routine exam as well. The physician discovered a lump the size of a marble in her right breast. Exploratory surgery was scheduled almost immediately. Betty was told a biopsy would be done, and if the tumor was found to be malignant, she'd be kept under general anesthesia, and a standard radical mastectomy would be performed.

"These were the dark ages for breast cancer surgery," Betty's daughter, Susan, said later. "When you woke up, you either had a Band-Aid or no breast."

Betty woke up with no breast. And just one strand left to the pectoral muscle underneath. It never crossed her mind to keep her diagnosis a secret; she was all too familiar with the damage done by secrecy—both personal and political.

"There had been so much cover-up during Watergate that we wanted to be sure there would be no cover-up in the Ford administration. So rather than continue the traditional silence about breast cancer, we felt we had to be very public."

Betty Ford stepped up to the White House Press Corps and shifted the old lexicon beneath their feet. Graciously but firmly, she informed them that the First Lady of the United States had breast cancer. No, not "cancer" and not "a women's cancer": *breast* cancer. What a conundrum! Those words were considered unprintable in print and unspeakable in polite conversation. Did she honestly expect Walter Cronkite to talk about *breasts* on the evening news?

Yes. She did.

After the surgery, the president and First Lady mugged for cameras outside her hospital room at Bethesda, and Betty gamely tossed him a football, which had been sent to her as a gift from the Washington Redskins. She's strong and smiling in those photographs. This was the face of a breast cancer survivor. While she was convalescing, Betty received almost fifty thousand letters of support. People applauded her courage. Patients thanked her for inspiring them to press on with treatment. Survivors shared their stories and expressed what a profound relief it was to finally hear the words *breast cancer* spoken out loud.

"It's never gone underground again, which is great," Betty said. "I've never regretted it."

That moment was like a glimmer of light shining through a keyhole. And all it takes is a keyhole to reveal that what looked like a wall is in fact a doorway. Time and time again, I've seen it happen: Make that leap in language, shake loose the words, information pours out, change rushes in. The next decade brought a sea change in the public perception of breast cancer.

In 1974, Betty Ford was one of over 90,000 American women diagnosed with breast cancer; 33,000 women died.

Mammograms were widely available in the early 1970s, but not routinely done, and a 1973 Gallup poll showed that less than 20 percent of women did regular breast exams, as recommended at that time by the American Cancer Society. The first First Lady to take a stand on an issue of public health, Betty Ford used every possible opportunity to talk about the numbers and instruct women on proper BSE (breast self-exam) technique. Through the turmoil of the coming years, even as she struggled with her own recovery from alcoholism and addiction to painkillers, even as she endured media horsewhippings for her pro-choice and pro–Equal Rights Amendment views, she remained practical, generous, and loving—and outspoken about the deeply personal aspects of her breast cancer experience.

"It isn't vanity to worry about disfigurement," she said in a television interview. "It's an honest concern. I started wearing low-cut dresses as soon as the scar healed, and my worries about my appearance are now just the normal ones of staying slim and keeping my hair kempt and my makeup in order. When I asked myself whether I would rather lose a right arm or a breast, I decided I would rather have lost a breast."

The year after Mrs. Ford's diagnosis, news correspondent Betty Rollin did a report on the effects of the First Lady's forthright response to her breast cancer experience.

"The terror women feel about breast cancer is not unreasonable," said Rollin. "What is unreasonable is that women still turn their terror inward. They think if they avoid investigating the possibility that they have the disease, they will avoid the disease. But as cases of such prominent women as Betty Ford become known, other women are turning their fear into the kind of action that can save lives."

A year later, Betty Rollin was herself diagnosed with breast cancer and took awareness another giant step forward with her groundbreaking memoir, *First, You Cry.* In 1976, the American Cancer Society honored Betty Ford with its Communicator of Hope award, and that's exactly what she was for my sister, Suzy. Betty was a lighthouse for Suzy at a moment when my sister was utterly out at sea, and as soon as Betty heard what we were attempting to do in Suzy's name, she was eager to help. She was a great friend to SGK from its early days. I'll never be able to fully express what she means to me.

That very first year, we were planning a women's polo tournament at Willow Bend as a fundraiser, and I wanted to put together an extraordinary luncheon as part of the weekend festivities. One of the original benefactors from my trusty shoebox was Norman's good friend Trammel Crow, a navy man who became a captain of industry. He warmly welcomed me into his office and listened intently as I shared my plans for SGK.

"I was wondering if you'd be willing to reach out to Betty Ford on our behalf," I said. "She meant a lot to my sister and me. We'd love to have her as our guest of honor."

Trammel picked up the phone and less than two minutes later was telling the former First Lady about Suzy, SGK, and our upcoming event.

"Will I have to play polo?" asked Betty.

Quite honestly, if I'd said yes, I think she would have given it a try.

13

Run the Good Race

Norman and I slept well together. We spent all our energy every day, collapsed into bed, discovered a second wind, as honeymooners do, then drifted off for six hours of sound, fulfilling sleep in which we breathed each other's dreams. I never dreamed as much without Norman, and to this day, I miss that terribly.

This particular dream of women running was so vivid that even after all these years, I can feel it when I close my eyes. Suspended just below the surface of morning, I saw a thin strand of pink light, and I was filled with hope and longing. The strand unfurled, a wide ribbon of light and movement that became a corpus of women in all their power and glory—beautiful, vibrant, moving as one. As they neared and enveloped me in a great rush, I felt the strength of their bodies and their bonds, and I was running with them, swept into their spirit, their accord. Surrounded by laughter and music, we reached a place—or a moment or a day, something—where there was great rejoicing and great resolve. We were still in motion; we never stopped for a moment. But the runners dispersed to throw shot puts and javelins, high jumping, long jumping, fencing, playing tennis.

"What stayed with me," I told Norman the next morning, "was how strong and yet how feminine the runners were. Powerful and energized, but with this very womanly esthetic. They were all wearing pink."

Norman was always on the go the moment his feet hit the floor in the morning, but I kept thinking out loud as we put ourselves together for the day.

"You know that feeling you get watching the Olympics," I said. "You see your flag and the torch runners and the sheer will it takes to be there. Most people never get a chance to be there, but they get it. You *feel* the

Olympics in that opening ceremony. We need to make people feel this cause the same way. They don't know what breast cancer looks like. They don't hear about it on TV or read about it in the paper. Even if they know someone with breast cancer, chances are she doesn't feel free to talk about it. And frankly, she probably doesn't feel all that powerful or beautiful—but she *should*. She should have an opportunity to celebrate the fact that she's alive and she's still the beautiful, sexual, strong woman she was before this thing invaded her body."

"So where are you headed with this?" asked Norman.

"I think we should have a women's sports day. A huge event with a 10K race, tennis tournament, horseback riding, track and field—and of course, we'd have an information fair, booths for support services, the traveling mammogram facility. And we'd come up with a great way to honor survivors in the opening ceremony. Maybe have them bring the torch! Oh, that's perfect. We definitely need a torch."

"Hold on, Bruni," said Norman. Not to be negative, just reeling in enough kite string to bring me back from dreamland. "I'm not saying don't do it, but—well, for starters, I smell liability issues. And confusion."

"That's dealt with all the time, though. Everybody has 5K or 10K races these days."

In fact, Cindy was organizing one for a children's cancer charity at the time. Before I brought it up to my band of angels, I checked with her, just to make sure she wouldn't feel like I was encroaching on her event, but she was enthusiastic about my idea. My band of angels was not. Halfway through an impassioned living room speech about the torch and all that, the two co-chairs of our upcoming luncheon gently but firmly dragged me into the powder room and closed the door.

"Nancy, this isn't a good idea. We don't have the people to do this. We'll end up complicating things and diverting resources and energy from doing the kind of events we do best. Events we know will bring in a lot of money."

"This wouldn't be about the money. This is about getting out there on our feet with people in big numbers. The grassroots support we need is out there." I pointed beyond the powder room door. "We can't take this to the next level if we stay locked into this one particular group of people.

A ticket to our luncheon event costs what some people pay for a month's rent. They're not going to come, and I don't want to see them excluded."

"You're risking the base we've been building, Nancy. Everything we've been working toward for the last year. Do you personally know any women who want to go out on a Saturday morning and tear around in the heat?"

"Our base will be just fine. And I love to tear around on a Saturday morning."

But they made some good points, I had to admit.

"What if we separate the two?" I said. "We'll do the luncheon as planned, and maybe do a scaled-down version of the sports day—a 5K or a 10K race—a week or so later. But connect the two so we can capitalize on the visibility from the luncheon."

Like the song says: You can't always get what you want. Sometimes you have to go for what you need, and I was convinced we needed this. There was no way we were going to get where we needed to be without the power of the people. On the other hand, we weren't going to get anywhere at all if I alienated the angel band.

One of Norman's Brinker Principles: Involve your people in the planning process.

It took me a few tries in life, but I eventually learned that you can't bully people into believing. You win people over—or you don't. And if you're never willing to be won over, it's a safe bet your supporters won't be open to it either. It's like a saloon door; it's got to swing both ways.

The powder room consensus: Focus on the luncheon first and foremost and follow it up with a little 5K "fun run" and information fair.

Plans for our second annual luncheon proceeded like a freight train. Co-chairing this event is a Herculean, plate-spinning, champagne magnum–juggling feat of superwoman prowess, and over the years, we've been lucky enough to find the right women for the job. Laura Bush was our invitation chair that second year. (Her father-in-law, George H. W. Bush, was vice president then.) She had two little girls, a husband on his way up, and a lot on her plate in general, but she stepped up like a trouper and volunteered to stuff and address hundreds of envelopes by hand.

Attire for the Annual Susan G. Komen Breast Cancer Foundation

Awards Luncheon was not business casual. From the very first year, it was big hair, done-out dresses, designer suits. It was vintage, over-the-top Dallas, loaded with unapologetic emotion.

"Create the place and take them there," Stanley Marcus said, and that's what we did.

A darkened ballroom. A single spotlight on an American flag. Cue music. The light expands as the colors are advanced. On a giant screen, portraits of courage, beauty, and faith—women with breast cancer—our reason for being.

By this time, I'd been to a few Washington events, and if there's one thing Washington knows, it's how to get out the ceremony. There's a reason for all that pomp and circumstance; I felt it as Suzy and I watched the Changing of the Guard at Buckingham Palace, but I didn't know what it was then or why it created such a lump in my throat. It made me think about all the small and large rituals that lend structure to our lives. We formalize connection with handshakes and weddings. We mark beginnings with bar mitzvahs and ribbon cuttings. We honor the life of an individual with a christening or a funeral. We pause and direct our attention for a moment because the moment deserves that. Words are optional. Ceremonies give us a framework in which to express something bigger than words.

We've gotten rather blasé about ceremony these days—we're all so determinedly cool, so afraid to display schmaltzy emotion—but I think we feel the lack of it. If you've run yourself ragged to raise $50,000 for a good cause, just knowing that the check has been dropped in the mail is pretty anticlimactic. You want to celebrate. You want to hand that giant check to someone in front of a cheering crowd. That giant check is a big deal! It deserves a moment of "*Wow! Big check!*"—just like you deserve a cake with candles on your birthday.

Our annual luncheons redefined *big* (and put a dent in "bigger"), honoring survivors and supporters, celebrating everything our scientists had accomplished, and setting the bar high for future efforts. If there was a dry eye in the house, I didn't see it. People came away filled with gratitude for their lives, inspired to give and live and love, believing in their own capacity for heroism.

This was the spirit I wanted to see at our little fun run, but truthfully, I wasn't certain anyone would show up. I'd tried to hustle some corporate sponsorship, but that effort fell flat. Even companies that had sponsored similar events in the past didn't want to attach their names to breast cancer. A few local businesses bravely ponied up a little money, and at the last minute American Airlines came through with a small grant. Some people would have been disheartened by that response; we were thrilled. We farmed out the task of creating a separate identity and some posters for the fun run to a small advertising firm in Dallas, and they came up with a name for the event: RACE FOR THE CURE.

The moment I heard it, I said, "*Yes!* Yes, you got it exactly right."

Feeling more optimistic, I dared to think two or three hundred people would come. That would be a starting point for us to build on. More important, Mommy was going to be there, and I couldn't stand the idea of her being disappointed.

She wasn't.

That Saturday dawned drizzly and threatening, but the morning sun burned through the clouds, and about eight hundred people showed up to cheer on the runners. Everyone involved in the planning process was fairly stunned by the turnout.

The atmosphere was positively buoyant—lighthearted, with a huge sense of *yes, finally*. The information fair was swarmed. You could feel the stories in the air, so many miles traveled, so many memories that never got a chance to happen. The hope was palpable. We tenderly passed armfuls of it back and forth the way sisters pass each other a newborn at a baby shower.

I felt another frisson of *Yes, exactly right*.

This was an event we could package and take to every city in America. This was how we would turn our little charity into a movement.

A t home in Dallas, Norman and I put in a full business week and then some. We bought a ranch in McKinney, Texas, and went there on weekends, all play. We rode horses and ate Mexican food. Norman pressed Eric into service baling hay and mucking out stalls, and the two of them spent many hours shooting skeet and chauffeuring Cindy, Brenda, and me around with a horse and buggy. In Palm Beach, we played polo and went boating with Mom and Dad.

Life was good, and as Norman and I grew together, I started thinking I'd like to have a baby with him. Norman wasn't immediately on board with the idea. Brenda and Cindy were grown up and on their own. His relationship with Christina and Mark, his two children from his second marriage, was less than he would have liked it to be, and that was painful for him. (Later on, when they were older, he did become close to both of them, and it brought him a lot of joy.) He and Eric spent a lot of time together, working and playing. Norman took Eric with him to scope out new properties. They visited various restaurants in the company to meet the people who made it all happen. Norman was grateful for the bonus opportunity to be a good father, and he was a very, very good father to Eric. Norman was satisfied with that—for the moment, anyway—and I was satisfied with simply keeping the door open. (For the moment, anyway.) Most nights, I lay down next to my husband feeling completely weary and completely content with my beautiful son asleep down the hall and the beautiful baby I'd already created in my mind tucked snug and safe at the edge of my dreams.

But on a particularly chilly night during the winter of 1984, as I lay down and pulled the comforter over us, my hand brushed across my left breast, and everything changed.

The next moment I was on my feet again, trembling, fighting panic. It was as if I'd touched a tarantula in the bed.

"*Oh, my God . . . oh, God. . . .*"

Norman was instantly standing beside me. "What's wrong? Calm down. Talk to me."

"It's a lump. I felt a lump. Right here. Feel. Do you feel it?"

I took his hand and moved it to the side of my breast, watching his face. His expression remained square and calm except for the smallest tick at the side of his mouth as his thumb located the small, pebble-hard lump.

"It's different, Norman. It's hard. It's—it's like Suzy said—not like before."

"All right. Let's just stay calm," Norman said evenly. "First thing in the morning, we'll call M. D. Anderson and get you on a flight to Houston."

"Yes. Okay. I'll call Fred Ames. He has my baseline mammograms. And I know he's the best. They don't get any better than him."

Norman coaxed me to lie down again and locked his arms around me. We both lay awake for a long time, and for a long time after his breathing relaxed to a slow, deep rumble, I lay there listening to my own heart pounding: *Not this, not now, not this, not now.*

Dr. Ames was a terrific surgeon who'd been monitoring my breasts, both for my own sanity and as part of that ongoing study of the female relatives of breast cancer patients. His hands were always sure and warm, like the man himself. Sitting on edge of the exam table in his office, I exhaled and inhaled, feeling calmer.

"Nancy, I don't think it's anything to worry about." Dr. Ames smiled and patted my hand. "Feels like another benign tumor to me."

"No. This feels different. I know what my breasts feel like. The other tumors were kind of rubbery. This is hard as a rock."

"That doesn't mean it's malignant," he said patiently.

"I know that, but I want to be sure."

"I'm not recommending another biopsy, Nancy. You've had this breast biopsied three times already. Even with a needle biopsy, which isn't always accurate, we keep building scar tissue. It makes the mammograms even harder to read—and that's already an inexact science. Let's watch it for a little while and see if it changes."

I nodded. That was a logical response. Good medical reasoning. Wait and see.

I went home to Dallas. I had things to do. SGK was sponsoring a seminar on breast cancer detection the next day, and there were a million details to keep me occupied the rest of the afternoon. One of the display tables featured an array of lifelike prosthetic breasts with lumps in them, and the next morning, as I welcomed our guests, I watched the women stand there, brows knit, palpating the different types of tumors. I don't know why I'd never felt those breast forms before, but that day I did. One of them felt chillingly familiar.

As I stood there, talking to our audience that day, the knot in my heart tightened.

"A biopsy entails the excision of a lump, from which thin samples are mounted on slides for microscopic examination. The 'permanent section' takes several days to analyze. Results from the frozen section are available within minutes. If a tumor is malignant, a test—the hormone receptor assay—is done to determine if the cancer's growth is influenced by hormones. There's a lot of important research being done right now in the field of hormone therapy, and you'll be helping to support that with your donations."

The women gathered there looked up at me, trusting what I was telling them, making notes on little yellow pads as I explained the difference between a mastectomy and the new lumpectomy surgery that had now gained wide acceptance.

"If you refer to your handout, you'll see the statistical differences in . . . in survival . . . with the various forms of adjuvant therapy. These decisions are deeply personal, and it's imperative that we get all the information before . . ." I cleared my throat, thumbed through my notes. "It's our responsibility to be vigilant about our own breast health. We can't just take a physician's word for it, even when it's a physician we know and like—a physician we respect and trust. You are the CEO of your own body. Just as a business hires consultants, you look to your physicians to provide you with an expert opinion, but ultimately the decision is yours."

By the time I left the podium, my face was burning with shame and fear, and I'd decided to practice what I preached. What kind of hypocrite could tell these women to do one thing, then go home and do another? I went home and called the surgeon who'd done my three previous biopsies in Dallas.

"Dr. Fogleman, it's Nancy Goodman Brinker. I need a second opinion."

Sitting on the edge of his exam table the next day, I felt considerably less calm.

"This doesn't feel good to me, Nancy. It's small, but . . ." He shook his head and thought for a moment. "If I were you, I'd get it out."

I nodded. That was a logical response. Good medical reasoning. Get it out.

Okay, Suzy. I pushed my palms together in my lap. *Now what do I do?*

"Let's head upstairs and do a transillumination," said Dr. Fogleman.

"Maybe," I said. "Let me think about it while I get dressed."

He left the room, and I put my blouse on and combed my hair, calmly instructing myself not to overreact. Dr. Fogelman had said the same thing about the other three lumps. Everything I'd learned in the last three years was very much in keeping with Dr. Ames's solid advice. I also knew from my research that this test, which illuminates the interior of the breast (it's also called diaphanography), was probably not going to shed any light, as it were. I never considered those three biopsies that came back benign to be "unnecessary"; there was a question that needed to be answered. The only unnecessary test is one that tells you what you already know, and unfortunately, this particular test has a history of doing that, but it might reveal something about the size and shape of the tumor. I opted to do it.

Reading the results on an infrared-sensitive camera, the radiologist reported a solid round tumor with a clearly defined exterior. Like a little candy-coated gumball.

"There's definitely something there," said Fogelman.

No kidding. I bit my lip, tried to swallow my frustration.

"The radiologist thinks it's benign." He shrugged. "That well-defined border is a very good sign. Maybe watch and wait is the way to go."

I forced myself to go about my business for the next ten days, pretending to the best of my ability that everything was fine. I didn't want Norman to look at me with that somber tick at the side of his mouth. I couldn't bear to drag Mom and Daddy through this whole thing again. I wanted Eric to feel happy and secure, knowing he was loved by an invincible mommy who'd always be there for him. I went riding with Norman on the weekend, wrote thank-you letters in the evening, fixed Eric's lunch, attended board meetings and moderated discussions, and spoke pleasantly with Mommy on the phone, even though she kept asking, "Are you sure you're all right? You sound tired."

It took every ounce of self-control to keep my hands away from my breast. Every moment I was alone, I prodded and poked it, thinking, *No. It's not growing. Or . . . is it my imagination or . . .*

Something was off. It was changing.

"I think it's getting bigger," I told Fogelman.

He moved my paper gown aside and ran his fingertips across it. "I think so too."

I immediately called Dr. Ames. "I don't care what this is. I want it out. Now."

"All right. No problem," he said, trying to soothe me, but I was no longer in a mood to be soothed.

"If you don't want to do it, that's fine. I can go elsewhere, but I've made my decision."

"Nancy, I'm as confident as I can be that this thing is benign, but if it's troubling you this much, then sure, let's take it out."

"Immediately? Tomorrow?"

He sighed, good-natured, patient with the impatient patient.

"Sure. Come on down. I'll give you a local and do it right here in the office."

Norman was out of town on business, and I didn't want to wait for him to come back.

"I'm not worried," I lied to him that night on the phone. "I'd rather just go by myself and get it out of the way."

I told Mommy the same thing, then called my friend Sandy and asked if she could go to the hospital with me. Doris Bechtold, the wonderful patient care coordinator who'd taken me and my family under her wing that first day we brought Suzy in to M. D. Anderson, greeted me at the door and took me to meet Dr. Ames, who walked with me to the day surgery room.

I lay back on the gurney, and a short curtain was placed under my chin so I wouldn't be able to see the procedure. Awake and aware, I felt the sting of a needle, then nothing as the local anesthesia took effect. Focused on the faces of Dr. Ames and the assisting nurse, I looked for any sign of emotion. Horror at a breast filled with cancer. Or bemusement at this silly, hysterical woman. There was only concentration, a strange sort of artistry.

"All done," said Dr. Ames. He smiled behind his surgical mask, and I saw the corresponding crinkle at the corner of his eyes. "I'll see you in a little while with the good news."

They wheeled me to the recovery room, where I stared at the ceiling, making occasional small talk with Sandy for what seemed like hours but was probably about seventy minutes. As luck would have it, Dr. Blumenschein was gone on a ski vacation. I'd have given anything to hear his voice on the other side of the curtain surrounding my bed.

Where is he? I kept thinking. *What's taking so long?*

Then the curtain slid aside with a metallic hiss, and there was Dr. Ames.

"Well, hello there," I said unsteadily. "Another false alarm, right?"

"No," he said. "It's not a false alarm. I'm sorry, Nancy. It's cancer. I sent it back twice. They confirmed that the tumor was malignant."

He was good. Didn't drop eye contact for a moment. I wish I could say I took it well. It's not like Dr. Ames was telling me anything I didn't already know in my heart of hearts, but the words broke over me like a swarm of red wasps, and I flailed to my feet, batting at them.

"*No!* Tell me that's not right. Tell me it's—it has to be a mistake." I choked and started sobbing. "*Please, say you're not telling me this. You can't tell me this. It's not true.*"

Rage and fear pushed everything else aside and consumed me. I think I'd actually convinced myself that it was going to go the other way, that somehow—by learning enough, doing enough, working hard enough, being good enough—I'd inoculated myself in some way. Or that Mommy had. The screaming unfairness of it forked through me, not for my sake, but for hers. Why should she have to face every mother's worst nightmare twice in one lifetime? The thought of telling her, ripping her world apart again—I pushed my fist against my side, crying so hard my ribs hurt. Sandy stood there horrified, gripping my hand, knowing there was nothing to say. After a moment, Dr. Ames put his arms around me.

"All right, let's be calm," he said. "Nancy, you know the drill here. It was small. We got it early. You've got plenty of options."

"Get them off me." I gritted my teeth, forcing myself to breathe. "I want them both off. Today. Get them off me right now."

"Nancy, calm down." Ames folded his arms in front of him. "We're not making any decisions like this."

"It's my decision, and I want them gone."

"We're going to sit down and talk about it. Rationally. After you get dressed and take a minute to call Norman and . . . you should call your mom."

I suspect he knew I wouldn't be moved. This day had been hanging over my head like the Sword of Damocles since the day my sister died. I was terrified of every step on the path she'd chosen, and I wasn't going to go the same way. I wasn't going to cling to my breasts or to false hope or misplaced trust.

"I'm sitting," I told Ames a few minutes later, facing him across the desk in his office. "I'm dressed. I'm rational. I want them off."

"Nancy, I don't think that's necessary."

"It's not your call."

"No, but I'm responsible for helping you make an informed decision."

"Fred." I almost laughed. "Do you know anyone who's as over-informed about breast cancer as I am? You know I think the lumpectomy is a great option for a lot of women. I've fought for that procedure to be accepted. I've given seminars on the advantages and disadvantages. I've memorized the statistical differences. Mastectomy versus lumpectomy, with radiation or without radiation, chemo or no chemo. I also know it's guesswork. Can you honestly look me in the face and tell me for a fact that this cancer hasn't already hit my lymphatic system?"

"You know I can't promise anything. But I can assure you . . ." He re-thought the words he was about to say, knowing I'd heard it before. "Let's run some tests to make sure it hasn't spread. We'll do a full body x-ray, bone survey, blood work. Take that time to really think this through."

"Oh, I've thought it through. A thousand times. I thought it through every day while I watched my sister dying. I thought it through every time I felt anything bigger than a mosquito bite on my breast." I took a breath, trying to ease the angry edge in my voice. "The tumor is close to the nipple. The cosmetic advantage of a lumpectomy doesn't even apply here. Why should I risk my life—to *any* statistical degree—in order to hang on to a breast that's going to be disfigured and misshapen anyway? For whose benefit would I be doing that?"

"I can agree with that, but what about the right breast? Removing it would be purely prophylactic."

"That's correct," I said without flinching.

"You know as well as I do, the jury's still out on the efficacy of that."

"Well, it's not the jury's call either."

I looked at my hands in my lap, cold but steady. I felt as poised as anyone prepared to jump off a cliff, hoping for deep water instead of rocks.

"Can you take the left breast off tomorrow?" I asked. "We can discuss the rest after we get the test results."

Dr. Ames nodded. "Sounds like a plan."

He and Doris Bechtold walked me through the battery of tests. Everything but my lymph nodes appeared clear. We wouldn't know about those until the mastectomy was done. I was admitted to the hospital, and Mom and Norman arrived that evening. I tried hard to be strong because I could see the weariness and fear in their faces, but the sedative I'd been offered (and gratefully swallowed) left me feeling weepy and philosophical. Every time I closed my eyes I could see Suzy, skinny, scarred, and shivering in the hotel bathtub, her translucent skin no longer able to contain the cancer that ravaged her.

"Mommy?" I didn't realize I was dozing until I jolted awake. "Where's Eric?"

"He's at home. Norman went home to be with him."

"Oh, God, he must be so scared. And Norman. And *you* must be so scared, Mommy. Are you okay?"

"I'm just fine. Does it hurt?"

"Not really. I just keep touching it because . . . I'll never feel it again."

"I know," she said, stroking my forehead. "But that's tomorrow."

"Tomorrow." I nodded. "Tomorrow, Mom, we declare war."

"Yes." She didn't look at me like I was dying. "Tomorrow, it's war."

"Tonight I just want to feel it." I cupped my hand over my breast, moving my thumb over the nipple the way Norman did sometimes in his sleep. "It isn't a bad-looking breast."

"It's beautiful," Mommy smiled. "You wear it well."

"What should I do about the other one?"

"You'll know when the time comes."

I rolled onto my side, and Mommy lay down on the bed with me, spoon-style. I closed my eyes again, allowing myself to be lulled. She talked quietly about being out on the water with Daddy, about the newly remodeled kitchen at Camp Tapawingo, and the matching butterfly blouses Suzy and I had when we were little. There was no pity or fear in her voice. Her hand on my back was relaxed and warm. She had a cot brought to the room so she could stay with me, and her confident, steady tone got me through the night. Every time I jolted awake, she was there beside me in the dark.

"Mom?"

"Right here, sweetheart."

"It's going to be just like Suzy."

"No. Don't even start down that road."

But I was already down the road and around the bend. No one could convince me otherwise. For the first time I think I truly understood how desolate Suzy must have felt.

"Mom, when I'm gone . . . you have to hold on to Eric."

"We'll both hold on to him. You're not going anywhere."

"I'll never have a baby with Norman. We were just getting started. Getting each other figured out. I love him so much, Mommy. What if he looks at me tomorrow and . . . what if he doesn't think I'm beautiful anymore?"

"He knows what's beautiful about you, and it'll still be there."

"He's already been through this once, and it tore his heart out. I can't stand the thought of doing it to him all over again. I can't stand hurting you and Daddy . . . leaving Eric . . . letting Suzy down. I promised her it would be different, and now here I am. Nothing's changed."

"Everything has changed," said Mommy. "You've changed. That's how I know you'll be all right."

I vaguely remember being wheeled into the operating theater early the next morning. Before they put me under, I touched my breast. I didn't feel warlike. I certainly didn't see my breast as the enemy. I felt mournful, and my breast felt soft as a rose hip. I tried to touch it one last time as I felt myself drifting away, but when I lifted my arm, it was as heavy and numb as the stone wing of a cemetery angel. The dulled tips of my fingers found the edge of a bandage and some plastic tubing.

It was over.

I'd taken that first terrible step toward survivorship.

Living One Step Ahead

Bridget Mooney Spence walks with purpose. Still in her twenties, she's come a long way, and she has every intention of going a lot further.

Growing up with three brothers, Bridget was as rough and tumble as she needed to be, but firmly grounded in girly-girlness in the tight-knit community of the all-girls school she attended in Baltimore. It was a loving sisterhood, and Bridget's upbringing—like Suzy's and mine—instilled in her a sense of stewardship. When she was in high school, she and her classmates participated in a Race for the Cure. Bridget remembers it as a lot of fun, everyone in pink, feeling good about the day, but she and her friends didn't take much notice of the survivors at that event. Those were mothers and teachers, older ladies—the ones who get breast cancer—and Bridget and her friends were busy being young and invincible. Which is exactly as it should be.

Bridget went on to Boston University to study international relations. Her dream was to travel the world in the Foreign Service, and the opportunity to study abroad during her junior year brought maturity and clarity to that vision. She experienced Europe with the same thrilled appreciation Suzy and I did and returned to Boston for her senior year in 2003.

She wasn't hypervigilant about doing a monthly breast self-exam. Why would she be? She was only twenty-one, not in any particular high-risk pool, no family history of breast cancer. But with all the reminders—all that pink flapping around every October—Bridget gave it a casual go once in a while, and one morning in the shower, she did feel something peculiar.

"The Mooneys don't get sick," she says. "We never go to the doctor.

I didn't even have a doctor in Boston. Mom made my regular appointments at home during vacation."

But when the small, firm lump didn't go away, she did confide in a friend, who encouraged her to go to the public health clinic for an OB/GYN exam. Bridget was reassured that this was a fibroma, nothing to worry about at her age—certainly not breast cancer. A mammogram was deemed unnecessary.

Bridget's biggest worry that semester was where to go for spring break. With all her credits nailed down, she was antsy for graduation, and she was six months into one of those euphoric First Great Romance sort of relationships with a tall, red-haired New Englander named Alex Spence. They'd said the *L* word. Life was good. But by the end of the school year, Bridget's stomach was unpredictable and her energy low. The lump in her breast, barely detectable at first, was clearly palpable now, almost protruding. She'd begun to notice a vaguely yellow cast to her complexion, a subtle warning of the cancer that had metastasized to her liver.

"I didn't know what jaundice is," she shrugs. "I kept thinking I was partying too hard or maybe had mono—the kind of stuff they tell you to worry about at this age. STDs. Stuff like that."

When Bridget's family arrived for graduation, her mother was startled and deeply concerned. She consulted the head of Johns Hopkins and had her daughter on the next flight to Baltimore. Arriving at the hospital with orders for an ultrasound and mammogram, Bridget was asked, "Why are you here?"

"They kept giving me a hard time," she says. "Everyone kept saying, *This isn't right. You're too young.*"

Bridget was diagnosed with Stage IV breast cancer. (And it *isn't* right. She *is* too young.)

"I'm well spoken, and I have a good handle on my emotions," she says. "I got through all those conversations just fine, but when I went to tell Alex, I was a blubbering mess. He's a button-down guy, a New Englander—not a gusher—but he scooped me up and let me cry, and then he said, 'Put on a party dress. We'll go out to dinner and talk about how to deal with this.' He's a high-school English teacher, God love him, so he has summers off. He moved into my parents' house and became best friends with my brothers."

"The first step is chemo," her oncologist told her. "We'll operate later. If at all."

The possibility of a cure didn't even enter the conversation; the objective was to keep her alive as long as possible, and the clear assumption was that she would be on some kind of chemo regimen for whatever time she had left.

"The worst part for me was having to move home," Bridget sighs. "I love my family, but I felt like such a dork, hanging out with my parents."

She started Adriamycin in combination with Taxol; results were immediate and better than expected. The tumor in her liver shrank to the extent that all visible traces of cancer completely evaporated from scans. After a lumpectomy and an intense course of radiation, Bridget went on Herceptin—a brand name for trastuzumab—a powerful new weapon in the breast cancer arsenal.

Herceptin is a monoclonal antibody therapy that uses ingeniously engineered molecules to create a smart little drug that attaches to specific defects in a cancer cell and mimics the natural immune response. Because cancer is essentially part of the host's body, the immune system—which is designed to spot and attack invaders—doesn't recognize it as dangerous. Monoclonal antibody therapies recognize cancer, attach to and reprogram growth receptors on the cell surface, and deliver radioactive particles that kill the cancer cell without damaging healthy cells nearby, which means the side effects are nothing like the havoc wreaked by treatments that are, of necessity, highly toxic.

The cancer cell is like a serial killer hanging out in a bar; he just blends in with everybody else. Herceptin walks in and—*hello*—knows him immediately for what he is. She lets him buy her a martini, takes him out for a tango, slips a toxic Mickey in his drink when he's not looking, and—*bam*—one less serial killer on the dance floor.

While Bridget was growing up, controversy swirled around clinical trials for this promising drug. Women who'd come to the end of their treatment options were frantic to get in; families tried to go over and under the table, angling for the right slot in the double-blind studies. Researchers (funded in part by SGK) fought to keep it all by the book, laboring through the rightly rigorous process of getting the drugs approved, available, and insured.

"I thank God every day for the people who took Herceptin before me—everyone who made it possible," says Bridget. "I felt like I'd bought myself some time. They were still negative. 'Oh, you won't live ten years.' But I felt positive."

She set out to get her life back: got an internship at a magazine, went to visit friends in New York, and landed a corporate job as an IT recruiter in Boston. Before she left home again, Bridget and her family threw a giant party, inviting everyone who'd sent her a card since she started chemo. It wasn't a going-away party; it was a celebration of moving forward.

A month later, the cancer in her liver revealed itself again.

Bridget attended her first Race for the Cure as a survivor in 2005 and connected with other young survivors, including Deb Kirkland, who started Breast Friends in Baltimore and later traveled with me to Budapest for the Global Advocate Summit. Our Baltimore affiliate was started by my stepdaughter, Brenda Brinker Bottum, whose mother—the famous tennis champion Maureen "Little Mo" Connolly—died of ovarian cancer at a heart-wrenchingly early age.

It's a small world for young survivors.

In this company, Bridget felt comfortable in her own skin for the first time since she was diagnosed. She hadn't even considered going without a wig before this. Deb immediately saw the potential in this bright, beautiful girl who was so able to articulate the challenges specific to young women with breast cancer—including the obstacles that delay diagnosis with catastrophic consequences.

"I want to take you to the sororities," she said. "They'll listen to you, and they need to hear that breast cancer isn't just something that happens to your grandmother."

Bridget got involved, stuffing envelopes, speaking to college students. She liked the IT job well enough, but started looking for an opportunity to become something more. In 2008, she decided to take on the Susan G. Komen for the Cure 3-Day event in Washington, D.C., and loved it so much, she turned around and did the San Diego 3-Day, walking a total of 120 miles to raise $6,000. Two weeks after she crossed the finish line, she and Alex Spence were engaged. A few weeks later, the cancer recurred in her lymph nodes.

"The fairy tale is supposed to be different." She talks about her lost innocence with some sadness and a thin edge of anger, but no bitterness. "I had to wake up to the fact that this happy ending I kept banking on was not going to happen. This isn't going to go away, but that doesn't mean we can't have a full and happy life together."

"I've integrated it into my life," says Bridget, "and I think I can keep it up for a long time, but I hate when people use the word *chronic* or compare it to diabetes. It's not like that, where you can find a baseline and maintain it. This is periods of *Hey, it's okay* and then fever-pitch emotion—this foreign thing is growing in you. I beg them to find some way to buy me another eighteen months, and somehow they do, and then we start all over again. I've managed to find a purpose in it, but I hurt for Alex. Who would choose this?"

Alex's answer to that question: "You don't choose who you can't live without."

The nodes were removed, and Bridget finished chemo just before the wedding. The two enjoyed an idyllic honeymoon and two months of wedded bliss—then another diagnosis, followed by a mastectomy. Bridget and Alex have accepted that cancer treatment is always going to be part of their life, but for the moment, Bridget is cancer-free. And for them, the moment is all that matters.

She doesn't dream of the Foreign Service anymore; the life she's fighting for is centered here at home. More than anything, she wants to have children with Alex and be there with him to see them grow up. She thinks about writing a book. She thinks about turning forty. She's no longer banking on the fairy-tale ending, but she has a great deal of faith that new, better treatments will continue to come along as she needs them. Meanwhile, she helps others cope with the specific challenges of being a young cancer survivor and works for us as a coach, facilitating participants in the Susan G. Komen 3-Day events. Having found her purpose, she's determined to keep putting one foot in front of the other.

Bridget Mooney Spence was born two months before the very first Race for the Cure event in 1983. When she was in high school, she helped us provide funding for self-exam education, awareness, and the clinical trials that brought monoclonal antibody therapies into common use.

Herceptin was made available to her just in the nick of time. Bridget considers herself incredibly lucky; each setback has occurred in the shadow of a hard-won advance. This remarkable young woman has been literally one step ahead of the disease her entire life.

I am desperate to keep up with her.

~ 14 ~

Purpose in Perspective

The morning after my mastectomy, an orderly stopped in to tell me a woman from Reach to Recovery was on her way up to greet me.

"Tell her if she does, I'll throw her ass out along with the damn falsies."

I wasn't in the mood to reach for recovery that day. Nothing against it—it's been a wonderful program for a lot of years, a trailblazer, God love them. But there's this idea floating around that people with cancer are obligated to be plucky about it. We're told to spackle on that positive attitude like television makeup, and here again I had to wonder, for whose benefit would I be doing that? The person who's patting my hand and telling me not to be upset? Why shouldn't I be upset? Moments like this are why God *created* upset.

Betty Ford was one of the first people to call me when this snowball started rolling downhill, and she gave me some very good advice.

"Take a day to cry. Get angry. Throw a tantrum. Feel terrible for yourself. Get it all out of your system, then get over it. Get on with it. Get through it." She mulled that for a moment, then pragmatically added, "You don't have to do it all in one calendar day. You could do it an hour at a time and spread it out over a few weeks."

She also warned me about lymphedema in my arm on the side where sentinel nodes (the lymph nodes closest to a malignant tumor) had been removed and talked to me about some of the other strange little nuts and bolts of the situation. Instead of telling me how I should feel, she shared with me what she'd felt, which reassured me that I wasn't going crazy. There was a strange burning over the front of my body—not the deep agony you'd expect when you're cringing at the thought of this surgery and certainly nothing like women must have endured after the old Halsted procedures—but the swarming sensation was insanely unpleasant.

Mostly, I was aching with inactivity and bristling at everyone hovering and scolding. I had things to do, a son to take care of, a flourishing foundation to build. We'd had a few successful events and were preparing for our second big luncheon, expecting seven or eight hundred people. Betty was presenting the award we'd named for her.

"Would it be all right if I bring my husband?" she'd asked.

It was all right, all right. We were thrilled! But adding President Ford to the head table took both expectations and logistics to a whole new level.

"I don't have time for cancer," I told Norm.

The first moment I was alone, I gingerly pulled on a robe, nipped my Sony Walkman out of my bag, and sneaked past the nurses' station to the stairway. I found my way to the physical therapy room where Suzy and I had spent hours gently working her wasting muscles and talking with other patients, particularly the children, who always loved Suzy and flocked to her the moment she showed up at the door.

Looking around the room, it seemed as if the very same people were there, trudging on treadmills and pedaling on stationary bikes, bald, bored, hollow eyed. A little boy who was maybe three or four years old bounced a ball against the wall while his mother spoke earnestly with the therapist nearby. His arms were spindle-thin, his little face lost and forlorn. I felt the nudge of Suzy's elbow.

"Hi there," I said.

"Hi!" He looked up and grinned, ready to play if anyone else was.

"Having fun today?"

He shook his head, then shrugged. "Do you want to play ball?"

"I wish I could. My arm feels kind of funny today." I touched the soft wisp of downy hair trying to grow back on top of his head. "We should be outside playing. It doesn't seem fair, does it?"

"We could go to the park," he volunteered hopefully.

"Another day. There will be lots of days at the park. You'll see. Today . . . do you want to listen to my music?"

He nodded enthusiastically. I handed him my Walkman and set the headphones over his ears. He waved brightly on his way out the door, and I waved back, hissing a little when I felt a corresponding burn. I climbed onto a stationary bike, settling into the new lopsided me, and managed to pedal a few miles before a nurse—the one Mommy called "Nurse Ratched" after the nurse from hell in *One Flew Over the Cuckoo's Nest*—found me and scolded me back to my room.

That sort of thing was very quickly making me crazy. I wasn't used to getting bossed around, and I didn't take it well. It chafed like sandpaper with the reeling lack of control I was already feeling. I'd have to accept that I couldn't wrangle my errant cells or mandate the future, but I needed to be allowed to call the shots. This was my body, and I'd gone to a lot of trouble to educate myself about this very situation. I needed my caregiving team to respect my decisions.

"I need to be on that bike every day," I told Norman. "I also need another Walkman. In fact, I need a dozen so I can give them to people."

The next day Blumenschein returned from his ski trip, thank God.

Straight talk ensued.

"I think you're in a good situation," he said. "There was no node involvement and your tumor was still small. I feel very optimistic about your case."

"George, I need to know I won't be . . . like Suzy."

"The first time I saw Suzy, it was a very different picture. You're nowhere near that place, and my goal is to keep you from getting there. I'm recommending that we treat this very aggressively for a number of reasons." He keyed them off on his fingers. "One: your age. As a rule, the younger the patient, the more aggressive the cancer. Statistically, thirty-seven is young to be diagnosed with cancer, and while your tumor wasn't wildly aggressive, it showed signs of being on the side of rapid growth. Two: Your hormone receptor assay was negative. Let's consider all our options and form an adjuvant therapy plan. Three: Your family history with the disease. That's paramount, Nancy. This is the same type of cancer Suzy had. We don't fully understand that genetic connection yet, but clearly it's cause for concern."

"Tell me about it," I said wryly. "From what I saw on the test results, I'm guessing my odds for long-term survival are about 85 percent. Would you agree with that?"

"I would. We can kick that up to 95 percent with chemotherapy. I'm recommending four cycles, starting as soon as the incision heals. Adria, Cytoxan, and 5-FU."

"The Adriamycin . . ." I tried to say it without wincing. "Is it still with the, um . . ."

"The subclavian catheter and pump." He nodded. "But there's been some improvement to it since Suzy had hers, and we're doing a better job with patient education on it. You'll take a class and learn everything you need to know so you can safely administer the drug to yourself outside the hospital. I know mobility is going to be important to you."

"So is staying alive."

Looking away from the sun streaks on the windowsill, I studied the ring on my finger, a get-well card Eric had drawn and taped to the wall, flowers from my parents on the nightstand. I thought about Suzy as she endured the ravages of chemotherapy. More than once I'd thought, *I would never choose to put myself through such torture. For such a slim chance at survival . . . how can she do this to herself?*

Now I knew how. Turns out it's not all that hard. The choice looked a lot less murky from my new perspective.

"I'll take the chemo," I said. "For a 10 percent boost . . . it's worth it."

A lot of people disagreed. To this day, people want to lecture me about it, and at the time, it seemed like everyone I knew in the cancer community felt entitled to render their opinion on my case. Going to board meetings, seminars, and symposiums over the next few months, I felt like a bug under a magnifying glass.

My amazing friend, Rose Kushner, was small and bony with a voice like a rusty trumpet. A pioneer. A tigress. She was out there irritating people and making them listen a long time before I came along. When Rose was diagnosed with breast cancer in 1974, she had to fight that old surgery roulette system. She went through nineteen surgeons before she found one willing to do the biopsy without the automatic mastectomy. When the biopsy came back malignant, she had to fight for a modified mastectomy instead of the Halsted radical that was still standard fare in a lot of places. And she kept fighting.

When Betty Ford was diagnosed, Rose bulldozed her way in as far as the presidential press secretary, trying to get word to Betty about modified mastectomies being done in Europe. In 1976, she was the first person to testify about breast cancer before the Senate Subcommittee on Health, and she took the opportunity to denounce the Halsted mastectomy and the single-step biopsy-mastectomy procedure, in which you went to sleep not knowing if you'd wake up with a breast.

She established the Breast Cancer Advisory Center in Maryland and was on the National Cancer Advisory Board, and by the time we met, she had a great, scrappy advocacy group she was trying to get fueled up. She instantly recognized me as someone who was annoyingly good at getting things fueled up; I instantly recognized her as a great woman who stood on the spirit of her convictions. We became fast friends, perhaps because we were very different but still had great respect for each other.

For all the reasons I was mobilized—radicalized, some would say— after Suzy's death, Rose was in there duking it out with anyone and everyone. She had strong opinions and didn't hesitate to voice them. Coming out of a contentious meeting, during which a battle had raged about clinical research versus basic research and the construction of clinical trials, Rose asked me about my treatment plans, and I told her.

"Nancy, chemo? That's crazy," she bluntly told me. "You're letting your fear rule."

"Yes, I am. But not the way you think, Rose. The more I learn about this, the more I wonder, if everything that could have been done for Suzy had been done, would she still be alive? Do you have any idea how bitter it is to live without an answer to that question? Imagine how it feels for my mother—the quintessential patient advocate—to live with the knowledge that one mistake after another was made, and that probably cost Suzy her life. This choice wasn't available to Suzy until it was too late. The fact that I have this choice at all—isn't that what we've been fighting for, Rose? A woman's right to make her own informed decision about what happens to her body?"

"Nancy." She sighed and squeezed my hand. "I know what you're going through. I know how scary it is, and I'm telling you, you don't have to do this."

"You know what it was like for you, Rose. Every person comes to this with unique parameters—genetics, histology, emotional history, resources—that's why the choice has to be in our hands and no one else's."

"It's like setting off a neutron bomb inside your body. For 10 percent."

"It's worth it to me. I need to know—and I want Mommy to know—everything that could possibly be done was done. I'm not waiting until that 10 percent advantage turns into a last-ditch effort." I chucked my notebook in my purse. "I'd rather get hit by a bus."

I started chemo and fought the downward spiral every inch, every drip, every lost eyelash of the way. Suzy used to tell me there was a metallic taste in her mouth; nothing smelled or tasted like it was supposed to. Now I understood what she meant. Along with the unpleasant aluminum foil tang at the back of my throat, I felt a creeping dread as my experience more and more closely paralleled my sister's.

"You're not Suzy," Mommy kept reminding me. "It may be the same cancer, but you're not the same person, and this isn't the same situation. Not at all."

But it tasted the same. It smelled the same. We were looking at the same sad pedestrian watercolors in the same uncomfortably cool waiting rooms. I don't know how Mommy stood it, walking those halls all over again, staying in the hotels, eating the dry cafeteria sandwiches and little crackers from the vending machines. The night after my first dose of chemo, I was wretchedly sick. Anti-emetics weren't what they are today, and the people living in the hotel rooms around us were cooking some kind of strong, pungent food on hot plates. Mommy almost took the roof off the place. She packed our things and moved us to another hotel in the middle of the night.

I cut my hair short, hoping to keep it, but it was coming out in the brush almost right away. I stepped in the shower one morning, pulled the rest off, and cleaned the shower drain, bald and weeping. Then I parked a wig on top of my head and fixed myself up to go out with Norman. I couldn't bear to have him look at me like I was pathetic. Thoughts of Maureen must have haunted him at times, but he never missed a beat. I've seen men pull away from their wives in that moment, grieving and separating from them as a measure of self-preservation. Not Norm. He made me laugh every day, and at night, he kept me in his arms and made me feel undamaged. If anything, our relationship took on an even deeper, more grown-up nature. The sexual connection of two like minds, two life forces, can withstand any impairment of the body. Cancer and aging are no match for that kind of love. I was strengthened by it every day.

Eric was nearly nine years old now: old enough to know, but too young to understand. Since he could remember, he'd been hearing about the ravages of breast cancer. He knew his Aunt Suzy had died of it. I took great pains to look and act as healthy and strong as I could in front of him. He walked in on me one morning before I had my wig on, and the sight of my bald head was a jolt. I could tell he was frightened, but also a little curious. But apparently more curious than scared. Before he left for school, I bent down to kiss him, and he nicked the wig off my head and ran off with it.

"*Eric!*" I charged after him. "Give me that thing! That's not funny!"

But of course, by the time I caught up with him and wrassled him to the ground, we were both breathless from laughing.

No matter how exhausted I was, I put myself together and plodded off to the auxiliary tea, luncheon, meeting, school function; whatever "everyday" meant, that's where I wanted to be. But I still got sicker. My mouth was full of sores; even warm broth felt like broken glass. Black, indecipherable dreams jolted me awake several times a night, and I'd lie there with my heart pounding, desperate to get some rest. It was like trying to sleep with jackals circling. At first, I'd get up and creep quietly to the kitchen, where I sat drinking wine and looking at clinical trial data. One glass became two, and on top of all the meds, that was the last thing I needed. I quickly realized I'd feel better if I forced myself to stick to a healthy eating plan and daily exercise.

I begged Blumenschein to just knock me out and give it to me all at once, but of course, that's not possible. It's one of those situations that calls for the old Winston Churchill approach: "When you're going through hell, keep going."

"Sometimes, I have to admit . . . I'm not sure this is worth it," I told Betty.

"You've studied this disease like no one else," she said. "Trust yourself. Believe in your good judgment. The rest is up to God—whatever 'God' means to you."

"Honestly, Betty, I don't know anymore."

"Remember that line in the Twenty-Third Psalm? *Yea, though I walk through the valley of the shadow of death* . . . Nancy, it says you walk *through* it. You don't stop. You get through it, one day at a time, and if a day is overwhelming, one hour at a time."

I'm more grateful than I can say for the friends who surrounded me with support during that year. Betty, Rose, Mommy, all the women who'd already given so much to SGK.

"Get out there and do things," Rose advised. "Keep a full calendar. Don't give yourself a chance to worry. And don't even entertain the thought that you might not be around to fulfill every single obligation."

I kept my hand in foundation activities, attending every organization lunch, every board meeting, every seminar and symposium, and wherever I was, I talked about what was going on with me. Some people thought I should have handled it privately and not talked about it to party guests or possible donors—not to mention the media. To their mind, I was a publicity hound, exploiting this opportunity to gain attention for the cause and money for SGK. I don't deny that. Cancer had taken a hell of a lot from me; it was about time it gave a little something back. I think there may have been a bit of smugness in their attitude: "Well, what did she *think* was going to happen if all she ever thought about was breast cancer?" As if I'd brought it on myself by speaking the words out loud, like saying "Open Sesame" outside the forbidden cave and *poof,* open it rolls.

So many dreams die with a cancer diagnosis. It's a loss of innocence, a shattering of our sense of security. My dream of having a child with Norman died with my diagnosis. The loss cut deep and still pains me. We have to honor those losses and grieve those dreams before we can truly open our eyes anew. It's natural for people to pull away from someone with cancer, simply because they don't know what to say. Or because they're terrified of it. Some need to believe that it's somehow your fault, because then they can believe it'll never happen to them. Of course, knowing that makes it no less isolating. The people who stick—those are your friends. There is a certain luxury in knowing beyond a shadow of a doubt who they are.

I'm actually far more comfortable talking about other people's cancer experiences than I am talking about my own. In fact, I *hate* talking about my own cancer experience. There's a little superstition, I suppose;

I'm frankly terrified of ever facing that cave entrance again. But more than that, I'm humbly aware and deeply grateful for the resources I had available to me, from the education and wherewithal to get a second and third opinion, right up to and including every soft pillow, room service call, and plane ticket. I had the best possible care. At the time, I was often weepy with gratitude and relief, and even now, the realization of how lucky I was leaves me with a lump in my throat. The cancer experience of a woman in a developing country—or even a woman living in poverty in the United States—is a different universe.

Never would I insult these women by pretending to know how they feel, and their plight weighed even more heavily on my heart after I'd made it through the dark valley. Every woman—no matter where she lives, whatever the color of her skin—is equally deserving of the best possible care. I doubled my resolve to make sure it would be there for her.

Love Will Find a Way

THERE'S NO such thing as a convenient time to get cancer. I've heard apocryphal tales of women diagnosed amid the choking dust of 9/11 or stranded with fresh mastectomies as water rose after Hurricane Katrina. A woman diagnosed the day before her wedding. A woman diagnosed the day her mother died. Even the quiet losses of cancer are cataclysmic, and every woman's experience is unique. No matter how much support she has, on a fundamental level, she's in it alone, and that makes her uniquely qualified to make decisions about how to go forward. Only she sees that cancer diagnosis in its true context: her life.

Kim Bloom's life was right on track. She'd started her career with a pharmaceutical giant, launching drugs and educational programs for women with osteoporosis, progressed to Wharton's executive M.B.A. program, and skyrocketed from there. In 2002, after several months of infertility treatment and in vitro fertilization, Kim and her husband were finally expecting a baby. The child they'd envisioned and fought for was growing inside her.

So was breast cancer.

Kim miscarried and in the blur of that heartbreak discovered the lump in her breast.

"I'd been doing routine self-exams all along. I knew what my breasts felt like. This wasn't right."

She was diagnosed with invasive ductile carcinoma. The lump itself was less than a centimeter in diameter, but the cancer had metastasized to six lymph nodes.

"My first question was 'Will I live?' And then I asked, 'Will I ever have a child?' My doctor responded with statistics. That's what I wanted. I'm data driven, trained by years in the drug industry. You arm yourself with the facts and go from there. I reached out to friends, family, colleagues in the industry, anyone who could help me understand and fight this disease."

The cancer was estrogen receptor positive; pregnancy was contraindicated. (A dry summation of dashed hope, if ever there was one.) Kim interviewed oncologists and surgeons, making clear that preserving her fertility was second only to fighting for her life. Before starting chemo, they used tamoxifen to stimulate ovulation, harvested four viable eggs, and froze four viable embryos. Kim chose the most aggressive treatment available to her, enrolling in a clinical trial at Sloan-Kettering: FEC (5-fluorouracil, epirubicin, and cyclophosphamide) followed by Taxol and taxane.

"Sitting in the infusion clinic, I kept thinking, *Why is this happening? I should be in a hospital having a baby.* Every week, I bought one children's book and put it on a shelf for my baby-to-be. That focus on the future helped me through the toughest days of treatment."

A year later, Kim was in remission. A gestational surrogate (who remains a dear friend) was implanted with one of the embryos. The pregnancy took, but the surrogate lost the baby Mother's Day weekend.

"It was just bitterly ironic," Kim says. "I felt like cancer had taken so much of my identity and now the last tiny bit of who I was before . . . it was gone."

But she couldn't let go of the idea that she was supposed to be someone's mother. She'd accepted long before that it wouldn't be easy or traditional. It would be a conscious, sometimes controversial, choice, and she'd have to fight for it. In her favor was the fact that she and her husband—through a combination of brains, opportunity, and hard work—had the knowledge and resources that made it possible for her to make choices when it came to both fertility and breast cancer.

It baffles me when third parties feel authorized to comment on—or hijack—women's decisions about breast health and childbearing, two deeply intimate issues. The so-called breast cancer wars tax my patience even more than the so-called mommy wars of the 1970s and '80s.

Suzy and I were the poster girls for those much-ballyhooed "mommy wars": she the traditional stay-at-home mom, I the full-time working mom. And Suzy and I were never at war. Some pundits wanted us to believe all homebound mommies were secretly immolated by dying ambition, but I knew Suzy was doing exactly what she wanted to do, and I was in awe of how well she did it. Other pundits wanted to cast workforce moms as feral cats who abandoned their offspring and thwarted God's will, but Suzy was thrilled to see me learning and growing in my work. She understood that was the only way I could be a good mother, because it was the only way I could be myself, and she was sad to see so many women conflicted about it.

First Lady Nancy Reagan discovered a lump in her breast in 1987 and opted for the old-school single-stage biopsy-mastectomy rather than the modern two-step procedure, telling physicians, "Look, if you get in there and find out what it is, please don't wake me up to have a conversation. It shouldn't take long to take it off," she added grimly. "Dolly Parton I'm not."

My friend Rose Kushner was terribly offended by this. She thought it set a bad example for women. I was worried about Rose at the time; she'd developed that odd little barking cough, just like Suzy. But the stand she was taking seemed so cruel to me. While I reached out to Mrs. Reagan with full support, Rose very publicly condemned her for making a treatment decision that, to enlightened lumpectomy proponents, seemed impossibly backward.

"She was a perfect candidate for lumpectomy and radiation," Rose fumed. "A tiny little tumor with no lymph node involvement . . ."

"In *her* breast," I said. "Which makes it her decision."

"She's as good as telling women to go out and mutilate themselves for no reason."

"No, she's telling women to go out there and *make their own decisions*. And you don't know a damn thing about her reasons, Rose."

"Neither does anyone else, Nancy. All they know is if the First Lady does it, it must be right. Just watch. . . ." Rose barked angrily into the crook of her elbow. "Watch the mastectomy numbers go up and the lumpectomy numbers go down."

Have you ever had a friend (or perhaps a sister) you wanted to gather in your arms one minute and the next minute shake her till her teeth rattled? That was Rose for me—and me for Rose, I'm sure.

Annoying little turf wars occasionally erupt in the cancer community, and when they do, I physically feel energy being drained from the important work before us. There are sharp—sometimes vehement—differences of opinion, but we're all on the same side. We all want the same thing, which is, bluntly, fewer dead women. As we engage in heated debate over health care reform in the United States, growing concern over the cost of breast cancer screening and treatment gives rise to the question of whether chemo is justifiable—morally or financially—in cases where the patient's odds of survival are statistically thread-slim. Does a thread-slim chance of malignancy justify a painful, expensive biopsy? Is a second opinion justified when a perfectly competent physician has already made an expert judgment call?

There are no cookie-cutter solutions. Every diagnosis is unique, and with all due respect to well-meaning loved ones, nervous insurers, and anyone else who feels some political, personal, or financial stake in the matter, *your* diagnosis belongs to *you*, as do your treatment decisions, and you're not obligated to justify them to anyone.

A woman's life is not a cost; it's a benefit.

Instead of devoting resources to telling women how wrong they are when they make decisions about their unique bodies from the unique perspectives of their unique lives, let's devote resources to advancing our understanding of this disease and improving the technology we use to detect and treat it. Let's make sure every woman has access to resources that provide a range of treatment options, along with the education she needs to make an informed choice about a situation only she can fully understand. Instead of asking why a woman needs a second opinion or complaining that her prophylactic mastectomy is really just a "boob job," let's ask why thousands of American families are bankrupted by cancer each year and rage about the millions of women all over the world who have no access to care or screening.

Rose was absolutely right; mastectomy numbers went up for a while. But so did mammogram numbers. There was heightened response, but heightened awareness came with it. Hopefully, Nancy Reagan's forthrightness and courage did as much good as Rose Kushner's forthrightness and courage. They both inspired women to be brave in the face of criticism and smart about their unique life and health decisions.

In her foreword to *I Love you, Ronnie: The Letters of Ronald Reagan to Nancy Reagan*, Nancy spoke eloquently about what it was like for her after President Reagan was diagnosed with Alzheimer's. It reminded me of how she spoke about her cancer experience back in the day.

"People are incredibly kind and sympathetic," she said, "in an elevator, on the street, everywhere. And the mail, which is tremendous . . . I can't begin to say how much this means to me and how helpful it is. There is a feeling of loneliness when you're in this situation. Not that your friends aren't supportive of you; they are. But no one can really know what it's like unless they've traveled this path. . . . Each day is different, and you get up, put one foot in front of the other, and go—and love; just love."

In January 2005, Kim Bloom's gestational surrogate was implanted with an embryo from a donor egg. In September, bouncing baby Ethan Bloom was born.

"For a long time I'd asked, *Why me?* and *Why is this happening?*" says Kim. "Ethan turned that completely upside down with all those *why* questions children ask. Why does a car have four wheels? Why is an elephant's nose long? It inspired me to think about the world in a vivid new way. I love his explanation of how babies are created: 'an egg from the mom and a spare from the dad.'"

Kim fully appreciates that her life is as much a miracle of modern science as Ethan's.

"After my diagnosis, I took time to listen, look, explore. I wanted to *give* and focus on family. I don't know if it was the thought of karma or the clock ticking. Maybe everyone gets to a place where you question the core of what you want to achieve."

Kim left the corporate world and bought Rosie Hippo, a little green toy company, so she'd have the flexibility to spend more time being a basically traditional mom.

"People thought I was crazy to walk away from my career, but this business is so *me*. It combines my interest in child development, my creative side, my marketing background, plus core values I want Ethan to learn: responsibility, generosity, respect. I'm developing resources for moms with cancer, because as much as I wish it wasn't, that's part of who I am now."

Over the years, I've seen many, many people—myself and Rose Kushner included—emerge from the cancer experience, flourishing with a passion and laser-sharp sense of direction they wouldn't have previously imagined. Does this mean cancer is a gift?

Not in my vocabulary.

"If cancer is a gift," writes Jen Singer, a young survivor mom, "where can I return it?"

The gift is a second chance at life and a new fulcrum from which to balance our options and priorities. We are more than the sum of our cells. More, even, than the sum of our dreams. We are, as Camus said, the sum of our choices, creating and re-creating ourselves day by day. When we choose an act of kindness, we are kind. When we choose an act of courage, we are brave.

Life goes on, and kindly, bravely, we must each find our own way.

~ 15 ~

To Market, To Market

No one, including Norman and Dr. Blumenschein, thought it was a great idea for me to play in our July polo tournament.

"You shouldn't be on a horse at all," said Dr. Blumenschein, following up with a litany of reasons why the potential risk outweighed the potential benefits. My immune system was compromised, so a broken finger or a skinned elbow could turn into a serious issue. Even a small bruise could bring on a major bout of lymphedema, an uncomfortable and sometimes irreversible swelling of tissue that occurs when lymph nodes have been blocked, damaged, or removed.

I chose to play anyway; for me the benefits outweighed the risk.

"Let me work with you," said Norman. "Start back easy and work up to it."

The hours he spent coaching me were a luxury. We were back where we began together. As worried as he was for my well-being, Norman loved my willingness to get back on the horse, as it were, and I loved that he still believed in our well-matched stride.

A few weeks after I finished chemo, I played in a polo tournament, pink helmet on my bald head and pink socks on my pony. What a glorious day! Oh, it felt good to fly down the field on that swift pony, fully engaged again, completely alive and finally outside. This was that day in the park I'd promised myself, and I said a prayer for that little boy from the PT room. I never saw him again, but I do hope he had many days, many years, of sunlight and air.

On the downside, I did bruise my arm, and it swelled up like an elephant's leg. The lymphedema from that day never fully went away. This is an issue that affects a lot of women with breast cancer, but I'd never fully appreciated what the impact can be. It's painful, and it's scary because a giant swollen arm that never goes away is frankly a lot more visibly disfiguring than a mastectomy, which can be reconstructed or compensated for with the right clothes. (I was still sporting the single-ton Righty; I didn't opt for immediate reconstruction like Suzy did.) Lymphedema can't be cured per se, but it can be controlled. I studied up and aggressively went after it with physical therapy, compression wraps, and pharmaceuticals. And a nice selection of three-quarter-length sleeves. Sometimes keeping up appearances is the best you can do for the moment.

In retrospect, once I got my arm back to a presentable size and shape, the polo match was worth it. I learned something the hard way, and those are often the lessons that stick with us. But more important, I stayed true to the woman I was before I had cancer. If it comes down to a choice between risking and settling, I'll take the risk. Cancer couldn't take that away from me—or perhaps I should say chemo couldn't cure me of it.

Norman understood this. Neither of us was hardwired to sit on the sidelines.

I was vigilant about my follow-up schedule. Walking out of your last radiation or chemo treatment is elating, but there's also the feeling of suddenly working without a net. Your support network goes on about their business, and so do you, but the fact that you're no longer actively fighting the cancer is a little unnerving. Limbo is my least favorite state of being, and the very word *remission* is uncomfortably open to possibilities. I was hypersensitive to every twitch and ping in my body. Dr. Blumenschein must have wanted to hide every time he saw me coming.

"You've got what I call 'toe cancer,'" said my friend Carolyn Walker, who'd been there and done that. "You start thinking every headache is a brain tumor, every tummy rumble is congestive heart failure."

Mom's diagnosis was "checkup crazies." Basically the same idea.

"What's the treatment for that?" I wondered.

"Time," said my wise mother.

I kept my sanity by expending every ounce of my energy every day. What I didn't give to my family, I gave to SGK—and not always in that order, I'm ashamed to say. I was always immersed in data, trying to get a handle on the freshest science, wanting to know everything that was going on in clinical research, patient advocacy, insurance issues, bills before Congress. As our visibility expanded, requests for help flooded in—grant proposals from researchers, patients wandering the wilderness, families frustrated and terrified—and we did everything we could, but there was never enough time or money to accommodate everyone.

"We have to do more," I kept telling Norman. "We have to do better." Trammel Crow has been much quoted:

There must always, always be a burning in your heart to achieve. In the quiet of your solitude, close your eyes, bow your head, grit your teeth, clench your fists, ache in your heart, vow and dedicate yourself to achieve, to achieve.

I tried to become that person.

Having Betty Ford on our side on a continuing basis exponentially increased our credibility and exposure, advancing both awareness and fundraising efforts. An army of volunteers came forward. Fabulously smart, dedicated women forming the core of the group put in countless hours, and I took shameless advantage of their generosity. It got back to me that some husbands had forbidden their wives to return my phone calls. They didn't want their names associated with breast cancer and worried that I asked too much of our corps of volunteers. Every time I met someone who was willing and able to help, I hugged her and gave her a fair, good-natured warning: "If you're going to run, run now. I'll be after you."

We decided that we needed to do a major event that would bring in a major influx of cash. Carolyn Williams took the lead, and we started putting together plans for a lavish, big-ticket auction. At our initial organizational meeting, someone cracked that old joke: "The only difference between men and boys is the size of their toys."

We all laughed, but then we looked at each other and said, "That's it."

I think there was an assumption that we'd be doing something very ladylike, given the subject matter and the unwritten rules that govern Southern ladies. We flipped that notion and went with the theme "Toys for Boys"—an auction loaded with manly merchandise, geared for Type A bidding. We went out and zealously shook down everyone we could think of for donated items we could auction off. Unusual, big-ticket items:

cars, hunting trips, motorcycles, leather chairs, power tools, horse tack and fishing tackle, a bass boat, tickets to major sporting events, natty wardrobes of Western wear and designer suits.

The television show *Dallas* was at the height of its popularity then. The luminous Barbara Bel Geddes played Miss Ellie, matriarch of the Ewing family, mother of antihero J.R. (played by Larry Hagman) and conflicted but adorable Bobby (Patrick Duffy), and grandmother of impossibly saucy Lucy (Charlene Tilton). In the early 1970s, Barbara had been diagnosed with breast cancer and had undergone a radical mastectomy. To her credit, she worked with the writers to incorporate her breast cancer experience into the *Dallas* story line in 1980. The episodes, one of the first glimpses of breast cancer in any mainstream television show, resulted in an Emmy for her and opened the door for sensitive, accurate portrayals of women coping with breast cancer. And this was more than a decade before *Murphy Brown* and *Sex and the City* featured breast cancer story lines that were called "groundbreaking." Both those were beautifully done, but Barbara was way ahead of them on the timeline.

She was a great friend to our little foundation from the very beginning, lending her voice and bringing major star power, including her television family, to those early events. Larry Hagman's ten-gallon hat was one of the hotly anticipated items on our "Toys for Boys" lineup, and several cast members—including Barbara, Linda Gray, and Larry Hagman—were attending.

Over the years, we've benefited from the refracted star-shine of many generous people from the entertainment and sports worlds, and over the years, I've found these people almost universally delightful to work with. I recently walked with Olivia Newton-John in the Palm Beach Race for the Cure and did a Passionately Pink for the Cure media tour with adorable Sarah Chalke from *Scrubs*, a bundle of energy in great shoes. Back in the day, Jill Ireland was a powerhouse, as was Jill Eikenberry. Linda Carter—well, what would you expect from Wonder Woman? Cynthia Nixon delivered a beautifully straightforward message as part of our breast health outreach to the lesbian community. I love Ricardo Chavira from *Desperate Housewives,* a chivalrous Texan who approached us after his mom died of breast cancer. The luminous Tejano Grammy-winner Soraya came to us before she was diagnosed and did such great good as our Latina ambassador right up until she died of breast cancer at age thirty-seven.

In a final message to media and her fans, Soraya said, "I know there are many questions without answers, and that hope doesn't leave with me, and above all, my mission does not end with my physical story."

There's a very tender spot in my heart for her always.

We were always careful about how we positioned celebrity voices, because we want the scientists to be the real stars of this talent show. We want our outcomes to be the cause for celebration. That said, the visibility celebrities bring to our events is PR platinum. You can't buy that kind of publicity.

We've had many, many memorable events over the years, but that first "Toys for Boys" auction stands as one of my favorites. We wanted to use this opportunity to convey the idea that breast cancer isn't a "women's" issue; it affects families, and men need to get involved. Everyone had so much fun. Spirits were high, and hearts were in the right place. As the crowd roared, Larry Hagman tossed his hat into the ring to be auctioned off. The moment it was sold, the buyer gave it back to Larry, who tossed it out to be sold again and again. We brought in almost $1 million that night, and just as importantly, we got a lot of attention.

The second year we did "Toys for Boys," Sharon McCutchin's husband, Jerry, whose daughter was diagnosed with breast cancer at age thirty-two, donated an ultralight aircraft, which he brought in, piece by piece, and assembled right there in the hotel ballroom—the most thrilling centerpiece of all time.

"You want to look bigger than you are," Norman said, and we accomplished that. We were still more David than Goliath, but now we were seriously on the map.

The first big cause-marketing payoff I know of was the brainchild of Bruce Burtch, who coined the friendly phrase "Do good to do well" to describe a 1976 partnership between Marriott and the March of Dimes. Three years later, a partnership between Famous Amos cookies and Literacy Volunteers of America brought about an awareness windfall for both organizations. (Cookies and a good book: the ultimate win-win.) As far as I know, the term *cause-related marketing* was coined by some great mind at American Express to describe a 1983 promotional campaign during which they donated a penny per transaction and a dollar for each new card to the Statue of Liberty restoration project. During the four-month campaign, transactions leaped by almost 30 percent, and Lady Liberty got $2 million worth of gorgeous.

As of this writing, cause-related marketing generates more than $55 million annually for Susan G. Komen for the Cure, which is why people refer to me as a "cause marketing pioneer" (when they're being nice); I never claimed to have invented it, but SGK certainly put some gas in its tank. In my mind, "pioneer" conjures a picture of Ma Ingalls riding across the prairie in a covered wagon. What we did felt more like NASCAR. Hold on to your sunbonnet, Ma.

My first big idea in this area was to get a major bra manufacturer to place attractive informational hang-tags on their bras. In one fell swoop, we'd be taking up residence in every major department store in America, promoting the American Cancer Society's breast self-exam technique and alerting women from A to double-D that the Susan G. Komen Breast Cancer Foundation was here for them with information, resources, and support.

With some help from Jack Cassidy, a friend at the Intimate Apparel Manufacturers Association, I jumped through the required hoops to get meetings with the CEOs of all my favorite lingerie companies in New York. On the way up to the first meeting, I shared the elevator with an exceptionally petite woman, who eyed me like I was a Cyclops.

Please don't let this be the meeting, I silently begged.

She was the meeting. And she was not amused. Feeling the full girth of my enormous hair and big red glasses, I found my way to the lowest chair in the room.

She asked, "What can I do for you?"

I delved into my pitch, but she cut me off.

"My customers aren't thinking about that," she said.

"Well, that's the problem. Awareness of—"

"Young lady," she said. "The meeting is over."

Ice burned and humiliated, I gathered my samples and slunk out the door. It had taken me a long time to set this up. The whole thing lasted all of ninety seconds and pretty much set the tone for the other meetings, which were often over before they began. A few had the courtesy to fiddle with the hang-tag sample as if they were actually listening to me for a minute before they threw me out.

"I appreciate what you're trying to do, but *no.*"

"Not to be insensitive, but *no.*"

"We want to help women celebrate their bodies, so *no.*"

"No. No, no. We want women to feel happy and sexy when they think of our product. We're selling beauty and femininity. You're selling disease and death."

"Not at all," I kept arguing, "We're encouraging breast *health.*"

"And yet I'm seeing the word *cancer.* Not a happy, sexy word."

It was terribly discouraging. I called Jack, who was also the president of a racing bra company, and he talked me off the ledge and donated a nice check plus several thousand cute plastic watches to put in our Race for the Cure swag bags. There never were any takers for the hang tags, but as we grew over the years, we had many great partnerships with bra companies and department stores, and several years later, ironically, I was honored with an award from the Intimate Apparel Manufacturers Association. It took a while to overcome those deeply ingrained ideas, and I wish I could take some credit for it, but the fact is, retailers changed their approach in response to a marketplace full of women who were evolving and making their voices heard.

"Grassroots," I told Norman. "That's the key. When they see how many people care about this, they'll come around. We just have to keep ringing that bell until we turn those old ideas upside down."

"Remember, Bruni, it's evolution, not revolution," Norm cautioned.

"Yes, Normie, but sometimes a little revolution is called for."

"Conventional wisdom says ten years to really get a nonprofit up and running."

I shook my head. "We don't have ten years."

In reality, it took a good seven or eight years to really get things rocking, and those were the hardest-working years of my life.

Our first real employee was our wonderful secretary, Barbie Casey. Linda Cadigan came on in 1984 as executive director and whipped our grant process into shape, not a moment too soon. As I explained to her the way we'd been doing things, she pressed her fingertips against her temples.

"Let me get this straight," she said. "You wanted to award a $100,000 grant to the University of Texas Medical School. So you wrote out a check, scrawled *Dr. Sprague* on an unsealed envelope and handed it to him—$100,000."

Well, when she put it like that, it really didn't sound right. At the time, I was just so elated about awarding the six-figure grant! This sort of casual-Friday practice was now a thing of the past. No more kitchen-table meetings, agonizing over every little check we wanted to write. Now there was a procedure, and we went by the book, but unlike other non-profits, the volunteers actually oversaw the staff; our power core was still very much in charge.

Jill Smith, one of three vice chairs who served with me as founding chair, remembers: "We had well-known Dallas women with famous names sitting on our board. That's how we built it up. They came in their dress suits and drank tea. But these women were so bright and so capable, we wanted to make it a working board. We changed the bylaws and required that they raise money and serve on a committee. I was scared they'd walk away, leaving us with no money and no support. Instead, they stayed and took responsibility for the organization. People started sending in résumés, asking to be on the board."

I stayed on to chair the board of directors, and I was unapologetically bossy about it. This was my sister's name. Human nature being what it is, and big organizations being what they are, shenanigans happen. I wasn't about to let them happen in my sister's name. I still feel the same way. In all the years of evolution (and a few moments of revolution, as well), Suzy has been the one constant in this organization. She anchored us to our vision from the beginning. Through the late 1980s, we saw rapid growth. The message caught fire and spread.

At our 1984 awards luncheon, we presented the Betty Ford Award to the beautiful and courageous Gigi Hill, who'd long been a pillar of Dallas society. The award recognizes those who've made significant contributions to increasing breast cancer awareness and is often presented to bravely outspoken survivors. Seeing Gigi there at the head table with Betty, people recognized her as one of their own. This wasn't an arm's-length charity to benefit the conveniently faceless "needy"; this was a fight for the lives of their own sisters, wives, and daughters.

"But we're never going to solve this problem if we stay in one city with one group of people," I told Mommy. "We have to raise awareness, raise money, and give it away the best way possible. We have to see it through, from the lab to the clinic, and translate that to the deepest, darkest reaches of the population where women aren't getting decent care."

Without knowing it, we'd already begun to spread our wings. In 1986, Nancy Paul founded the Canadian Breast Cancer Foundation, which was patterned after SGK and later became our staunch ally. That same year, we had our first Race for the Cure outside of Dallas. Of course, this had to happen in Peoria. Suzy's dear friend Linda Washkuhn stuck by Suzy to the very end, and as soon as she heard what we were doing, she told me, "I don't know what I can do, but I'll do something!"

She got the Peoria chapter rolling and her fabulous posse put together an amazing event. The weather was nothing short of glorious. We'd hoped for a thousand people, and twelve hundred came. Dr. John Miller organized what would later be called "3 Miles of Men," a line of great guys in tuxedos, handing out swag bags, cheering on the walkers and runners. The decorations were feminine and fun—totally Suzy—and it was incredibly moving to see this demonstration of public affection for her. Peoria loved Suzy as much as she loved Peoria. Memories were all around us. I must have heard a hundred Suzy stories that day, big and small acts of kindness for which she'll always be remembered in her hometown.

The first year, the Peoria Race for the Cure brought in about $20,000. In 2004, they brought in $600,000. In 2006, the twenty-year total for the Peoria Race for the Cure had come to more than $6 million. I can't begin to tell you how proud I am of my dear hometown and the vibrant, unstoppable crew Linda and company have built there. That 1986 Peoria race was an important first step out of Dallas.

Scott was a solid and industrious sixteen-year-old by this time. It hardly seemed possible. He would have towered over Suzy, and she would have loved that. Steffie was twelve, and she seemed fairly overwhelmed by the day. She was touched and appreciative of all the stories about her mom, but she said later, "I was kind of jealous. All those strangers knew her better than I did. I was the only one who didn't remember her."

This might be the appropriate moment for me to explain that I've purposely written and spoken very little about Scott and Steffie in public. Their father is a private man who never wanted them to be "poster children" for a cause, famous for the worst thing that had ever happened to them. I've always respected that and will continue to do so.

I hope it goes without saying that they're an important part of my life, in my thoughts daily, and always close to my heart.

In 1986, reactor number 4 at the Chernobyl Nuclear Power Plant melted down, *Oprah* debuted, Jill Eikenberry and Gloria Steinem were diagnosed with breast cancer. V. C. Andrews (author of *Flowers in the Attic* and other chiller-thriller blockbusters) died of the disease, along with 40,534 other women in the United States.

That same year, Rose Kushner, Ruth Spear, Diane Blum, and I got together and formed the National Alliance of Breast Cancer Organizations. I was proud to be part of it, but we were a scrappy bunch with wildly differing political views, and no fear of speaking our minds. Sometimes we giggled like eighth graders at a slumber party; other times we went at it like gladiators, but we were in the trenches together with a common goal and the same burning zeal. With Race for the Cure events coming together in several cities, we put together planning and support materials that would make it an eminently doable and consistently participant-friendly event. The first Race for the Cure logo featured an abstract runner outlined by a pink ribbon, and we liked it so well, we kept it for almost ten years.

We were making more and bigger research grants, and in addition to researching the best places to put that money, I was puzzling my way through two difficult decisions women face after breast cancer treatment and recovery: reconstruction and hormone balance. The hormones and other "female troubles" were a bit of a struggle; long story short, I ended up having a hysterectomy. I discussed the reconstruction issue with Mommy, who completely understood both my motivations and reservations. I discussed it with Norman, who let me know he was going to love and desire me with or without my left breast. If anything, he found my battle scar strangely sexy. In his mind it represented triumph, not loss;

it was a symbol of overcoming. Riding the far reaches of the ranch in McKinney, I discussed it with Suzy and finally came to a decision.

My research turned up an excellent surgeon in Atlanta: John Bostwick, co-author with Karen Berger of *A Woman's Decision: Breast Care, Treatment, and Reconstruction.* After reading *A Woman's Decision* and weighing all my options, I went to Atlanta and had my left breast rebuilt and my right breast reshaped to match it. A few months later, I went back and had Dr. Bostwick install a beautiful nipple, using a tattooed skin graft from my thigh. When it healed, I went to Neiman's, as giddy as a thirteen-year-old, and bought my new breasts their first bra.

In 1987, Margaret Thatcher was elected to a third term, AZT and Prozac hit the pharmaceutical market, and Kate Jackson and Nancy Reagan were diagnosed with breast cancer.

In 1988, Benazir Bhutto became the first Islamic woman prime minister of Pakistan, *A Fish Called Wanda* was in movie theaters, and Eileen Brennan and Sandra Day O'Connor were diagnosed with breast cancer.

In 1989, the Berlin Wall was torn down, and *The Joy Luck Club* was published. Bette Davis and another 40,000 women died of breast cancer. We launched the Susan G. Komen National Toll-Free Breast Care Helpline. Our first chapter beyond our core group in Dallas opened its doors in San Francisco, and this affiliate is still humming with that fantastic energy unique to the Bay Area. Our first major corporate relationship began when New Balance joined us, and they've stayed with us for more than twenty years now, sponsoring Race for the Cure, our Breast Cancer 3-Day, and Marathon for the Cure in addition to a massive in-store promotion, Lace Up for the Cure. The lasting relationships with our local affiliates and sponsors mean so much to SGK and to me personally. I'm continually inspired and held accountable by their unshakable belief in what we're doing.

Later that year, I was appointed by President Reagan to serve on the President's Cancer Panel, the first breast cancer advocate at the table.

Rose said, "It's about time."

Lesions in her lungs had metastasized throughout her body, but she was still fighting with every breath, making phone calls and rabble-rousing from her hospital bed.

"Go to M. D. Anderson," I tried to tell her. "I'll go with you, Rose. You could get into a clinical trial."

"I'm not going to do that to myself just to buy a couple of months," she said.

It was her choice. There was never any question in anyone's mind about Rose Kushner's ownership of her own body.

In 1990, Lech Wałęsa became the president of Poland, and *Seinfeld* made its debut. Jill Ireland and Rose Kushner died of breast cancer. Jill had lent her fabulous face and poignant voice to SGK over the years, and Rose—well, her contribution to the breast cancer movement is historic. She'd been shunned and ridiculed in the beginning; now the Society of Surgical Oncology posthumously awarded her one of their highest honors, the James Ewing Layman's Award, in recognition of her outstanding contribution to the fight against cancer.

One of the hazards of my work is that I end up loving a lot of women with breast cancer, and every time another great woman dies, it's like losing Suzy all over again. It's happened more times that I can stand to think about, and even though I know it's coming, it crushes me and makes me feel like such a failure.

By 1990, we'd been shouting from the rooftops for seven years. That year 54 percent of American women over forty received a mammogram, which was an improvement over the bad old days, but we still had a long way to go. A lot of insurance companies routinely denied coverage for screening tests, even when a woman presented with a lump in her breast, and as studies raised questions about the efficacy of mammograms—false positives and missed tumors—we started wondering about the equipment being used and the competency of the people reading the results. We'd made some strides in the awareness department. The research piece was growing more and more exciting. It was time to focus on advocacy.

"Politics is the art of the possible," said Max Fisher.

A great Jewish leader, philanthropist, and Republican statesman, Max had taken me under his wing. He and his wife, Marjorie, were important mentors in my life, good friends with great souls. Max lived by a philosophy of patriotism and giving, and he knew how to get things done without being a bully. I plagued him with questions, and he schooled me on the workings of Senate subcommittees and appropriations and the deal making that happens over dinner and out on the links. We talked for hours about the imperative of integrity and dedication to the greater good.

"We have to do more," I told Norman, "and we have to do it better."

Over the years, I'd been watching the way Norman scouted locations and opened new restaurants. Expansion. Evolution. He was always looking at the next step.

The moment I walked into Judah Folkman's lab, I said, "We have to fund this research."

While Dr. Folkman was still at Harvard, he'd pioneered the design of an early pacemaker. While he was in the navy, he'd developed a time-release drug delivery device and donated it, patent-free, to the worldwide Population Council, who used it to develop the Norplant birth control method. At Boston Children's Hospital, he got the idea that cancer could essentially be starved to death by inhibiting angiogenesis, the process whereby a tumor generates blood vessels that feed it. For more than twenty years, his theories had been scoffed at, but the year SGK was founded, he indentified a capillary growth stimulator, and less than two years later, a capillary growth inhibitor, which laid the foundation for an entirely new thought process when it comes to metastatic disease. Another twenty years of research, trials, and the refining fire of scientific process resulted in FDA approval of bevacizumab (Avastin) for the treatment of metastatic colon and lung cancers in 2004 and metastatic breast cancer in 2008.

We were also among the supporters of Australian biologist/bioethicist Elizabeth Blackburn, who won a Nobel Prize in 2009 for co-discovering telomerase, an enzyme that affects the stability of chromosomes. Early in her career, we recognized the importance of her work in molecular and cellular biology.

In our first fifteen years, SGK awarded a little over $11 million in research grants. The lion's share—three-quarters of that—went toward biology. We felt there was a need to increase basic biological knowledge of this disease to lay the groundwork for advances in treatment and detection. In 2008 and 2009, we awarded more than $160 million in grants, and well over half of that went toward the translation of that hard-won knowledge to treatment, detection, and prevention.

As Eric made his way through elementary and middle school, Norman was tough on him, but Eric took it in stride. His childhood was a wide-ranging wealth of experiences that included mucking out stalls in the barn, attending city council meetings, and dining with political figures, entertainment luminaries, and giants of industry. When Norman received the Horatio Alger Award, Eric and I were seated next to Governor Mario Cuomo. Eric was about ten years old, and he impressed everyone at the table; he knew when, how, and how much a kid could appropriately contribute to an adult conversation. Governor Cuomo excused himself after most of us had finished eating, but he'd hardly touched his lamb chop, and my growing boy was still hungry, so I scooped it over onto his plate. Much to my surprise, the governor came back, and much to the governor's surprise, my knife and fork were on his empty plate. Perhaps not the greatest example of state dinner etiquette, but a teachable moment in which Eric saw that everyone's just folks when it comes right down to it. Someone snapped a wonderful photo of the three of us just as Governor Cuomo and I burst out laughing.

Eric had the same learn-outside-the-classroom style I did. Norman and I expected good grades, and Eric worked hard to deliver, but numbers were hard for him at first.

"If you work hard enough, you can learn anything," Norman insisted.

"But sometimes you learn it a different way," I tried to tell him. Norman came from a mindset and a generation where the only two learning disabilities were "lazy" and "stupid," and Norman knew Eric wasn't stupid, ergo . . .

"Three times seventeen," Norman was constantly drilling. "Six times twelve."

I had to bite my tongue sometimes. I knew it wasn't right for me to get in the middle of their relationship, and their relationship overall was pretty great. Eric adopted a stray dog, and Norman was impressed with the patience and responsibility that brought out in Eric. He named it

Underdog—"Undie" for short. The two of them immediately had that "boy and his dog" rapport. Life was a lot of fun. We played polo, traveled, and skied. Brenda, Cindy, and I threw several Annual Forty-Ninth Birthday parties for Norman. We all worked hard, but we always made time for each other.

When Eric was twelve, he wanted to start working for Norman, and Norman agreed to find him something in the mailroom, but he didn't cut Eric one inch of slack, and I knew I couldn't either. On the day he was to start work, Eric came into the kitchen freshly scrubbed and ready to take on the world.

"Are you taking me to work or is Dad?" he asked.

"You're taking the bus," I said. "And you'd better hurry and pack a lunch. You won't have any lunch money until you get paid."

Naturally, Eric reacted as if I'd thrown him off the lifeboat. "You're so mean!"

"Eric, you don't want people to see you ride up in the boss' car. While you're at work, you're an employee, and Daddy is Mr. Brinker, just like he is to all the other employees. The only difference is you'll work twice as hard as anyone else there because you know they're all watching you."

He set his jaw, packed his lunch, and went off to meet the bus. It was good for him. Sometimes he didn't get home until a little later than I would have liked, but he was happy. He quickly made friends with all the regulars on the bus, working people, men, women, young, old, black, white, and Hispanic. They loved him because he was polite and respectful and loved to listen to their stories. Everything was great until the night he didn't come home. I came unglued.

"Why did you make me do this?" I raged at Norman. "He's gone! He's kidnapped!"

Norman went out to look for him, but an hour later, Eric trudged in with his blood-spattered shirt in his hand.

"*Oh my God!*" I ran to him. "What happened? Where are you hurt?"

He wasn't hurt at all.

"The bus was in an accident," he said. "A lady got hurt, so I took off my shirt and wrapped it around her."

Eric wasn't into polo, but he loved being at the field with us, talking to people, industriously selling programs, and listening in on grown-up conversation. He and Norman would go out driving on scouting excursions, checking out possible locations for new units. Norman would ask Eric, "What do you think of this corner?" Eric would say, "I like it" or "I don't know, Dad. Traffic pattern doesn't look right."

"He's got a good eye," Norman told me. "And I think he's getting better with his numbers."

"Business in Wichita is improving," Eric remarked at dinner one night. "Dallas is taking off too. And Boca Raton is zooming."

"See?" Norman said proudly. "I told you he was getting better at numbers. He's been reading the sales reports!"

"Oh, no, Dad," said Eric. "It's because I'm in the mailroom. Those receipts are heavier than they used to be."

We had a good laugh about it, but it was an interesting comment on the way they worked together. They made a good team. Eric saw forests; Norm saw trees.

The numerical and the empirical. The statistical and the anecdotal.

That's the crux of the ongoing—and going and going—debate about screening. A study pops out, demonstrating with statistics that screening is next to pointless, and on the heels of it come a rush of stories from women whose lives speak quite the contrary. It's not conflicting information; it's the same information sifted through two different value systems.

For me, it's a moot point. What it comes down to is a woman's right to establish her own value system when it comes to her own body. If she wants a mammogram, she should have a mammogram. That's what we were fighting for, and the state of Texas was the first to change laws, requiring insurance providers to cover mammograms. In 1992, we helped push through the Mammography Quality Standards Act, which requires facilities and technicians to be meet certain standards to be accredited. (Just the beginning of our continuing quest to make mammography more accurate, more accessible, and more technically precise as a diagnostic tool.)

Meanwhile, Eric grew to be a tall and capable young man. He was becoming more and more frustrated in school, being pulled out of class half the time for tutoring. Searching for resources that might help him, Norman and I heard about Landmark School in Boston, which specializes in teaching high-potential students with learning differences. It was an adjustment—more for me than for Eric—when he went off to school, but his confidence soared along with his reading and math scores. He was part of a community. He was excelling. I missed seeing him every day, but it was wonderful to hear his voice on the phone, thriving and happy, as he grew by leaps and bounds. We made the most of every weekend and vacation that he spent with us. During the summer, he learned to wait tables and earned his own spending money. When he wanted a car, we told him we'd pay half. He worked hard, saved his money, and ferreted out a secondhand but still functional Jeep. Eric graduated from Landmark and went on to Bradley University in Peoria. He loved being close to Mom and Daddy, who divided their time between Florida and Peoria, and I loved that he was living in the Land of Milk and Honey.

More Race for the Cure events were popping up all over the country—seven in 1990, including the National Race for the Cure in Washington, D.C., where we launched our National Series Breast Cancer Survivor Recognition program with the help of Vice President and Marilyn Quayle. Turnout was massive. Every survivor was given a pink visor, and they were as countless as cherry blossoms. At our Tenth Anniversary Gala in 1992, Senator Connie Mack and his wife, Priscilla, were presented with the Betty Ford Award, with Betty Ford doing the presentation, as always. Vice President and Mrs. Quayle were there, along with President Ford, Nancy Reagan, and Lady Bird Johnson. We presented our first Brinker International Awards for Breast Cancer Research to Dr. Bernard Fisher, who'd advanced the science of adjuvant therapies, and Dr. V. Craig Jordan, who discovered the preventative properties of tamoxifen. Support flooded in from diverse sources, many of whom remain friends and partners to this day, including the Zeta Tau Alpha fraternity and the ZTA Foundation.

SGK was such a huge part of our lives. It would have been impossible for me to have both my family and this all-consuming decade of work had I been married to anyone else. Sitting next to Norman at the monthly board meetings, I'd feel his knee nudging mine. He always held my hand, but kept it under the table, so I wouldn't look like a woman who needed hand-holding.

Every once in a while, he'd look at me as if I'd hung the moon and say, "I knew you had this in you."

Over the early years, people kept telling me we'd never survive unless we allowed ourselves to be absorbed by a larger organization, but that was no longer the vision. Our vision was to *be* the larger organization, and instead of absorbing the small foundations that sprang up, we'd help them grow—or at least not get in their way. We'd come a long way in a short time. Now there was no stopping us, and as stingy as we were with our operating costs, we weren't about to hand a bag of money over to an umbrella organization for the privilege of having them tell us what to do. Our foundation stood on its own feet.

Others keep trying to convince me that what we really need is to build a big building. I see where they're going with that idea, but why would we invest all that money in a facility that would stand for a hundred years? Our greatest hope is to finish what we came to do, eradicate breast cancer forever, and close up shop. I dream of the day we're no longer needed. I hope I live to see it. When the work is done, I'll happily walk away, put my feet up, gaze at some great Hungarian art, and celebrate the promise kept.

SGK celebrated a great milestone in 1991: For the first time, we made more than $1 million in grants funding breast cancer research projects in a single calendar year. The grassroots grew; our corporate partnerships flourished. Every once in a while, I'd remove my nose from the grindstone just long enough to notice how much things had changed.

It was astonishing.

Between the beginning of 1988 and the end of 1992, the world changed more than a little. Tiananmen Square became an icon, apartheid ended, the Warsaw Pact dissolved, the iron curtain collapsed, the Soviet Union foundered and fell apart.

Evolution and revolution everywhere.

And another 215,039 American women died of breast cancer.

From Point A to Point B

"Everybody has a story about why they do what they do," says Dr. Fredika Robertson. "Science is a very personal endeavor. Believe me," she adds wryly, "we're not in it for the money and glory."

About fifteen years ago, Dr. Robertson was invited to join an epidemiologist friend in a study related to anti-inflammatories and the cyclooxygenase-2, or "COX-2," gene.

"I said *sure*," says Fredi, and you can hear in her voice how completely fascinated she is with her specialty, molecular biology. "We designed experiments, obtained samples from patients with early metastatic disease, and learned that this COX-2 gene is unregulated in patients whose disease has spread."

She would go on to establish links between COX-2 and estrogen and the enzyme aromatase, which is key to estrogen production. The study, published in 1997, caught our eye because of promising data we were seeing in the field of aromatase inhibitors. Less than a year later, while conducting a lab meeting, Dr. Robertson reached down to pick up a pen, and everything burst into shooting stars. A tumor in her brain had caused a massive hemorrhage.

"It hurt," says Dr. Robertson, who is not one for hyperbole.

The physician at the urgent-care "doc-in-a-box" facility happened to be a resident she'd trained. He asked her if she thought she had spinal meningitis.

"No," Fredi managed. "Do an MRI."

After what seemed like a long time, she saw a flurry of white coats rushing into the room.

"Later on I saw the brain scans," she says, "but you can't even really see the brain. They told me in front of my sixteen-year-old daughter that

I wasn't going to make it, and I said, 'No, I don't accept that.' That's something I've learned over and over from the patients I've worked with. They come into M. D. Anderson with a terrible prognosis, Stage IV, looking for a second opinion after someone told them nothing could be done—and yes, some of them die, but some of them get through it."

The chemical treatment of the tumor and recovery process that followed was laborious and slow. Fredi sat at the computer for hours, learning her own language from the beginning, her head pounding, the words hanging just out of reach, tantalizing and torturing.

"I'd tell myself *just fifteen minutes more* and after that *just fifteen minutes more*. It took a lot of persistence. I was forty-four years old and learning like a first grader would learn."

She battled her way back and was eventually able to resume her work.

In August 2008, Dr. Robertson stood in a hangar at Dallas/Fort Worth International Airport, celebrating the award of the first SGK Promise Grant. Parked out on the tarmac like a mommy, daddy, and half a dozen hatchlings were an American Airlines 757, a 777, and a group of American Eagle commuter jets, gleaming in the sunshine, freshly painted with their new livery. A vivid pink ribbon unfurled the entire length of each fuselage from one end to the other, and each tail fin was emblazoned with our trademark "running ribbon."

In addition to flying our color all over the world, American Airlines was funding an important five-year study of IBC inflammatory breast cancer—to the tune of $8 million. Fredi and her co–principal investigator, Dr. Massimo Christofanilli, are conducting transitional research using critical blood and tissue samples from IBC patients, advancing our understanding of the disease and identifying IBC biomarkers.

"The collaboration between patients, physicians, and laboratory scientists has created a one-of-a-kind environment for robust team science," said Dr. Christofanilli.

"The day they pulled those planes up in Dallas," says Fredi, "what a thrill. A few months later, I gave a talk in Dresden, and coming into the Frankfurt airport, there was one of those planes. I got tears in my eyes. That support means everything."

The Promise Grant will enable her team at M. D. Anderson to continue studies that bring her into daily contact with the women whose lives are at stake. One of those patients is Jenee Jongebloed Bobbora, who was diagnosed in 2003—a thirty-two-year-old woman with a two-year-old daughter.

"The survival rate at that time was about 5 percent," says Dr. Robertson. "But seven years later, she's NED—no evidence of disease—and life is good. She knows what it is to be a survivor; she sees what could have been, and she's grateful for what is. She has this tremendous life force, and she's so funny."

Jenee was a teacher before, and now she's on fire to educate women about the factors that contribute to misdiagnosis, which is a factor in the low survival rates for women with IBC. It's rare, and those who get it are generally much younger than the average breast cancer patient. Instead of presenting with a lump in the breast, it often appears as a rash or redness. It's often invisible on a mammogram or ultrasound. And it is hellishly aggressive. Early detection is key, but IBC is most often diagnosed at Stage IIIB, which is most often too late. Jenee helped establish the Inflammatory Breast Cancer Foundation, whose mission is to advance understanding of this rare but virulent cancer.

In 2006, M. D. Anderson opened the world's first dedicated Inflammatory Breast Cancer Clinic. Fredi Robertson still suffers from searing chronic headaches, but there's nowhere else she'd rather be.

"I've had friends who opted to retire early, but how could you possibly? I learn every day," she says with obvious relish. "From advocates, from patients, from team members. M. D. Anderson is Disneyland for scientists. I feel really blessed to be here."

We take a lot of flack (speaking of searing chronic headaches) from people who feel our corporate sponsors get more from the relationship than they ought to. I wish I could personally introduce each of those critics to Dr. Fredi Robertson.

People are fond of saying, "It's not personal; it's business." But in my experience, those who achieve the greatest success in business take it very personally. They see a personal stake in the welfare of the customers from whom they derive their bottom line. At the end of the day, of course, they're in business to make money. When we started down the road toward significant use of cause-related marketing, Norman cautioned me never to lose sight of that fact, and I never have. Susan G. Komen for the Cure is a nonprofit organization; our corporate sponsors are not. Their raison d'être is profit. Every one of our corporate sponsors has a fiduciary duty to its stockholders, and stockholders are hoping for a pleasant retirement. We want them to thrive, because we need their help. We give and take, and if all goes as it should, we help each other muddle through to duel another day. That's how money and love make the world go 'round.

In 2008, our corporate sponsors enabled us to invest an additional $55 million in discovering and delivering the cure for breast cancer. Whatever goodwill American Airlines realizes from its continued partnership with us—however many times that translates into someone buying a ticket from American instead of another provider—the airline deserves it. I value every yes I get. Our corporate partners do a lot of good for us, and I believe in the adage "what comes around, goes around." I strive to be as tenacious and unflappable as my father, but he told me from the time I was young: "For every five *yes*es you get in life, you hear a hundred *no*s."

Certainly, if the people critical of cause-related marketing were to offer to provide us with $55 million a year, we'd be happy to stay home and put our feet up. Till then, we'll keep knocking on doors. In the early days of SGK, I pursued meetings with CEOs I admired, but I didn't go to them with my hand out; I went to them asking for advice. Their wisdom was a great asset to us, and one of those benefactors was Bob Crandall of American Airlines. He gave me a lot of sound advice that stayed with me, but one particular point resonated with me.

"Don't put all your eggs in one basket," he cautioned. "When you see a source of revenue on the rise, it's tempting to put all your energy there, but that's a mistake."

At the time, the Race for the Cure was really catching fire all over the country, and we were already seeing how it could go global. It was thrilling, but I was a little nervous about it taking over the organization. Without taking any energy away from that effort, I redoubled my outreach to corporate partners, and we've worked hard over the years to keep all the plates spinning.

When Eric was working with his teammates at JetBlue to design a new sort of customer experience, he said, "You have to go where you need to go. That's the first thing. But getting there is more than just Point A to Point B."

The same could be said for research. It's a spiral staircase, not an elevator. The give-and-take goes around and comes around, peopled by scientists, physicians, patients, and supporters.

Mary Woodard Lasker has been called the "fairy godmother of medical research" for the way she facilitated symbiotic connections between the will and the way. Jonas Salk said, "She is a matchmaker between science and society." When Suzy and I were growing up, Mary Lasker was a role model, and as I was beginning my career in business, I recognized the political savvy and social grace she wielded with the precision of a scalpel. She was responsible for the perennial daffodils visible from Lady Bird Johnson's window at the White House—and for the congressional declaration of a national War on Cancer. The lesson wasn't lost on me back then, but I only recently grasped its full meaning.

Not long ago, while visiting our affiliate in Orange County, California, I met Leslie Whitfield, who's survived eighteen years since being diagnosed with Stage IV breast cancer.

"*Eighteen years?*" I gasped. "After the worst possible prognosis? That's unheard of!"

"It hasn't been easy," she said, "but I'm alive, and I'm having a good life."

"Tell me about your treatment. Walk me through it from the beginning."

As she described her journey, every protocol, every chemo regimen, every blast of radiation, every setback and step forward, I was overwhelmed with emotion. Every therapy she'd received had been funded by SGK grant money. And now, against all odds, here she stood telling me about her family, working to raise money for research, reaching out to help other women with breast cancer.

I consider her an excellent investment.

16

My Kingdom for a Horse

If you want a crash course in Activism 101, observe the efforts on behalf of AIDS awareness. I paid close attention, was continually inspired, and learned a lot. On December 1, 1989, the Visual AIDS Artists Caucus of New York City staged their first DWA—Day Without Art—an eloquent and powerful "national day of action and mourning" that garnered a tremendous amount of attention. In 1991, they launched the Red Ribbon Project, purposely keeping the campaign creator's name anonymous and the copyright for the image free. They wanted to preserve it as a sincere, personal symbol of compassion. At the 1991 Tony Awards, the red ribbon was seen on Jeremy Irons and other Broadway denizens. Within months, it was the must-have fashion accessory of the season.

A few months later at the New York City Race for the Cure, inspired by the elegant simplicity of the red ribbon loop, volunteers pinned loops of our signature pink ribbon on participating survivors. We were still using the logo with the runner outlined by a pink ribbon. It wasn't something we did on purpose, but it was so poignantly reminiscent of the pink ribbon sash on Suzy's homecoming queen dress. Low-cost, easy to execute, and pleasing to the eye, the loop of pink ribbon quickly caught on as a way to identify participants, survivors, and supporters at Susan G. Komen events. Following the example of the Red Ribbon activists, who welcomed all comers (including sponsors who enabled them to take their important work into schools, museums, galleries, and parks), we didn't trademark the ribbon or any particular derivation of it at that time.

The following year, when *Self* magazine editor Alexandra Penney teamed up with Estée Lauder to promote the second annual Breast Cancer Awareness Month issue for October 1992, they went back and forth over the rights to a peach ribbon, but Penney was advised to pick another color, and she chose pink. Understandably, there was some rumbling from our camp, but when the subject was raised at a board meeting, I held up my hand like a traffic cop.

"We have no dog in that fight. They distributed 1.5 million breast self-exam cards. Why should we be unhappy about that? We have a lot of work to do. Let's not waste energy being territorial about less than a penny's worth of pink ribbon."

I felt Norman's hand on my knee under the table. A quick squeeze of approval. Breast Cancer Awareness Month—a collaborative effort involving many terrific organizations—was a whirlwind, as every October has been since BCAM began, and after that Norman and I waltzed through the holiday party season. As we did every year, we spent New Year's Eve in Norman's office. Knowing the restaurant managers would be working hard, he spent the evening at his desk, calling every single one of them to ask after their families, thank them for their dedication, and wish them a prosperous New Year. I lay on the couch, listening to a master manager in action. At first I thought he did this to make his people feel important. Then I realized he did it to acknowledge that they *are* important.

That year, 1993, promised to be a thrilling year for SGK. U.S. Olympic runner Francie Larrieu Smith was our National Honorary Chair of the Race for the Cure Series. We were funding some amazing research, and with the passage of the Mammography Quality Standards Act, we were looking into the art of the possible, considering alliances and actions that might have a great effect from Capitol Hill.

About to celebrate our twelfth wedding anniversary, Norman and I headed for our home in Florida. Norman was leading the Chili's polo team in the Challenge Cup Tournament at the Palm Beach Polo and Country Club. The first week, play was postponed because of a relentless rain that had the players pacing in the bar and horses stamping restlessly in the stables.

January 21, 1993 was bright and beautiful. Perfect weather for polo.

Norman and his teammates—Stewart Armstrong, Fortunato Gomez, and George Olivas—rode out looking tan and invincible to face the Cadillac team led by Joe Henderson. The field was still a bit mucky, but the players went at it with their typical fervor. At the end of the second chukker, it was Chili's 3, Cadillac 2. The horses huffed and whinnied, visibly winded from slogging in the mud. Stewart and Norman both decided to change mounts during the break. When the players rode out again, Norman was on a quick and pretty little horse named Kachobie.

I'd been tending to some business, but before the third chukker began, I pulled my Land Cruiser into a spot right about midfield and climbed up to sit on the roof. The whistle blew, but play was suspended almost immediately. One of the horses had kicked up a dollop of mud that hit Norman in the face. The horses shuffled and hedged and the players ribbed each other in good nature while Norman dismounted and wiped his eye with a clean towel.

He glanced my way, and I waved, but I don't know if he saw me.

Norman swung back into the saddle and loped down the field. The ball was back in play with Cadillac in control. Henderson hit a cut shot, and Norman countered from a defensive position, but the ball clipped off at an angle between Kachobie's dancing feet. Norman turned and blazed after it. I'm not sure he even realized that Henderson's mount was coming at him. It's possible he was having trouble seeing because of the mud in his eye. Or maybe Kachobie, who was usually fleet and fierce, was lumbering a bit because of the field conditions. Norman and Henderson were both galloping at breakneck speed. In the split second before they came together, Norman and Kachobie reeled to the side.

T-boned is the term for what happened next.

Henderson's mount screamed like the braking of a freight train. The impact smashed Kachobie to the ground. Norman took the blunt force of the fall directly to the side of his head and was instantly rendered unconscious with the full weight of his horse on top of him. Kachobie lay stunned for a moment, then began heaving in panic. She struggled to find her legs, but couldn't and rolled back on Norman's body, crushing his ribs. The other players scrambled from their mounts and rolled her onto her back, trying to gentle her thrashing.

By this time I was off the roof of the SUV and running down the field, my boots pounding over the hardpan areas, slipping and stumbling in the mud between. Norman had fallen about a hundred yards from where I was sitting. He always raised his hand when he fell, even if he couldn't get up right away—all I needed to see was his hand—but he lay motionless.

Don't scream. Don't scream. He'll be embarrassed.

I reached Norman just as the little medical van bumped up across the sod and lurched to a stop. Someone with the best of intentions had rolled Norman onto his back and removed his helmet. When I fell to my knees beside him, he was gray and lifeless.

"*Oh, God—Norman! Norman, can you hear me?*"

Norman's eyes were closed, his mouth bluish gray.

I shrieked over my shoulder to the attendant climbing out of the medical van. "*He's not breathing!* Get oxygen! Get the oxygen and bring the board! He has to be immobilized."

The young man looked at me wide-eyed. He was used to splinting broken fingers, maybe slinging a broken arm firmly enough for the ride to the hospital. Nothing like this.

"It's—it's locked." He pointed at the back of the van. "I don't know where they keep the oxygen."

His partner finally got the door open and located the oxygen bags.

"Do you know how to activate it?" I asked.

"Um . . . I think you pull this . . ."

"Give it to me."

He cleared Norman's mouth while I activated the bag. (Suzy had used a similar device. It's not something you forget.) As soon as it was strapped over Norman's face, he dragged in a deep, tortured breath.

"Norman? *Norman.*" I stroked his face and kissed his forehead. "Norman, hang on."

Someone had volunteered to run to the clubhouse to call for an ambulance, but I knew that would take at least thirty minutes. I gripped Norman's hand, cursing myself for leaving the Land Cruiser back at midfield.

"Get him in the van," I told the attendant. "We're taking him to the hospital."

"We can't transport patients. It's against state law."

"*Screw the state law! Get him in there.*" I heard myself roar like a wolverine. I struggled to my feet, fists clenched at my sides. "I accept full responsibility. Whatever the consequences—just—just *help me*. Please."

We got him on the board and into the van.

"Take him to Wellington Regional," I told the attendant. "I'll follow you."

There was a mobile phone in my car. (This was back in the day when the damn thing was the size of a brick and tethered to a base under the dashboard.) I ran for the Land Cruiser as fast as I could, fighting for calm, for a thought process. It had been about five minutes since he hit the ground. How long had he stopped breathing? Three minutes? I got in, gunned the engine, and peeled out of the gravel parking lot, groping for the phone. I bumped up onto the road behind the medical van and called Dr. Sandy Carden, a friend at St. Mary's Hospital in Palm Beach.

"*Sandy.* Sandy, thank God you're there. Please, help me. Norman's hurt. It's bad. He's unconscious. We're taking him to the Wellington ER."

"I'm calling a neurosurgeon. He'll meet you there," said Sandy.

His voice was even and cool. That helped. I hung up the phone but tried to hold on to that even, cool undertone as we wheeled into the breezeway at the small hospital. My heart sank. It was late in the afternoon. I wasn't even sure there would be a doctor on deck. It was a sleepy little facility back then. If the doctor was on call . . .

It had been almost twenty minutes now.

I threw open the car door and ran for the van. A male nurse pushed through the double doors and strolled out toward the curb in no particular rush. A combination of *Medical Center* reruns, panic, and a lot of time spent in cancer wards took over.

"*Code Blue! Code Blue!* I'm Dr. Brinker. This is my patient." I didn't think about it. I just did it. "He's in respiratory arrest. Get him to ICU. Get him intubated. *Stat! Let's move!*"

The ER staff instantly mobilized with a deference they don't show hysterical wives. Within moments, Norman was on a respirator, and though he didn't open his eyes, his color warmed from ash gray to a mottled flush as his vital signs stabilized. I scribbled through the paperwork, glancing nervously toward the door. *Where's the neurosurgeon?*

"We'd better get some x-rays," I told the nurse. "If this is a spinal cord injury, he'll need a steroid injection right away, won't he?"

"Yes, Doctor." He looked at me oddly but nodded and handed me a form for the x-ray.

There were no broken bones in his back or neck. Still no neurosurgeon. And not so much as a flicker of Norman's eyelids.

"I want him moved to St. Mary's. Call the trauma hawk." I called

Sandy from a phone at the nurse's station. "This is . . . this is Dr. Brinker. We're bringing that patient I told you about."

Sandy was waiting for us with a team of specialists. Norman was whisked to the ICU. I stood in the hall, shaking in my muddy boots. One of the merciful sisters came and spoke quietly with me, reassuring me. Over her shoulder, I watched them splay Norman out spread-eagled with monitor wires snaking out from his neck and torso, ventilator hose to his mouth and nose, IV tubing taped to his arm, catheter between his legs. A hole was drilled in his forehead, and a four-inch pipe protruded from it, standing straight up. The ICP, I would soon learn, the intercranial pressure monitor.

The coming and going settled into a quiet dusk. I pulled a plastic chair next to Norman's bed. The room fell still except for the soft beeping of the heart monitor and the librarian scold of the ventilator: *shush-hushhhh, shush-hushhhh*. Norman was in a deep coma. I stroked his arm and pressed my dry lips to his hand, listening with all my heart for any echo of where he might have gone, aching to follow. Wherever he was, I hoped there were horses.

This is that part of the movie they don't show. They insert a montage of cross-fading images, the terrified wife pacing, the shattered son and daughters lingering in the hallway, the doctors with their grave faces and endless jargon—a babble of technical terms and hope-crushing numbers. "On a scale of one to ten, he's a one." All this has to be compressed from days to moments, the space of a moving piece of music. To sit through it in real time would be unbearable. It *was* unbearable.

Dr. Phil Williams, a dear friend and neurosurgeon, came from Dallas, examined Norman thoroughly, and discussed the prognosis with us.

"If he comes out of the coma—and that's a big if right now—he'll likely see some progress initially. He might be able to recover some mobility and be quite functional as far as speech and cognition. Typically, with this type of injury, there's improvement, then a plateau, followed by steady decline."

Periodically, the ICP protruding from Norman's forehead issued a shrill warning, and the attending physician rushed in and administered a drug that kept the swelling of his brain in check. The rest of the time nurses and orderlies came and went quietly, maintaining him in this terrifying suspended animation. Norman's attorney came with the president of Brinker International, and we crafted a press release. Norman was the CEO of a fast-growing, publically held company. We had to be circumspect but truthful in the statement that would be released late in the afternoon on Friday, after the stock markets closed.

"He's still undergoing tests," I said. "He's stable. He's strong. I'm going to assume that he's going to be all right."

It was agreed. They faxed me the statement. We made copies, and Eric took them to a little bank of pay phones in the hall. The phones rang one after the other. Eric, Daddy, and Margaret and a few others kept a rotation going, sitting there answering the phones, reading the statement to media people and others who called.

> Norman E. Brinker, chairman and chief executive officer of Brinker International, Inc., was involved in a polo accident at the Palm Beach Polo Club in Florida on Thursday, January 21, 1993. Exact details of the incident are not yet known. Brinker is in the hospital, where he is being treated for his injuries. His vital signs are stable and the prognosis appears favorable.

On Sunday, the Brinker board met and named an interim chairman and CEO.

Instead of satisfying curiosity or settling rumors, the statement opened the sugar bowl for the ants. Reporters tried to sneak in and get pictures. Eric saw a "doctor" in surgical scrubs at the nurse's station outside Norman's room and recognized him as a man he'd seen down in the gift shop.

"Hey, that guy's not a doctor," Eric told Mommy and me. "Mom, when I went down to mail your letters, he was at the counter asking about Dad."

Mommy strode over to the guy, jammed her finger into his sternum, and said, "You get the hell out of here! I'm about to call the cops. In fact—no! You stay right where you are. I'm going to have you hauled out of here."

The guy was already sprinting down the hall, and for the first time in days, I found myself laughing.

"Oh, Mommy, that was stellar." I dabbed tears from the corners of my eyes. "That was a great moment. I can't wait to tell Norman."

The neurologist told me to watch the EKG and blood pressure monitor while I talked to him. I don't know if he really thought something was going to happen or he was just trying to keep me busy, but I did it.

"We usually do a tracheostomy by the ten-day mark," he told me.

"Can you wait? He won't like it if he wakes up with that thing. He'll hate it."

"We'll give it ten days."

We settled into a daily routine. I insisted they help me get Norman dressed. The hospital gown was just not him. He wouldn't have wanted his children to see him like that. I'd rallied his friends so we could keep a steady rotation of stimulating conversation going on around him. Polo game videotapes on a VCR. The *Wall Street Journal* read cover to cover every morning. I rotated in with medical journals and research, but instead of continuing on the path of discovery I'd been on during the fifteen years since Suzy was diagnosed with breast cancer, I did a deep dive into the perplexing science of brain function and dysfunction, ravenously consuming everything I could find on decerebrate rigidity and decorticate posturing (the tortured poses that indicate severe brain injury) and the Babinski response (what the toes do or don't do when the sole of the foot is stimulated). I was trying to assimilate a daunting amount of information, and none of it was very comforting.

The physical therapist helped me work every muscle in his arms and legs. The radiologist's team came and took him for daily CAT scans and MRIs. I rotated his wrists and massaged his hands, telling him about his horses at home.

"Kachobie's going to be all right. The vet says you can ride her again in a month or so. Juanita and Little Delta miss you. Every time I walk into the barn, they come nosing over, wanting to know where you are." I flexed his fingers one at a time and whispered, "Where are you, Norman? Where are you?"

He'd been perfectly still for ten days and was beginning to look gaunt.

"He has a very high metabolism," I told the nutritionist. "He needs more calories. I don't want him to wake up and find himself wasted away."

I brought in a St. Anthony icon and a St. Jude to boot, fixed a mezuzah on the doorframe and set a Hindu prayer wheel on the nightstand. I played John Philip Sousa marches on a little tape deck during his exercise time and stirring classical pieces the rest of the day. No "Moonlight Sonata" or baroque quartets; I played "Hall of the Mountain King" and "March of the Toreadors"—Grieg, Mahler, Wagner—music that demands *get up, get up, go forth,* while I sat by Norman's side, writing dozens of thank-you notes for flowers and gifts and well wishes that poured in from all over the world. We weren't allowing visitors other than family ("family" included Margaret Valentine, of course), but the Fords, Reagans, and Bushes called, along with Larry Hagman and his wife, Maj, and a host of celebrities who'd been feted at our annual luncheons over the years. Norman's friend Ross Perot went to Chili's in Dallas, had his picture taken surrounded by a bevy of shapely young waitresses, blew the photo up to the size of a panel truck, and posted it against the wall in the hospital room.

The Sunday after the accident, a great crowd of people turned out for the Race for the Cure in Palm Beach. The day Norman got hurt, I'd spent the morning completely preoccupied by the details and doing of it, but I'd hardly thought about it since. I heard there was a minute of silent prayer for Norman.

On February 3, he flexed his hand. The whole room cheered. Mom and Margaret and I whooped and cried and hugged each other. But no matter how we begged, he didn't do it again. I asked Ray Martinez, another good friend, to come in every morning and talk about polo. Still not a flinch from Norman. Another three days went by.

Norman's physician was pushing for the tracheostomy now. I'd been begging for another day, another day. We were sixteen days out now.

"Norman," I whispered in his ear. "Wake up. *Wake up,* Norman. They're going to put a hole in your throat tomorrow, and you're not going to like it. Norman. *Norman.* I'm selling the polo ponies. Do you hear me, Norman? If you don't wake up, they're gone. The horses and everything that goes with them. So you have to wake up. Please, Norman, wake up."

Nothing.

The next morning, Ray Martinez came in as usual.

"Good morning, Norman."

"G'morring, Ray."

I uttered a sharp, involuntary cry. Ray and I stood there, frozen in the moment, waiting for . . . anything. There was no sound or movement in the room for what seemed like a long time. Then Norman flexed his right arm.

"*Norman?*"

He turned his head slightly toward the sound of my voice. He opened his eyes, just a drowsy slit, but enough for me to see the color there.

"Oh, God, Norman. You're awake. You're here." I gripped his hand, weeping, kissing his face. "Thank God . . . thank God . . . you're here . . . oh, Norman."

He tried to mumble something, but I couldn't make it out with the tube in his throat.

"Don't try to talk. Just squeeze my hand if you understand me."

I gripped his hand the way you'd grip your brother's hand if you found him hanging off the side of a cliff. Norman took hold of my hand and didn't let go.

Norman had lost about twenty-five pounds while he was out. The left side of his body was paralyzed. He lay there without speaking for several days, drifting in and out of a fitful but normal sleep. Then he started talking incessantly in a strange, liquid language that cobbled together clicks, hums, and fragmented English. His body thrashed and flailed with all the kinetic energy he hadn't spent during those weeks of lying still. It was the tightly wired, slightly impatient, fully charged energy I'd always found exhilarating (and not just a little sexy)—the energy Norman and I had in common—only now it crackled, hissed, and twisted like a downed power line. Norman had to be restrained for his own safety.

"Please," I begged the neurologist, "there must be a better way. To be tied down like this is torture for him."

They started him in language and occupational therapy, and he didn't do well. They expected him to do things like make a bed, make coffee, recite the ABCs. It wasn't Norman.

"He doesn't even drink coffee," I said. "He runs restaurants. Ask him about that."

I told them to assign him to the youngest, prettiest physical therapists and engage him in conversations about polo horses and business. He did respond better to that, but his progress was two steps forward, one step back—and sometimes three steps back. It's ironic; if Norman had had cancer, I'd have been completely in the know. I'd have been up front with the action plan, on the ground and mobilized from day one. Brain injury was something I knew virtually nothing about. I was starting from zero, and while I'd grown a lot as a patient advocate in general terms, I felt dwarfed by everything I didn't know about his condition. I'd amassed a stack of books and publications and was wading my way through them, but I felt as if I were searching for my husband in some vast unknowable wilderness.

Eventually, he began putting together words that made sense but which came from some cubbyhole in his memory, as if doors and windows to the past thirty-five years were randomly opening and closing. Every once in a while he'd let loose a stream of profanity and X-rated jargon—words I'd never once heard from his mouth. He kept wondering what to do about his rabbits. He'd ask about his polo ponies, then want to go ashore on leave. Sometimes he thought I was his dead mother.

"Norman?" The neurologist leaned over him, shining a light in his eyes. "Do you know where you are?"

"On a boat. San Diego," Norman muttered.

"Do you know where you work?"

"Steak & Ale."

The neurologist held a mirror in front of Norman's face. "Norman, who is this?"

He studied the image in baffled annoyance. "It's some old man."

Standing off to the side by the machine that monitored his vitals, I felt an ice-cold trickle at the back of my neck. I had a box of home movies brought in and sat for hours, watching with him, narrating and prodding while Norman jerked and fought with his restraints, his eyes searching the room.

"Norman, look, there we are skiing at Vail. Look how beautiful Brenda is. She reminds me so much of her mom. Look at Eric and you, playing with Undie. Look, Norman. Here's us at our engagement party. And then we told everyone we were already married. Remember? Mommy said,

'Look, are you adults? How old are you? What are you waiting around for?' so we went to city hall and instead of an engagement party, we had a wedding reception." I leaned in and whispered to him about that night, everything we were to each other in our private moments. "We've been married twelve years tomorrow, Norman. Do you know that? How many days is that? Help me figure it out. Twelve years times 365 days . . . that's more than 4,000 days, Norm. Think about that."

He touched my face and smiled at me with all the affection a man has for his dead mother. The next morning, I heard Eric coaching him.

"Dad, what are you going to say when Mom gets here?"

"She talks too much."

"No, Dad, say *Happy Anniversary.*"

"She needs to calm down. Too high strung."

"Dad, can you say that? Happy . . . C'mon, Dad. Happy Anniversary. Easy."

I smiled, remembering how Norman had plagued Eric with math drills when he was little. When I walked into the room, Norman grinned his old grin.

"Happy Anniversary, Bruni."

I laughed and cried and hugged them both.

"I brought all the *Wall Street Journals* from while you were out." I set the stack beside him on the bed. "We have a lot of catching up to do. There's an article here saying the story of your injury generated more queries than any other CEO injury they'd ever reported. It's because your people love you, Norm. You should see the cards and letters. I've got them all in boxes according to region."

The support of Norman's corporate family meant so much to him. Their affection for him and dedication to the company lit a fire under him. The neurology team told us it would be a year or more before Norm would achieve any meaningful recovery, and that he was going to have to accept certain limitations in his life now. He was sixty-two years old, they told him, and couldn't expect to bounce back like a kid.

"You're wrong," he said flatly.

But they weren't.

It's so difficult for me to describe the years that followed. The first several weeks, we worked all day every day on simple cognitive functions and basic motor skills. He'd spend hours with the physical therapist while I took care of household matters and foundation business; the rest of the time we were together, drilling photographs and flash cards. I brought in videotapes of polo matches, and those calmed his restless limbs. With sheer grit, he kept excavating, drilling, grinding ahead, fighting for every small victory.

Norman did make a dramatic comeback. He had to accept that he'd never play polo again or ride horses in anything approaching the way he'd ridden before, but he worked at walking on his own, and he had realistic hopes of eventually resuming a role in his company.

April 29, 1993, we flew home. It was just the two of us, and Norman was very emotional. We flew into Love. (One of the reasons I still dig Dallas: you get to "fly into Love" over and over.) It was a forty-five-minute drive to the house, and Norman stayed wide awake.

"Good to be home," he said again and again. "Oh, boy, it's good to be home."

Norman had always embodied—and always will embody—everything about Texas that speaks to my soul. This was where he thrived, and I was so happy to see him back in his natural habitat. I had hopes for a while. When he's home, I kept telling myself, he'll remember who he is. We arrived at the house, and Norman stared out the tinted window, waiting for the driver to open his door.

Slowly, laboriously, he moved his legs, set one foot on the driveway, then the other. The driver made a move to help him, but I cleared my throat sharply and shook my head. Norman struggled to stand, got his bearings for a moment, then made his way to the front door without a cane or crutches, stitching one step onto the next, his arms taut as a tightrope walker's but hanging straight down at his sides. I stayed behind him and didn't make a sound. He rattled the front door open and stood in the foyer, breathing, steadying himself after the great effort.

"Well. I'm not Superman," he said. "But I'm back."

"You're home." I put my arms around him, kissed his mouth, stroked his neck. "We're home, and we've got a lot of work to do."

There was a Brinker International board meeting scheduled for

May 4. I made flash cards with photographs of the board members and drilled Norman relentlessly on their names. We practiced shaking hands and making small talk. Reassuring phrases, pleasant conversation. The meeting went well, and he was officially reinstated as chairman and CEO. Some people had reservations, and I understood that, but it was the right thing to do for the stockholders' sake, and more important (more important to me, anyway), it was something Norman desperately needed. This company was the culmination of his life's work. If they'd taken it from him, he would have felt defeated and betrayed. We had to surround him with full confidence now, full faith, full support.

The next day, Margaret and I took Norman to his office at the company headquarters. There was a massive banner: WELCOME BACK, NORMAN!—WE LOVE YOU! Margaret and I led him out to a patio on the ground floor. Four hundred employees had gathered on the lawn, and they greeted him with a roaring ovation. Norman spoke briefly, telling them how much he loved and appreciated them. People were moved to tears by his determination and that *grit*, that true, true grit. He cracked everyone up with a story about the team of specialists telling him he'd never be back on his feet by the May 1 deadline he'd set for himself.

"They didn't support me until five days ago. Then they started saying, 'Good idea, Norm, good idea!'"

Another roar of approval. The outpouring of emotion and support from his people was like an infusion of red blood cells for Norman. He started back with half days at the office, devoting hours every day to his physical therapy, and I continued to work with him on his memory, still searching in the wilderness for . . . something. His indefinable *Norm*ness seemed to be missing.

The continuing process over the years was unbearably frustrating to him. He was angry sometimes, and he could be cruel. It was as if the injury had sprung the lock on the normal filters that keep you from saying things you can't help thinking. The kindness I'd always admired in him was tinny and false now. He was lucid enough to know how to be polite, but his personality was unmistakably altered.

Lying in bed at night, I repeated the great Brinker Principles, everything he'd taught me as he mentored me through the launching of SGK and taught Eric as our boy grew to be a man. I recited those high concepts back to Norman now, reminding him of who he was, what he believed in, how he inspired people.

"*Dream the idea.*"

In 1994, Susan G. Komen Breast Cancer Foundation grantee Mary Claire King, Ph.D., discovered the gene mutation BRCA1, an indicator for inherited forms of breast cancer.

"*Get out in the field.*"

In 1995, Race for the Cure events were held in fifty-seven U.S. cities. We now had twenty-seven local affiliates from New York to Los Angeles.

"*Create the culture.*"

In 1996, we advanced our efforts and exponentially broadened visibility with two dozen corporate partnerships, cause-marketing initiatives, and sponsorship of the Race for the Cure Series. Pink was the new black. I sat on a sofa in George Michael's condo with Susan Carter Johns (now our vice president and chief of staff), eating potato chips with one of the Spice Girls, wondering how we got there.

"*Encourage innovation.*"

In 1997, in the world of crawling dial-up access and 5 1/4-inch floppies, we launched our first website, the world's first online resource specifically dedicated to breast health and breast cancer information.

"*Be growth oriented.*"

In 1998, the first Race for the Cure event outside the United States was held in Costa Rica, making the Race for the Cure Series the largest registered 5K in the world. We also helped the U.S. Postal Service launch its Breast Cancer Research stamp—the first stamp to generate funding for disease awareness and research. Funds were earmarked for the Department of Defense Breast Cancer Research Program and for breast cancer research at the NIH.

"*Listen, listen, listen.*"

In 1999, we established the African American National Advisory Council to further support the breast cancer needs of the African American population and to help reduce their mortality rate. The Interdisciplinary Breast Care Fellowship was established with the University of Texas Southwestern Medical Center to better educate clinicians about the special needs and care of breast cancer patients. Our first international affiliates opened their doors in Germany and Greece, and telomerase, an enzyme instrumental in a chromosome's ability to divide and replicate was discovered by SGK grantee Elizabeth Blackburn, Ph.D., who went on to win the Nobel Prize a decade later.

"Take a leadership role in your industry."

In 2000, one of our top legislative priorities was achieved when President Bill Clinton signed an executive order mandating that Medicare coverage include clinical trials. We provided $1.5 million in funding for a state-of-the-art research study on the quality of cancer care, collaborating with the American Society of Clinical Oncology, Harvard, and the Rand Corporation. Our new Italian affiliate, helmed by the indefatigable Riccardo Masetti, hosted a Race for the Cure event in Rome, and we established the Breast Health Advisory Council, bringing together internationally recognized breast cancer experts. For the first time in a single season, more than 1 million people crossed the finish line in the Race for the Cure Series.

"Delegate and empower."

At the turn of the century, our volunteer tour de force was 75,000 strong and growing. It always was and always will be our greatest asset.

Volunteer recognition was always an important part of our annual luncheon, and I'll never forget the year we honored Kris Plunkett and her teenage daughter, Sarah.

"We couldn't believe it," Sarah told me recently. "We did things like bake cookies, stuff envelopes, make copies. Mom always said if we did the ordinary tasks, that would free up the people at Susan G. Komen to do important things: raise money, help people, find a cure." (I must have coffee with Sarah soon, so we can discuss the meaning of the word *important*.)

Kris Plunkett was a seamstress, so she'd made smartly tailored suits for herself and Sarah, who was as thrilled as any Dallas kid would be when legendary Dallas Cowboys coach, Tom Landry, escorted them to the head table, where they hobnobbed with Lynda Carter, President and Betty Ford, and the Fords' daughter, Susan. Kris was never comfortable being the center of attention, and an arduous course of chemo and other treatment was beginning to wear on her, so she'd decided Sarah should give the acceptance speech when the time came.

"Mom thinks that Bette Midler song, 'Wind Beneath My Wings,' is about her children. That we're the wind beneath her wings, but we feel like it's the other way around. She's the one who lifts us up, being a home-room mom, Girl Scout leader, just being there when we need her. And it's like that with Susan G. Komen. We're so grateful for all the amazing things you all do for us and for a lot of other families. We always . . . we know that you . . ."

Sarah bit her lip and welled up with emotion, but her mother was there for her.

"We know where we can go when we need a hug," Kris said, slipping her arm around her daughter's waist. "Thank you."

Kris Plunkett died the following year, but as long as she had the strength to get out of bed, she and Sarah continued to step up for all those extraordinary ordinary tasks. They also went out wherever they were called to go, sharing their story, reminding audiences that when cancer happens to one person, it happens to an entire family.

"Most women dread the thought of becoming their mother," Sarah says. "I strive to be half as amazing as my mom."

She and I have that in common.

Carl Sagan wrote, "The secrets of evolution are time and death."

The truth of this is clear in cellular biology. Cancer cells are lethal because they proliferate beyond control and refuse to die. This isn't a foreign object in your body; this is *you*, your own biology going so against your nature, it can actually kill you. We all have cancer cells roaming silently through our bodies. They are part of what we are, and they're only dangerous when a genetic mutation allows them to take control.

In a strange way, this is how it was with Norman's personality. Just as Dr. Phillips had predicted, his brain repaired itself on a functional level and reached a plateau where he was reasonable, insightful even. He had wise answers for good questions and wise questions for good answers. His brilliance for business still flashed when he was well rested and feeling focused. His visionary edge was blunted, but he was competent enough to know that, and it pained him. Without question, even on his worst days, he was still smarter than 99 percent of the people in the room.

But then, as predicted, he began to decline. Subconscious impulses—the murky proclivities and flickering inclinations we all have in us—slowly, invasively reached *karkinos* tentacles into the very tissue of his *self*, and his conscious mind was too wounded to fight it. The man I'd loved for four thousand nights was right there, flesh and blood in front of me, and I still loved him with every fiber of my being. But the man who loved me was gone.

Cancer and age couldn't have torn us apart. As long as our minds were connected, we were indivisible. Had his injury been anything other than what it was, I believe our marriage would have survived. For seven years, I refused to let go, but as the old century limped to a close, the death throes were undeniable, and we divorced early in 2000.

Not the way either of us had dreamed of celebrating our twentieth anniversary.

Candidly, I would have stayed married to him. I'd have thrown down my pride and let people say whatever they wanted to say about me. Let them shake their heads and tsk-tsk behind their hands in the ladies' room about the idiot wife who's the last to know. Newsflash: The wife is the *first* to know, but she's the last to give up on a man and judge him on that one criterion.

I'm not making excuses for men who philander, but I knew Norman had an image as a vital and virile and active man. I wanted him to feel that way about himself again, but there was much about his presence that undermined his powerful image now: the stitched gait, the slur of his speech when he was tired, the extra moment it took for him to come up with a one-liner, and the labor it took for him to get from Point A to Point B. He eventually had to retire, and even though it was at an age when a lot of people *want* to retire (and he did retain the title of chairman emeritus at Brinker International), retirement had never been part of Norman's plans. It made him feel old and unmanned, out of the running. If other women could have fixed that for him, I would have endured it, but it came to my attention that he was allowing one of them to bleed him for money. Enough money for me to notice. Beyond the fact that my fate was inextricably bound to his, it terrified me because this behavior was so antithetical to who Norman was.

"Get rid of her," I told him. "If you need to pretend that these women are—that they do something for you . . . do what you have to do, but not with her."

"I'll do as I please. No one's stopping you from doing the same."

"If you don't get rid of her, I want my finances segregated from yours. I don't want to leave you, but I'm not going to let this parasite take what you've worked for."

"That's not what I worked for." There was a twitch of disgust in his upper lip.

"Please, Norman, don't do this. *Why are you doing this?*"

"What do you expect me to do?" he said bitterly. "Spend the rest of my life going to your award ceremonies?"

"If you push me out of your life, who'll take care of you?" I realized too late it was the cruelest thing I could have said. I covered my face with my hands so he wouldn't see me begging. "We can do whatever you want, Norman. What do you want?"

"I want her."

The secrets of evolution. Time and death.

Knowing when to grow and when to let go.

Words are such shallow containers for human emotion, barely a tea-cup dipped in a deep blue sea. Pages can't name what this man meant to me or how deeply agonized I was by the loss of him. Norman Brinker didn't create me, but he planted me like a tree. Fed and pruned by him, I grew, branched out, bore fruit, experienced seasons of winter rest and spring glory. But because I took such deep root in this place where I belonged, when he walked away, I couldn't follow. To take me with him, he would have had to cut me down, and Norman was still enough himself that he couldn't bear to do that.

At the same time, he wasn't born to be anybody's wingman; he couldn't follow me either. The gossip mill ground out rumors that I'd abandoned him in his hour of need, that I'd run off with a younger man, that I was too consumed with my own ambitions to care about my family. It tore my heart out, but there was no point in saying anything about it, and I didn't expect him to step in and defend me. I understood why he had to tell people, "I just couldn't handle her anymore." This clichéd explanation went down as easily as an oyster with men who fancied themselves "handlers" of their wives.

Texas is famous for its epic high-dollar and high-drama divorces, but ours was quite unremarkable. I didn't fight for money; he insisted on giving me more than I asked for. We had an accountant suggest a settlement and didn't even engage attorneys until the official documents were drawn up. Immediately after the papers were signed, the woman who'd been influencing Norman's finances disappeared. I was baffled at first, even felt a stab of hope that we might reconcile. But then I understood. This was the only crowbar he could have used to pry me away.

I asked Norman to stay on the SGK board, and he readily agreed. He attended board meetings faithfully, sitting next to me as he always had, and his hand always found mine under the table. He and Eric remained closer than ever as Eric's career thrived. They had a lot to talk about now, a lot in common. Just three years after he graduated from Bradley, Eric became director of brand management at JetBlue Airways. Norman was incredibly proud of him, but for a long time, Eric struggled to understand what had happened to his dad.

"He always says he loves you and that you'd still be married if not for that accident," he told me. "I don't know why he'd sacrifice everything for . . . for what? A *game*? He knew how dangerous it was. Why would he take that risk?"

If there's no risk, what fun would it be?

That's who Norman was. I wouldn't have had him any other way.

The following year, as I prepared to leave for Hungary, I asked Norman to go with me. I didn't really expect him to say yes, but I had to ask.

"They still remember you in Budapest," I said. "Norman Brinker, *kitűnő lovas*. The great horseman. They'd be thrilled to see you. And I could use the benefit of your wisdom."

"You'll do fine." With genuine gladness, he added, "You're really soaring now."

"Don't I know it." I had a fleeting thought of Suzy, taking flight for Spain with her Dramamine and vodka.

"I love you, Bruni."

"I love you, Norman."

Two years later, he married a blonde.

III

Revolution

17

Bridge of Light

Among the fables and myths that surround the Szechényi Chain Bridge, which spans the Danube connecting Buda and Pest, is the misconception that the stately stone lions flanking the imposing cast-iron structure have no tongues. One tall tale has the disillusioned sculptor flinging himself into the Danube after being mocked by critics.

In another story, he retorts, "You wish your wives had tongues like my lions!"

That always gets a big laugh. The Eastern Bloc equivalent of "Take my wife—*please*."

The truth is, the Chain Bridge lions do have tongues. You can't readily see them because instead of arching up or lolling out, they lie flat on the floor of the lions' mouths. I liked that the sculptor designed them that way. To me, it was a symbol of the tremendous strength of the Hungarian people, despite the way they'd been dominated and silenced. There's strength to be found in self-restraint. One should have a tongue, but know when to keep it low in the mouth. There's a time to roar and a time to purr. The necessary art of knowing the difference is called *diplomacy*, and I'm proud to say this is a trait the president recognized in me.

I'd known Laura and George W. Bush since the 1980s, when they came to Dallas with his baseball team, the Texas Rangers. Norman had been a supporter of "41"—President George H. W. Bush—since the 1960s, when he first ran for the Congress. Laura and I both have that volunteer gene, so we got along just fine, and I liked her husband, who always seemed smart, funny, and full of energy. When he was running for governor in 1994, he invited me to his office and asked for my support, knowing it was going to be a tough call for me.

I liked our current governor, Ann Richards. I supported her. She was smart and tough; she had integrity and a good, good soul. And not too fine a point, but SGK was less than a dozen years old. I didn't want to jeopardize our advocacy efforts by alienating the most powerful woman in the state. Ann Richards had a rock-solid base; I honestly didn't know if George Bush could win against her. But when we sat down and talked about the issues that mattered to me, I liked what he had to say.

Over the next several years, politics became so polarized, it was a bit of a flying trapeze act maintaining friends and allies on both sides of the aisle. Norman was well known for his support of conservative Republicans, but everyone who knew me knew that my priorities were advancing the science of cancer treatment and improving consumer access to it. I served on the Steering Committee for the National Dialogue on Cancer, and we did our best to keep it exactly that: a dialogue. I spoke at the Republican National Convention and was still welcomed to work with U.S. senators Dianne Feinstein and Ted Kennedy, U.S. congressman John Dingell, and other Democrats on cancer-related legislation over the years. Later on, serving as President George W. Bush's chief of protocol during the 2008 changing of the guard, I worked with incoming vice president Joe Biden and his wife, Dr. Jill Biden, who hosted special events surrounding the Washington, D.C., Race for the Cure. In my experience, people who keep their eyes on the ball have very little trouble engaging in the nonpartisan conversation about cancer.

"We can respond with anger and destruction and get nothing done," I told a House subcommittee hearing, "or you can take the energy and channel it into something productive. I believe we can make a difference here."

Shortly after the 2000 presidential election, I was informed that President Bush was considering me for an embassy post. It was either the best possible timing or the worst. Norman and I had just finalized our divorce, and though I was dating, I was in no emotional shape to get entangled in a serious relationship. Better to fall in love with a country, I suppose, and for better or worse, that's what happened.

When one becomes an ambassador for the U.S. State Department, the first step is being invited, but a lot goes on behind the scenes of every appointment; the president doesn't just call you up and pop the question. There is, of course, some political "You scratch my back, I'll scratch yours" sometimes. Optimally, it isn't all about payback, however, because anyone in an embassy position overseas has a duty to represent the citizens of the United States along with the foreign policy of the president and the National Security Council, and I've never met an ambassador who took that less than seriously. It's prudent for the president to appoint a friend, someone he knows and trusts, because each ambassador serves "at the pleasure of the president." The president has to know that if you are told to go and deliver a message to the people of that country, you're going to say, to the letter, exactly what you were told to say. There's a great deal of vetting, interviewing, and assessing leading up to the appointment, and (one would hope) a great deal of soul-searching on the part of the appointee.

For me, the most conflicted aspect of the decision was leaving the daily running of SGK. Being appointed an ambassador means you have to step away from any ties to corporate or nonprofit organizations to avoid any possibility of even the appearance of impropriety. I'd always felt fiercely protective of Suzy's name and the organization by extension, and of course, I wanted things done the way I wanted them done, but there was no doubt in my mind that my colleagues would be able to carry on the work we'd set out to do.

"A hallmark of great leaders," Norman had told me long before this, "is that they're not indispensible."

My mentor Max Fisher had given me the same advice: raise up lieutenants and mentor strength within the organization. It's bruising to the ego to think the world will continue to rotate just fine without you, but if you care more about your organization than you care about your ego, that's not a problem. I knew Norm and Max were right, and I tried hard from the beginning to bring in the best people I could find, then step back and let them do what they're good at.

It was a painful but healthy recognition: My leaving was going to hurt me more than it would hurt them. Norman would stay on the board, along with a dear friend and founding board member, Bob Taylor. I trusted them. Susan Braun was our CEO, and I probably owe her a dozen roses quarterly for life.

Once I'd made the decision to serve, I was asked if there was somewhere in particular I might be best qualified to serve, and I immediately thought of eastern Europe. I'd traveled there when Eric went to study at the University of Economics in Prague, Czech Republic, while working on his degree at Bradley. I loved the spirit of eastern Europe, the challenges of a newborn democracy, the sharp-chiseled men and bold, alto women. I felt an inexplicable connection to the bone structure of the art and architecture of Hungary.

At the time, genetic evidence was emerging about the profile of the BRCA carriers; a significant percentage of those carrying the mutation were Ashkenazi Jews descended from a key group of about six thousand people who lived in northern Europe before the Diaspora of the early 1900s. I made a wide study of cultural and technological assets and needs in eastern Europe and concluded that Hungary was perfectly poised for a major step forward in breast cancer awareness and response. Their medical facilities were underfunded, but staffed with willing hands, sharp minds, and all the technology needed for modern screening and treatment. The women were not ignorant by any stretch of definition, but they were very modest and personally conservative. They weren't very vocal about their bodies, and the importance of early detection simply hadn't been talked about.

"We could help Hungary lead the charge and really advance the cause of women's health care in eastern Europe," I told the president. "Not just breast cancer—women's health care in general, and I'd even include the problem of sex trafficking in that. I'm very concerned about what I've learned about young women who are taken across international borders, swindled into handing over their passports, and then bought and sold like cattle. We have to speak out against it. We can't make them change their laws, but we can shine a light on what's happening there and make it an embarrassment if they allow it to continue."

I received the appointment, went through rigorous training, and spent months immersed in all things Hungarian, eating the food, educating myself on their history and politics, drilling key phrases in the difficult language. The first week of September, I was sworn in by my new boss, Secretary of State Colin Powell, and that was a terrific day for my whole family. Mom and Daddy were there, button-bursting proud. When he was young, my father's dream was to serve as an officer in World War II, but migraines and poor eyesight prevented him from enlisting.

He'd always secretly (and sometimes not very secretly) wanted a boy, and after a lifetime of trying, this was the closest I ever came to being the son he never had. Eric held the Bible while I was sworn in, and Norman stood off to the side, beaming like nobody's business.

As I prepared to depart, I studied the weather and planned my wardrobe accordingly. I'd read something about a river flooding in the city and had purchased a pair of rubber camouflage boots, imagining myself hurling sandbags with my Hungarian friends. The State Department's Art in Embassies Program had curated a spectacular collection of twentieth-century American women artists, which was to be installed in the embassy gallery on my arrival, and I'd looked forward to hosting schoolchildren and women's groups, thinking this would be a way for me to begin my health care outreach. I packed suits and dressed with those occasions in mind. *Nothing too fancy,* I could hear Suzy saying, *but certainly nothing frumpy.*

I was up early on the beautiful September Tuesday I was scheduled to leave for Budapest. My assistant came to take me to the airport, and as I settled the last of my bags in the trunk, I decided to dash back to the kitchen for a couple of water bottles. The little television set on the counter had been left on, and though the volume was low, I could tell something was terribly wrong the moment I walked into the room. That image that was to become horribly familiar caught my eye for the first time.

Bright blue sky cut with fire. Smoke billowing over the New York skyline.

I ran out to the car and told my assistant, "Come inside. Something terrible is happening."

A few days later, an acquaintance with a private plane received permission to fly to Budapest, and she allowed me and several business leaders to fly over with her. When the flight touched down in Hungary, people there assumed the private jet was mine, and they were all terribly impressed.

The world in which I'd eagerly agreed to serve was an economically stable, peacefully turning planet. Post 9/11, everything had changed— from the process of getting on an airplane to the messages I would be

charged with bringing to these people and this government. My thoroughly planned agenda for helping Hungary lead the charge and advance
the cause of women's health care in eastern Europe was now on the back
burner. In fact, if there was something even farther back than the back
burner—like a brick wall separating the kitchen from the garage—my
agenda would have been well behind it.

To say I was nervous is a gross understatement. Odd as this may
sound, I hadn't spent much time working in a real job since Eric was a
toddler. Almost everything I'd done since I married Norman, I'd done
as a volunteer. This position was already a dramatic departure from everything familiar, and now all my meticulous preparations applied to a
universe that no longer existed. But as we approached the embassy gate,
I saw a field of flowers, candles, stuffed animals, and homemade gifts
spread in front of the wrought iron fence with cards, letters, and posters
welcoming me and expressing love and support for the United States. It
was one of the most humbling and precious moments of my life. I arrived
with my hat in my hand, and the citizens of Hungary surrounded me
with generosity and understanding.

Our first order of business revolved around the heightened security
measures worldwide, which caused innumerable logistical headaches for
Hungarian companies doing business in the United States and American
companies doing business in Hungary. There was much to do every day,
much to learn. As a member of the diplomatic corps, I was also charged
with the inspection of Hungarian military exercises. Late one night there
was a pounding at my door. I was told it was time to do the inspection,
and what could I do? I pulled on my rubber camouflage boots, and off
we went.

My goal was to get to know people in the government before trying
to drag some attention back to my health care agenda, but one of my first
assignments was part of our government's effort to promote democratic
principles. I was given a strongly worded message to deliver regarding increased sensitivity toward hate speech, anti-Semitism, and inflammatory
rhetoric in the media. I was to speak to a gathering of business leaders,
government officials, and members of the press at the Harvard Club about
our responsibility to support freedom and to confront hate and terrorism.

"That's going to create trouble for you," Daddy worried, and I knew he was right.

I didn't want to do it. Not so soon. I would have liked a little time to make friends and create a rapport with the government leaders. The room was full of seriously manly men who weren't going to appreciate being scolded by a Jewish American woman about anti-Semitism. But I did what was asked of me. The Hungarians didn't love me for it, but I think they were pleasantly surprised at my grit, and I followed it up with every gesture of goodwill I could think of in an effort to make friends. I talked with my father every day, and he coached me with calm, solid advice.

The spectacular exhibit of women's art was stranded somewhere in wounded New York City. Curators were reluctant to ship it with the heightened terror alerts and security concerns. It would be a while. No one could tell me how long.

"This could actually be an excellent opportunity for me to do something for the artists here," I told Mom and Daddy. "The embassy could host an exhibition of Hungarian artists who haven't gotten enough face time in the world market. There's wonderful art here, Mommy. Suzy would have loved all that living color. All the great movements are represented—everything from Impressionists to modern poster art—and none of it has gotten the attention it deserves."

I went to my friend István Rozsics, a historian and art consultant who'd been instructing me on Hungarian culture in preparation for this post, and asked him if some contemporary Hungarian artists might want to display their paintings. The answer was an enthusiastic yes, and soon the place was filled with works by Lázló Fehér, István Nádler, Károly Klimó, Imre Bak, Tamás Soós, and Attila Szűcs. Once I'd spent a little time living with these paintings, I knew I'd never want to live without them again.

The people, seen and unseen, in these paintings spoke to me like soul mates and kindred spirits. They were vibrant and engaged. Energy born of anger, determination born of loss. But there was a playfulness there as well, a sporting sense of joy and, sometimes, a dignified but darkly knowing sensuality.

Ich bin ein jelly doughnut.

I couldn't speak the language, but I knew I belonged there.

The American Embassy residence had fallen somewhat into disrepair. If you're a guest in someone's house, you're not going to insult them by painting the place while you're in town, but this isn't a Hungarian guest-house; it's a little piece of the United States within their country. Letting it get shabby is like parking a wreck of a car in someone else's driveway. It should be a symbol of who we are. I raised a bit of money and used some of my own to renovate the bathrooms and update the ancient electrical features and employed local craftspeople to restore the elegance and shine to the wood and glasswork.

Slowly but surely, I did forge friendships in the Hungarian government, and I was able to nudge the topic of women's health care into conversation, advance my ideas across the table, and win a few powerful allies, including the Hungarian president's wife. Eventually, I gained the trust and cooperation of many heads of state and of the good people of Hungary.

Our goal for the Bridge of Health Alliance Against Breast Cancer was to connect the million or so Hungarian women most at risk with the information and facilities that would offer them significantly improved odds for survival. The only thing standing in our way was a system in need of transparency and repair. For generation upon generation, breast cancer had been unspeakable, untouchable. Hungarian women suffered and died quietly, just as American women once had—before Betty Ford and Rose Kushner started shaking things up. I sensed that this country was ready to make that leap in language, and now I'd seen firsthand that if we could shake those words loose, change would be unstoppable.

I proposed an educational symposium followed by a Sunday evening walk across the Chain Bridge, from Adam Clark Square on the Buda side to the Hungarian Academy of Sciences, a spectacular Neo-Renaissance building in Pest. Nearby Roosevelt Square would serve as the perfect place for a celebration of life and offer a rabble-rouser's-eye view of Parliament.

"Wouldn't it be dazzling," I suggested, "if the bridge were illuminated in pink?"

It was a plan that purred on paper, but which in practical reality would roar.

The formidable pillars of the Chain Bridge had towered virtually unchanged for more than 150 years as the clatter of horse-drawn carriages evolved to streaming urban traffic. Even when Hitler's retreating forces swarmed and destroyed every bridge in Budapest, the pillars stood, and the majestic lions maintained their silent resolve. The bridge itself embodies survivorship and was built as a symbol of national awakening. All this made it the perfect place to begin our journey. The visual transformation would pack a tremendous wallop, generating a buzz of curiosity—and yes, a little controversy—without leaving so much as a chalk mark on a single stone. Every eye in the city would widen just a little. Media across the country would ask the obvious questions, and we would be ready to answer with solid facts and accessible resources. Bathed in pink light, the path would be plain, and we would take the first steps together, beginning in the garden square in Buda, at the stylized Zero Kilometer Stone.

The actual lighting of the bridge turned out to be as complicated and expensive as all other aspects of the event combined. I'd gotten the technology and cost covered by a company owned by General Electric, but Hungarians have great reverence for their monuments. The powers that be weren't eager to endorse the disruption of history or rush hour traffic. "That's never been done" is the reason I'm most often given for why one can't do a thing I'm already convinced I can and most assuredly will do. The second most frequent speed bump is "People won't like it," and I'm equally happy to circumnavigate that one, but gently. With diplomacy.

My respect for the magnificent city of Budapest and for this historic landmark was genuine, and I made a point of expressing my appreciation to everyone from the mayor to the maintenance workers. There was an endless exchange of forms, phone calls, meetings, and e-mail. Coffee and protocol. Lots of sit-down, face-to-face time with the event committee, the health committee, the diplomatic committee. For months, I lay awake, agonizing over the permits, permissions, and logistics. Having secured the necessary paperwork, I assembled an energized team of people to accomplish the task. Then I lay awake agonizing over whether anyone would come.

The day of the event, the first subtle rumblings of thunder nudged through the clouds just before sunset. A light drizzle settled over the stone lions as they lounged, circumspect, atop the grand abutments that bookend the bridge. Shielding my forehead with a gloved hand, I scanned the threatening sky above the rolling river.

There would be rain; there often is.

It's uncanny how many times I've seen this happen in the years—the decades—that have flown by. It starts with hazy precipitation. We're all nervously glancing back and forth from our wristwatches to the gathering weather. The teasing drizzle sets us on edge; it keeps us acutely mindful of the importance of our cause and the fragile, no-guarantees nature of life, but from that first foot over the starting line in Dallas to the moment our millionth runner crossed the finish line in Rome almost twenty years later, it seems like the actual downpour always waits until we've done what we came to do. Then the torrent comes down with unbroken spirit, drenching the scattering crowd, dripping off the drooping balloons, melting the crepe paper decorations.

Those are the moments I feel closest to Suzy. It's as if she's holding an umbrella over our heads. The rain always holds off until after the event.

Well, almost always.

It'll hold off, I assured the taciturn lions. They glowered down at me, wet and skeptical, and I thought about the gloomy skies over Willow Bend. But the people came that day, and kept coming for twenty years.

By sunset, we were eight hundred strong. Despite the chilly wind and persistent drizzle, we gathered in the square, linked arms, lit candles. And Suzy held back the rain until we reached the other side, marching arm in arm. In remembrance of our sisters. In honor of our mothers. In defense of our daughters. Passing beneath the gaze of the guardian lions, we reached the opposite shore and sent up a great roar. My throat ached with the nearness of my sister, the beauty of the evening, the commitment of all those assembled here. For that moment, we all understood each other. Without this moment, nothing explored or explained inside the Academy of Sciences would have made a bit of difference.

Think globally; act locally, the saying goes. So we began, I and my small circle of friends in Dallas. Never underestimate the power of so-called Ladies Who Lunch. Twenty years and more than $1 billion later, I stood beside the stone lions on the other side of the world, and that old saying had rotated on its axis. We were poised to *think locally; act globally,* but the message and mission remained the same. My heart still burned with Suzy's singular resolve and stammered with all my old uncertainties.

"Ambassador?"

A small woman touched my elbow. The gesture was tentative, but the face was brave. She met my eye with the piercing blue gaze I'd come to appreciate since assuming my post at the U.S. Embassy in Hungary. She might have been a doctor or a survivor or a sister; we all looked the same in our heavy winter coats. Rich and poor, men and women, young and old, we were all bundled in leather and down, chins tucked low in our wool scarves, cheeks and noses glowing from the light but biting wind.

"Hello," I said, leaning in to close the ten-inch gap between my tall frame and her small one. "I'm so glad you're here."

"I just wanted to thank you," she said. "I don't know if we would have had the courage to do it without you."

My Hungarian was sparse and labored, and because I love the sound of the language, I'm reluctant to butcher it. I put my arms around her, wishing I had the vocabulary to tell this woman there was never a doubt in my mind regarding the courage of the Hungarian people. Their natural tenacity and stubborn pride, their resilience through tortured centuries of wars and rumors of wars, the eagerness of their young scholars, and a general willingness to progress—everything I loved about this great country—surrounded me every day of my sojourn with its beautiful people and spoke to me through its magnificent art.

While I was still living in Budapest, I began the collection of paintings that now sojourn with me.

Béla Czóbel's *Reclining Girl* rests in a jumble of rich, womblike colors, brushstrokes, shadows, and textures. Up close, it's chaotic; she doesn't come easy. But step back ten feet, and she makes complete sense. Much like any real woman, I suppose. Her creator was prolific and painted for a long time. She wasn't his only love, but his affection for the reclining girl is lush and apparent.

Róbert Berény's contrasting images in *Still Life with Pitcher and Fruit* and *Still Life with Blue Pitcher* tell two love stories: The pitcher in *Pitcher and Fruit* suggests a naked (and well-endowed) man strutting his stuff while the mordantly female fruit lies nearby playing hard to peel. The *Blue Pitcher* pitcher keeps his pants on, behaving properly in a formal setting, but his apple admirers are vibrating inside their skin. You get the feeling they're about to jump off the platter.

When I look at these works, I'm reminded what a revelation it was for Suzy and me when we spent that summer exploring Europe's tapestry of art and politics.

There's a Rembrandt feel to Mihály Munkácsy's *Tin Drum* boy, who stands barefoot and grinning in a dark, stubbled field. His clothes are ragged but clean, and he beats his battered drum with found sticks— thumb-thick twigs he's picked up off the ground or broken from the branch of a dead tree. You've never seen anyone with so much nothing and so much something all at the same time. He's there where everyone else isn't, making whatever noise he can.

You can't help wanting to follow him.

Higher Learning

ACCORDING TO *Webster's Dictionary*, the verb *commence* comes from the Vulgar Latin *cominitiare*, meaning "to have or make a beginning." People tend to think of commencement exercises as the end of high school or college, but as I watched Eric cross the stage to collect his high school diploma at Landmark and again to collect his degree from Bradley, it did feel very much like a starting point.

Maura de Souza, a bright and beautiful twenty-two-year-old, earned her degree in music from Sam Houston State University, completing her last year of studies after being diagnosed with a high-grade unclassified sarcoma, a virulent, invasive cancer in her abdomen. Maura's parents and sisters formed a phalanx of support around her. Her friends made paper cranes, wore teal wristbands, and gave to sarcoma research. Members of the Dynamo, Houston's professional soccer team, could be seen sporting Maura's teal wristbands as they loped down the field. Her oncologist worked feverishly to get her into a clinical trial that might buy her a few more months, but the week before graduation, it was clear Maura wasn't going to walk the stage with the rest of the class of 2009. Faculty and administration from the School of Music came to M. D. Anderson with her cap, gown, and honor cord, filing into her hospital room, "Pomp and Circumstance" playing on a CD player, all participants in full regalia.

Dr. James M. Bankhead, chairman of the School of Music, gave a brief commencement address.

"This is a beginning, a celebration of new and wonderful things. While commencement may indicate the culmination of a great deal of work, many years in school, work done in classrooms with many wonderful teachers, wonderful classmates, it is mostly the result of the work of the individual student—a student who is gifted, beautiful, really intelligent, and fun—a student who is about to go on a wonderful journey that most of us right now can only dream about and hope about. This is about a life well lived . . . and life yet to come . . . and we celebrate this life, knowing we will see you again."

He cleared his throat and added gruffly, "Normally, at this point the commencement speaker is given a gift."

There was laughter and applause, then the director of choral studies presented a framed diploma, conferring upon Maura Cassiana de Souza the degree of bachelor of music. Crowding into Maura's room and spilling out into the hall, musical friends and family led by Maura's high school choir teacher closed the ceremony with "The Lord Bless You and Keep You" in full harmony.

"It was the best graduation ceremony I've ever attended," says Maura's mom, Erin de Souza. "One of the happiest moments of my life."

Hospice arrangements were made at home. Erin and the rest of the family surrounded Maura with love and music. She died peacefully on May 19, 2009 with her head on her father's shoulder.

Watching my mother's response to Suzy's cancer experience was an education in co-survivorship for me, beginning with her staunch patient advocacy and ongoing with her care for our family after Suzy died. Erin faced the same journey as she struggled to shift her focus from the overwhelming needs of her daughter to the overwhelming needs of the rest of the family and, last (but not least, dear caregivers, you are not the least), to her own needs. She made her first tentative steps back into life that summer. She went to the gym with a friend, reconnected with her coworkers, and eventually returned to her job as an academic counselor specializing in international students.

"I love hearing stories about Maura," she says. "Little glimpses into pieces of her life that I didn't personally witness, her songs and laughter and smile and how she affected others. I heard from someone who made Maura's chili recipe for a cook-off and took second place. And from the lead guitarist of a local rock group who once jumped off the stage to dance with Maura, leaving his bandmates to finish the song without him. On Maura's birthday in June, two of her friends released a portion of her ashes from the top of the Eiffel Tower. Another friend sent me a picture of a little boy in Cambodia wearing one of Maura's teal wristbands."

October rolled around, and the pervasive pink was oppressive for Erin. Why, she wondered, was so much being done for breast cancer and so little for sarcoma?

"When Maura was diagnosed," says Erin, "I was stunned to find that drugs being used for sarcoma now are pretty much what they were in the 1950s. So few people have it, it seems like nobody cares."

The myth of the "magic bullet" that would "cure cancer" arose in the 1970s before we understood the true extent of the diversity of this disease. Now we know the word *cancer* actually describes a family of more than two hundred different diseases, from astrocytomas to Waldenström macroglobulinemia. There will never be a one-drug-fits-all cancer treatment, and if we parse resources into buckets according to histology, statistically rare cancers are always going to come up with a very small bucket.

If there is a magic bullet that will come to the rescue of anyone diagnosed with any kind of cancer, it's not a medicine. It's a mindset.

As little girls in the 1950s, Suzy and I watched Lucy and Ricky Ricardo puffing cigarettes, and—what can I say? We loved Lucy. While neither of us developed a major habit, we both lit up over cocktails in Paris. But in the late 1960s, major awareness efforts (including the Surgeon General's warning applied to cigarette packages in 1970) ingrained the indelible connection between smoking and lung cancer in the minds of the American public. At the time Suzy was diagnosed, I felt the same way Erin de Souza did. *Why*, I wondered, *are we hearing about lung cancer as if that's the only cancer there is? Why are we still struggling along with these antiquated treatment options?* But at the same time, I saw the power of that awareness effort to completely upend a cultural norm.

Flash forward a few years to the *Surgeon General's Report on Acquired Immune Deficiency Syndrome* in 1986, which was frankly slow in coming. Red Ribbon activists were instrumental in forcing the conversation on AIDS and HIV, making people pay attention, ramping up research funding, and shifting cultural biases against those infected with the virus.

From the time I was a teenager, I'd watched and learned, taking lessons in grassroots activism from people like Martin Luther King Jr., Harvey Milk, Gloria Steinem, and Lech Wałęsa. When the time came, I beat my tin drum until somebody listened.

"If I have seen further than others," said Sir Isaac Newton, "it is because I have stood on the shoulders of giants."

We at SGK gratefully stood on the shoulders of giants, and we hope others will stand on ours. Thirty years ago, there was agonizingly little awareness of breast cancer; now it occupies a giant pink plat of real estate in the collective consciousness. The global breast cancer movement resulted from a perfect storm of cultural, political, and personal influences. The moment, the messengers, and the methodology clicked into place. People were empowered. Will met way. What's unfolded over the last thirty years is a template for the democratization of a disease.

Breast cancer isn't an island. The overarching dynamics of this movement have created a rising tide.

"For many women with low resources," says SGK board chair Alexine Clement Jackson, "breast cancer screening is the only doorway into a health care system from which they've previously been excluded. Prostate cancer screening based on the breast cancer model does the same thing for men. Our focus is breast cancer. We have to do what we do. But the greater goal is to solve the disparities that plague health care access in general."

On the advocacy front, amid the maelstrom of conflicting ideals that formed the health care reform debate in 2009, our Advocacy Alliance stood beside Republican senator Kay Bailey Hutchison of Texas and Democratic senator Sherrod Brown of Ohio, who linked arms across the aisle and put forth an amendment pushing for access to clinical trials, and we'll continue to push hard for legislation that would require Medicare, Medicaid, and private insurers to pay for clinical trials, not just for breast cancer, but for all types of cancer. Clinical trials are the best—sometimes *only*—hope for patients with rare cancers, and the knowledge we gain from trailblazers like Maura de Souza is the best hope for the more than ten thousand people diagnosed with sarcoma the year she died.

In the scientific arena, breast cancer funding has opened doors and windows in the fields of molecular biology, immunology, and research method. We've supported many projects that bring together patients and scientists, and since 2008, our knowledge has expanded with donations of healthy breast tissue to the SGK Tissue Bank, a one-of-a-kind research facility at Indiana University's Simon Cancer Center.

To chart the journey of a cell from a normal to malignant state, it's imperative that we have healthy tissue for comparison. In January 2010, forty members of the Zeta Tau Alpha fraternity traveled to the IU Medical Center in Indianapolis. There technicians drew blood, administered lidocaine, and through a small incision, collected about a gram of healthy breast tissue from each of the sorority sisters. Talk about "giving of yourself"—I wish I could have been there to hug every one of these extraordinary young women as they got off the bus. Researchers at Dana-Farber Cancer Institute in Boston and Walter Reed Army Medical Center in Washington, D.C., are already benefiting from their contribution to this critical research.

We commence.

We move forward with a common spirit of seeking, a desperate need to learn, and a selfless desire to help. Maura de Souza, the Zeta girls, and a legion of giants go with us. As we explore the vast, perplexing cartography of cancer, each tissue sample and each molecular slide offer a tiny piece of the map, and every day is a new beginning.

18

Pride and Protocol

While I was in Budapest, Laura Bush came to visit, and we spent our days together visiting hospitals and cancer wards. I can't overstate what it meant to these women who so often felt forgotten and pushed aside to have the First Lady of the United States sit on the edge of their beds and hold their hands, chatting with them through the inter-preter, asking about their treatments and their children, and telling them how much she appreciated their beautiful city.

If I'm ever lost in the woods, Laura is the one I want with me. She's the kind who can read a compass, identify the edible berries, craft a Jeep Cherokee out of a piece of driftwood, and have us on our way before nightfall. She'd have my back. That I know for certain. With both our busy lives, Laura and I didn't get to talk as often as we would like, but I've always known she's there if I need her, and I hope she knows that about me.

I think we're always attracted to people who have the qualities we wish we had ourselves. Laura is extremely intelligent and doesn't forget anything. Unlike me, she is patient. She understands people and always says the appropriate thing. More than anyone else I know, she has a way of articulating what needs to be articulated, always in the nicest possible way. She's not a grandstander, never pushy, but she has a presence that brooks no nonsense. She's a lady. She *gets* it. She took a lot of pride in doing the small things—for her daughters, her home, her husband—and as a volunteer, she was always willing to do the jobs no one else wanted to do. Even when she was First Lady of Texas, she stayed active and devoted time to SGK, coming to events and staying until the last dog was hung. She knew it meant a lot to the other volunteers to spend time with her, and she was glad to spend time with them.

I suppose I'm biased, but I think she was a great First Lady.

"Thank you for coming," I told her during a quiet moment in Budapest. "It's so nice to hear someone speaking English."

"Have you had a lot of visitors?" she asked.

"A few. Some American and European CEOs, congressmen. Bob Taylor called and filled me in on everything at home. Eric came. Mom and Daddy had a lot of reservations about my being here, but they came and had a wonderful time. Daddy's not well. I'm worried about him."

Ultimately, though I would have liked to remain in Hungary for another year, I came home in the fall of 2003 because I had a feeling there was something seriously wrong, and there was.

Daddy had stomach cancer.

He kept working through his treatment, and Mommy rose to the occasion as always. I bought a house in Florida so I could be close to them. Daddy and I talked every day. He was always my first stop for advice. He never tried to tell me what to do or to spoon-feed me an answer; he asked the right questions and listened while I talked it through for myself.

At the seventh annual SGK Mission Conference in 2004, every session felt electrified with purpose. The astonishing growth of our organization had made it possible for us to fund a wide range of research projects and community-based services. Along with new and innovative clinical studies, we were looking for new and innovative ways to address disparities in underserved populations. There was a lot going on in the world, and it was an election year. We were doing our best to stay focused and certainly not looking for trouble, but we got into a political dustup that would turn into a frustrating distraction when one of our valued corporate sponsors, Curves (a chain of workout centers for women), withdrew their support and denounced SGK because some of our local affiliates had made grants to their local Planned Parenthood chapters.

When you donate to a local SGK affiliate or support a walker in a Race for the Cure, 75 percent of that money stays right there in your neighborhood to serve local women. We don't spend money building Susan G. Komen Breast-Cancer-R-Us facilities; we get the most bang for our buck by funding services that can be offered through existing local infrastructure. The grants in question supplied breast health counseling, screening, and treatment to rural women, poor women, Native American women, many women of color who were underserved—if served at all—in areas where Planned Parenthood facilities were often the only infrastructure available. Though it meant losing corporate money from Curves, we were not about to turn our backs on these women. Somehow this position translated to the utterly false assertion that SGK funds abortions.

As controversy swirled, several pro-life advocates, including Catholic bishops and Sister Carol Keehan of the Catholic Health Association, sprang to our defense. Unfortunately, the false assertion has persisted for years, hopping around the blogosphere like a poisonous frog to this day, frequently coupled with the ridiculous old wives' tale that abortion causes breast cancer.

"Well-conducted research consistently fails to support this claim," our chief scientific adviser, Dr. Eric Winer, said in an open letter. "We agree with the bulk of scientific evidence—from the National Cancer Institute, Harvard, a rigorous study in Denmark and from Oxford University—that there is no conclusive link between breast cancer and induced abortion or miscarriage."

I was sad to lose the corporate support of Curves, and I have the utmost respect for its founder's religious convictions—as I do for all people of every faith—but we remain focused on our mission.

A happy footnote to that whole brouhaha: Even though Curves withdrew its corporate support, I continue to see many terrific women at Race for the Cure events walking or running with their Curves workout groups. I applaud the daily, proactive commitment of these women to their own health, and I appreciate their continued support. With all eyes on the prize, they've risen above the fray and taken to the streets. I stand ready to follow their example.

The White House chief of protocol is responsible for facilitating a smooth experience for the president, vice president, secretary of state, and their spouses when they interact with foreign dignitaries. When we mix with other cultures, there's always potential for embarrassment, faux pas, or a general lack of communication. The chief of protocol and her (or his) team research key phrases, customs, cuisine, taboos—everything and anything we can do to make sure a visiting head of state feels welcomed and respected from the moment he or she steps off the airplane to the official handshake photo with the president. If a queen has an allergy to roses or a prince has a deathly fear of heights, the chief of protocol makes sure the daisies and ground-floor accommodations are in place. The position is part ambassador, part Emily Post, the diplomacy of etiquette and the etiquette of diplomacy.

I knew several people who'd done the job, including Shirley Temple Black, who served under Gerald Ford, and Lucky Roosevelt, who served under Reagan. There was no learning curve in this position; mistakes have far-reaching consequences, so only perfectionists need apply. Also required are research skills, social graces, the stoic patience of a stone lion, and a genuine respect for people of all cultures from all over the world.

In spring 2007, the White House reached out to see if I was interested in the position. I thought long and hard before I accepted.

"If it was something in Health and Human Services, I wouldn't even stop to think," I told Mom and Daddy. "But this would be a complete disconnect from the direction I've been moving my whole life."

"The connection might not be obvious," said Mommy, "but you'll find it. Women of my generation didn't have all the open doors. Sometimes we had to climb in a window."

It occurred to me I'd be learning about diverse cultures from every corner of the globe, interacting with their leaders, and getting to know their wives. It wouldn't be appropriate for me to use the position as a lobbying platform for women's health, but I'd be building a foundation and forging relationships that might later help me to advance breast cancer treatment and awareness on a global level.

But here was my father. I couldn't leave Mommy to take care of him by herself. And selfishly, I was rather enjoying my life the way it was at the time. I was back on the SGK board, seeing an interesting man, traveling, and adding to my burgeoning collection of Hungarian art. My friend Barbara Rogoff and I spent hours poring over auction catalogues and excavating dusty basement archives far and wide.

"I don't know," I said. "The timing isn't great."

"There's never a convenient time to serve," said Daddy. "You do it because you were called. Your president asked you to serve, so you serve."

I let Laura know I was willing and ready, President Bush called to pop the question, and we made it official. I immediately immersed myself in study and preparations. My father remained sharp as a bullwhip and kept working to the very end. He was in a horrific amount of pain, but he didn't complain. Two days before he died, he was sitting up in his hospital bed, reading the *Wall Street Journal* and reviewing profit-and-loss statements.

"That's how I want to go," I told Mommy.

My father taught me how to live, and he taught me how to die. He finally slipped into a coma and passed away on a June Sunday in 2007, the day before I was to give a speech in front of fifteen thousand physicians, administrators, and others gathered for the annual conference of the American Society of Clinical Oncology. Mommy held off the funeral for a day so I could go and deliver the talk.

I won't say I did it because Daddy would have wanted me to (though he would have); I did it because I wanted to, and I wanted to because I am the woman he raised me to be.

On September 14, 2007, I was sworn in as chief of protocol. The following two years were an adventure, an education, and a tremendous challenge; it would take me another two years to recount every great leader I was honored to greet and every thrilling stamp I added to my passport.

Visiting presidents and prime ministers stay at Blair House, the presidential guesthouse just across Pennsylvania Avenue, and it was my responsibility to see that everything was in order there. I organized visits and activities and coordinated with the kitchen staff to make sure the right food was being served. Mrs. Bush was responsible for selecting gifts suitable for the recipient, and she had an impeccable sense for choosing the exactly right bike or Fabergé egg or painted porcelain dish. I made sure the staff was well versed in personal and political issues so the conversation would be amiable and appropriate, never "How was your flight?"

When visiting heads of state came to meet with the president, I usually met them and their entourages at the South Portico outside the White House and escorted them to the West Wing, but when the Dalai

Lama arrived, he flew into Washington on a commercial flight, and I met him at the gate. He waved and greeted me, jolly and laughing. As we walked down the concourse, it was as quiet as a stroll through a bamboo forest. People recognized him, but they didn't rush toward him or call out. Peace and happiness radiated out from him, and even those who didn't know who he was seemed noticeably affected by it.

According to Tibetan tradition, he'd brought me a *kata*, a long white scarf used for offerings and greetings, which he blessed. I bent my knees and scrunched down a little so he could reach up and place it over my shoulders, and as he did, he noticed the little pink ribbon on my lapel.

"What does it signify?" he asked.

I told him about Suzy and about SGK, and he blessed me with the nicest compliment possible.

"You did a good thing," he said, smiling that wonderful crinkled smile.

The pope made a six-day visit to the United States while I was in office, and I was the first one to greet him when he arrived. For months my team and I prepared for his arrival. For the first time ever, the pontiff would be met by the president out on the tarmac on his arrival, along with a huge crowd. The daunting logistics of it occupied my every waking thought from the moment the plans were announced. It was a brisk and beautiful April day in Washington when Shepherd One landed at Andrews Air Force Base. The boarding stairway was wheeled into place and secured, but a gusty wind kept whipping the red carpet away from the foot of the steps. A few people made nervous jokes about the winds of the Holy Spirit, but I was more than a little anxious at the thought of this eighty-one-year-old man negotiating those steep steps only to have the rug literally pulled out from under his feet.

Just before President Bush and the First Lady came out onto the tarmac with their daughter Jenna, I climbed the staircase with a representative of the church to greet the pontiff and make sure everything was as it should be. As we boarded, he looked up and smiled at me.

"Your Holiness," I said, bowing my head slightly, returning his smile. "On behalf of the president and Mrs. Bush, welcome to the United States."

He took my hand between his palms. The gesture was warmer than a handshake, fatherly and generous. During his stay in the United States, the pope took time to bless a box of silver ribbon-shaped pins and had them sent to my office. The day he left, I was at Andrews to see him off, and I thanked him for the ribbons that would mean so much to the men and women of faith who would receive them. He took my hands and blessed me for my work.

I couldn't help myself. I burst into tears. All I could think of was Suzy, standing breathless on a street corner in Rome, clutching those two little statuettes to her heart.

Priceless, Nanny. Blessed by the pope.

P resident Bush allowed me to expand my job description a little to include a cultural exchange called Experience America. This grand adventure threw a group of foreign ambassadors all on the same bus, taking them out of the status quo and squiring them from sea to shining sea. We'd taken a beating in the foreign press over the last few years. My objective was to share my love and wonder for this great country and show our guests the America that Americans have made, the America Walt Whitman heard singing, blithe and strong. We visited Ground Zero, the NASA jet propulsion lab at Cal Tech, an ethanol plant in the Midwest, and miles of Americana in between, ending up at College Station, Texas, where we all had lunch with President "41" and Barbara Bush. People said they never had so much fun, but more important, they saw the verdant green America beyond the Beltway.

The year 2008 was a contentious one in American politics, and I tried to exert a calming, nonpartisan influence. Winding down my time at the White House, I was already looking outward into the world where I knew I belonged now, and I saw the vital connection, this bridge I'd crossed. I had friends and allies in every corner of the globe. I'd sought first to understand; now I was ready to seek their understanding.

Laura Bush and I had done a lot of traveling together, and we talked a lot about the particular challenges facing women in developing nations. Together we formed the U.S.–Middle East Partnership for Breast Cancer Awareness and Research, forging relationships with remarkable men and women who were positioned to help us launch awareness-building campaigns, grassroots advocacy and support efforts, and technical training. We orchestrated outreach that would include tasks as tangible as needle biopsy training and as esoteric as empowerment for girls and women.

In October, Laura and I hosted a breast cancer conference at Blair House, and in celebration of the event, the White House was illuminated in pink. Meanwhile, Katrina McGhee, SGK's VP of Global Partnerships, traveled to Africa with other staffers, preparing for the launch of the Ghana Breast Cancer Alliance with actress Gabrielle Union; Malaak Rock, Chris Rock's philanthropist-activist wife; and Billye Aaron, the gracious wife of baseball great Hank Aaron. SGK's CEO announced a grant of $250,000 and plans for a symposium that would bring together the great minds and hard resources needed to bring breast cancer care to women in desperate need.

Barack Obama took office on January 20, 2009, and the next day I was on a train and back to work at SGK, which had been christened Susan G. Komen for the Cure two years earlier, a rebranding that captured a fresh vision encompassing so much more than we originally dreamed it would. I'd met with political and spiritual leaders from all over the world and laid the foundation for important dialogue to come. I'd also worked with many amazing people in the State Department and at the White House and was lucky enough to bring some of them along as this new phase unfolded. It felt good to be back at board meetings, my focus back where I wanted it to be, but with a whole new perspective. I'd been appointed to a position with the United Nations as the World Health Organization's Goodwill Ambassador for Cancer Control. In addition to advocating for cancer awareness and prevention, I would investigate and report on the state of cancer care in all parts of the world and help form WHO's global strategy for prevention and control of noncommunicable diseases.

I had a lot on my plate, but compared with the pressures and pace at the White House, the 60-hour weeks felt like a pleasure cruise. It occurred to me that I could have a bit more of a social life now.

It had taken me a while to learn how to date again after Norman remarried. I did see a number of interesting men and was actually pretty fond of a few of them, but none of them had me flying into Love as he had once upon a time. I've always had a penchant for bad boys, and I was now in a position where any indiscretion on my part might reflect poorly on others. I couldn't allow myself to be led down the garden path.

After I'd been seeing one wonderful fellow for a while, I came to the conclusion he wasn't the right fit for my life. Instead of trying to reform him, I sat him down at his private club and said, "You're fired."

"Fired?" he echoed.

"Yes. You're fired. From dating me. From my life. I'm sorry, I have to let you go."

"Oh." He looked like he wanted to laugh but wasn't sure he should. "I've never been fired from somebody's life before."

I saw a long black car arrive outside the window.

"Well. There's my date for the evening," I said. "Best of luck to you."

He looked a bit shell-shocked as I gathered my things and walked away, but we actually laughed about it later, and we've remained the very best of friends. (Bad boys make wonderful best friends.) When I told Norman about it, he laughed, but then he told me very seriously, "No one will ever love you like I do."

He'd told me this many times over the years, and it always felt like both a blessing and a curse. I certainly didn't want it that way, but I knew it was true. I knew I'd never marry someone else as long as Norman was alive.

"Don't settle," he said. "Somebody out there will see what a great package you are."

"I'm not everyone's cup of tea," I reminded him.

I'm afraid some men viewing my life from a rotunda perspective don't see how they'd fit in. Friends try to fix me up and coach me to be "less intense," which rankles me; men are never told that their accomplishments make them less desirable. I don't sit around waiting for a man to give my life meaning, but I'm always willing to find time and energy for the right relationship. I'm an able ally for a strong man, and I must say (because Suzy's not here to say it for me) I still look pretty good in a sports car. I've had a little work done, but just before the anesthesiologist put the mask over my face, I stopped the surgeon's hand and said, "Don't give me my money's worth." I aspire to the kind of beauty my mother has; it's physical and classic, and comes from taking care of herself with the same tender vigilance she extends to others.

Norman's health had deteriorated over the years. He was increasingly unstable on his feet and often used a motorized scooter now. Along with the progressive effects of his brain injury, he'd had cancer in his throat and a host of other complications that accompany a lifetime of high mileage, but he made the Herculean effort it took to participate in every SGK board meeting, even if he had to come in a wheelchair or tune in via video conference. He always held my hand under the table and always parted with "I love you."

I'm so grateful those were the last words I heard from him.

The last board meeting Norman attended was in March 2009. Margaret Valentine (who works for us at SGK now) told me that on his way home, he said to her with great satisfaction, "Boy, oh boy. They are on *fire*."

Norman died that summer. June 2009. The news left poor Eric utterly bereft, but Norman would have been proud of how fiercely protective he was of me in the difficult days that followed. There was a huge memorial service planned at Meyerson Symphony Center in Dallas, but I was bluntly uninvited. A close friend of Norman's who knew it wasn't his style to exclude anyone interceded on my behalf so I could attend the memorial, but I wasn't allowed to sit with my son or accompany him to his dad's gravesite.

Eric arranged private visitation the night before the service, but when I saw Norman laid out in a pedestrian suit and tie, I was stricken with the same heartsick reaction I'd had to seeing Suzy in her coffin. He'd always said he wanted to die with his boots on, and if it had been up to me, that's how he would have been buried. White jeans, fresh polo shirt, stick by his side. Ready to ride. But it wasn't up to me. I had no standing here, no right to feel as profoundly widowed as I did. I was reminded of the way I'd felt when Jake, the man I'd dated during my early days at Neiman Marcus, died just as our relationship had begun to blossom. Polite society knows what to do with a widow or an orphan, but who are we when etiquette hasn't invented a word for our particular form of bereavement?

During the funeral, a famous friend of Norman's got up and made a statement about how "the last few years of Norman's life were the happiest," and my face burned as if I'd been slapped. The platitude was such an insult to Maureen, to Norman's beautiful children, and to the man Norman was when he was *Norman:* the vital, brilliant businessman, the spring-step entrepreneur, the empire builder, athletic lover, and fearless horseman. How small and chauvinistic to eulogize him as someone who prized dotage over powerful partnerships that produced amazing human beings. Among the thousands who came to honor Norman that day, in addition to the hundreds who knew and loved him as a tour de force in the restaurant industry, were hundreds of others who knew and loved him because of the work he'd done during his twenty-six years on the board of Susan G. Komen for the Cure, people who knew the organization wouldn't be what it is if not for this man who gave me a platform and taught me how to use it. Nothing was said about the lives he'd saved.

That night, Larry Lavine, Norman's partner in Chili's and beyond, brought together all of Norman's protégés, the people of whom Norman was proudest. Managers and innovators he'd raised up and mentored. Entrepreneurs and restaurateurs who'd thrived on his guiding principles. There was Eric, who'd delighted his dad by leaving a handprint on JetBlue's unique branding, then found his way back to Peoria, where he carried my father's work into the future. I was so honored to be included. We toasted Norman's memory, shared stories and laughter, and warmly agreed to come together every year to celebrate that little bit of Norman's great heart still beating within each of us.

A week or so later, Brenda's daughter Connolly graduated from junior high in San Francisco, and I was slated to give the commencement address. Norman and I had both been looking forward to it. Now the occasion felt so weighted with emotion, I wasn't sure I'd be able to speak. But standing at the podium next to the wide-open water, looking at this beautiful grandchild Norman Brinker and Maureen Connolly were kind enough to share with me, I felt nothing but joy and humble gratitude. I dedicated my remarks to her grandfather and did my best to let this girl know what extraordinary love and valor resided in her DNA.

Those two events were the fitting tribute Norman had earned, the fruit of his best and happiest years. I didn't need to be part of his burial; I was part of his living legacy.

Where We Aren't, Where We Are, and Where We Want to Be

I RECENTLY found myself on *Meet the Press*, seated next to a physician I've known and respected for a long time, rehashing those controversial "Don't bother with those inconvenient mammograms" recommendations issued by the U.S. Preventive Services Task Force in fall 2009. This was the physician who called breast self-examination a "search-and-destroy mission," so I suppose they were expecting a good mud wrestling match. I brushed off my note cards and armed myself with the same truths and ideals with which I gird my loins every five years or so when a similar study makes similar statements for similar reasons and similar broadcasts seat me next to similar physicians for similar discussions.

Not my first time at the rodeo, nor my last, I'm sure.

We were collegial and polite as we squared off. The moderator chuckled and finessed us, hoping the gloves would come off and good television would ensue. But I'm not a gloves-off sort of guest. In fact, I'm not a gloves-*on* sort of guest. I don't wear gloves unless it's with a nice winter coat or on the back of a horse at full gallop. I'm not looking to box anyone's ears. I know what I know, and I won't back down, but I always hope to forge some common ground where we can plant a support and start building a bridge that will serve women in some way.

I started by pointing out that my life was saved by early detection, and my sister died without benefit of screening. Anecdotal evidence, but compelling nonetheless.

"Cancer is personal. *I get that*," the physician said. She went on to make the valid point that we have to screen 1,900 women for ten years to reliably prevent one death. A lot of effort, some would say, for a relatively small return.

"But one out of 1,900," I protested. "That's a lot of women!"

The physician seated next to me bumped past that thought like a busy yellow school bus.

"This is about *science*," she said.

I get that. But do the math.

In a town the size of Auburn, Maine, losing one woman out of 1,900 over ten years would be a little more than half a dozen women: the entire staff at Betty Lou's Beauty Nook. In a city the size of Billings, Montana, that's about two dozen women: all the altos and sopranos in a Full Gospel Church choir. In a metro area the size of Detroit, that's about 1,500 women: all the mothers of all the fourth graders in a sizable school district. In New York State, it's the Metropolitan Opera, filled to capacity from cheap seats to orchestra pit, including the fat lady singing.

Approximately 17 million people visit Disney World's Magic Kingdom each year. One out of 1,900 would be 8,947 people over ten years. If "Pirates of the Caribbean" killed *75 people every month*, would anyone argue against implementing life-saving precautions?

One woman counts. One woman adds up.

The science of cancer is fascinating when applied to the enigma of cause and the intricacies of treatment. But the medical reality of breast cancer itself—the disease in its rawest form, advancing undetected until it can't be denied, then advancing unimpeded until the death of its host—defies scientific thought. There's no histology that can fixate sorrow. Human suffering can't be mapped on a mammogram. Statistics that detail losses say nothing about loss.

Breast cancer unnamed is a spiritual death by isolation; breast cancer untreated takes a physically hideous course. But that's just rhetoric until the one woman with breast cancer is you or someone you love.

Thank goodness, there are many physicians out there who get *that*.

Sitting across the table from Dr. Eric Winer, I can't believe my good fortune. He's brilliant and pleasant to listen to, a man of good humor and great integrity, dedicated to his precise and compassionate science and to his wife and children. They say a good man is hard to find. A good oncologist is even harder.

I first met Dr. Winer in 1995 at Duke; I was exploring Duke's bone marrow transplant program, and he was an earnest young scientist. Eventually, he moved on to Dana Farber in Boston, and I ran into him there half a dozen times over the years. As SGK grew, surpassing the billion-dollar mark for project funding, we decided we needed to put someone in charge of our scientific position. This person would advise me and other spokespersons on the official scientific stand of SGK, assist us in the grant-making process, and act as an interpreter between the scientists we sought to fund and the patients we sought to serve.

When we talked about assessing people, looking for what you need in a team member—or a team leader—Norman always said, "If you always agree, one of you is unnecessary."

SGK offered the position to Dr. Eric Winer, but he turned it down.

"I don't think you want a chief science officer," he said, off to a good start on that disagreement thing. "You need a committee with a chair as adviser. And you want that person to be actively working in the field, rather than someone who's left the field to work for you."

We followed his recommendation, formed the SGK Scientific Advisory Board and asked him to chair. This time he accepted the offer. (Off to a good start on disagreeing only half the time.) I knew we could count on him to render a thoughtful, science-based opinion, not the SGK party line. Of course, this makes me want to shake him every once in a while, but only in those moments when I'm so damn tired, I just wish someone would tell me what I want to hear and not befuddle my righteous wrath with facts. Fortunately, Dr. Winer understands the need to deliver hard information with tact and good humor, another job skill you look for in a good oncologist.

"I view this organization as a large steamship," he says. "When maneuvering a great ship, it's important to move slowly and deliberately."

I don't know where he finds all the hours he requires each day, but Dr. Winer still sees patients, and more important, his patients see him. He insists that "mission" is too lofty a term for what he does, but will reluctantly concede "calling."

"It's the work I do. It's a privilege to be able to do work that helps others and gives me a lot of gratification."

Dr. Winer came to his calling early, and it was hard earned.

"I had a lot of exposure to medicine as a child. A kid with hemophilia—that meant I was chronically having bleeding into my joints. I missed a great deal of school and could not play sports or participate in most activities. When I was eleven years old, treatments became available that made me essentially normal for the first time. I witnessed a revolution in the way we care for people with hemophilia and experienced a dramatic change in my own life. That really brought me into it and made me want to forge a practice where I'd have the opportunity for those close relationships."

He considered pediatrics, but ultimately became fascinated with the chemistry of cancer—cellular, psychological, and emotional. Sitting across the table from him, I'm always energized by his blood-borne vitality and a weltanschauung I can only describe as *healthy*. Even with the complications he's had to deal with, he looks at the complications that might have been, and he's grateful.

"What drew me to oncology was really the incredible need I thought existed on the part of patients and the fact that so much progress might be made," says Dr. Winer. "Most important, there's that intimate, intense experience with patients. When you become someone's cancer doctor, you enter their lives in an extraordinary way. People who go into oncology want to take care of people—take care of families—at a time when that's very difficult, getting involved in the nitty gritty. But of course, some degree of emotional detachment, or perhaps emotional neutrality, is critical," he adds. "Objectivity is paramount. Once you lose that objectivity, you just can't make the best decisions."

When the Preventive Services Task Force rolled out those controversial recommendations that seemed to fly in the face of everything we'd been telling women about the importance of yearly mammograms, there were some complaints that Susan G. Komen for the Cure was slow to respond—and I'm proud to say, we were. Rather than leap into the fray, our Scientific Advisory Board took a few days to wade through the panel's recommendations and all the small print of their supporting documentation. A lot of people, including me, were surprised to find that there was really nothing groundbreaking or even particularly fresh about the research from which the task force had extrapolated their opinion, and nothing all that new about the opinion itself. They'd just innovated a new and extraordinarily ham-fisted way of talking about it.

I can't speculate on their motivation, but the immediate effect was the heaving of an international sigh, women all over the world rolling their eyes as if to say, *Make up your mind already.* Our switchboard lit up. E-mail flooded in. Women weren't confused; they were angry.

Editorials editorialized and bloggers flogged away, all true to their agendas. Health care reform was the hot political topic at the moment, so those in favor of reform held up the recommendations and said, "You see? This is why we need reform!" and those opposed to it held up the recommendations and said, "You see? This is why reform is evil!"

As is always the case, the truth was in the quiet middle ground, where people like Dr. Eric Winer reside, and that voice of reason is our only hope of breaking the gridlock of resentment between people who could—and should—be working together toward the same goal.

"The thing they got most wrong," Dr. Winer told me, "is the rollout. The rest is more complicated, but what we agree on is the technology gap. They're saying mammography is inadequate, and they're right. We've been looking at the same studies and coming to the same conclusion for years."

"So let's talk about improving mammography," I said.

"Exactly."

"Meanwhile, how do we get some spin control on it? I'm not suggesting we ignore the science when it doesn't fit our talking points, but we can't be naïve about what insurance providers are going to do with this. Whatever a woman decides to do with this information, it ought to be her choice."

"Then say that," said the good doctor.

The following week, I stood before the National Press Club, told the women of America our recommendations hadn't changed, and reminded the insurance companies that the all-seeing eye of Susan G. Komen was upon them.

No matter where a woman is in this world, help is nearby—agonizingly close to her reach in many cases. What ends up separating her from her life and the people who love her is often a lack of knowledge, but more often, a lack of money. Awareness and access. It almost always comes down to these two issues, whether you're talking about women in the United States who are stuck outside a broken health care system, women in developing nations who are deprived of education, or women everywhere who are marginalized by poverty and politics.

At the 2009 UN Economic and Social Council Summit, Secretary General Ban Ki-moon appealed to the citizens of a world in crisis. Everything goes south in an economy like this; funding stumbles, the food chain breaks down. He touched on "cancer and other noncommunicable diseases" in the context of global health. Translation: It'll be a long time before this subject bubbles up through the immediate issues of food, clean water, and rampant communicable diseases. That year's focus, however, was global health, and that felt like a handhold. Now something innovative was needed, something that would capture the public consciousness.

In October of 2009, we pinked the Pyramids.

We planned a week of groundbreaking, silence-shattering events in partnership with the Suzanne Mubarak Women's International Peace Movement, the Breast Cancer Foundation of Egypt, and other organizations as deeply committed as we are to the health and well-being of women. There was an unfortunate tempest in the teapot a few days before we arrived; two Israeli attendees were told—quite incorrectly—that they were no longer welcome to attend. That morphed into false reports that we'd slammed the door in the face of the Israelis. The blogosphere was abuzz with misinformation, calls for boycott, howling for my head on a platter, but those of us on the ground (and occasionally on camels) remained focused on our common purpose.

"Who's the purse?" my Man Friday, John Pearson, always asks when we arrive at whatever far-flung airfield we're landing on. If no one else volunteers, he shoulders the large pink bag I schlep around wherever I go. I have no idea what all is in it, but I'm fairly certain I could perform an appendectomy if called upon. Someone else usually has to carry the purse because I still have trouble with my arm from that damned old lymphedema after my mastectomy. It's a good metaphor for how I do what I do. Over the course of a lifetime, I've amassed my proud pink toolkit. It's portable, versatile, and I depend on strong, smart people to help me wield it.

The moment we heard about the misinformation circulating, we pulled everything we had out of the diplomatic bag, clarified facts, and made sure everyone understood that no one would be excluded from this event. Sadly, the Israelis opted not to attend, but they remain our allies as we move forward in the region. We supported their important clinical research and community programs prior to this misunderstanding, and we continue to support them now. I was scheduled to visit Israel the following week to discuss plans for a major international think tank and our first Israel SGK Race for the Cure. My travel plans didn't change and at this writing, I'm very much looking forward to those events. Did I win the heart of the blogger who said I was Adolf Eichmann's lap dancer? Probably not. Hopefully, he's moved on to how the moon landing never happened. We can't be distracted by misinformed chatter or by political differences that don't involve us.

The week-long series of events in Egypt brought together physicians, advocates, scientists, and survivors from all over the Middle East and northern Africa. The Great Pyramids at Giza were illuminated in pink light, and the following morning, walkers and runners gathered for the first Egyptian SGK Race for the Cure.

We'd hoped for two thousand participants. Ten thousand people came.

As I traveled to Israel and beyond in the following weeks, I felt the clock turn back. A familiar sense of opportunity shivered down my spine. And then the monkey chorus of old doubts reminded me that I'm not as young as I used to be. The necessary commitment, effort, and creative energy are daunting, and to be perfectly frank, my feet hurt.

Well, I hear Suzy tease à la Laurel and Hardy, *you really got us into it this time.*

Have I committed, I sometimes wonder, to a battle that can't be won? Is it even possible to gain an inch of ground? But then I feel my mother's steely gaze in the rearview mirror. I think of the women who've caught my hand and searched my eyes as I walked by.

"Am I going to die?" so many of them ask.

Or "Does this mean my daughter will get it?"

"Is my disease contagious?" a woman in India recently asked me. Her face was ashen with fear. Crusted black tumors pushed through the skin beneath her bright magenta sari.

In those moments, I know that doubt is an unaffordable luxury. Defeat is unthinkable. Inaction is not even an option. I hear the echo of great words: *How long? Not long.*

When SGK board chair Alexine Clement Jackson and I discuss where we'd like this organization to be in twenty-five years, Alexine states un-equivocally: "Out of business. Because the cure for breast cancer has been found and it's a chronic, treatable disease for all women, everywhere in the world."

It's a challenge. But in the words of JFK, "That challenge is one that we are willing to accept, one we are unwilling to postpone, and one which we intend to win."

On a wide world stage in a complicated environment, the well-being—in many cases the very survival—of 2.5 billion people is threatened by a horizontal system that needs to be vertical, a lack of access that needs to be an open door. There are places in the world that haven't progressed much beyond that first rudimentary diagnosis and treatment of breast cancer recorded by the ancient Egyptians, places where women's bodies are shrouded in shame and silence. Angels of mercy die as a matter of in-convenience, and their passing doesn't even leave a hash mark on statistical analysis. At this writing, the UN's Millennium Development Goals do not include the word *cancer*. And beyond all that is the bald reality that at the end of the day, I'm tired and I miss Suzy, my touchstone, my best friend. At the end of the day, a stinging sense of *not enough* always lingers.

In Shakespeare's *Much Ado About Nothing*, a nobleman tells a returning soldier, "A victory is twice itself when the achiever brings home full numbers." He asks how many were lost in battle, and the war-weary soldier says, "None of name."

My numbers can never be full because I wasn't able to bring my sister home. But the mothers and sisters know that every one of the fallen had a name, and I've heard those names spoken as I marched beside the few who became the many. We see the long road ahead and feel the loving presence of those who fought the good fight. We remember their faces and carry their love with us into the future, not because of how they died but because of how they lived. In my heart, I speak to each of them the words I spoke at Suzy's funeral:

Sister, I thanked God today for taking you into his peaceful eternity. I thanked Him for giving you to us, even if for too short a time. And I thanked Him for relieving you of your suffering and pain. But for all of us who loved you so dearly, the pain will continue. Losing you is overwhelming. Many beautiful words vanish like snowflakes as they fall. But not your familiar beautiful words. The ones you wanted to say to us one more time: *Thank you . . . I forgive you . . .* and always, *I love you.* Those words will remain in our hearts forever. No accolades or rewards, Suzy, just us whom you loved so well in death as in life. Go with God, in peace, my dear sister, and know that with you goes a part of each of us.

19

Promise Me

I knew President Obama wasn't calling to offer me a job because there was no call before the call. Just a call from his office. "Ambassador Brinker, the president would like to offer you the Presidential Medal of Freedom."

It had been twenty-nine years, almost to the day, since Suzy died. This was one of those moments when the enormity of everything that's happened since then crystallized and overwhelmed me.

The Presidential Medal of Freedom is the highest civilian honor in the United States, given for "an especially meritorious contribution to the security or national interests of the United States, world peace, cultural, or other significant public or private endeavors." I was stunned, indescribably honored, and humbly amazed when I learned what exceptional company I'd be keeping. Justice Sandra Day O'Connor of the Supreme Court. Dr. Joseph Medicine Crow, the last living Indian Plains war chief. Geneticist Janet Davison Rowley and Dr. Pedro José Greer Jr. were being celebrated for their contributions to medicine, Stephen Hawking for science, Chita Rivera for dance, Sidney Poitier for film, and Billie Jean King for sports. Harvey Milk was being posthumously recognized for activism.

During the awards ceremony, President Obama said,

One of the last things Suzy Komen did before she died was to have her sister Nancy make her a promise. Nancy promised that she would prevent other families fighting breast cancer from suffering the way that her family had. What began as a shoebox with $200 and a list of friends has become a global Race for the Cure; a campaign that has eased the pain and saved the lives of millions of people around the world. In the months after making that promise, Nancy lay awake at night wondering if one person can really make a difference. Nancy's life is the answer.

Stepping behind me, he lowered the medal on its wide ribbon close to my heart and worked the clasp at the nape of my neck. I bit the inside of my cheek, trying hard to keep my face from crumpling, thinking what this moment would have meant to my father, to Norman, to Suzy—grateful at the same time that Mommy, Eric, Brenda, and Connolly, and so many other people I loved were there and that a banquet hall full of friends and colleagues waited for me at the Hay-Adams across the street from the White House.

Later, as I greeted people at the reception, the daughter of a friend said, "Love the necklace, Ambassador. Did you get it from someone special?"

"Maddie! Abbie!"
        "Aunt Nan!"
Suzy's granddaughters come running in ruffles and ribbons. Scott and his wife, Marnie, laugh at how adeptly the girls invest me with their grandmother's gift for silliness. Sitting in pint-size chairs at the American Girl store in Manhattan, we get down to the serious business of our tea party.

"When your Grammy Suzy and I were little girls," I tell them, "our daddy built us a playhouse in the backyard with a little table so we could have lunch with our dolls."

"And important meetings?" says Maddie.

"Yes, very important meetings."

Abbie declares her dolly administrative assistant. I excavate my spare BlackBerry from my big pink bag and place it between dolly's stiff but capable hands. We eat cookies and giggle and tease. All too soon it's time to leave. I pull the girls close so Eric can take our picture, and before I let them go, I kiss each of them on top of the head.

"Abbie, I'm counting on you to be a good girl."

She nods gravely.

"Susan Madeline Komen?"

"Yes, Aunt Nan?" she answers with tea party decorum.

"Promise me you'll always take care of your sister."

"I promise," says Maddie, and she dances away.

BREAST CANCER TIMELINE

1600 B.C.E.	Earliest mention of breast cancer in Egyptian surgical papyrus.
400 B.C.E.	Greek physicians observe crablike tentacled tumors in autopsy and coin the term *cancer*.
1700s	Trend toward surgical medicine popularizes mastectomy as most effective treatment for breast cancer.
1880s	Mastectomies are routinely performed without anesthesia or antiseptic until 1850s. Halsted innovates radical mastectomy technique in 1880s.
1890s	Marie Curie discovers radium in 1898, laying foundation for radiation treatment for cancer.
Early 1900s	Halsted radical and super-radical mastectomies push limits of survivable surgery.
1940s	American Cancer Society Research Program launched with $1 million raised by Mary Woodard Lasker.
	Chemotherapy emerges with development of Cytoxin (cyclophosphamide) and Adriamycin (doxorubicin).
1958	5-fluorouracil synthesized.
1960s	The less invasive lumpectomy gains favor.
1970s	Dr. Brian McMahon analyzes epidemiological evidence linking breast cancer to lifetime exposure to reproductive hormones.
	American Cancer Society promotes mammography as best tool for early breast cancer detection.

1974   First Lady Betty Ford speaks openly about her breast cancer diagnosis.

Studies by V. Craig Jordan, Ph.D., show tamoxifen prevents cancer in rats by binding to estrogen receptors.

1977   Susan Goodman Komen is diagnosed with breast cancer.

1978   U.S. Food and Drug Administration approves tamoxifen for treatment of estrogen receptor–positive breast cancer.

1980   American Cancer Society sets early detection guidelines for breast cancer.

Susan G. Komen dies of breast cancer at age thirty-six.

1982   Susan G. Komen Breast Cancer Foundation founded on July 22 in Dallas, Texas. SGK awards grants totaling $30,000 to M. D. Anderson in Houston and Baylor University Medical Center in Dallas. Dr. Ronald Levy successfully treats lymphoma with monoclonal antibody therapy.

1983   First SGK Race for the Cure is held in Dallas, Texas, with 800 participants.

First SGK National Awards Luncheon in Dallas.

1984   Nancy G. Brinker diagnosed with breast cancer.

1985   Studies by Dr. Bernard Fisher demonstrate lumpectomy plus radiation survival rates are equivalent to mastectomy survival rates.

1986   First SGK Race for the Cure outside of Dallas takes place in Peoria, Illinois.

First National Breast Cancer Awareness Month (NBCAM) is held in October.

1989   SGK grantees Dr. Harold E. Varmus and Dr. J. Michael Bishop receive Nobel Prize for oncogene behavior discoveries, a breakthrough that provides foundation for many treatments to come.

Nancy G. Brinker is first breast cancer advocate named to the President's Cancer Panel.

First SGK local chapter (later called "affiliates") opens in San Francisco, California.

SGK National Toll-Free Breast Care Helpline established.

1990 SGK grantee Mary-Claire King, Ph.D., isolates gene mutation on chromosome 17, setting the stage for discovery of BRCA1 and BRCA2.

SGK affiliates award first community grants for education, screening, and treatment projects.

1991 For the first time, SGK reaches $1 million in research and project grants in a single year.

1992 SGK 10th Anniversary gala includes Vice President and Mrs. Dan Quayle; U.S. senator Connie Mack and his wife, Priscilla Mack, receive the Betty Ford Award.

SGK plays key role in passage of Mammography Quality Standards Act.

V. Craig Jordan, Ph.D., D.Sc., and Bernard Fisher, M.D., receive first Brinker International Awards for Breast Cancer Research.

1993 U.S. Olympic runner Francie Larrieu-Smith is National Honorary Chair of the SGK Race for the Cure series.

1994 Studies by Dr. Brian Henderson show that exercise reduces breast cancer risk in premenopausal women.

Research by David G. I. Kingston, Ph.D., leads to FDA approval of Taxol (paclitaxel).

1995 SGK Race for the Cure events in 57 U.S. cities; SGK local affiliates in 27 cities nationwide.

1996 Research by David G. I. Kingston, Ph.D., leads to FDA approval of Taxotere (docetaxel).

1997 SGK launches first website solely dedicated to breast health and breast cancer information.

Thomas Čech, Ph.D., and Robert Weinberg, Ph.D., each clone gene for telomerase.

Dr. Judah Folkman and Dr. Timothy Browder cure cancer in mice with angiostatin and endostatin.

1998 FDA approves monoclonal antibody Herceptin (trastuzumab) for breast cancer treatment.

SGK supports issue of U.S. Postal Service Breast Cancer Research stamp.

First SGK Race for the Cure outside of the United States in Costa Rica (SGK Race for the Cure series now the largest registered 5K in the world.)

1999   Studies by SGK grantee V. Craig Jordan, Ph.D., show that raloxifene reduces breast cancer risk by 76 percent in postmenopausal women.

SGK establishes the African American National Advisory Council (AANAC).

Interdisciplinary Breast Care Fellowship established at University of Texas Southwestern Medical Center.

Telomerase, an enzyme instrumental in a chromosome's ability to divide and replicate, is discovered by SGK grantee Elizabeth Blackburn, Ph.D.

First international SGK affiliates are established in Germany and Greece.

2000   President Clinton signs executive order mandating Medicare coverage for clinical trials.

SGK provides $1.5 million in funding for a first-of-its-kind research study on the quality of cancer care in association with the American Society of Clinical Oncology (ASCO), Harvard University, and the Rand Corporation.

SGK affiliate established in Italy; first international affiliate-hosted Komen Race for the Cure is held in Rome in May.

SGK establishes the Breast Health Advisory Council (BHAC), consisting of internationally recognized breast cancer experts.

For the first time in a single season, more than 1 million people cross the finish line in the SGK Race for the Cure Series.

2001   SGK volunteers total more than 75,000. FDA approves first digital mammography devices.

Male breast cancer survivor and honorary Team New Balance member Mark Goldstein participates in his 100th Komen Race for the Cure.

Representatives of SGK participate in an official White House roundtable discussion on breast cancer with President George W. Bush, Laura Bush, physicians, scientists, advocates, survivors, and members of the Bush administration.

Worth magazine names Komen one of "America's 100 Best Charities" out of more than 819,000 charities in the United

States. (Of twenty-seven health organizations named to the "100 Best" list, SGK was one of two solely focused on women's health.)

2002   SGK commemorates twentieth anniversary.

2003   SGK celebrates the twentieth anniversary of the SGK Race for the Cure, a series of more than one hundred races around the world, the largest series of 5K runs/fitness walks in the world.

2004   With affiliate network, corporate partners, and generous donors, SGK has raised $750 million.

2006   More than forty SGK affiliates participate in Champions for the Cure, a grassroots program designed to educate Congress, the president, and other policy makers about breast cancer. More than 100,000 Americans become SGK eChampions on ActNowEndBreastCancer.org, a virtual advocacy forum.

2007   FDA approves raloxifene, used to reduce risk of invasive breast cancer in postmenopausal women.

SGK marks 25th anniversary, changes name to Susan G. Komen for the Cure; the "running ribbon" logo adopted to symbolize energy and forward momentum.

SGK reaches milestone of $1 billion invested in the breast cancer movement and pledges to invest another $2 billion in the next decade.

SGK Community Challenge launches twenty-five-city campaign to rally leaders around the country to put breast cancer back at the top of the national agenda.

SGK launches first-ever Global Advocate Summit, connecting delegates from the United States and thirty other countries to discuss the global state of breast cancer.

SGK establishes its Scientific Advisory Board, a small group of top-level scientific and medical advisers led by Dr. Eric P. Winer.

SGK changes grants process to focus on four categories: Promise Grants, Investigator-Initiated Research Grants, Career Catalyst Research Grants, and Postdoctoral Fellowships.

First-ever *State of Breast Cancer* report discusses the breast cancer movement in lay terms.

2008   FDA approves Avastin (bevacizumab) for treatment of metastatic breast cancer.

SGK Course for the Cure first utilized to train advocates from nine pilot countries as part of SGK's Global Initiative for Breast Cancer.

Global Promise Fund established, allowing donors to contribute specifically to Komen's global work.

SGK celebrates $100 million awarded in research grants, the largest single-year investment in research in the organization's twenty-six-year history.

2009   SGK grantee Elizabeth Blackburn, Ph.D., receives Nobel Prize for discovery of telomerase.

Nancy G. Brinker receives Presidential Medal of Freedom and is made United Nations Goodwill Ambassador, overseeing Cancer Control for World Health Organization.

SGK Tissue Bank established at the Indiana University's Simon Cancer Center.

SGK sponsors major international breast cancer conference in Egypt. Pyramids at Giza illuminated in pink for Egypt's first SGK Race for the Cure.

2010   Having invested over $1.5 billion in research, services, and advocacy, Susan G. Komen for the Cure brings together millions of volunteers around the world, continuing the fight to end breast cancer forever.

Resources for Families Dealing
with Breast Cancer

1–877 GO KOMEN (1–877–465–6636) is the resource for any and all things relating to breast health, breast cancer, and Susan G. Komen for the Cure. On the web, log on to www.komen.org.

HELP WITH CLINICAL TRIALS
Susan G. Komen for the Cure has a strategic relationship with BreastCancerTrials.org, which operates as a program of QuantumLeap Healthcare Collaborative, a nonprofit corporation. This site educates patients and families on clinical trial advantages and procedures and offers a trial matching service that helps patients locate trials in which they may want to participate.

> https://www.BreastCancerTrials.org.

RISK FACTORS AND PREVENTION
Facing Our Risk of Cancer Empowered (FORCE)
Information for people at higher risk of breast cancer.

> http://www.facingourrisk.org

National Cancer Institute (NCI)—Breast Cancer Risk Assessment Tool
Interactive breast cancer risk assessment tool.

> http://bcra.nci.nih.gov/brc/q1.htm

National Cancer Institute (NCI)—Genetic Testing
Information on genetic testing.

> http://www.cancer.gov/cancertopics/factsheet/Risk/BRCA

National Cancer Institute (NCI)—Genetics of Breast and Ovarian Cancer
Information on the genetics of breast and ovarian cancer.

> http://www.cancer.gov/cancerinfo/pdq/genetics/breast-and-ovarian

National Institutes of Health (NIH)
Information on clinical trials recruiting people with BRCA or other genetic mutations.

> http://clinicaltrials.gov

State Cancer Legislative Database Program
Information on state legislation requiring coverage for prophylactic mastectomy.
http://www.scld-nci.net

EARLY DETECTION AND SCREENING
National Breast and Cervical Cancer Early Detection Program
Information on free or low-cost mammograms.
http://www.cdc.gov/cancer/nbccedp

National Cancer Institute (NCI)
Interactive breast cancer risk assessment tool.
http://bcra.nci.nih.gov/brc/q1.htm

Susan G. Komen for the Cure
Information on free or low-cost mammograms and other sources of financial assistance.
http://www.komen.org

U.S. Food and Drug Administration (FDA)
List of FDA-approved mammography facilities.
http://www.fda.gov/cdrh/mammography/certified.html

DIAGNOSIS
American Society of Clinical Oncology (ASCO)
Clinical guidelines and information on diagnosis.
http://www.cancer.net

Inflammatory Breast Cancer Research Foundation
Information on inflammatory breast cancer diagnosis and care.
http://www.ibcresearch.org

National Cancer Institute (NCI)
Information on different types of breast cancers as well as other types of cancer that can occur in the breast, such as Phyllodes tumor.
http://www.cancer.gov

Triple Negative Breast Cancer Foundation
Information on the triple negative breast cancer.
http://www.tnbcfoundation.org

TREATMENT—CLINICAL TRIAL INFORMATION
CancerConsultants.com
Free and confidential clinical trial matching and referral services.
http://www.cancerconsultants.com

CenterWatch
Information on participating in clinical trials and a searchable list of current clinical trials.
http://www.centerwatch.com

ECancerTrials.com
Free and confidential clinical trial matching and referral services.
http://ecancertrials.com

National Cancer Institute (NCI)
Information on participating in clinical trials.
http://www.cancer.gov/clinicaltrials

National Institutes of Health (NIH)
Information on current clinical trial research and participating in clinical trials.
http://www.cc.nih.gov
http://www.clinicaltrials.gov

Susan G. Komen for the Cure
Information about clinical trials. Clinical Trials Fact Sheet.
www.komen.org

University of Pittsburgh Medical Center (UPMC)—University of Pittsburgh Cancer Institute
Interactive website with information about clinical trials and personal stories.
http://www.upmccancercenters.com/trials/index.html

TREATMENT—INFORMATION ON TREATMENT OPTIONS
American College of Radiology
Information on current radiation therapy treatment options.
http://www.acr.org

American Society of Clinical Oncology (ASCO)
Treatment guidelines and information on treatment options.
http://www.cancer.net

American Society of Plastic and Reconstructive Surgeons
Information on breast reconstruction.
http://www.plasticsurgery.org

U.S. Food and Drug Administration (FDA)
Consumer information on breast implants.
http://www.fda.gov

COMPLEMENTARY THERAPY—GENERAL INFORMATION AND SEARCH TOOLS FOR SCIENTIFIC STUDIES
National Cancer Institute (NCI)—Office of Cancer Complementary and Alternative Medicine (OCCAM)
Detailed information on complementary and alternative medicine therapies for people living with cancer.
http://www.cancer.gov/cam

National Institutes of Health (NIH)—National Center for Complementary and Alternative Medicine (NCCAM)
Detailed information on complementary therapies.
http://nccam.nih.gov

National Library of Medicine—PubMed
Search tools for scientific articles on complementary therapies.
http://www.pubmed.com

Natural Medicines Comprehensive Medicine Database
Information on complementary therapies.
http://www.naturaldatabase.com

Natural Standard
Detailed information on complementary therapies.
http://www.naturalstandard.com

COMPLEMENTARY THERAPIES—SAFETY INFORMATION
National Institutes of Health (NIH)—Office of Dietary Supplements
Information and safety alerts on dietary supplements.
http://ods.od.nih.gov

U.S. Federal Trade Commission (FTC)
Safety alerts on complementary and alternative medicine therapies.
http://www.ftc.gov/bcp/menus/consumer/health.shtm

U.S. Federal Trade Commission (FTC)—Cure-ious Resource Page
Information on false cancer treatment claims; how to file a complaint.
http://www.ftc.gov/curious

U.S. Food and Drug Administration (FDA)
Safety alerts on complementary and alternative medicine therapies.
http://www.fda.gov/opacom/7alerts.html

U.S. Food and Drug Administration (FDA)—Fake Cancer Cures
Information on scam treatments.
http://www.fda.gov/cder/news/fakecancercures.htm

U.S. Food and Drug Administration (FDA)—MedWatch
Information on drug and medical products; how to file a report on a drug or medical product safety concern.
http://www.fda.gov/medwatch

U.S. Pharmacopeia (USP)
Information on whether a dietary supplement has been tested and USP verified for integrity, purity, and safe manufacturing.
http://www.usp.org/USPVerified/dietarySupplements

COMPLEMENTARY THERAPIES—LICENSING STATUS OF COMPLEMENTARY AND ALTERNATIVE MEDICINE PROVIDERS

American Association of Naturopathic Physicians
Information on the licensing status of naturopathic physicians.
http://www.naturopathic.org

American Massage Therapy Association
Information on the licensing status of massage therapists.
http://www.amtamassage.org

Federation of Chiropractic Licensing Boards
Information on the licensing status of chiropractors.
http://www.fclb.org

National Certification Board for Therapeutic Massage and Bodywork
Information on the licensing status of massage and bodywork therapists.
http://www.ncbtmb.com

National Certification Commission for Acupuncture and Oriental Medicine (NCCAOM)
Information on the licensing status of providers of acupuncture and Oriental medicine.
http://www.nccaom.org/find/index.html

COMPLEMENTARY THERAPIES—CLINICAL TRIALS

National Center for Complementary and Alternative Medicine
Information on and a listing of clinical trials of complementary therapies.
http://nccam.nih.gov/research/clinicaltrials
See also Treatment—Clinical Trial Information.

COMPLEMENTARY THERAPIES—INTEGRATED HEALTH CARE ORGANIZATIONS AND CENTERS

National Library of Medicine—Directory of Health Organizations
Information on local health care organizations and centers offering complementary/integrative therapies.
http://dirline.nlm.nih.gov

GETTING GOOD CARE

Administrators in Medicine—Association of State Medical Board Executive Directors
Information on finding a licensed physician.
http://www.docboard.org

American Board of Medical Specialties (ABMS)
Information on verifying whether a physician is board certified.
http://www.abms.org

American Cancer Society (ACS)
Information on care for people living with cancer.
   http://www.cancer.org

American Medical Association (AMA)—DoctorFinder
Information on finding a licensed physician.
   http://www.ama-assn.org/aps/amahg.htm

American Society of Clinical Oncology (ASCO)
Information on finding an oncologist.
   http://www.cancer.net

Health Care Choices
Information on many breast cancer care issues, including patient volume data and insurance coverage.
   http://www.healthcarechoices.org

Intercultural Cancer Council
Promotes programs and policies to remove ethnic/racial barriers to breast cancer care.
   http://iccnetwork.org

Joint Commission for the Accreditation of Health Care Organizations
Information on finding a health care organization that meets the commission's safety and quality standards.
   http://www.qualitycheck.org/consumer/searchQCR.aspx

National Cancer Institute (NCI)
Information on care for people living with cancer.
   http://www.cancer.gov

National Center for Quality Assurance (NCQA)
Information on the accreditation rating (based on quality standards) of health management organizations (HMOs).
   http://reportcard.ncqa.org

National Coalition for Cancer Survivorship (NCCS)
Teamwork: The Cancer Patient's Guide to Talking with Your Doctor.
   http://www.canceradvocacy.org

U.S. Food and Drug Administration (FDA)
Information on FDA-approved mammography facilities.
   http://www.fda.gov/cdrh/mammography/certified.html

AFTER TREATMENT
Fertile Hope
Financial aid for women with breast cancer whose insurance will not cover fertility treatment.
   http://www.fertilehope.org

National Cancer Institute (NCI)
Information on genetic testing for inherited gene mutations related to breast cancer.
   http://www.cancer.gov/cancer_information/prevention/

National Heart, Lung, and Blood Institute
Information on weight control and physical activity.
   http://www.nhlbi.nih.gov

National Lymphedema Network
Information on lymphedema.
   http://www.lymphnet.org

Young Survival Coalition
Information and networking services for young breast cancer survivors.
   http://www.youngsurvival.org

SOCIAL SUPPORT
American Cancer Society (ACS)—Cancer Survivors Network
Online community for cancer survivors and caregivers.
   http://www.acscsn.org

American Cancer Society (ACS)—Reach to Recovery
In-person and telephone support for people living with cancer.
   http://www.cancer.org

American Cancer Society—I Can Cope
Support for people living with cancer, their spouses, and partners.
   http://www.cancer.org

Association of Cancer Online Resources
Information on online support groups.
   http://www.acor.org

Cancer and Careers
Information for working women with cancer.
   http://www.cancerandcareers.org

CancerCare
Information on online support groups.
   http://www.cancercare.org

Gilda's Club Worldwide
Support services for people living with cancer, their family, and friends.
   http://www.gildasclub.org

Living Beyond Breast Cancer
Information on breast cancer support and care.
   http://www.lbbc.org

Mautner Project for Lesbians with Cancer
Social support services for lesbian women living with cancer and their partners.
   http://www.mautnerproject.org

Men Against Breast Cancer
Services to help men be good caregivers of women with breast cancer.
   http://www.menagainstbreastcancer.org

National Coalition for Cancer Survivorship (NCCS)
 Teamwork: The Cancer Patient's Guide to Talking with Your Doctor.
   http://www.canceradvocacy.org

National Hospice and Palliative Care Organization
Information on local hospice care.
   http://www.nhpco.org

Susan G. Komen for the Cure—Talking with Your Health Care Provider
Visit the "Questions to Ask Your Doctor" section.
   http://www.komen.org

The Wellness Community
Support for people living with cancer and their families.
   http://www.thewellnesscommunity.org

Well Spouse Foundation
Social support for spouses and partners.
   http://www.wellspouse.org

FINANCIAL ISSUES—GENERAL INFORMATION
Agency for Healthcare Research and Quality (U.S. Department of Health and Human Services)
 Choosing and Using a Health Plan.
   http://www.ahcpr.gov/consumer

A.M. Best Company
Information on insurance company ratings.
   http://www.ambest.com

American Association of Retired Persons (AARP)
Information on health issues, Medicare, and health insurance programs for people over age fifty.
   http://www.aarp.orghealth

American Cancer Society—Taking Charge of Money Matters
A financial workshop for people living with cancer.
   http://www.cancer.org

America's Health Insurance Plans
National directory of health insurance plans and information on types of coverage.
   http://www.ahip.org

Association of Community Cancer Centers
Cancer Treatments Your Insurance Should Cover.
   http://www.accc-cancer.org

Medicaid
Find your state's Medicaid toll-free hotline.
   http://cms.hhs.gov/medicaid

Medicare (U.S. Department of Health and Human Services)
Information on the Medicare health insurance program, including Medicare prescription drug plans.
   http://www.medicare.gov

National Association of Insurance Commissioners
Find your state insurance commissioner.
   http://www.naic.org

National Coalition for Cancer Survivorship
Working It Out: Your Employment Rights as a Cancer Survivor; What Cancer Survivors Need to Know About Health Insurance; and *A Cancer Survivor's Almanac: Charting Your Journey.*
   http://www.canceradvocacy.org

Patient Advocate Foundation
Legal and advocacy help for disputing insurance claim denials; financial assistance information.
   http://www.patientadvocate.org

FINANCIAL ISSUES—MEDICAL ASSISTANCE
Breast Cancer Network of Strength
Financial assistance for wigs, prostheses, and mastectomy bras.
   http://www.networkofstrength.org

CancerCare
Financial assistance for diagnostic workups; information on specific prescription drug assistance programs.
   http://www.cancercare.org
See also Transportation Assistance.

NeedyMeds.com
Information on drug assistance programs .
   http://www.needymeds.com

Partnership for Prescription Assistance
Information on drug assistance programs.
   https://www.pparx.org

Pharmaceutical Research and Manufacturers of America
Directory of drug manufacturers' assistance programs.
   http://www.phrma.org

Social Security Administration
Find your local Social Security office.
   https://s044a90.ssa.gov/apps6z/FOLO/fo001.jsp

Susan G. Komen for the Cure and CancerCare's Linking A.R.M.S.
Financial assistance for some medications and medical supplies.
   http://www.cancercare.org

Susan G. Komen for the Cure and Patient Advocate Foundation's Co-Pay Relief (CPR) Program
Insurance copayment assistance.
   http://www.patientadvocate.org

FINANCIAL ISSUES—TRANSPORTATION ASSISTANCE
Air Charity Network
Air travel assistance for people living with cancer and their caregivers.
   http://aircharitynetwork.org

American Cancer Society (ACS)—Road to Recovery
Local transportation assistance.
   http://www.cancer.org

CancerCare
Financial assistance for transportation to and from treatment. Childcare when a parent is having tests or treatment.
   http://www.cancercare.org

Corporate Angel Network
Air travel assistance for people living with cancer.
   http://www.corpangelnetwork.org

Lifeline Pilots
Air travel assistance for people living with cancer and their caregivers.
   http://www.airlifelinemidwest.org/index2.htm

Mercy Medical Airlift
Air travel assistance for people living with cancer and their caregivers.
   http://www.mercymedical.org

National Patient Air Travel HELPLINE
Air travel assistance for people living with cancer and their caregivers.
   http://www.patienttravel.org

Raquel's Wings for Life
Air travel assistance for people living with cancer and their caregivers.
http://raquelswingsforlife.com/default.html

LODGING ASSISTANCE
American Cancer Society (ACS)—Hope Lodges
Lodging for families during cancer treatments.
http://www.cancer.org

ABOUT THE AUTHORS

Nancy G. Brinker

Ambassador Nancy G. Brinker is regarded as the leader of the global breast cancer movement. Her journey began with a simple promise to her dying sister, Susan G. Komen, that she would do everything possible to end the shame, pain, fear, and hopelessness caused by this disease.

Shortly after Susan's death from breast cancer at the age of 36, Brinker founded Susan G. Komen for the Cure® in 1982. Today Komen for the Cure is the world's largest grassroots network of breast cancer survivors and activists fighting to save lives, empower people, ensure quality care for all, and energize science to find the cures.

In 1983, Ambassador Brinker founded the Susan G. Komen Race for the Cure®, which is now the world's largest and most successful education and fundraising event for breast cancer. To date, virtually every major advance in breast cancer research has been touched by hundreds of millions of dollars in Komen for the Cure funding.

Brinker has enlisted every segment of society—from leaders to citizens—to participate in the battle. In 2009, President Barack Obama honored her with the Presidential Medal of Freedom, the nation's highest civilian honor, for this work. The same year, she was named Goodwill Ambassador for Cancer Control for the United Nations' World Health Organization, where she continues her mission to put cancer control at the top of the world health agenda.

Brinker was named one of *Time* magazine's "100 Most Influential People" in 2008. She served as U.S. Ambassador to the Republic of Hungary from 2001 to 2003. Most recently she served as U.S. Chief of Protocol from 2007 to 2009, where she was responsible for overseeing all protocol matters for visiting heads of state and presidential travel abroad. In 2008, President George W. Bush appointed her to The Kennedy Center Board of Trustees.

She has received numerous accolades for her work, including the prestigious Mary Woodard Lasker Award for Public Service, the Trumpet Foundation's President's Award, the Independent Women's Forum Barbara K. Olson Woman of Valor Award, the Champions of Excellence Award presented by the Centers for Disease Control, the Porter Prize presented by the University of Pittsburgh Graduate School of Public Health, and the Forbes Trailblazer Award. She was named one of *Ladies' Home Journal*'s 100 Most Important Women of the 20th Century and *Biography* magazine's 25 Most Powerful Women in America.

Joni Rodgers

New York Times bestselling author Joni Rodgers was born into a family of gospel/bluegrass musicians and grew up on stage, opening for country music legends of the 1960s and '70s. She continued performing, directing, and teaching creative drama until 1994, when she was diagnosed with non-Hodgkin's lymphoma, an aggressive blood cancer. Rodgers used the chemo downtime to complete her first two novels, both of which were published to critical acclaim. Her memoir, *Bald in the Land of Big Hair* (HarperCollins, 2001), is the story of her cancer experience and how it led to the publication of her first book. Rodgers continues to write fiction, speak to audiences about survivorship and creativity, and coauthor memoirs with extraordinary people. She lives with her family in Houston, Texas. Thanks in part to treatments developed through SGK funding, her cancer has been in remission for thirteen years.